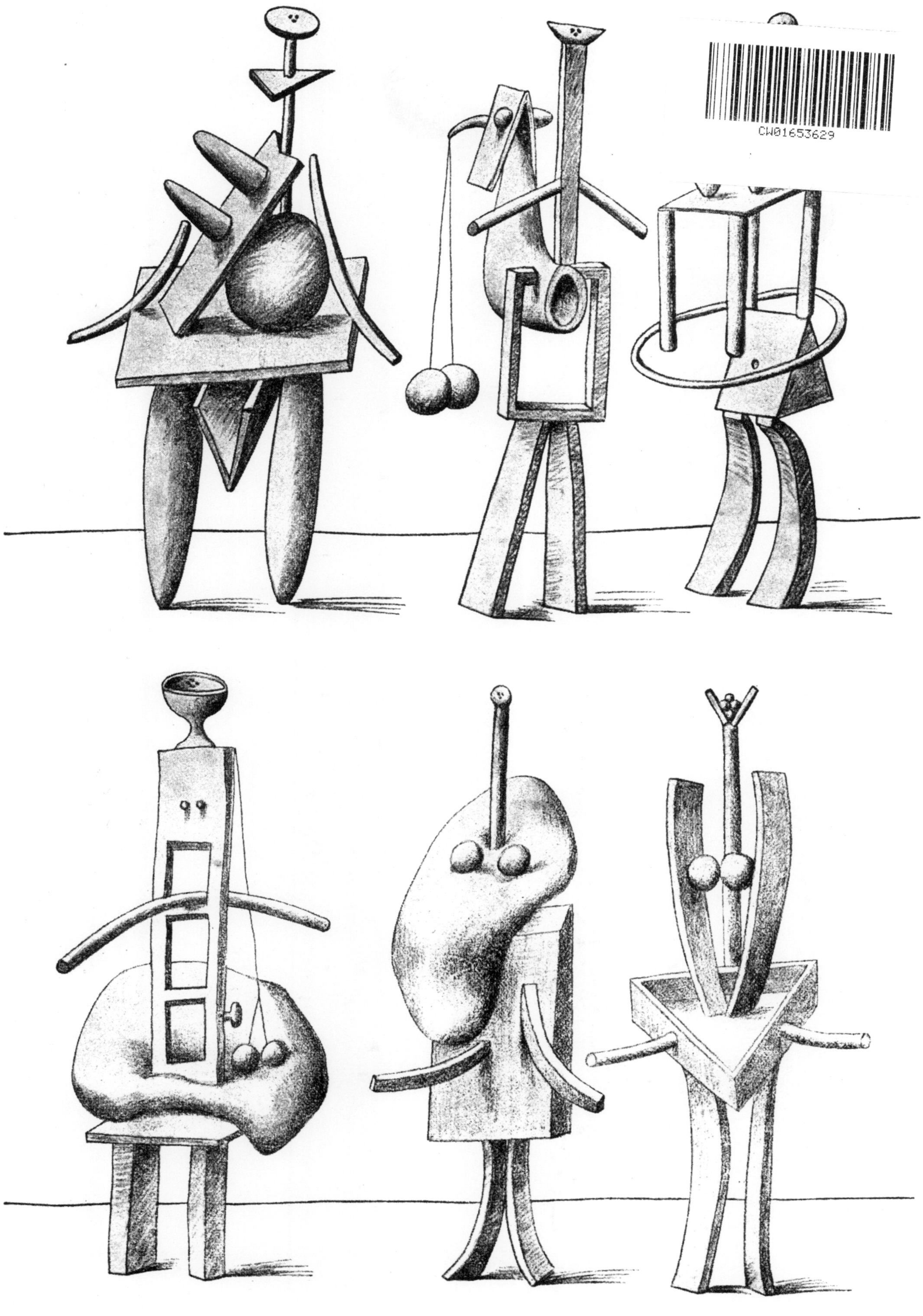

MARVELOUS OBJECTS

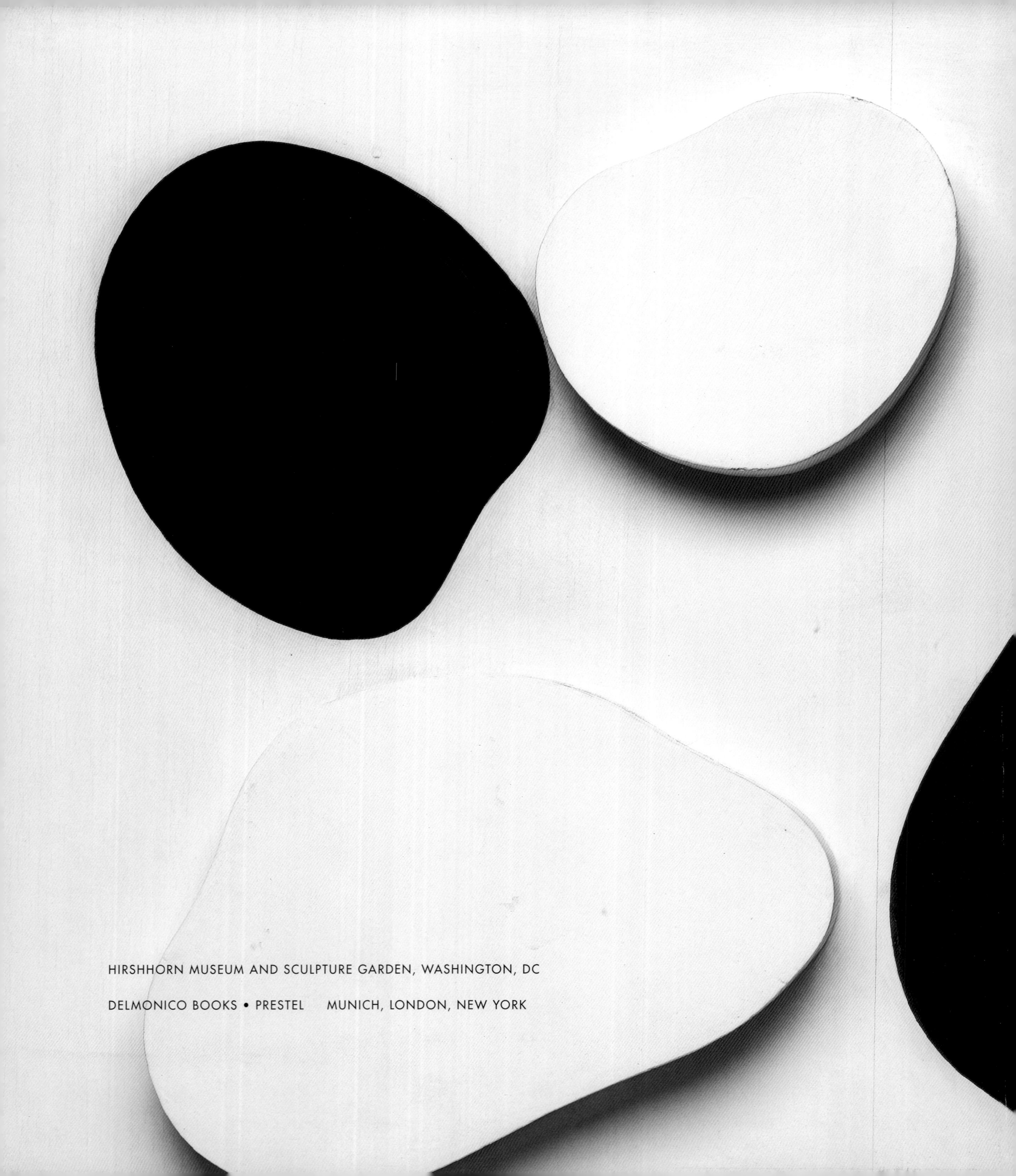

HIRSHHORN MUSEUM AND SCULPTURE GARDEN, WASHINGTON, DC

DELMONICO BOOKS • PRESTEL MUNICH, LONDON, NEW YORK

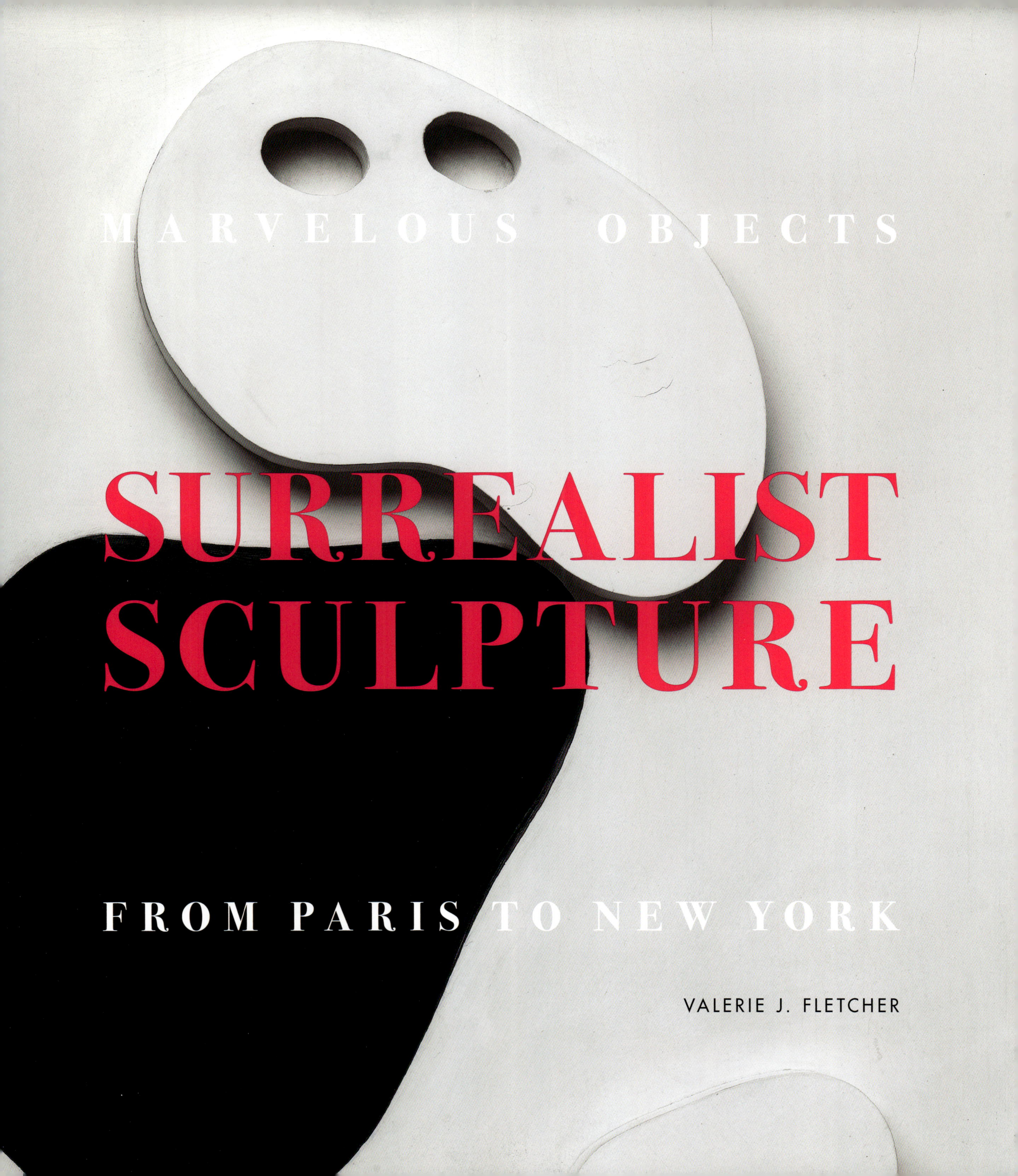

MARVELOUS OBJECTS

SURREALIST SCULPTURE

FROM PARIS TO NEW YORK

VALERIE J. FLETCHER

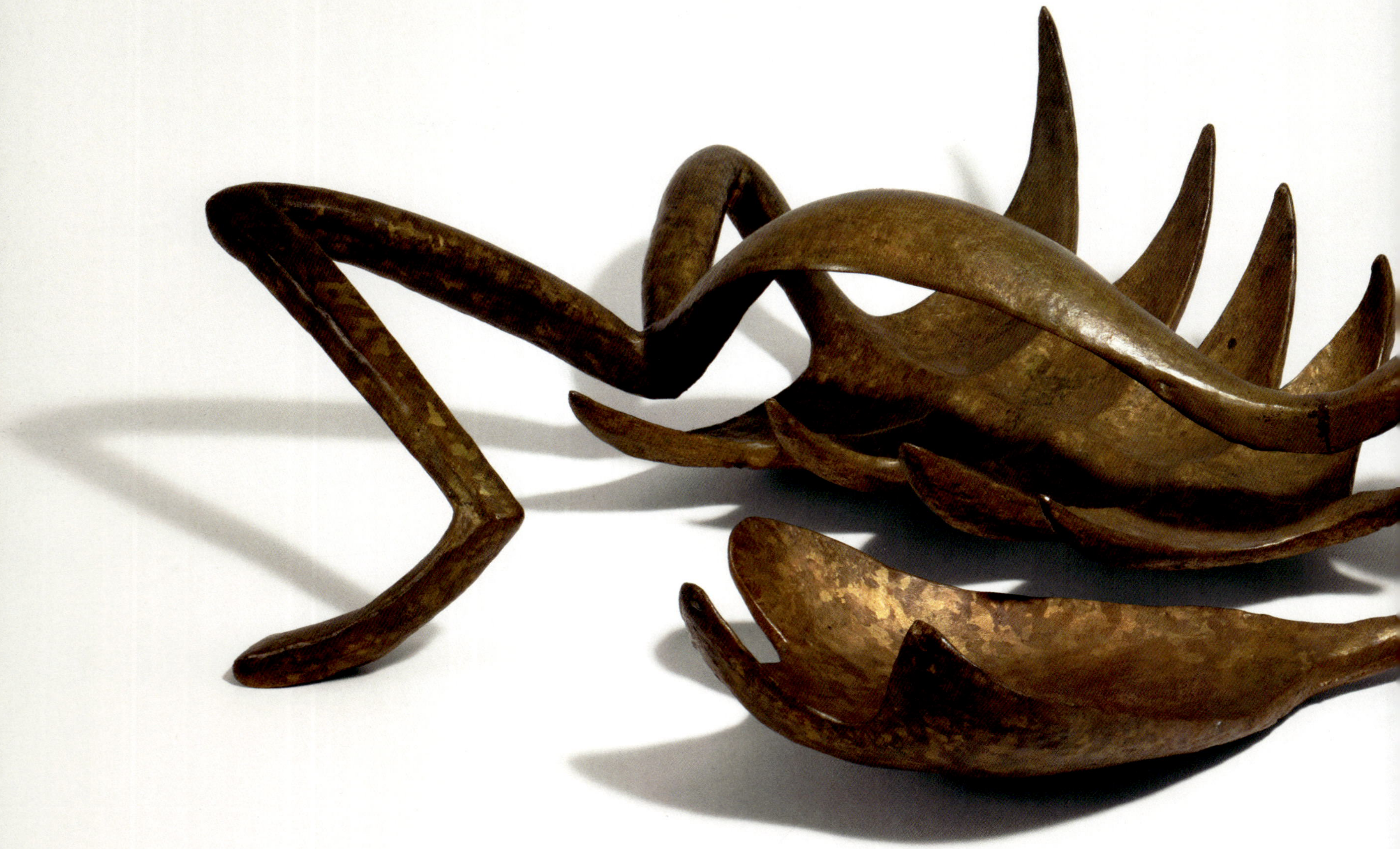

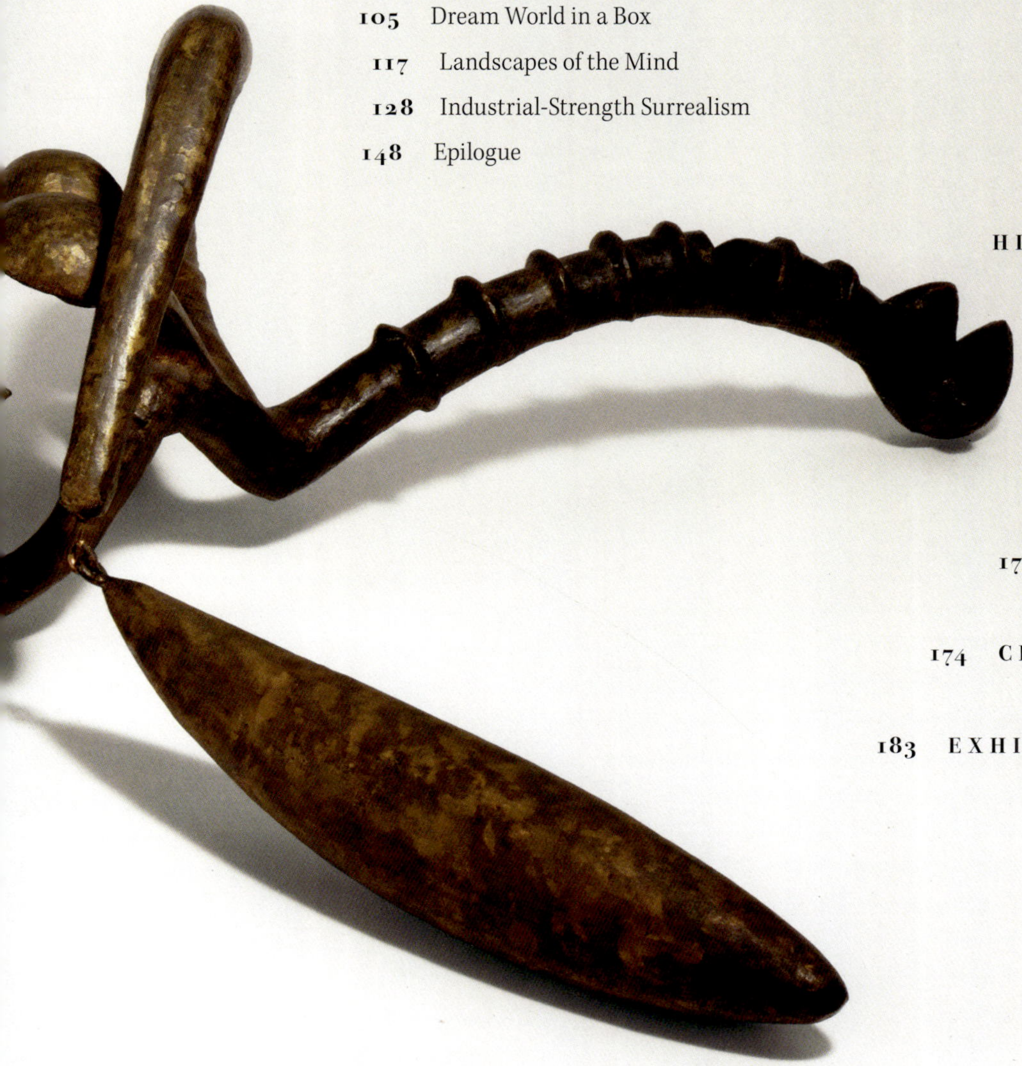

FOREWORD

Marvelous Objects: Surrealist Sculpture from Paris to New York is the first major museum exhibition to present a comprehensive analysis of Surrealism's three-dimensional works. One of the most innovative and influential cultural phenomena of modern times, the Surrealist movement has been the subject of numerous studies. The sculptures, however, have tended to be overshadowed by the paintings and drawings from the period, and when the three-dimensional works have been the focus, most scholars have approached them with a less inclusive scope.

In a boldly revisionist exploration of the topic, *Marvelous Objects* proposes an expanded assessment of the sculptures from this period. While Surrealism is usually recognized as a French movement that originated in 1924 and eventually spread to other parts of the world, the Hirshhorn's project offers a continuous narrative of contributions by both Europeans and Americans from the early 1920s through the late 1940s. *Marvelous Objects* also presents a more wide-ranging definition of Surrealist sculpture, incorporating biomorphic works as well as found-object assemblages. The two modes were equally valued by specialists and the public, and they each inspired crucial inspiration for subsequent generations of artists.

On behalf of the Museum's Trustees and staff, I wish to express our profound thanks to the organizations and individuals who stepped up to make this complex project a reality. We are extremely grateful to the lenders who have entrusted us with works from their collections, and we are indebted to those who funded the exhibition. Leading support for *Marvelous Objects: Surrealist Sculpture from Paris to New York* has been provided by the Jerome L. Greene Foundation, with major funding from the Terra Foundation for American Art, and lead corporate sponsor Altria Group. Additional support has been provided by the Swiss Arts Council Pro Helvetia, the Hirshhorn International Council, and the Smithsonian Institution's Scholarly Studies Program, and from Barbara and Aaron Levine and Robert Mnuchin.

Recognition should also be given to the outstanding staff at the Hirshhorn, almost all of whom contributed to the realization of the show—firstly, Valerie Fletcher, senior curator, who has had the idea for this exhibition for many years, and Stéphane Aquin, chief curator. We also extend thanks to the Smithsonian leadership, particularly Undersecretary for History, Art, and Culture Richard Kurin, Smithsonian Secretary David Skorton, and former Acting Smithsonian Secretary Albert G. Horvath, for the institutional support of *Marvelous Objects*, which wonderfully fulfills the Hirshhorn's mandate to provide fresh and challenging perspectives on modern art.

MELISSA CHIU

Director
Hirshhorn Museum and Sculpture Garden

ACKNOWLEDGMENTS

Organizing an exhibition of sculptures made by more than a dozen artists on two continents poses a serious challenge to any curator's stamina and dedication. Bringing it to fruition is accomplished only through the cooperation, expertise, and generosity of many individuals and institutions.

Marvelous Objects: Surrealist Sculpture from Paris to New York culminates nearly three decades of my work at the Hirshhorn. I am profoundly grateful to countless individuals in the Museum and in the broader Smithsonian Institution for their willingness to support in-depth research for so many years.

Marvelous Objects had an unusually long gestation period, starting with the initial concept in 1998. James T. Demetrion, who was then the director of the Hirshhorn, encouraged me to develop and clarify the show's content and goals. Subsequently, as the director's position passed through several hands, the project was put on hold, but it ultimately survived the tumultuous years of staff downsizing and uncertain federal funding. No words can fully express my gratitude to Richard Koshalek, director from 2010 to 2013, who enthusiastically revived and empowered this project. During the past year, our current director Melissa Chiu and our chief curator Stéphane Aquin have helped to shape and finalize the exhibition in ways that enabled it to be realized at last. I am also grateful to Elizabeth Duggal, deputy director, for her efforts during a transitional period, and to Melissa Ho, associate curator, for her research on Marcel Duchamp and her overall assistance.

A project of this scope owes its very existence to the participation of lenders, both public and private. A number of institutions and individuals have made special efforts on our behalf: allowing us to borrow rare and fragile works that normally do not travel, lending more works than usual, and graciously continuing to lend despite several changes in schedule. Many, many thanks to all of you.

Very few curatorial activities are as stimulating and satisfying as conversations with other experts and generous colleagues. My research on the topic of Surrealist sculpture included consultations with scholars in Europe and elsewhere. Although I cannot mention everyone, special appreciation goes to Dawn Ades, whose expertise in Surrealist art and artists is unsurpassed. As she has done for several generations of scholars, Dawn encouragingly pointed me toward other experts, including Jennifer Mundy and Christopher Stephens, curators at the Tate who have greatly expanded our knowledge of Surrealist sculpture in Britain. Camille Morandi at the Centre Georges Pompidou provided access to research files and introductions to other scholars in France. Walburga Krupp, formerly at the Stiftung Hans Arp and Sophie Taeuber-Arp, has compiled tremendous amounts of data on Arp's oeuvre, including the rarely discussed issues of dating and restorations. Marcel Fleiss of Galerie 1900–2000 in Paris kindly shared information on specific works and private collections. The archives of the Mayor Gallery in London was a delightful surprise; unrestricted access allowed me to absorb the ambiance of Surrealism in Britain.

Here in the United States, I am particularly grateful to Anne Umland, curator at MoMA and authority on Joan Miró's works; William Jeffett, curator at the Salvador Dalí Museum in St. Petersburg and author of their collection catalogue; Michael Taylor, then-curator at the Philadelphia Museum of Art; and Stephanie D'Alessandro, curator at the Art Institute of Chicago, who shared her research on Dalí's original and editioned *Venus de Milo with Drawers*. Adam Boxer and Caitlin Suarez at the Ubu Gallery patiently tutored me on the complexities and nuances of Hans Bellmer's vintage photographs. Lynda Hartigan took time from her responsibilities as chief curator at the Peabody Essex Museum to advise me on Cornell's often undated serial box assemblages. Peter Stevens and Susan Cooke at the Estate of David Smith brought my attention to a surprising number of sculptures and drawings that chart the artist's ongoing dialectic with Surrealism; the full extent of that dialectic has yet to be revealed. And, despite the demands of other exhibitions throughout the world, Alexander S. C. Rower and Lily Lyons at the Calder Foundation made crucial loans available, even as the dates of *Marvelous Objects* changed. I also want to express my gratitude to Museum Services, Sotheby's New York.

Behind the scenes, the Hirshhorn's dedicated staff provided crucial expertise, efficient actions, and much-appreciated encouragement. First and foremost, I want to acknowledge Lawrence Hyman, our indefatigable manager of exhibition and curatorial planning; quite simply, without him, the project would not have been possible. I am also grateful to the directors of collection management, Susan Lake and Sarah Stauderman, and their staff. A special thanks goes to our sculpture conservator, Gwynne Ryan, whose skills enabled us to secure several extremely fragile loans to *Marvelous Objects*. As for our extraordinarily talented exhibits department, led by Al Masino, I would like to paraphrase Winston Churchill: never has any curator owed so much to so few for so long. The installation project manager and designer for *Marvelous Objects* was Scott Larson, a colleague of many years; working with him has been an unmitigated pleasure.

Among the unsung heroes behind *Marvelous Objects* are the Hirshhorn's registrars, especially Rosemary DeRosa; Jennifer Barrett and the development department; Kelly Carnes, Bob Allen, and the other members of the communications team; our librarian Anna Brooke, and our photographer Cathy Carver. I would like also to acknowledge the graduate-student assistants who searched libraries and databases, checked details, photocopied images, and brought youthful enthusiasm to the process: Natalia Miskisko, Kathrin Halpern, Cicie Sattarnilasskorn, Abigail Winograd, and Molly Harrington, who also assisted with procuring images for the book.

We are delighted that DelMonico Books • Prestel partnered with us to publish the catalogue accompanying *Marvelous Objects* and appreciate their enthusiasm for a revisionist and scholarly examination of Surrealist sculptures. Under Mary DelMonico's leadership, Ryan Newbanks, Karen Farquhar, and Luke Chase steered the project through changing iterations with patience and tact. Rhys Conlon, editor and publications manager at the Hirshhorn, worked with tireless devotion to see this book through to completion. She and Amy Pastan gently nudged the ungainly first versions of the manuscript into a publishable state. A special thanks goes to designer Eileen Boxer, who produced a stunning book design in an exceptionally short time frame.

Finally, I would like to express my gratitude to all of the other individuals whose efforts helped make *Marvelous Objects* a reality.

VALERIE J. FLETCHER

Senior Curator
Hirshhorn Museum and Sculpture Garden

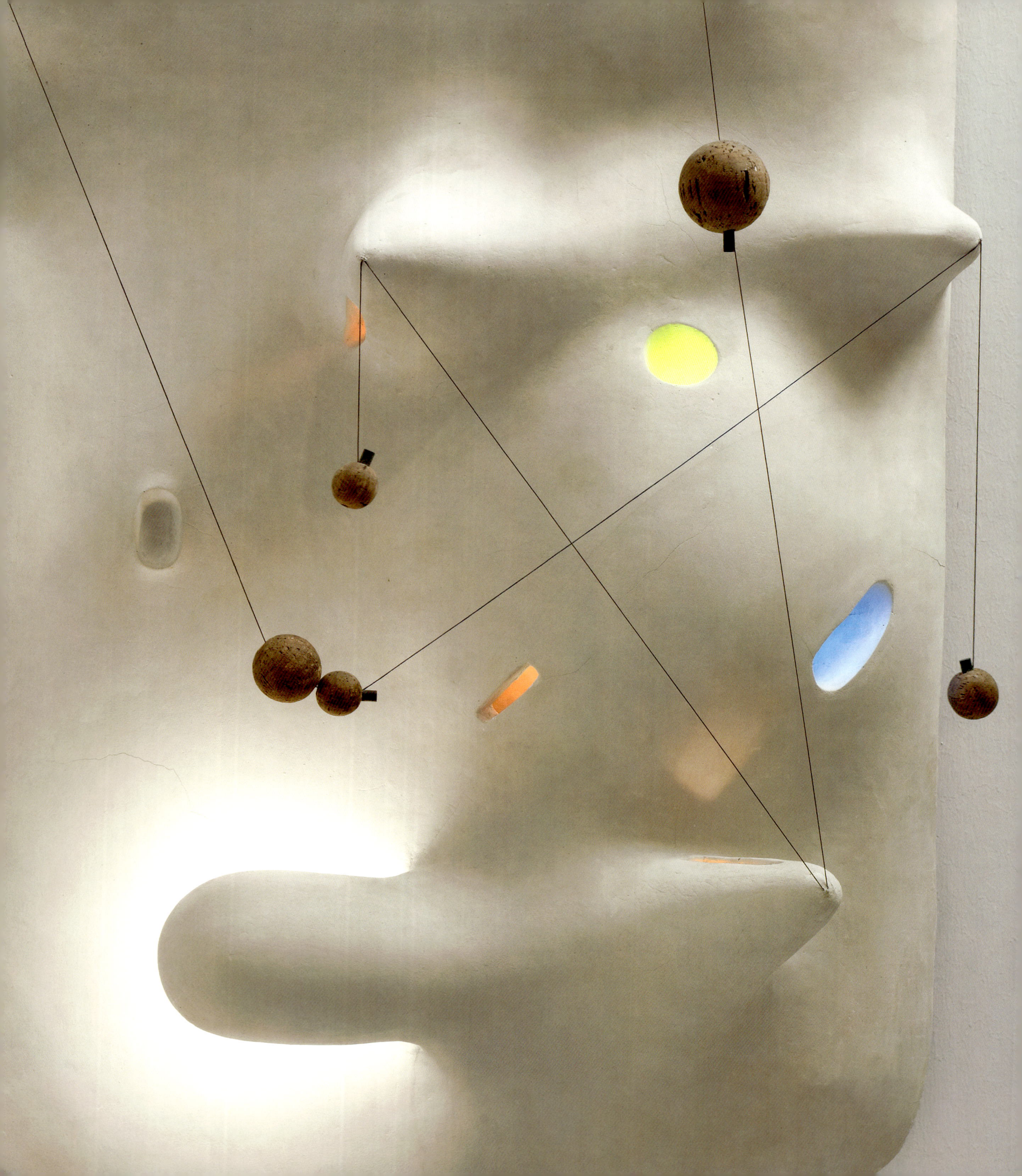

SURREALIST SCULPTURE

VALERIE J. FLETCHER

As one of the most influential literary and artistic movements of the modern era, Surrealism has permeated popular culture and contributed much to art since the 1920s. Most film buffs can describe the scene of a human eyeball being sliced by a razor in *Un Chien Andalou*, 1929, the film by Luis Buñuel and Salvador Dalí. Art aficionados are familiar with the image of melting watches from Dalí's painting *The Persistence of Memory*, 1931. Exhibitions of Surrealist art attract huge audiences, and the scholarly details have been extensively documented in essays, chronologies, and theoretical interpretations ranging from political and biographical to psychoanalytical and sexual. But prominence has nearly always been given to paintings and drawings, then to photographs and films, while sculptures appear mostly as adjuncts to the other media.

Occasionally, especially in the past decade, Surrealist sculptures have emerged as a subject of interest, but they have still not been researched in a comprehensive way. Curators and historians have tended to lavish attention on only one kind: those consisting of ordinary items assembled into three-dimensional compositions. Known as *Surrealist objects* or *assemblages*, these wondrously surprising constructions opened up new paths for generations of artists. Yet there was another, equally significant approach within Surrealism: *organic abstraction*, now known as *biomorphism*. The two methods might be defined as curiously antithetical: one reflects the prevalence of material goods in modern society, whereas the other expresses the forces of nature, but their origins and goals were similar. Both modes originated in Dada, evolved in tandem, and were exhibited together. Both spread internationally and eventually entered mainstream aesthetics.

To some extent geography and nationalism have obscured the big picture. Most histories of Surrealism focus on developments in France, while regional specialists have separately researched what happened elsewhere, particularly in Belgium, Britain, Germany, Switzerland, and the United States. *Marvelous Objects: Surrealist Sculpture from Paris to New York* introduces a more inclusive narrative of international developments. Whether or not an artist was officially affiliated with Surrealism is less important than how sculptors developed, adapted, and transformed the movement's core ideas, images, practices, and intentions.

In French the term *surréalisme* means "above reality," and the Surrealist movement—which officially began in Paris in 1924—was based on a communal search for enhanced awareness and creativity. Ideas were formulated by the French writers André Breton, Louis Aragon, and Paul Eluard. At first, there were few artists, mostly painters from other countries, such as Max Ernst from Germany and Joan Miró from Spain. Surrealist artists pursued a diverse range of styles; variety was prized over conformity. Works of art were intended not as paragons of beauty but as portals to our intuitions and imaginations, enabling us to develop perceptions and insights beyond logic and reason. Breton explained in the *Manifesto of Surrealism*, published in Paris in late 1924, that people are "inveterate dreamer[s]" who can escape drudgery by rediscovering the unfettered curiosity and open receptivity of childhood. Children "are weaned on the marvelous" but then lose the ability to live within their fantasies. Surrealist methods promised to restore access to imagined realities and "to set up [our] abode in those distant regions." Breton declared that "there are fairy tales to be written for adults," noting that "the mind which plunges into Surrealism relives with glowing excitement part of its childhood."[1]

Their goal was defined as a search for *the marvelous*.[2] A person experiences the marvelous as an instantaneous flash of recognition or revelation triggered unexpectedly by an external stimulus. Breton once described the desire for such encounters as almost addictive; he sought to discover things that "introduce me into an almost forbidden world of sudden parallels, of petrifying coincidences . . . of lightning flashes that make one see, really *see*. . . . [These are events] of pure observation, but *every* time possess all the appearances of a signal."[3] Such affective episodes resonate within us, although their specific meanings may remain indefinable.

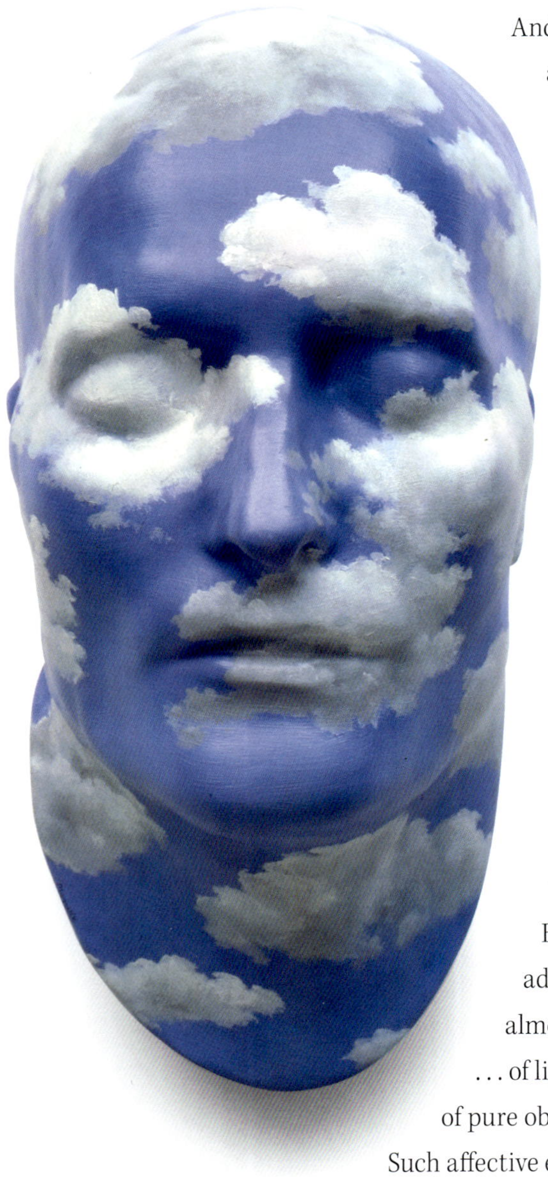

1
RENÉ MAGRITTE
THE FUTURE OF STATUES, 1937
Tate Gallery, London

Eager to precipitate these random occurrences, called *objective chance*, the Surrealists wandered around Paris, their eyes and minds openly receptive to any place or thing. They discovered a strange magic in mundane sights, from shop-window displays and advertising signs to old junk in the flea market. Virtually anything could speak to an observer, abruptly opening a conduit to one's unconscious and revealing a startling network of correspondences, somewhat like a drug-induced vision. Over time these episodes would accumulate into a more invigorating and satisfying awareness. Surrealists would eventually master the ability to move at will between the conscious and unconscious realms, which Breton described as connected permeable vessels. The term *Surrealist desire* originally meant a yearning for these transient moments of illumination; only later was its meaning more narrowly defined as erotic.

The Surrealists' quest for the marvelous was predicated on what was then a revolutionary concept: the sub- or unconscious mind as a font of perceptions, memories, and associations. Proudly proclaiming that Surrealism was "getting into the area of psychology," the manifesto averred that "if the depths of our minds contain strange forces capable of augmenting those on the surface . . . there is every reason to seize them [and] then, if need be, to submit them to the control of our reason."[4]

That the Surrealists were inspired by the ideas and practices of Sigmund Freud is an established fact.[5] But over the decades, as some Freudian tenets have been superseded by other theoretical and clinical approaches, many art historians have shied away from this aspect of Surrealism and thereby have limited the possibilities for experiencing the marvelous. On a very basic level we cannot understand why the Surrealists created works of art, nor how we perceive them today, unless we accept the premise that the subconscious permeates our thoughts and actions. Conscious reality is limited; exploring the hidden mysteries of our unconscious enriches our lives and expands our minds. Thus the Surrealists eagerly shared and interpreted each other's dreams, at least at first. More enduring was the practice of *free association*: emptying the mind to facilitate spontaneous responses to an image, as in a Rorschach test. The Surrealists inferred that accessing this reservoir of associations would help liberate us from the constraints of ordinary reality. Their mantra was a descriptive phrase written decades earlier by the French poet Isidore Ducasse: "as beautiful as the chance encounter between an umbrella and a sewing machine on a dissecting table."[6]

As modern neuroscience has confirmed, the human brain is hard-wired to understand what it sees. When confronted with an unusual image, such as the juxtaposition of two or more unrelated things, our minds instinctively try to make sense of it. Does Ducasse's image offer a metaphor for the unimportance of material objects or the pointlessness of a life that must inevitably end in death? Is it perhaps a confrontation of male and female genders (the long furled umbrella versus the sewing machine), and might their relationship be so toxic that it requires an autopsy?

There is no single or correct answer. Rather, because our reactions arise from individual life experiences, there can be as many indirect and subliminal responses to a work of art as there are observers of it, and the Surrealists placed great faith in that limitless potentiality. But their goal differed from psychoanalysis. Whereas psychotherapists analyze dreams and memories in order to strengthen the role of conscious thought over debilitating emotions, the Surrealists wanted to weaken the hold of reason and empower our intuition and imagination.

The Surrealists were particularly intrigued by the pervasive and mysterious ways that memories affect how we observe and think. From the 1880s on, Edgar Degas alternated between working from observation and from recollection, ultimately concluding that the latter produces stronger results. In 1896 the French philosopher Henri Bergson published *Matter and Memory*, a study of relations and interactions between "the reality of spirit and the reality of matter." He asserted that pure observation is fundamentally impossible because perception "is impregnated with memory-images which complete it as they interpret it." This remarkable insight provided the basis for the modern philosophy of phenomenology, which developed parallel to the Surrealist movement. Subsequent decades of brain scans and other tests have confirmed that memory, conscious or not, plays an active role in our interpretations of all works of art.

FORMATION IN PARIS, 1919–24

Surrealism had its intellectual and stylistic roots in the international Dada movement, which vehemently reacted against the pointlessness and destruction of World War I. At first "the war to end all wars" was expected to last only a few months in 1914, but it raged for four years in stalemate after stalemate. New weapons were appallingly effective, including long-distance cannons, hidden landmines, and poison gas. Soldiers also died from rampant diseases in open-air trenches and from the incompetence of those commanders whose rank reflected social status rather than military experience. No wonder, then, that respect for the societal status quo collapsed.

Dada emerged almost simultaneously in Switzerland, the United States, and Germany during the war. Critical mass occurred when artists and writers flocked together to form a very active but short-lived Dada group in Paris from 1919 to 1924. Aragon summarized their state of mind as rebellious, ironic, and emphatically negative: "No more painters, no more writers, no more musicians, no more sculptors, no more religions, … no more politicians, … no more armies, no more police, no more fatherlands, enough of all these imbecilities, no more anything, no more anything, nothing, NOTHING, NOTHING, NOTHING."[7] Over time such negation offered limited creative possibilities, and eventually Breton and some former Dadaists opted to expand their horizons in a more hopeful direction.

The difficulty lay in defining what new forms Surrealist art should take. Certain methods and motifs revealed in small gallery exhibitions provided inspiration. Ernst's collages of bizarre juxtapositions showed that magic can inhabit the mundane. The artist later recounted how, in 1919, he had an epiphany:

> I was struck by the way my excited gaze became obsessed with the page of an illustrated catalogue showing objects designed for anthropological,

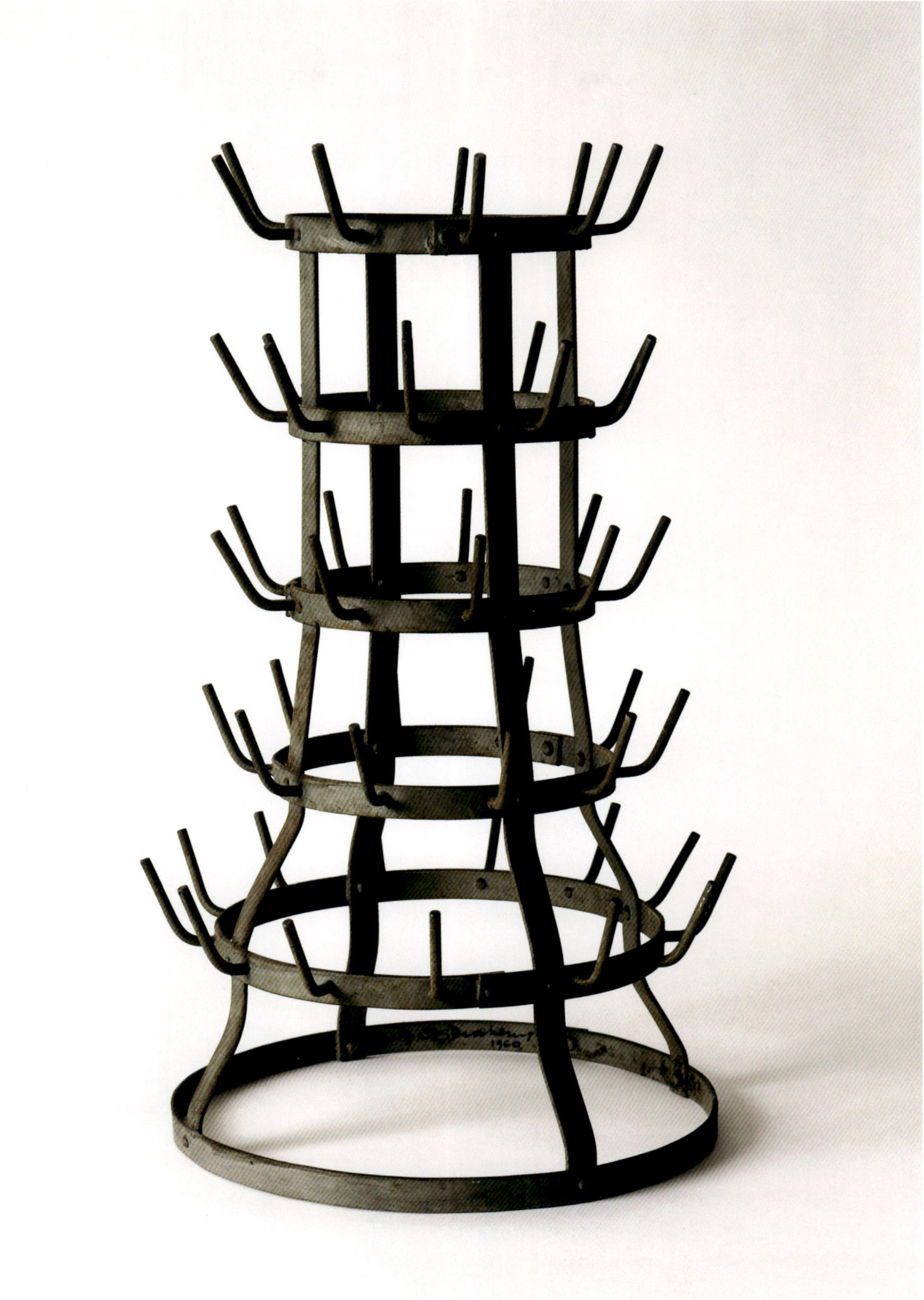

2
MARCEL DUCHAMP, *BOTTLE RACK*, 1914
Robert Rauschenberg Foundation, New York

> microscopic, psychological, mineralogical, and paleontological demonstrations. . . . the sheer absurdity of this assemblage caused a sudden intensification of my visionary faculties and brought forth a hallucinating succession of contradictory images: double, triple, and multiple images overlaying each other with the persistence and rapidity peculiar to love memories and visions.[8]

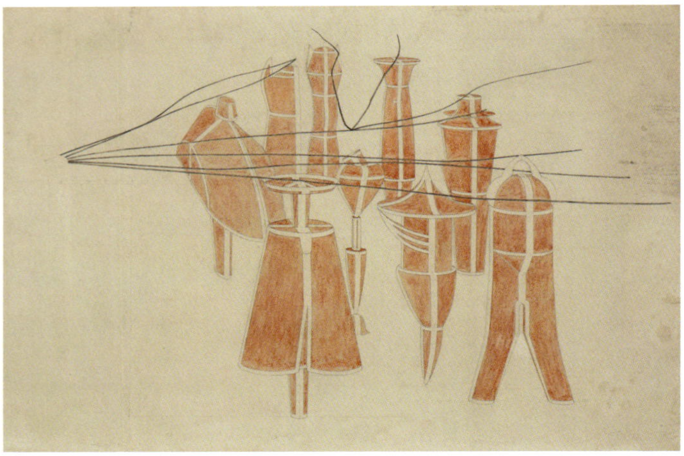

3
MARCEL DUCHAMP
CEMETERY OF UNIFORMS AND LIVERIES, NO. 2 (THE BACHELORS AND NINE MALIC MOLDS), 1914
Yale University Art Gallery, New Haven; gift of Katherine S. Dreier to the Collection Société Anonyme

He cut out images of manufactured items from commercial and industrial catalogues and juxtaposed them in puzzling combinations that seem to suggest a narrative but defy logical interpretation. When Breton learned about an exhibition of these collages in Cologne in 1921, he arranged to show them a few months later in Paris and wrote the catalogue text praising Ernst's images as visual manifestations of the irrational recesses of the artist's mind.

Several years previously in New York, Marcel Duchamp had used mass-produced objects in a similar spirit. He shocked American audiences by selecting less-than-lovely items, inscribing them, and proclaiming them art. His *Readymades*—a term he coined in 1915—began with a bottle-drying rack devoid of bottles (fig. 2) and a snow shovel called *In Advance of the Broken Arm*. The concept that any ordinary thing could become art was aggressively revolutionary, and Duchamp soon developed more complex works, culminating in *The Bride Stripped Bare by Her Bachelors, Even*, 1915–23 (a.k.a. *The Large Glass*; fig. 5). Sandwiched between plates of glass are reproductions of mechanistic objects excerpted from advertisements and technical publications, including a chocolate grinder, water mill, and chest-expanders. *The Bachelors and Nine Malic Molds*, also known as *Cemetery of Uniforms and Liveries, No. 2*, 1914 (fig. 3), depicts nine men as metal containers for acidic chemical reactions. The artist identified them as a department-store delivery boy, policeman, priest, stationmaster, undertaker, and other bachelors who are destined to play a licentious role in the unwritten narrative of a bride being serially deflowered.

4
MARCEL DUCHAMP
WITH HIDDEN NOISE, 1916
Collection Timothy Baum, New York

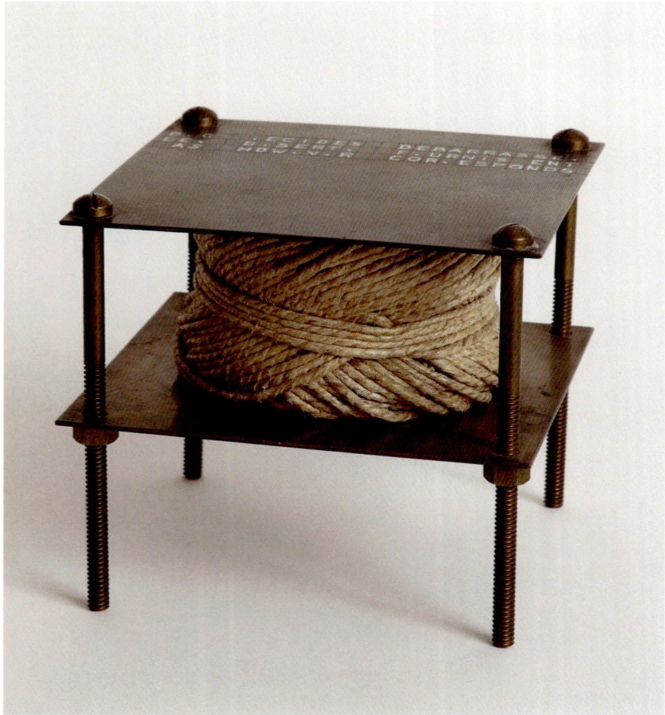

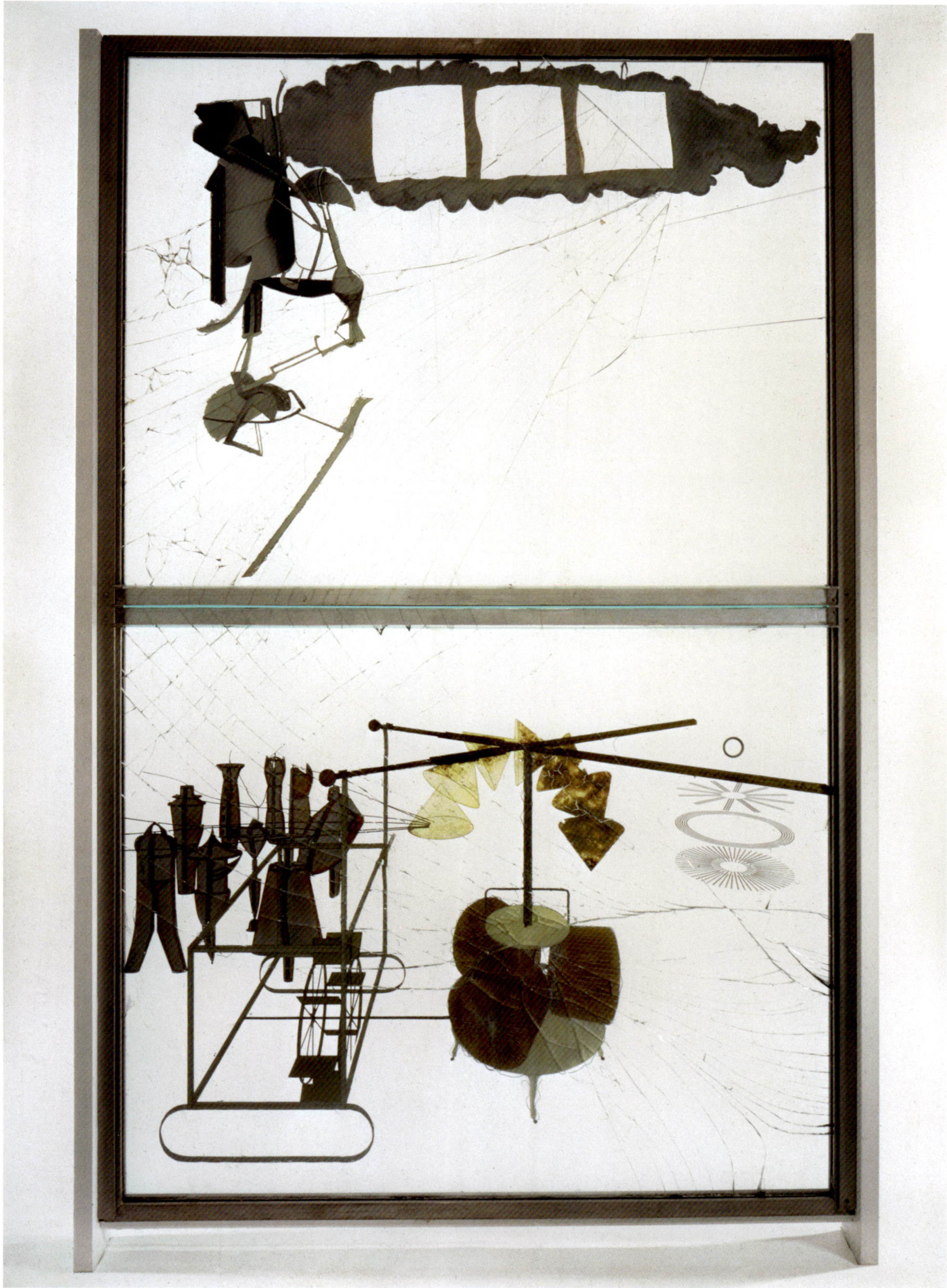

5
MARCEL DUCHAMP, *THE BRIDE STRIPPED BARE BY HER BACHELORS, EVEN (THE LARGE GLASS)*, 1915–23
Philadelphia Museum of Art; bequest of Katherine S. Dreier

Duchamp's *Assisted Readymades* juxtapose two or more mundane objects in seemingly random—yet also premeditated and complex—combinations. For *With Hidden Noise*, 1916 (fig. 4), a friend of the artist secreted an undisclosed object inside an ordinary ball of twine, which Duchamp secured between metal plates bolted together. Like a wrapped present, the identity of the object inside might be deduced by someone handling the sculpture—shaking, smelling, and listening to it. As the puzzle remains inviolate, it elicits a subtle sense of frustration at the impossibility of knowing, even though it is an utterly unimportant thing. Of course, a viewer could get a screwdriver to undo the four bolts, free the ball of twine, and reveal the hidden object, but then the sculpture would cease to exist, annihilated by a wanton act of destruction, which in itself is an ironic metaphor.

Fresh Widow, 1920 (fig. 7), consists of a reduced-size replica of a typical French window. For centuries artists had depicted windows as symbols of visual and spiritual aspirations toward other realms better than the one in which we live. Duchamp covered the glass panes of his window with black leather, denying the possibility of access or escape. Instead of a vista, viewers are confronted with an opaque darkness that conjures associations with evil, death, fear, and nothingness. The punning title may seem amusing but, in fact, it is a somber reference to the millions of women recently widowed by the war.

6
MARCEL DUCHAMP
WHY NOT SNEEZE, ROSE SÉLAVY?, 1921
Collection of Aaron and Barbara Levine, Washington, DC (exhibited work). Photo of original courtesy Philadelphia Museum of Art; the Louise and Walter Arensberg Collection

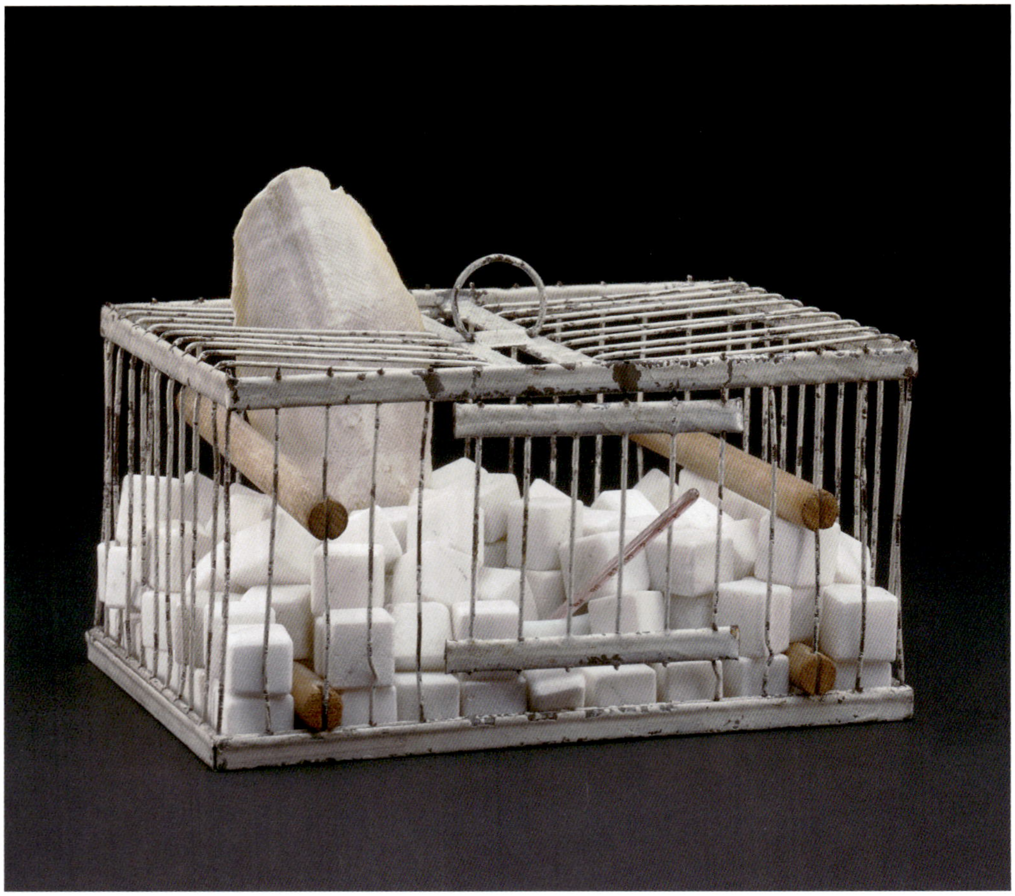

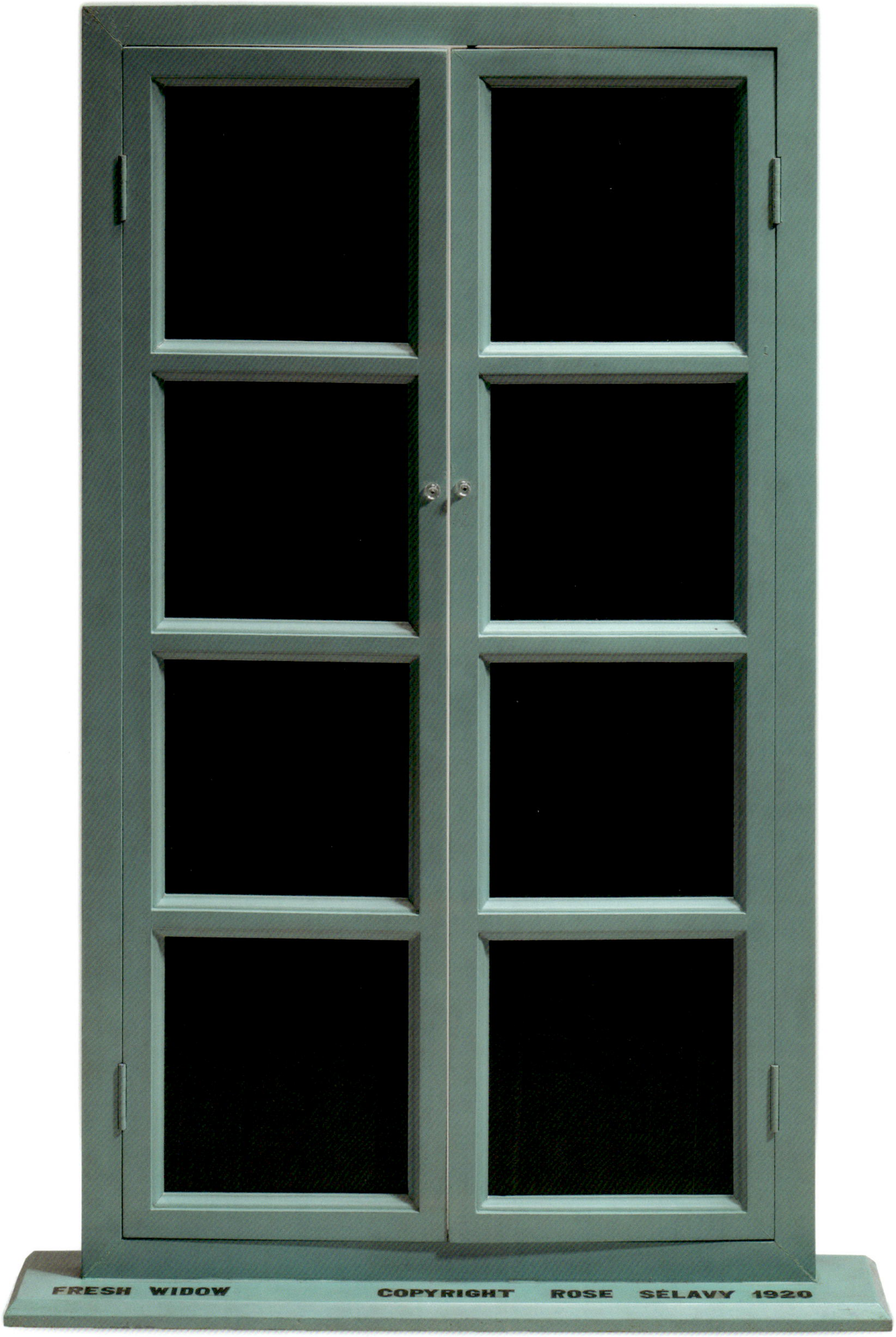

7

MARCEL DUCHAMP, *FRESH WIDOW*, 1920

National Gallery of Art, Washington, DC; gift of Deborah and Ed Shein

For *Why Not Sneeze, Rose Sélavy?*, 1921 (fig. 6),[9] Duchamp meticulously constructed an interactive object predicated on a childish prank. Breton described its effect when the artist showed to some friends "a cage which seemed to contain lumps of sugar rather than birds. He asked them to lift the cage, and they were surprised at its heaviness. [The sugar cubes] were really small lumps of marble which at great expense Duchamp had had made specifically for [this trick]."[10] Two other items stick out from the cubes: a cuttlebone (an avian chewing toy) presumably alludes to the former inhabitants of the birdcage, and a glass thermometer appears to be taking the sugar-marble's temperature, a pointless and silly act. The title adds to the puzzle: what has sneezing to do with birds, cages, sugar, or marble? Perhaps the question "Why not sneeze?" is a metaphor for yielding to a sudden impulse to release any kind of internal pressure.

8
MAN RAY, *GIFT*, 1921
Smithsonian American Art Museum, Washington, DC; gift of Juliet Man Ray

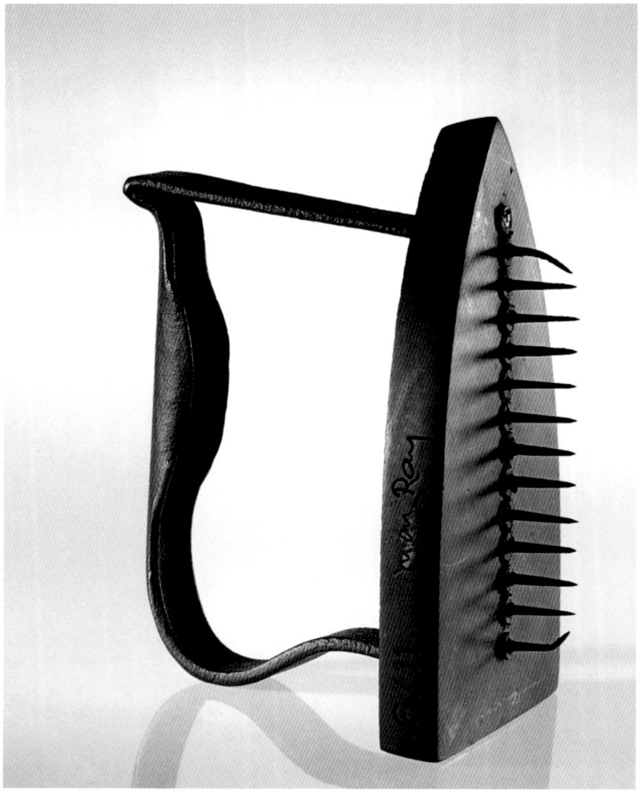

Aside from a very small circle of Dadaists, few people knew of Duchamp's object assemblages, even after he and his American colleague Man Ray (Emmanuel Radnitzky) came to Paris in 1921. Audiences were therefore startled when Ray included an object in his exhibition of paintings and photographs in December. *Gift* (fig. 8) is childishly malicious: using it would rip clothes to shreds rather than smooth out wrinkles. Equally surprising were his photographs of kitchen implements puzzlingly titled *Man* and *Woman* and his camera-less *rayographs* (his term for photograms), which he made by exposing objects on light-sensitive paper (fig. 9). Although the choice of objects appears random, some rayographs invite our unconscious minds to find meanings. For example, from an image of a handgun juxtaposed with a hotel-room key, might we infer that something violent is about to occur behind closed doors? The pairing of a fast-moving filmstrip and a gyroscope—a compass mounted on gimbals, which maintains accurate directional headings even when tilted—becomes an oblique yet cogent symbol of stability and perseverance in a tumultuous environment.

In addition to the Dada contributions from Germany and the United States, another major inspirational factor was the art of Jean (Hans) Arp. A co-founder of the Dada group in Zürich, Arp had reacted against the horrific destruction of World War I by inventing an anti-rational aesthetics based on nature rather than man-made objects. His goal was

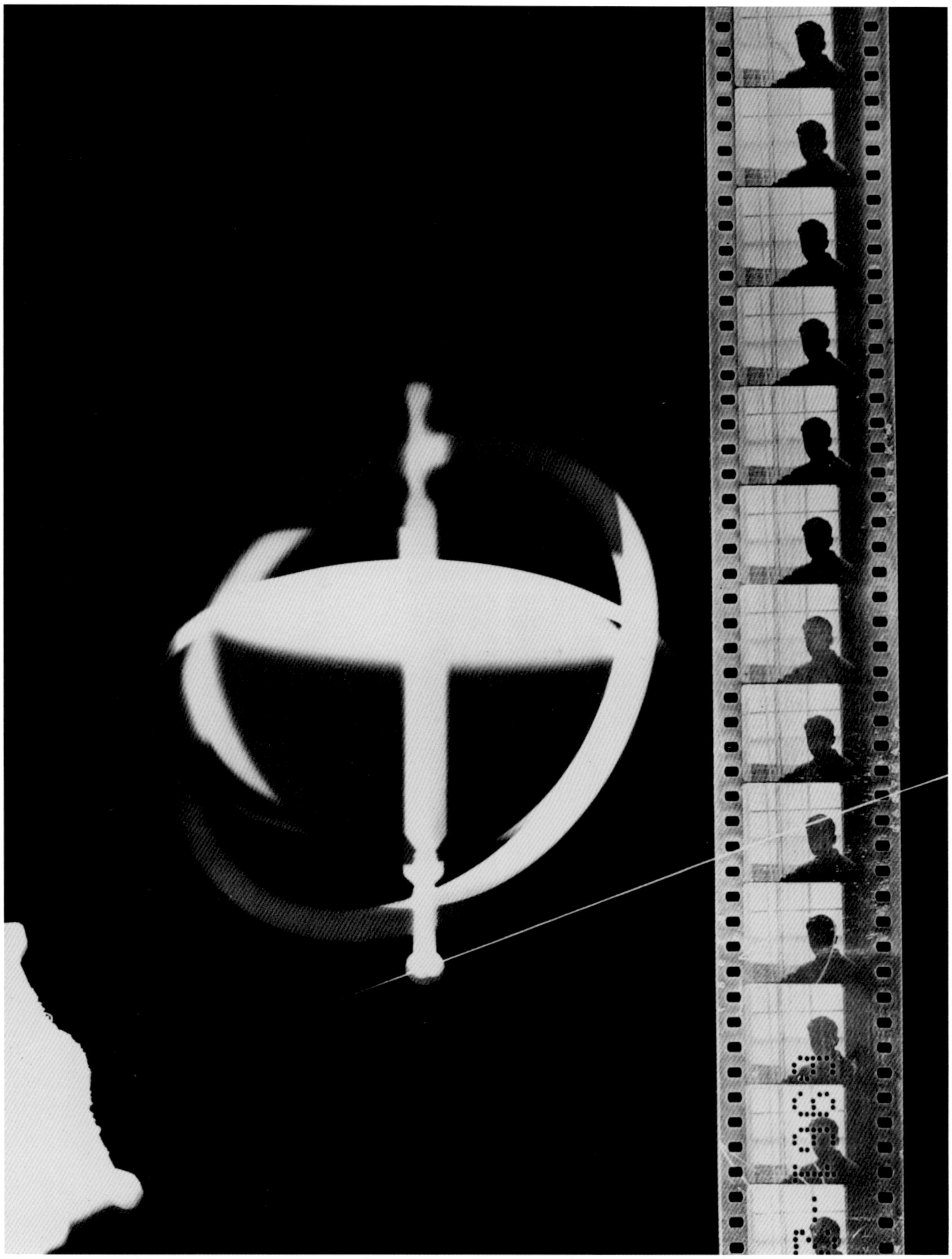

9

MAN RAY, *UNTITLED*, 1921

Smithsonian American Art Museum, Washington, DC; gift of Juliet Man Ray

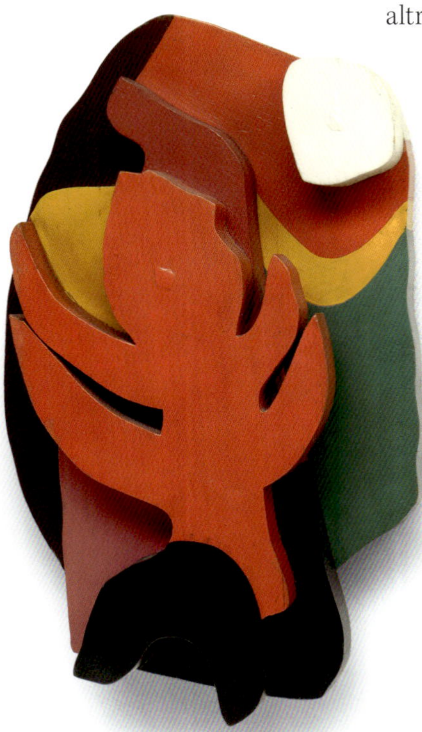

altruistic: to develop "an elementary art [that would] save men and women from the furious madness of the times. We aspired to ... establish an equilibrium between heaven and hell." Arp believed that "art should lose itself in nature, and even merge with nature. In this way art rids itself more and more of self-centeredness, virtuosity, and absurdity."[11] He started by sketching motifs from nature more from memory than from observation, a practice that allowed him to simplify the forms and give them a fluid vibrancy, as if caught in the process of becoming. His method was *automatist* (allowing his hand to start drawing without a preconceived subject), a practice that the Parisian Surrealists would enthusiastically embrace several years later. Arp preferred to title his compositions when they neared completion and believed that the process of creation and the interpretation of ambiguous forms were more important than the finished work. These, too, became fundamental principles in Surrealist art.

11
JEAN ARP
ENAK'S TEARS (EARTHLY FORMS), 1917
The Museum of Modern Art, New York; Benjamin Scharps and David Scharps Fund and purchase

In Zürich, Arp had begun a series of reliefs constructed from superimposed layers of wood, usually painted, which he called *Earthly Forms*.[12] He intended the amorphous forms in *The Forest*, 1916–17, and *Enak's Tears*, 1917 (figs. 10–11), to evoke rather than describe a subject. Instead of portraying an entire landscape, *The Forest* features only one lively tree on a receding background. The mellifluous forms in *Enak's Tears* are entirely abstract and bafflingly indecipherable. "Enak" sounds like the name of a fictitious creature, somewhat like the *orcs* and *ents* in J. R. R. Tolkien's writings; the term is also an Indonesian word meaning "delicious." Presumably, Arp was alluding to a biblical personage who fathered giants, though it remains for us to speculate why Enak is weeping.

10
JEAN ARP
THE FOREST (EARTHLY FORMS), 1916–17
National Gallery of Art, Washington, DC; Andrew W. Mellon Fund

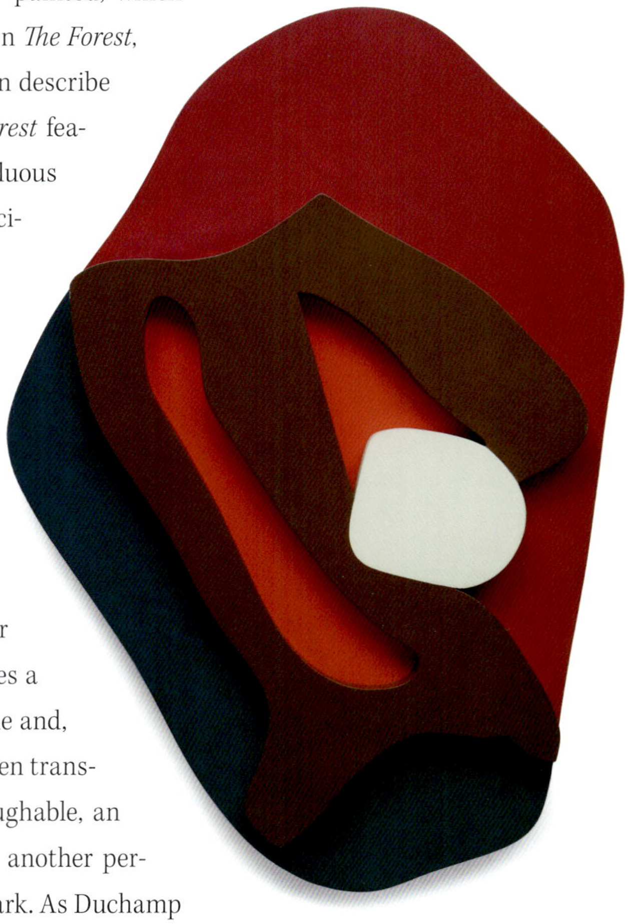

After the war, Arp defined and developed his aesthetics in compositions such as *Torso-Navel*, 1921 (fig. 12). Two blue forms stand out in relief on a large gray mass: the upper one appears to represent the head, and the lower one indicates a navel. The navel was Arp's favorite motif: every human has one and, as a visible marker of birth, it symbolizes new beginnings. When translated into English as "belly button," the symbol becomes laughable, an effect the artist would have undoubtedly appreciated. From another perspective, the blue shapes resemble an inflated exclamation mark. As Duchamp

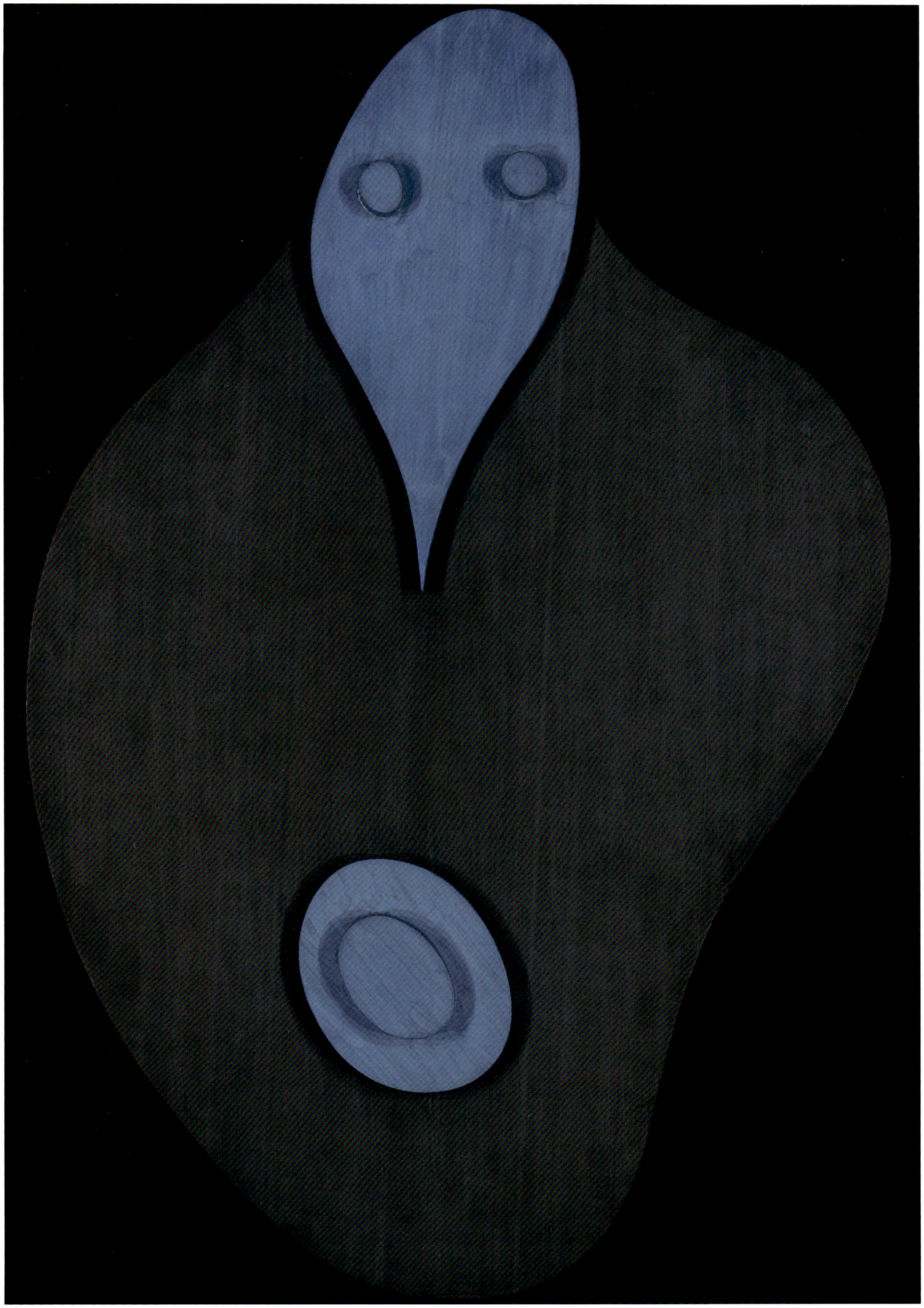

12
JEAN ARP, *TORSO-NAVEL*, 1921
Yale University Art Gallery, New Haven; gift of Katherine S. Dreier to the Collection Société Anonyme

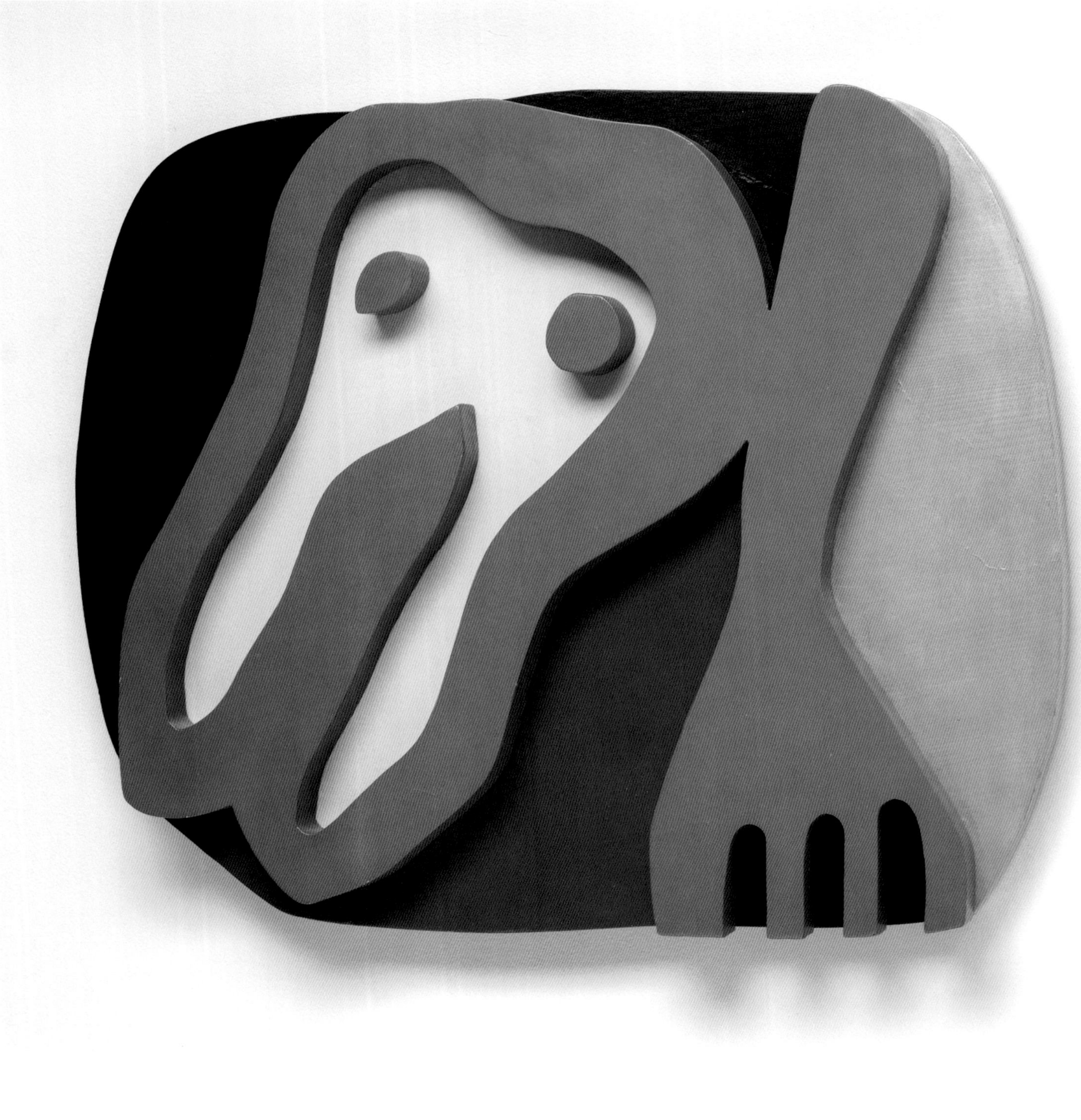

13
JEAN ARP, *SHIRT FRONT AND FORK*, 1922
National Gallery of Art, Washington, DC; Ailsa Mellon Bruce Fund

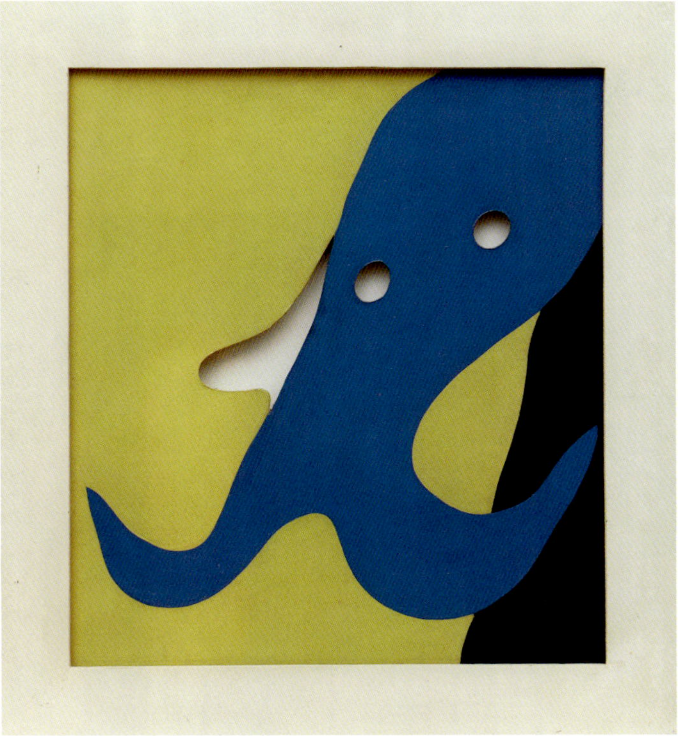

14
JEAN ARP
MAN-MUSTACHES, 1925
Private collection, courtesy
Acquavella Galleries, New York

later recalled, "the important element introduced . . . by Arp was humor in its subtlest form: the kind of whimsical conceptions that gave . . . such an exuberant liveliness. . . . Arp showed the importance of a smile."[13] The artist's fondness for nonsensical images and unexpected transformations also characterize his poems, as in "It Will Turn into a Head," 1922: "if you sew a cackling bouquet on this happy holiday / it will turn into a head / that instantly looks at itself in a mirror / and wonders: is that me or isn't that me."[14]

Even when Arp portrayed inanimate objects, like articles of clothing, they swell and swirl with vitality. He described one motif, a bottle with a belly button, as a "monstrous household implement" derived from a bicycle, a brassiere, a spoon, and a sea serpent.[15] These are the kinds of subliminal associations that he hoped viewers would respond to. In *Shirt Front and Fork*, 1922 (fig. 13), the shirt looks like a very peculiar head with two eyes or a giant molar with cavities. In *Clock*, 1924 (fig. 15), the numerals have been replaced by squiggly pictographs, and the minute-hand by a tumescent penis or molten cigar. To further tease us, the artist intended to hang *Clock* in randomly changing orientations, even upside down, to mock the importance we place on time and schedules.

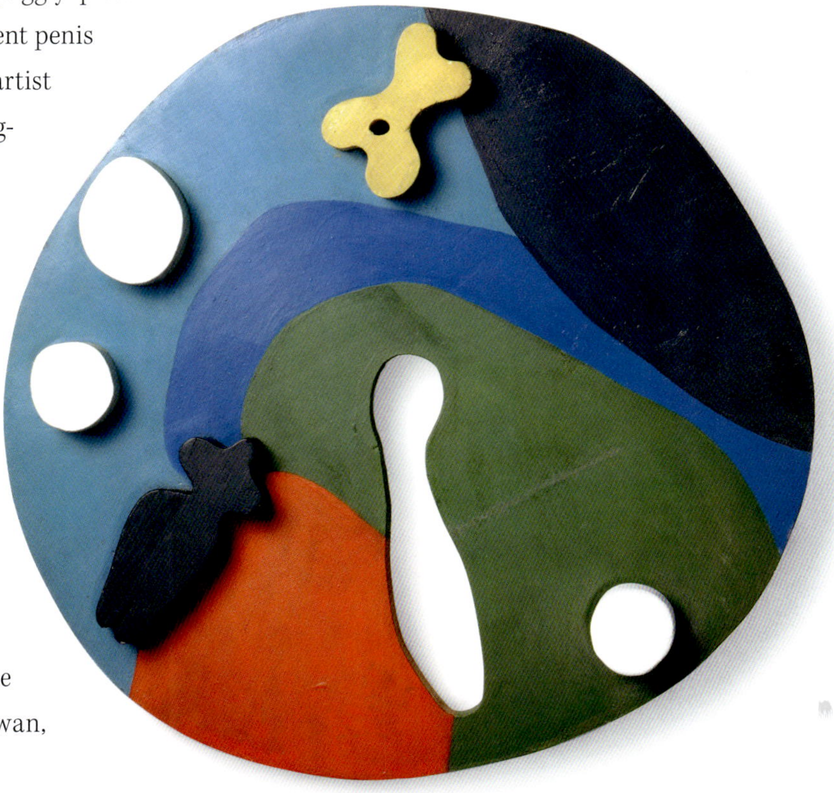

15
JEAN ARP, *CLOCK*, 1924
Kunstmuseum Basel; gift of
Marguerite Arp-Hagenbach

Arp usually depicted his subjects as if caught in the act of changing into something else, a process known as metamorphosis—the Greek term for the transmutation of reality. Classical myths and modern fairy tales provide many examples of humans changing into different entities through magic or divine intervention: Zeus transformed into a swan,

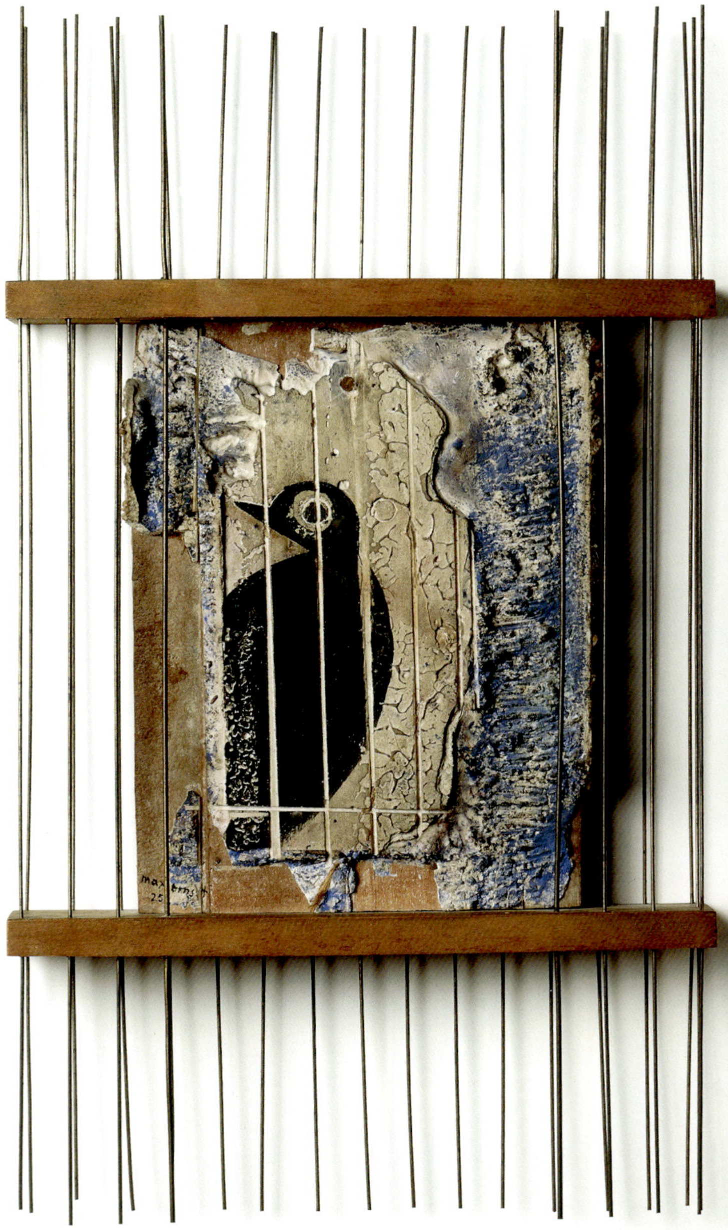

16
MAX ERNST
CAGES ARE ALWAYS IMAGINARY, 1925
Kunsthaus Zürich

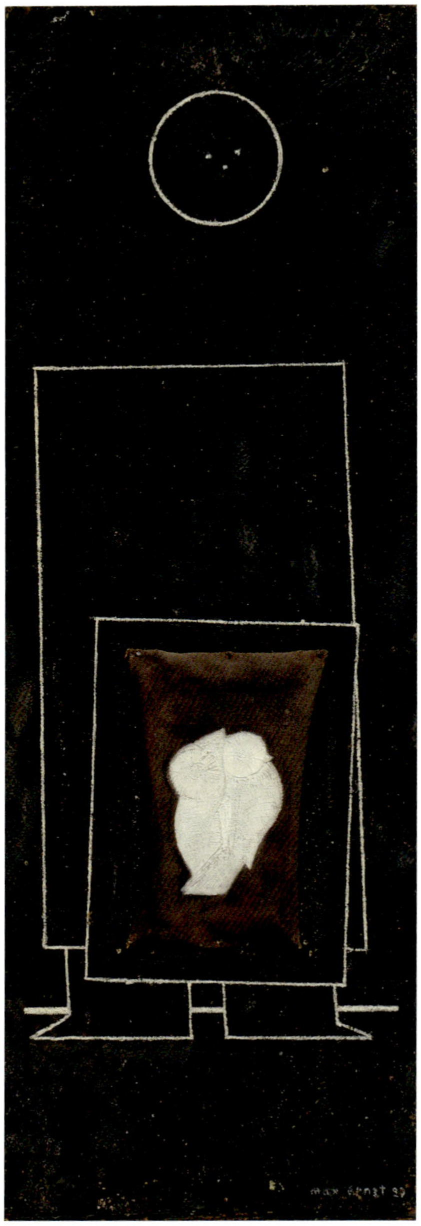

17
MAX ERNST
HUMAN FIGURE WITH TWO BIRDS, 1925/1929
The Art Institute of Chicago; through prior gift of the Albert Kunstadter Family Foundation

Daphne into a laurel tree, and Arachne into a spider. Nature shows us many metamorphoses: a tiny acorn grows into a massive oak, cocooned caterpillars emerge as butterflies, eggs hatch into turtles, and black carbon compresses into clear diamonds. In European fairy tales—especially those by the brothers Grimm—a pumpkin turns into a carriage and a frog into a handsome prince. The titles of Arp's reliefs remind us of magical events in our world and nudge us to imagine others: *Torso with Flower Head, Lunar Frog, Head-Landscape, Phantom Chasing a Navel.*

When Arp arrived in Paris in early 1925, financial difficulties forced him to make reliefs from cardboard rather than wood. *Man-Mustaches*, 1925 (fig. 14), presents a large blue head with two frontal eyes and a profile nose defined as negative spaces cut out to reveal the white wall behind. The head merges with its exaggeratedly large mustache, a fluid shape that can also be perceived as a squid or octopus walking on floppy limbs. Such spontaneous perceptions, like those of a creative child, invite us to laugh at ourselves and perhaps to question our presumed superiority over other creatures.

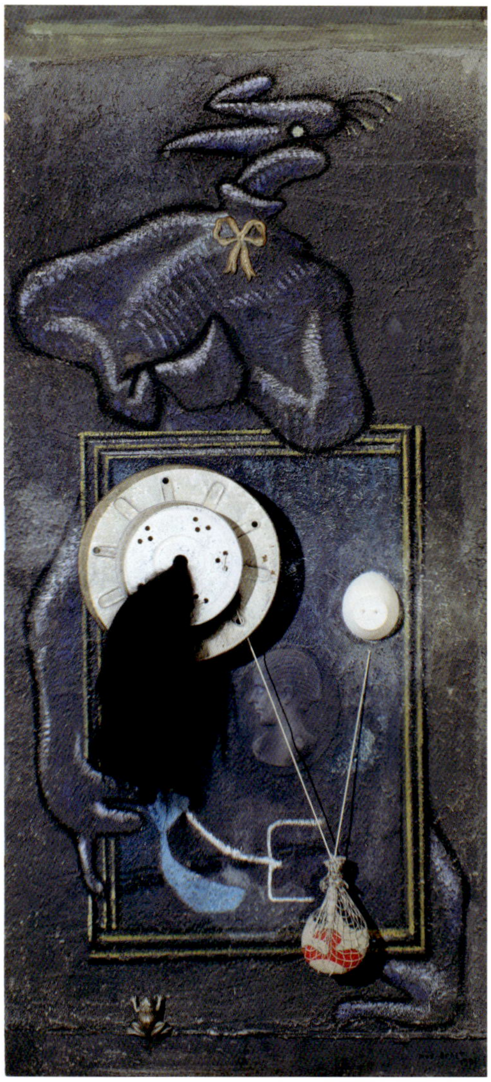

18
MAX ERNST
LOPLOP INTRODUCES A YOUNG GIRL, 1930/1936
Musée national d'art moderne, Centre Georges Pompidou, Paris

PERIOD OF EXPERIMENTATION, 1924–29

When the *Manifesto of Surrealism* was written, only a few artists—all of them painters—had formulated a style that fit the conceptual criteria. Experimentation became an end in itself. In the early and mid-1920s, Ernst painted many images of birds, which have traditionally symbolized freedom. Sometimes he sketched dark vertical lines over the birds to simulate cages. He also constructed relief frames that exceed mere decoration to function as physical enclosures, although it is not clear whether they are protective or punitive. On several thick chunks of concrete and plaster, the artist painted birds and then superimposed actual objects. In *Cages Are Always Imaginary*, 1925 (fig. 16), for example, heavy black metal bars heighten the effect of a bird forcibly held in captivity. Yet the title offers hope, suggesting that no matter how constrained we may be by physical limitations, debilitating fears, or socio-political events, our spirits can still soar. A similarly optimistic message is delivered without bars in *Human Figure with Two Birds*, 1925/1929 (fig. 17), where Ernst painted small white doves on a piece of gray sandpaper, which he attached to a large black window shutter. The birds appear to glow with an inner light that bespeaks a sense of power, even transcendence, over their dark and gritty environment.[16]

Soon the artist invented a biomorphic bird, called Loplop, as a symbol of himself. In *Loplop Presents*, 1929, the large creature cavorts around a very small birdcage, as if triumphantly gloating. *Loplop Introduces a Young Girl*, 1930/1936 (fig. 18), shows the biomorph standing above and amid small domestic items attached to the canvas. The dominance of Loplop's curving forms over the banal objects might be construed as nature triumphing over the man-made or the spirit over flesh. Ernst's erudition and nuanced imagery helped Breton formulate Surrealist concepts and encouraged others to seek complexity, ambiguity, and symbolism in art.

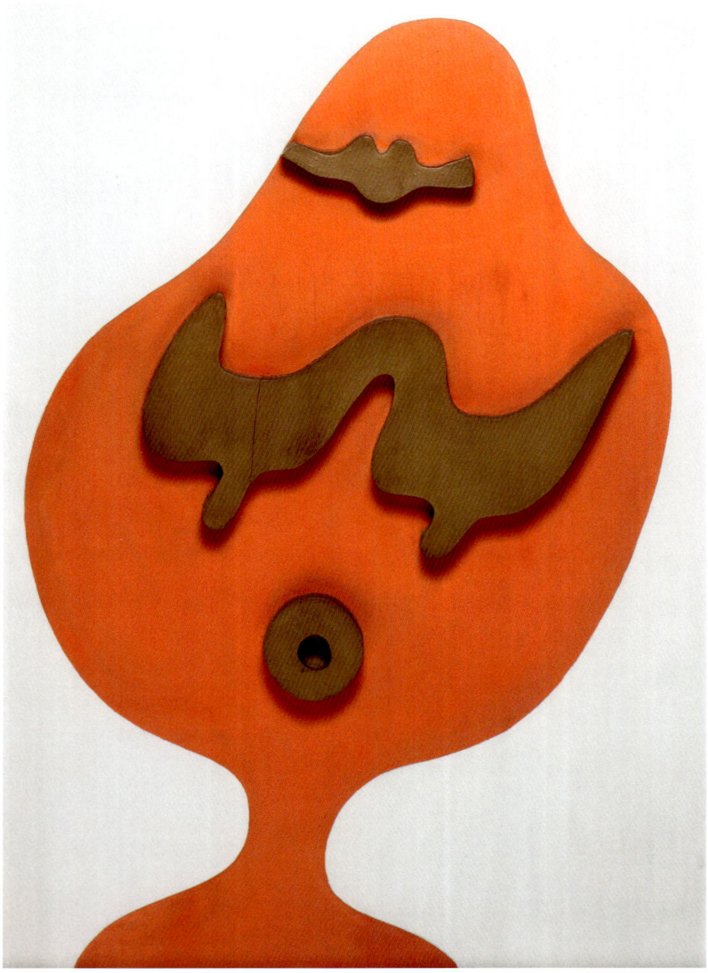

19
JEAN ARP
WOMAN, 1927
Musée national d'art moderne, Centre Georges Pompidou, Paris

The shapes of Ernst's Loplop figure evolved directly from Arp's aesthetics. The two artists had become close friends in 1914, corresponded throughout the war, and vacationed together in mid-1922. When Arp moved to Paris three years later, Ernst introduced him to the Surrealists, and Arp participated in the *Surrealist Painting* exhibition at Galerie Pierre in November 1925. In addition to influencing Ernst, the impact of Arp's biomorphism on Miró was immediate and profound, encouraging the Spaniard to move beyond the stylized forms he had derived from Romanesque and Catalan folk art. The transformation of Miró's style is evident in the progression from *The Farm*, 1921–22, to *Harlequin's Carnival*, 1924–25, and then to full-blown organic abstraction in *Painting (Circus Horse)*, 1927 (fig. 20).[17] Prior to Arp's presence in Paris, artists interested in abstraction had turned to mathematical paradigms, particularly the angular geometry of Cubism and the austere grids of De Stijl. Arp introduced the first viable alternative: an abstract language based on nature and humor. Whereas geometry speaks to the rational mind, evocative organisms should (in theory) appeal to our biological selves and communicate with our subconscious minds on a subliminal and intuitive level.

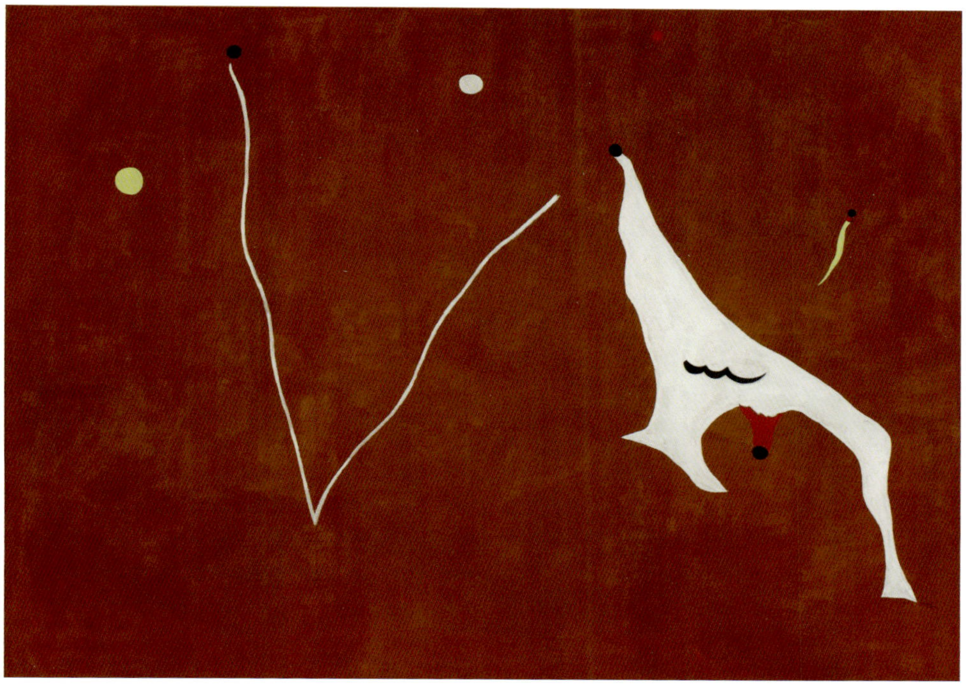

20
JOAN MIRÓ, *PAINTING (CIRCUS HORSE)*, 1927
Hirshhorn Museum and Sculpture Garden, Washington, DC; gift of the Joseph H. Hirshhorn Foundation

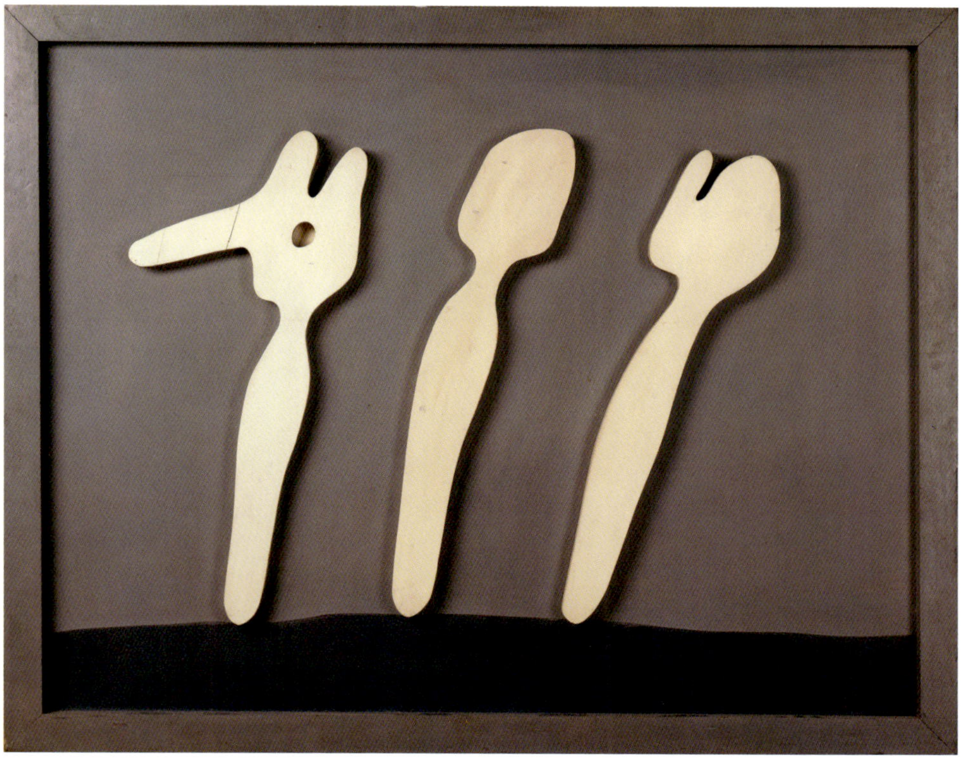

21
JEAN ARP, *THREE WALKING STICKS*, 1927
Kunstsammlung Nordrhein-Westfalen, Düsseldorf

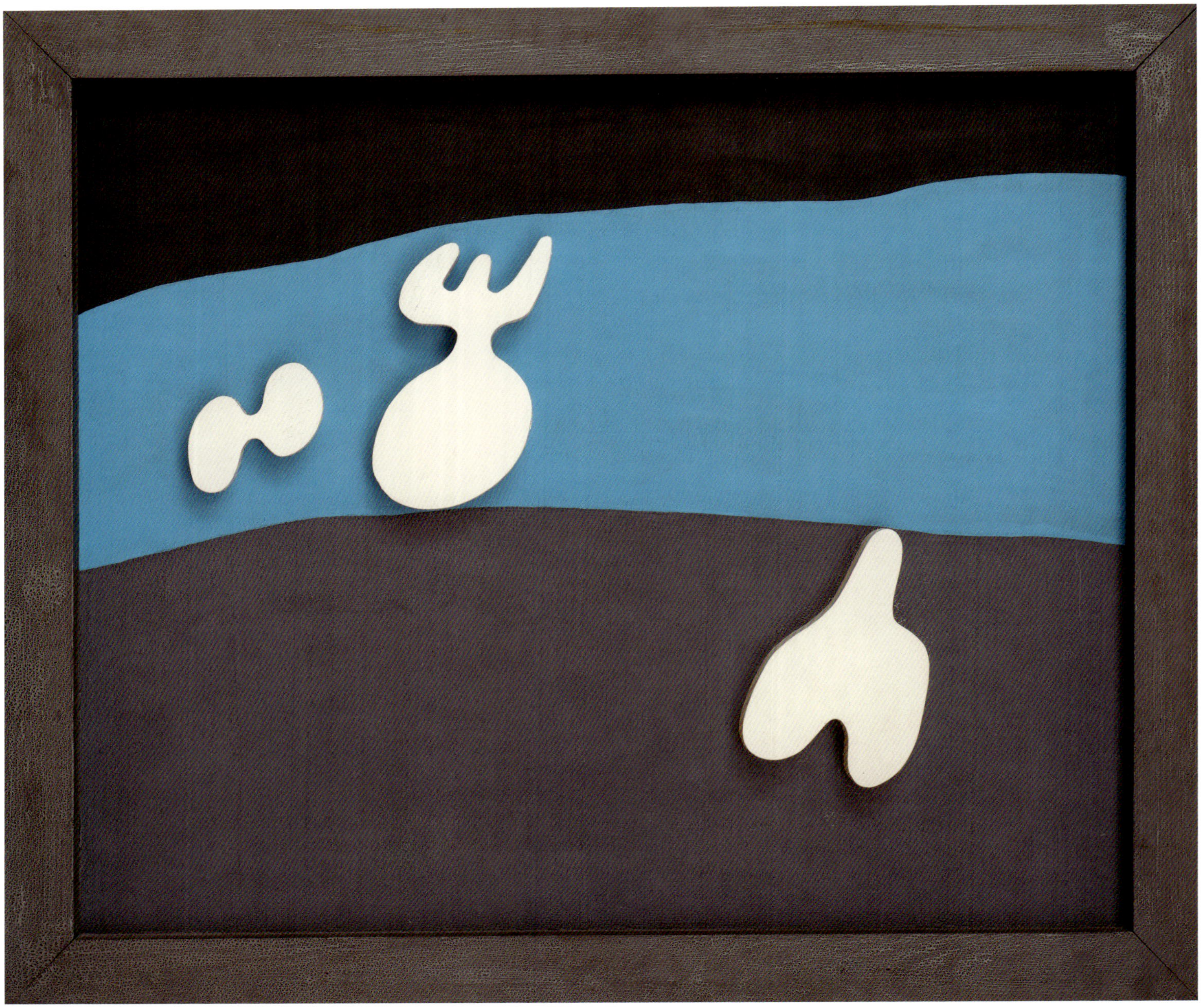

22
JEAN ARP, *OBJECTS PLACED ON THREE PLANES LIKE WRITING*, 1928
Wadsworth Atheneum Museum of Art, Hartford; purchased through the gift of James Junius Goodwin

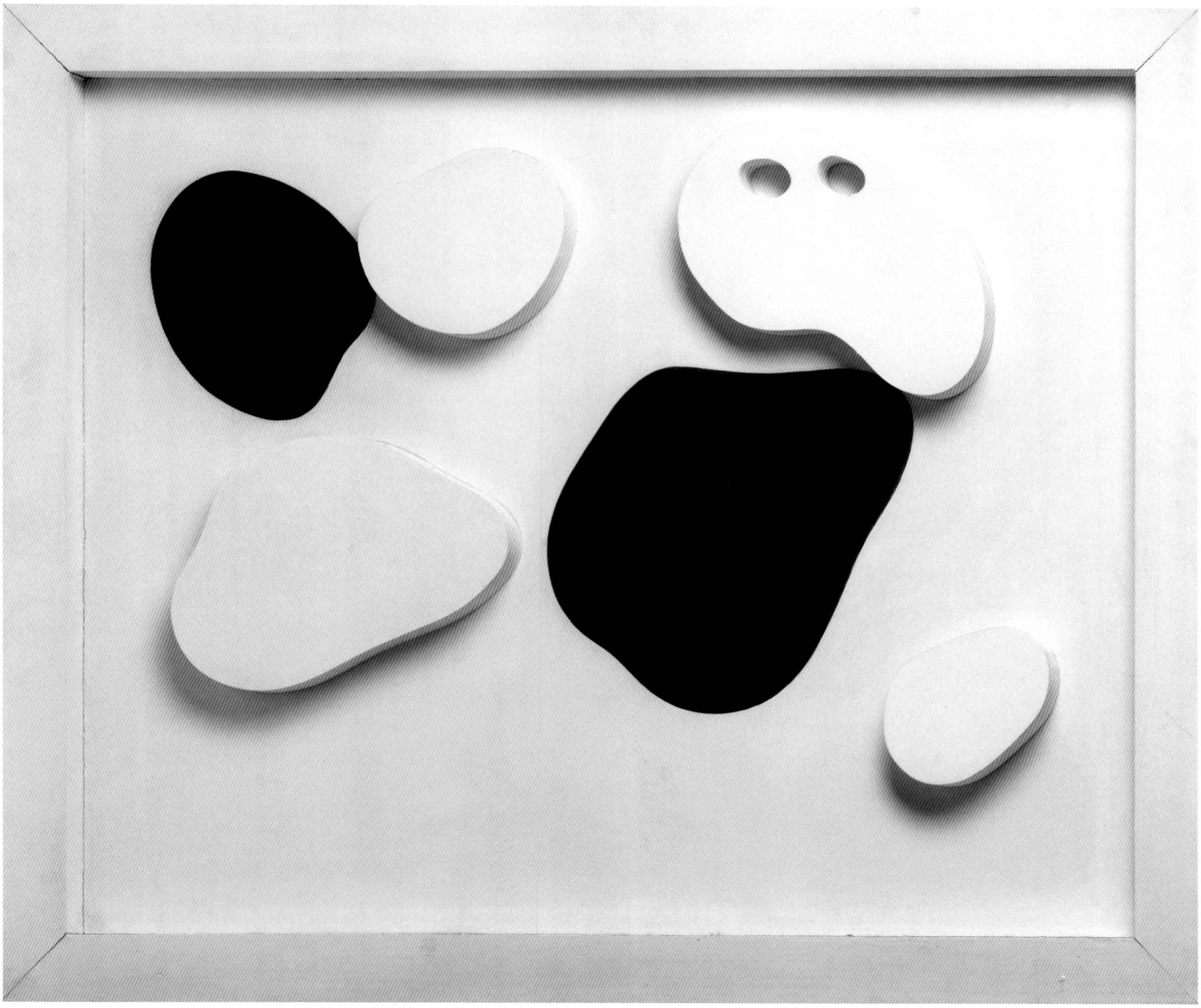

23
JEAN ARP, *CONFIGURATION WITH TWO DANGEROUS POINTS*, c.1930
Philadelphia Museum of Art; A. E. Gallatin Collection

Arp's metamorphic inventiveness became known to a wider audience in his exhibition of forty-six works at the Galerie Surréaliste in November 1927. By this time the artist could afford to make larger reliefs from better-quality materials and have them professionally fabricated by a carpenter. Examples include *Three Walking Sticks*, *Dancer*, and *Woman*, 1927 (the latter two acquired by Breton; figs. 21 and 19). *Objects Placed on Three Planes Like Writing*, 1928 (fig. 22), features three white forms superimposed on a background of three horizontal bands, suggestive of lines on paper or an abstract landscape of the kind favored by Miró in his contemporaneous paintings. Arp's protoplasmic forms appear to hover weightlessly and to squirm as if alive and eager to convey some calligraphic meaning, much like the mental energy of a written text or the vitality of a musical performance. The entities may be read as amoebic abstractions or as shorthand notations for a bow tie (on the left), a figure with arms raised or wearing a flower hat (in the center), and a torso or bifurcated bottle (on the right). Another flight of fancy might see the forms as child, father, and mother in a story like "Goldilocks and the Three Bears." No interpretation is wrong; an observer can see whatever she wants to—the further from rational reality, the better.

OBJECTS: THE REAL AS UNREAL

At the end of the Roaring Twenties several events precipitated a greater interest in sculpture among Surrealists. Breton's *Second Manifesto of Surrealism*, published in the last issue of *La Révolution surréaliste* in December 1929, coincided with a divisive split among the group's members over Marxist politics.[18] The new manifesto redefined the movement's aspirations and methods. Instead of seeking refuge from reality by escaping into dreams and fantasies, Surrealists should henceforth find inspiration in concrete things. Ordinary objects, when deprived of their normal function and placed in odd combinations, could trigger a collision between conscious reason and subconscious intuitions, shocking us out of habitual thinking. Objects would therefore be chosen for their psychic resonance and ability to evoke voluntary and involuntary associations. As Breton explained in *Communicating Vessels*, 1932, "the finding of the object rigorously fulfills the same function as the dream in the sense that it frees the individual from affective, paralyzing scruples." Although commodity-based, these new sculptures should be "utterly unjustifiable both in terms of their usefulness and their entertainment value." That the Surrealists used the word "object," rather than "thing," is significant. In French and English the word can mean not only a physical entity but also a goal, as in "the object of our quest is freedom."

Along with the *Second Manifesto of Surrealism*, the December 1929 issue of *La Révolution surréaliste* featured an illustrated text by the Belgian painter René Magritte entitled "Words and Images" (see pp. 162–63), which succinctly summarizes how depictions of ordinary items

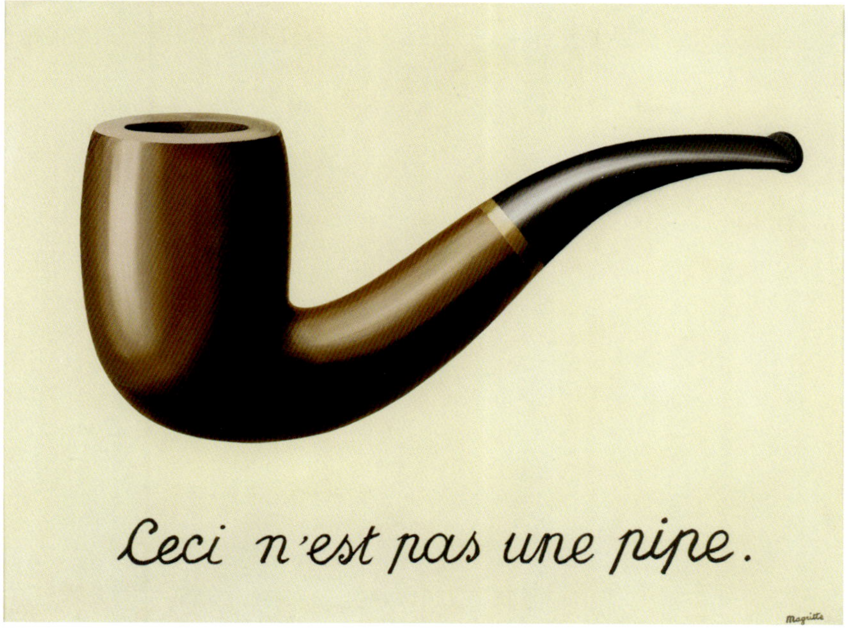

24
RENÉ MAGRITTE
THE TREACHERY OF IMAGES (THIS IS NOT A PIPE), 1929
Los Angeles County Museum of Art; purchased with funds provided by the Mr. and Mrs. William Preston Harrison Collection

can challenge our dominant sense of logic. By captioning an image of a leaf with the word "cannon," Magritte demonstrates his belief that "an object never fulfills the same function as its name or image." In *The Treachery of Images*, 1929 (fig. 24), an image of a tobacco pipe is captioned "Ceci n'est pas une pipe" (This Is Not a Pipe). The title is quite literal: the painting is an image of a pipe, not an actual one. In another sense, the phrase is an admonition not to believe what we see. Magritte would later expand the idea into sculpture with *This Is a Piece of Cheese*, 1936–37, a small painting of cheese inside a glass serving dish. Although Magritte left Breton's group and returned to Brussels in July 1930, his confrontational portrayal of ambiguously identified objects helped change the direction of Surrealist art.

These new ideas fortuitously coincided with the Surrealists' discovery of the Swiss-born sculptor Alberto Giacometti, who had worked in obscurity since arriving in Paris in 1922. Several years later he discovered the totemic frontality, stylized forms, and fertility symbolism of African wood carvings. *Spoon Woman*, 1926 (fig. 25), presents a narrowly defined concept of woman as a large womb topped by geometric forms that may be understood as a bust and a tiny head (or hairdo). The figure's identity is equated almost entirely with her reproductive capacity rather than any intellectual function. The artist pursued the theme of gender symbolism in a series of nearly flat abstractions entitled *Woman* or *Man*, 1929–30 (fig. 26), which brought Giacometti to the attention of the so-called "dissident" Surrealists who operated more or less separately from Breton's coterie.

Centered on the writers Georges Bataille and Michel Leiris, this other group delved into the darker recesses of the human unconscious. Their fantasies of aggression, eroticism, and violence complemented Giacometti's own obsessions and encouraged him to explore them in sculptures such as *Reclining Woman Who Dreams*, 1929 (originally titled *Woman in*

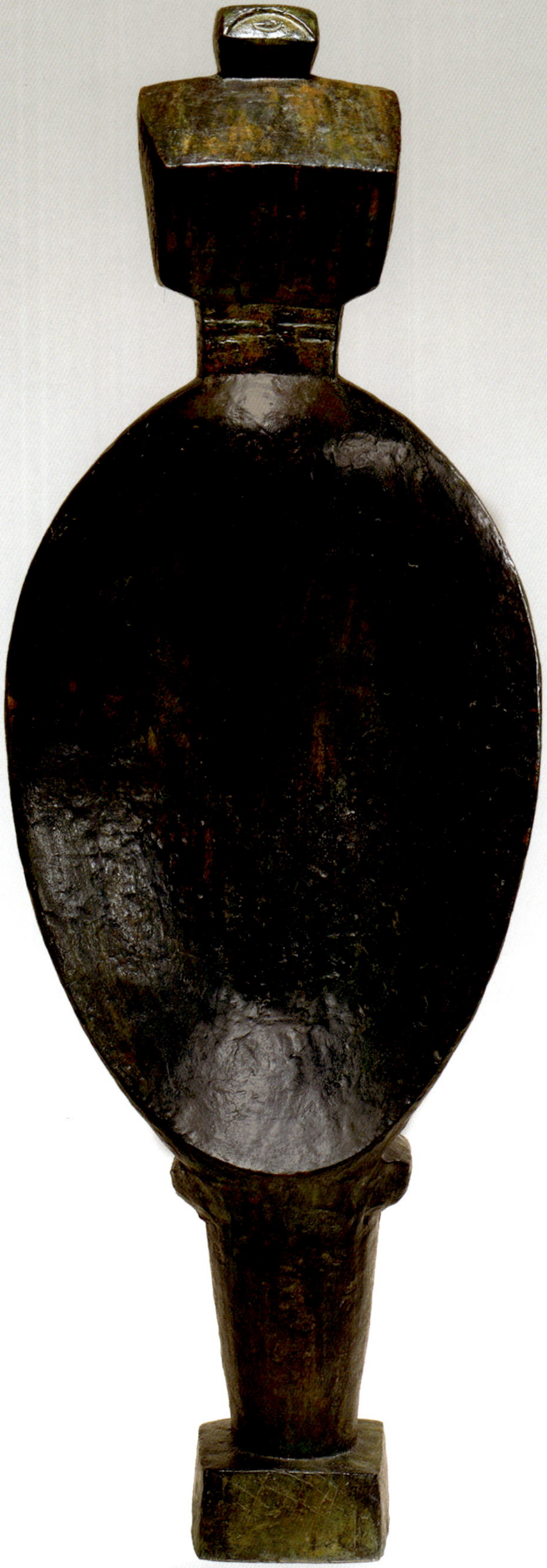

25
ALBERTO GIACOMETTI
SPOON WOMAN, 1926
Raymond and Patsy Nasher Collection,
Nasher Sculpture Center, Dallas

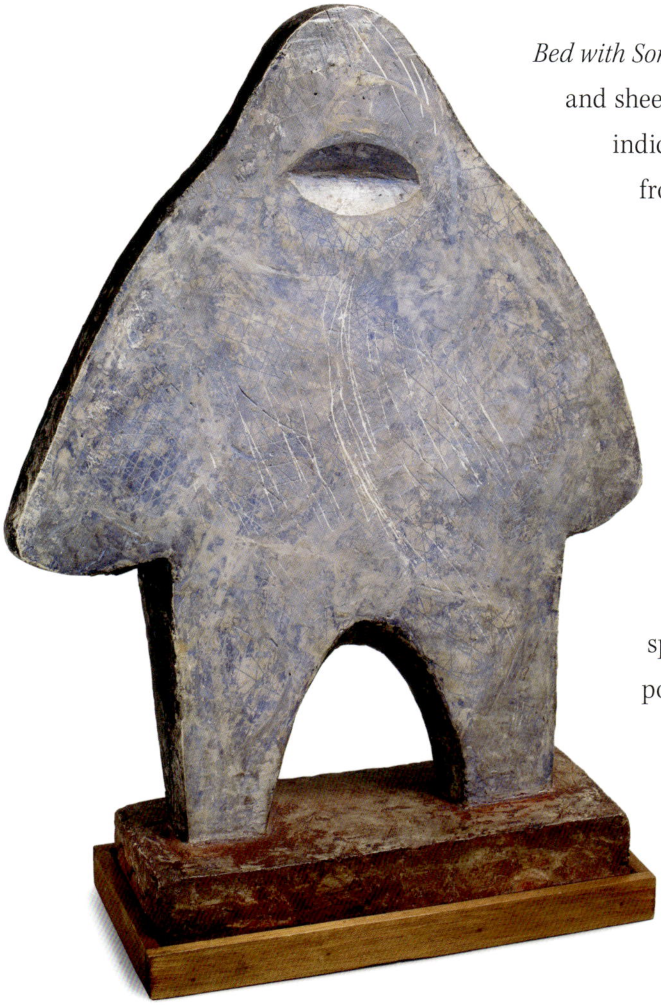

Bed with Someone Else; fig. 27). Two horizontal planes represent a figure and sheets moving rhythmically in bed, with an empty half-sphere indicating the woman's head. When a viewer shifts position in front of the sculpture, the phallus-shaped bedpost overlaps and appears to penetrate the head. Giacometti developed this theme of erotic reverie more aggressively in *Man and Woman*, 1929 (fig. 28), where two linear figures confront one another. The male is depicted as an elongated, sharp, and bent prong that thrusts threateningly toward the female's vagina, while her body recoils in fear—a succinct, if somewhat brutal, visualization of the primal urge to procreate.

Giacometti translated these themes into more spatially complex constructions in 1930–31. The ovoid and pointed forms in *The Cage* (fig. 29), are arranged on diagonals to suggest dynamic tension, as if locked in some undefined conflict. From a crossbar in the iron frame of *Suspended Ball* (fig. 30), a sphere hangs above a recumbent elongated crescent. Its upper surface matches the groove cut in the underside of the sphere. At rest the composition might be described as a geometric abstraction comparable to contemporaneous vanguard movements in the Soviet Union and Germany. But when the viewer—an active participant—sets Giacometti's sphere in motion like a pendulum, it glides up and down the crescent in a way that is highly suggestive of sexual intercourse. Instead of the aggression implied in *Man and Woman*, here the theme is frustration; the two forms do not ever actually touch because the string is too short.[19] That Giacometti had introduced movement and thereby managed to evoke erotic desire astounded the Surrealists; Breton bought the sculpture and invited the artist to join his circle.

26
ALBERTO GIACOMETTI
MAN, 1929–30
Hirshhorn Museum and Sculpture Garden, Washington, DC; gift of Joseph H. Hirshhorn

By spring 1930 the newcomer was fully immersed in the Surrealist ethos and displayed recent sculptures in the *Miró—Arp—Giacometti* exhibition at the Galerie Pierre Loeb. No catalogue or installation photographs exist, but presumably the overall aesthetic was biomorphic. Miró's *Relief Construction*, 1930, for example, presents two superimposed layers of wood elements dominated by a central white form akin to Arp's enigmatic torso motif. But Miró added a hint of aggression by forcing metal staples into the form's surface, reflecting his desire to avoid the seduction of pure beauty in his art. The fluid contours of Giacometti's *Man* and *Reclining Woman Who Dreams* bore some resemblance to organic abstraction, but any similarity was as superficial as his acceptance of the Surrealists' term "object." In the

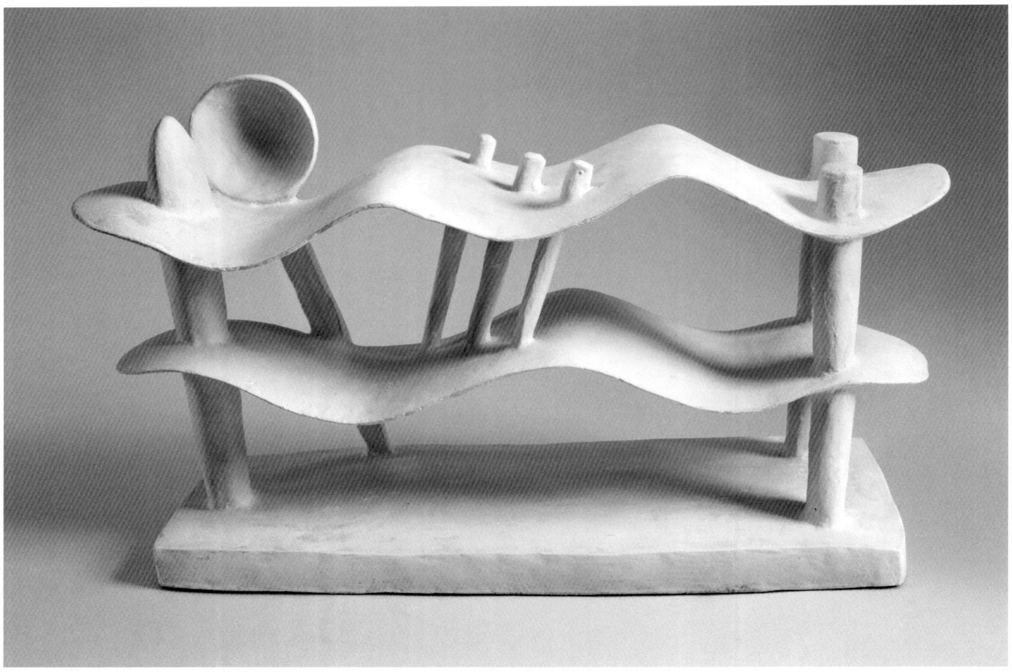

27
ALBERTO GIACOMETTI
RECLINING WOMAN WHO DREAMS, 1929
Hirshhorn Museum and Sculpture Garden, Washington, DC; gift of Joseph H. Hirshhorn

28
ALBERTO GIACOMETTI
MAN AND WOMAN, 1929
Musée national d'art moderne, Centre Georges Pompidou, Paris

December 1931 issue of *Le Surréalisme au service de la révolution* he published drawings of seven sculptures—including *The Cage*, *Suspended Ball*, and *Disagreeable Object*—as "Moving and Mute Objects" (fig. 35). None incorporated found items; rather, Giacometti modeled them in plaster and had them executed in wood by a local carpenter.

In the same issue Dalí published "Surrealist Objects," an essay proclaiming new categories of sculpture, including "objects for throwing" and "wrapped objects."[20] He defined "objects functioning symbolically" as constructions whose potential meanings are not revealed until a viewer sets them in motion or otherwise plays with the components. One of Dalí's first assemblages presents a woman's red shoe containing a glass of milk, along with sugar cubes. Adhering to the artist's paranoiac-critical aesthetics, which demanded that both attraction and revulsion be manifest, the glass rests on top of a brown turd.

Giacometti's *Disagreeable Object* could be considered a plaything for women, as in Ray's photograph (fig. 31). The ridiculously sized penis flaunts the artist's sometimes desperate aspirations toward sexual prowess, and the thorn-like bits on the tip allude to his fantasies of sadomasochism.

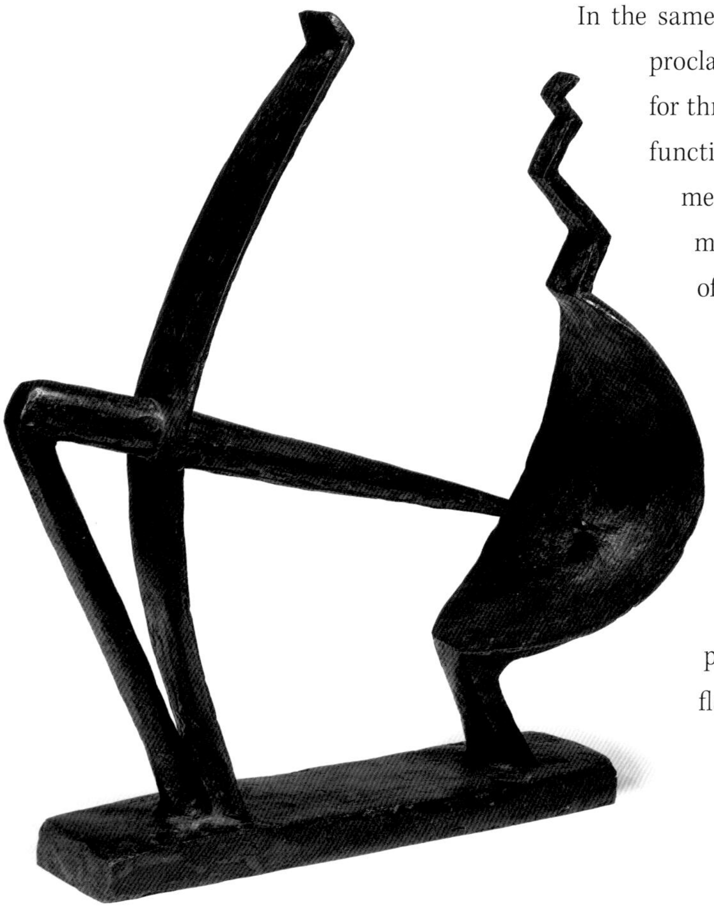

29
ALBERTO GIACOMETTI
THE CAGE, 1930–31
Moderna Museet, Stockholm; purchase

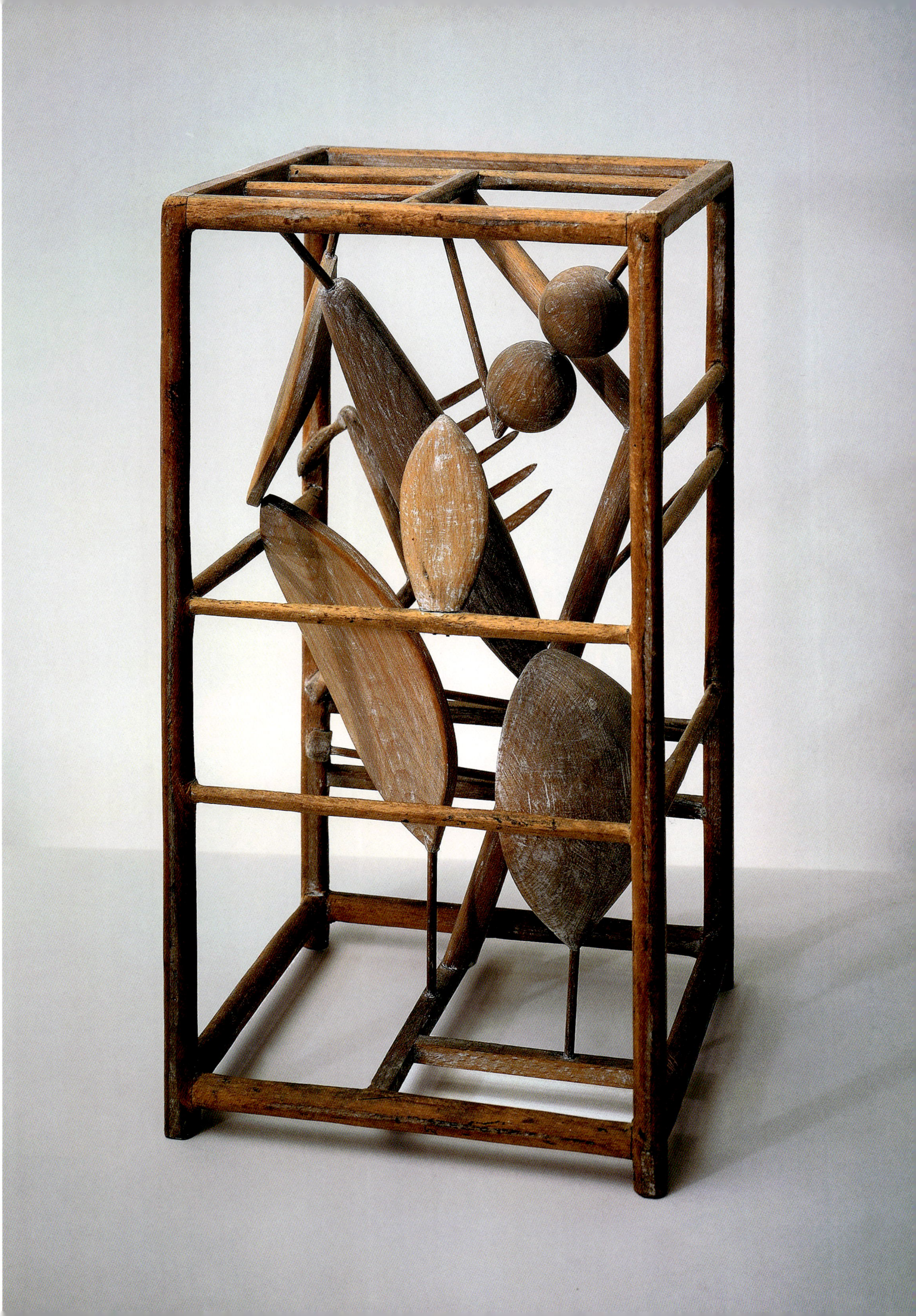

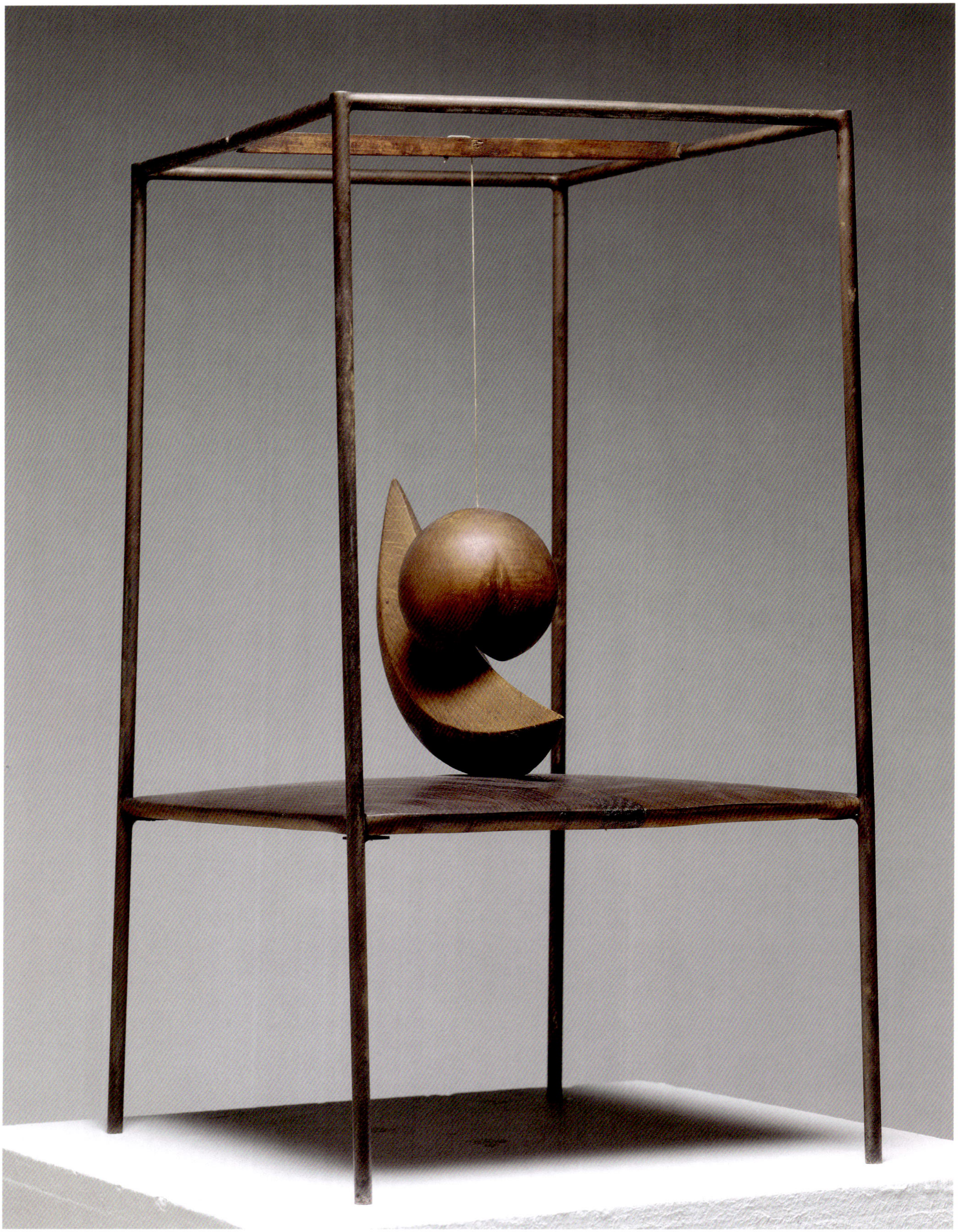

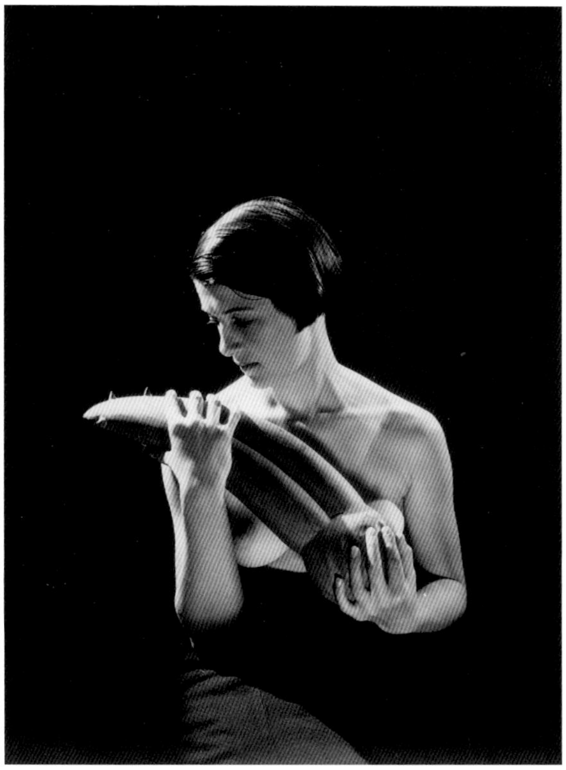

31
MAN RAY
WOMAN HOLDING GIACOMETTI'S "DISAGREEABLE OBJECT," 1931
Musée national d'art moderne, Centre Georges Pompidou, Paris

In comparison, Miró's contemporary *Personage with Umbrella* (fig. 32)—a coat rack "figure" with a large horizontal rod projecting outward at hip level—appears more comical than aggressive, perhaps reflecting the fact that the happily married Miró was not plagued by gender and potency issues. [21]

Giacometti's solo exhibition at the Galerie Pierre Colle in May 1932 revealed an astonishing range of unprecedented subjects and formats that are neither biomorphic nor assemblage. Rather, his Surrealist sculptures metaphorically express his neurotic anxieties and ambivalence about relationships. Outwardly a devoted son, Giacometti feared being hindered by his parents; in *Family Portrait*, 1930, three standing posts of varying heights are firmly yoked together. Yet another sculpture, now known as *Caress*, represents in white marble a woman's pregnant abdomen, gently held by two incised hands—an image of joyful expectation.

In *Point to the Eye* a sharp phallic weapon aims directly at a small head on a spike, a dramatic image of aggression and imminent harm. *Caught Hand* suspends a wooden arm inside a mechanism, facing a gear-like wheel that presumably can be set in motion by the attached hand-crank (possibly an echo of Alexander Calder's contemporaneous kinetic constructions). *Flower in Danger*, 1932–33 (fig. 34), presents a curved wooden rod resembling a catapult or archer's bow, which is held in tension by a filament connected to a trigger mechanism. If the taut string were suddenly released, the rod would whiplash viciously and possibly hit the white plaster blossom hanging precariously from its metal stalk (which also eerily resembles a standing figure with a white head). But the release mechanism does not function, so the violence is held in abeyance, a clever metaphor for how innocence and purity are ever-menaced. None of these sculptures is interactive; rather, they each focus on the threat (and perhaps the sadistic pleasure) of anticipated pain, instead of the destructive act itself.

Giacometti carried the idea of sculptural drama further in *The Palace at 4 a.m.*, 1932 (fig. 33), where the format is a theater stage or the inside of a building. The actors are a female figure, a large pod

32
JOAN MIRÓ
PERSONAGE WITH UMBRELLA, 1931
Reproduced in *Le Surréalisme au service de la révolution*, no. 3 (December 1931)

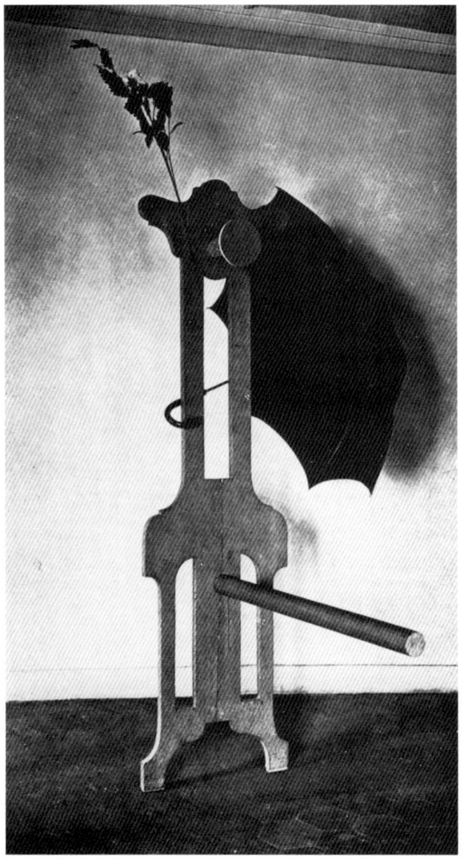

30
ALBERTO GIACOMETTI
SUSPENDED BALL, 1930–31
Musée national d'art moderne, Centre Georges Pompidou, Paris

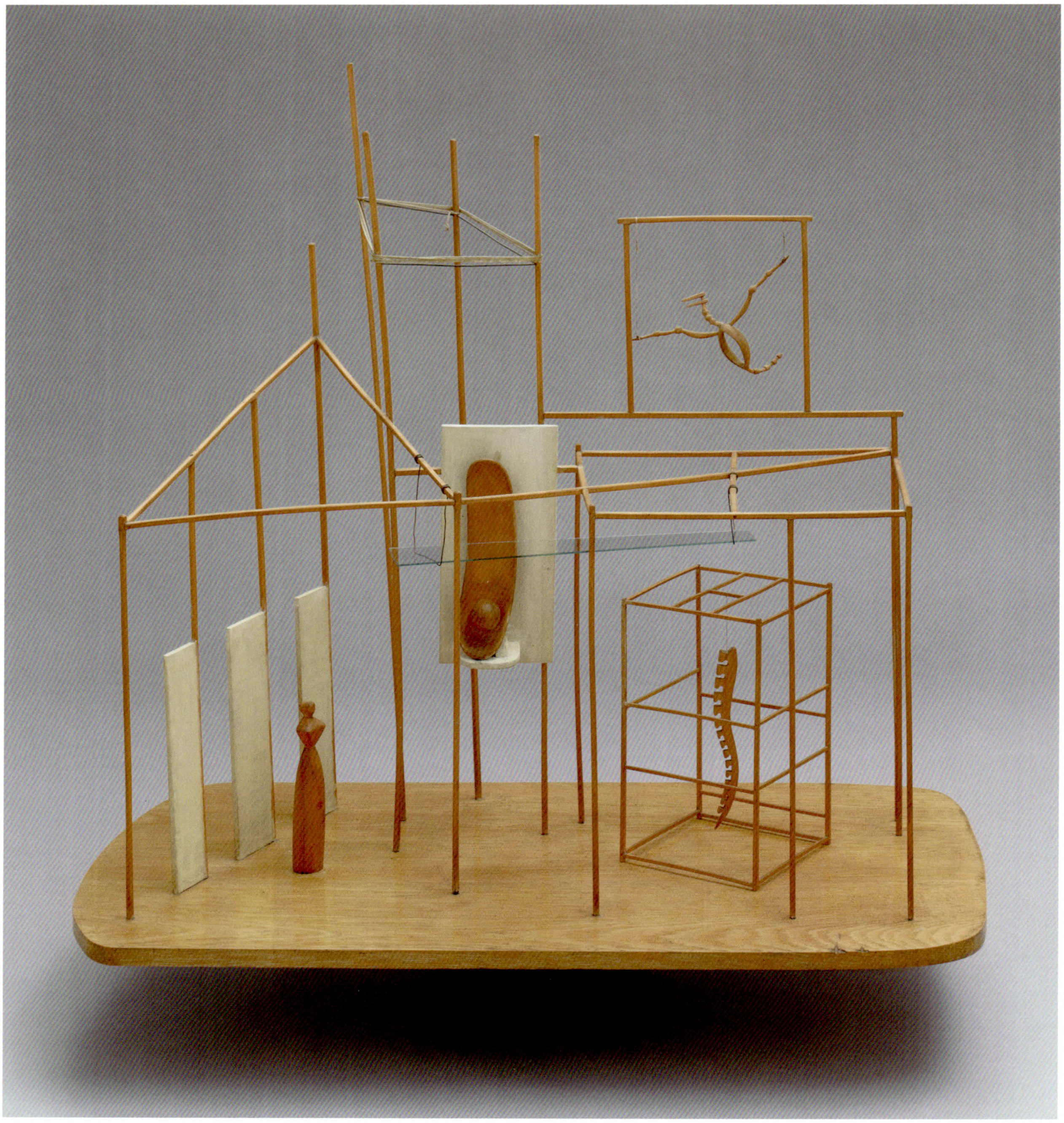

33
ALBERTO GIACOMETTI, *THE PALACE AT 4 A.M.*, 1932
The Museum of Modern Art, New York; purchase

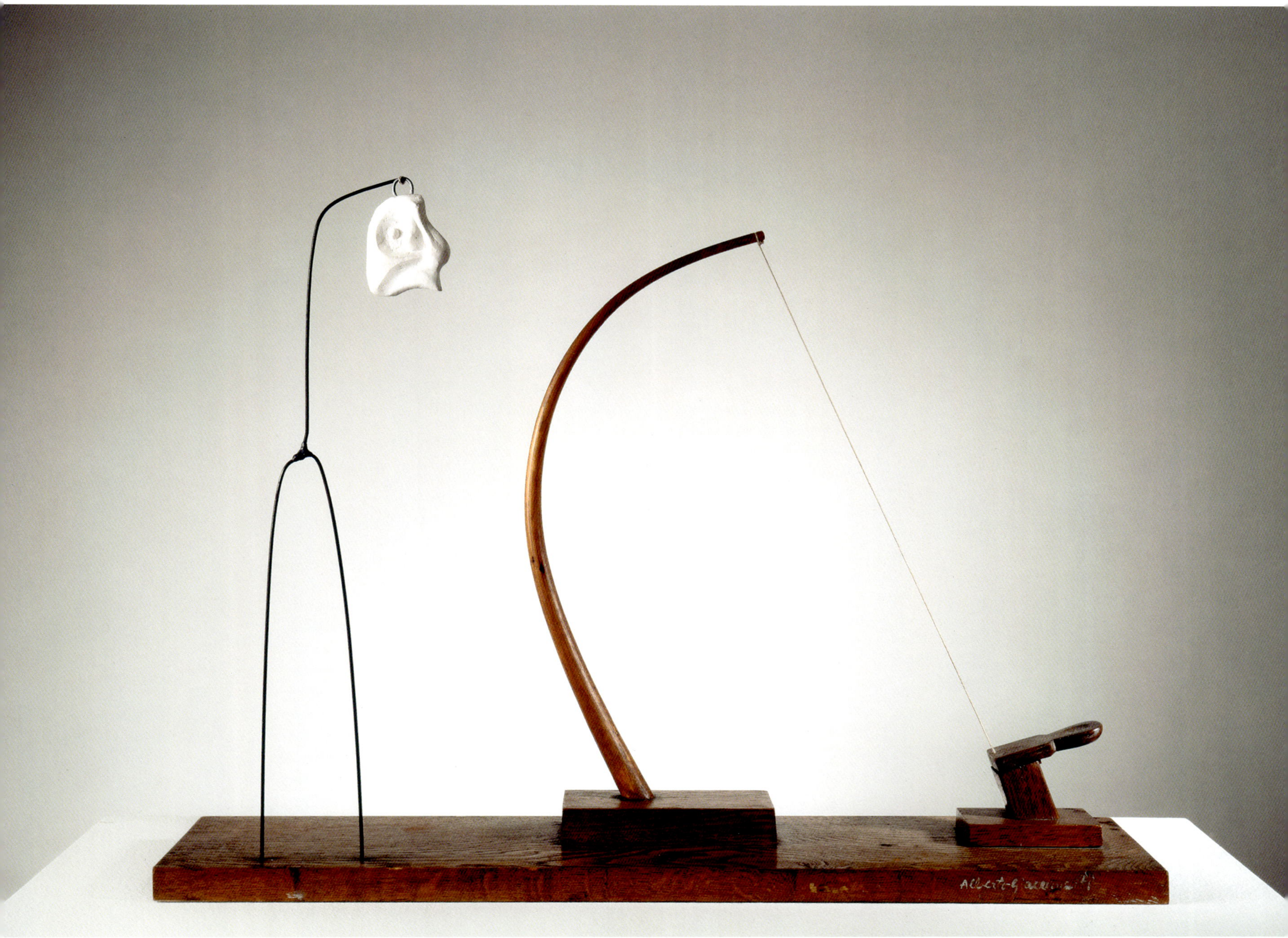

34
ALBERTO GIACOMETTI, *FLOWER IN DANGER*, 1932–33
Kunsthaus Zürich

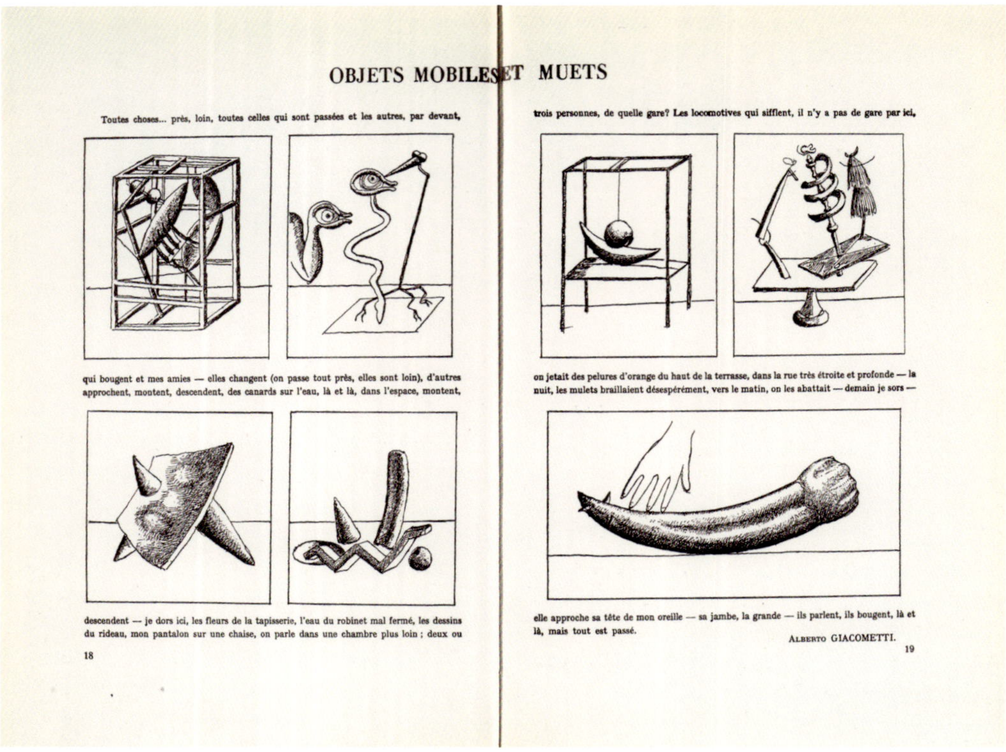

OBJETS MOBILES ET MUETS

Toutes choses... près, loin, toutes celles qui sont passées et les autres, par devant,

qui bougent et mes amies — elles changent (on passe tout près, elles sont loin), d'autres approchent, montent, descendent, des canards sur l'eau, là et là, dans l'espace, montent,

descendent — je dors ici, les fleurs de la tapisserie, l'eau du robinet mal fermé, les dessins du rideau, mon pantalon sur une chaise, on parle dans une chambre plus loin ; deux ou

18

trois personnes, de quelle gare? Les locomotives qui sifflent, il n'y a pas de gare par ici,

on jetait des pelures d'orange du haut de la terrasse, dans la rue très étroite et profonde — la nuit, les mulets braillaient désespérément, vers le matin, on les abattait — demain je sors —

elle approche sa tête de mon oreille — sa jambe, la grande — ils parlent, ils bougent, là et là, mais tout est passé.

ALBERTO GIACOMETTI.

19

35
ALBERTO GIACOMETTI
"OBJETS MOBILES ET MUETS," (MOVING AND MUTE OBJECTS),
Le Surréalisme au service de la révolution, no. 3, (December 1931)

or phallus on a shelf, a pterodactyl escaping through a window, and a spinal column dangling inside a cage. Individually the motifs elicit all kinds of associations and memories—an archetypal woman who is mother or lover or both; sexual power; royalty; a wish for a stronger backbone (psychologically); imprisonment; the age of dinosaurs; and the human urge to escape constraints. The structure itself is extremely fragile: thin sticks mounted precariously in tiny holes and a piece of glass held together by threads. Like a house of cards, it could collapse at any moment—an analogy for the uncertainties and dangers of life.

Giacometti's sculptures had a galvanizing effect. Almost overnight the Surrealists discovered that sculpture could be non-representational yet express complex metaphors and states of mind. At the same time Dalí advocated the use of found items, notably in "The Object as Revealed in Surrealist Experiment," an essay published in English in September 1932 (see pp. 164–67). The text recommends various practices to develop a more intuitive knowledge of objects, such as handling unknown items while blindfolded and making automatist sculptures by manipulating malleable materials. In response to objects like a rocking chair or a piece of soap, artists should play free-association word games that may factor in considerations such as "what happens to it if it is put in urine [or] vinegar, etc." Moreover, items could be inscribed with "writings devoid of any obvious or intentional relation to the object," for instance "a mysterious manuscript written in white ink and completely covering the ... surfaces of a brand-new Rolls Royce." He also discussed the potential for monumental outdoor sculptures, such as "having a colossal loaf (fifteen yards long) baked and left early one

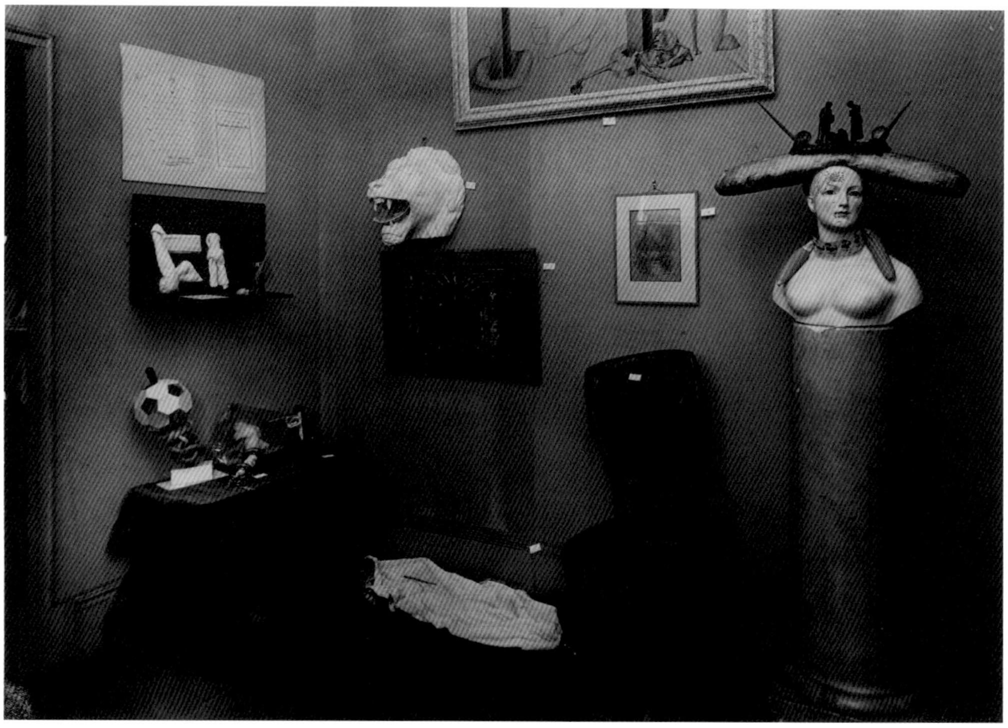

36
MAN RAY
SURREALIST EXHIBITION,
GALERIE PIERRE COLLE,
PARIS, 1933
Philadelphia Museum of Art; 125th anniversary acquisition, the Lynne and Harold Honickman Gift of the Julien Levy Collection

morning in a public square, the public's reaction . . . to be noted." Previously, he had proposed, "Let some huge motorcars, three times as big as actual ones, be made in plaster or onyx with thoroughness of detail. . . . Let them be wrapped in women's underwear and buried in a graveyard, the spot being indicated merely by a thin yellow clock." The essay concludes that "What matters is the way in which the experiments revealed *the desire for the object*, the tangible object." [22]

To some extent the Surrealists' fascination with objects may be considered a political or philosophical rejection of the materialism of modern society, but the artists were not, in fact, so pure. Especially in the 1930s, their activities were very much a part of the glamorous world of wealth and fashion. The Great Depression, caused by the collapse of the American stock market, took several years to seriously affect France, and until it did, the glitterati threw lavish parties and encouraged attendees to wear provocative and amusing costumes. At one soirée in July 1930, a guest wore a telephone attached to the side of his head. Another party was held in a structure entirely wrapped in silver foil and adorned with silver cages holding stuffed birds. One host placed temporary sculptures of farm animals on his lawn. Another installed aquariums with live fish, and a guest obligingly came dressed as a coral reef. [23] Ray provided a crucial link between art and fashion through his commercial photographs, such as his *Electricity* portfolio for a French power company (figs. 37–40). Society's conspicuous consumption and flair for the dramatic provided the backdrop for Surrealist object-based art.

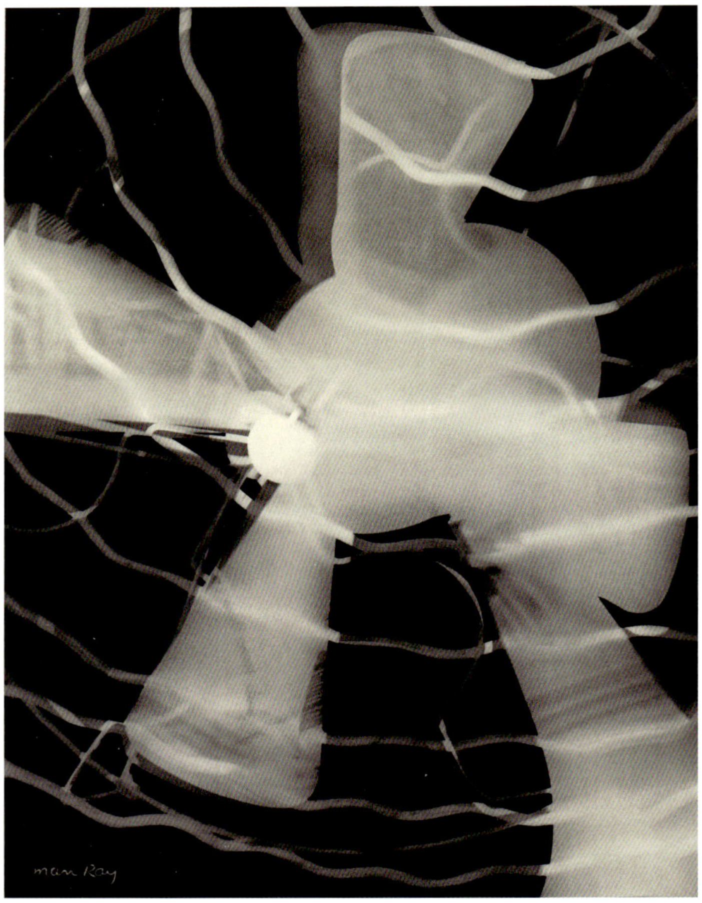

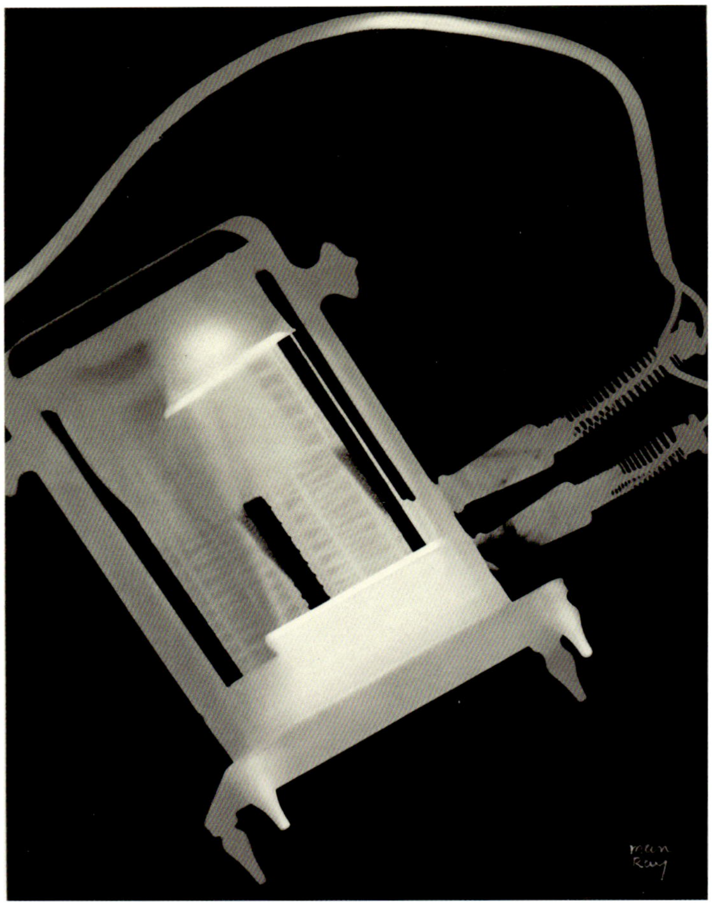

37
MAN RAY, *ELECTRICITY: BREEZE,* 1931
Smithsonian American Art Museum, Washington, DC; museum purchase

38
MAN RAY, *ELECTRICITY: DINING ROOM,* 1931
Smithsonian American Art Museum, Washington, DC; museum purchase

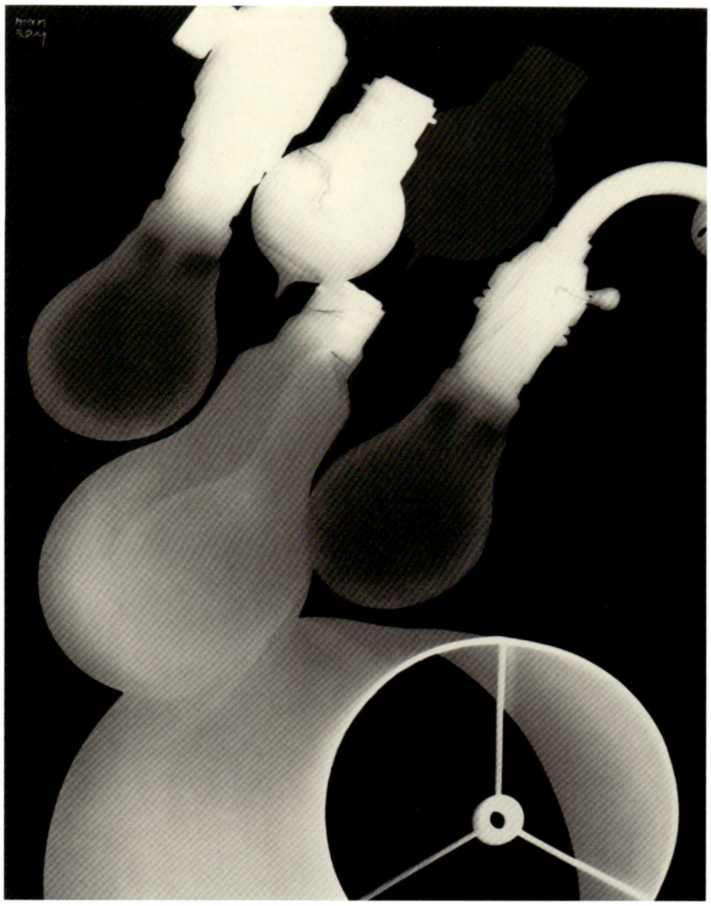

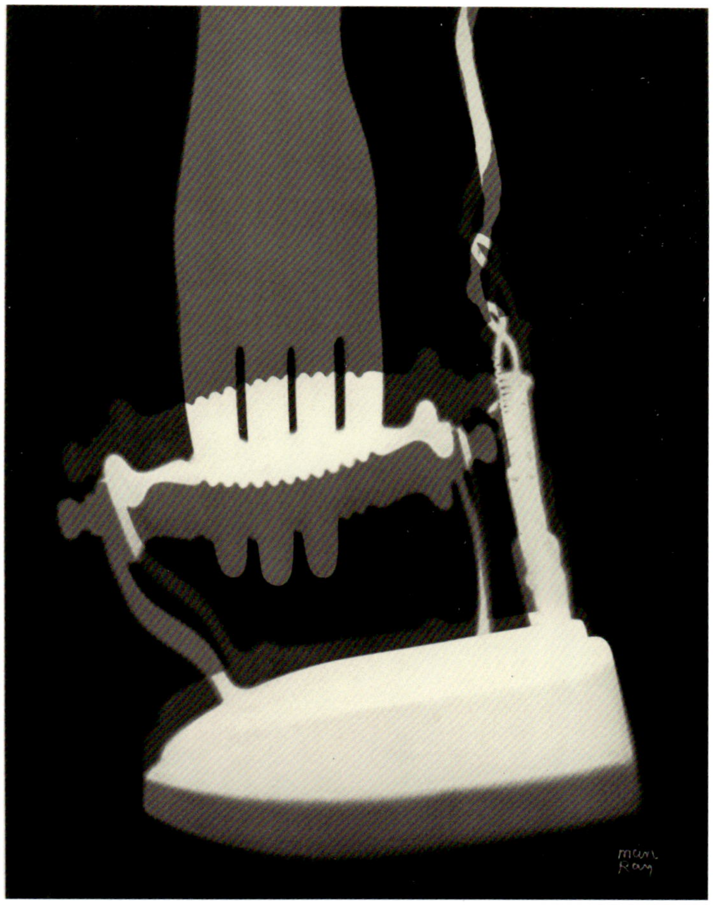

39
MAN RAY, *ELECTRICITY: HOUSE*, 1931
Smithsonian American Art Museum, Washington, DC; museum purchase

40
MAN RAY, *ELECTRICITY: LINGERIE*, 1931
Smithsonian American Art Museum, Washington, DC; museum purchase

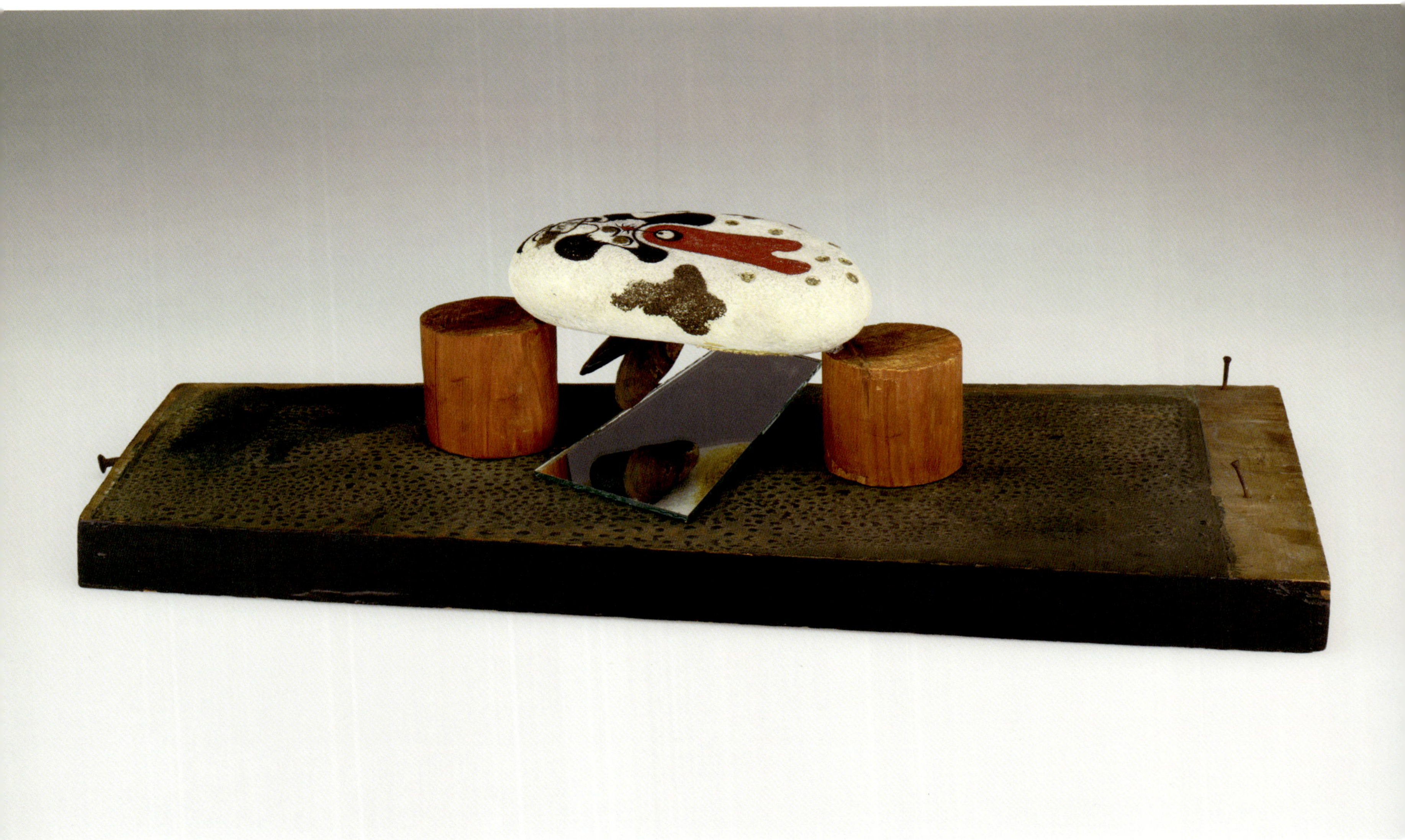

41
JOAN MIRÓ, *OBJECT*, 1932
Philadelphia Museum of Art; A. E. Gallatin Collection

The Surrealists' newly expanded definition of sculpture as assemblages had an enormously liberating effect. Anyone—regardless of academic training—could make works of art from inexpensive things. The ensuing deluge was revealed in the *Surrealist Exhibition: Sculptures, Objects, Paintings, Drawings* at the Galerie Pierre Colle in June 1933 (fig. 36).[24] Only fourteen of the seventy exhibited items were titled *Object*, including recent assemblages by Miró, which were similar in style to those he had shown as early as December 1931 in *Miró Sculptures-Objects* at the Galerie Pierre.[25] All are small in scale and consist of elements ranging from a tree fragment to string and rusted bits of metal, which he gathered during walks in the countryside during annual visits to Spain. One composition (fig. 41) features a smooth stone adorned with a stylized image of a female figure. The natural grace of the stone contrasts with the crude wood of the base, a forced union of opposites. By using detritus (the mirror is only a shard), Miró further developed the idea of his "anti-painting" collages of 1928. He described how he chose the elements for his assemblages: "I feel myself attracted by a *magnetic* force toward an object, and then I feel myself being drawn toward another object which is added to the first and their combination creates a poetic shock." [26]

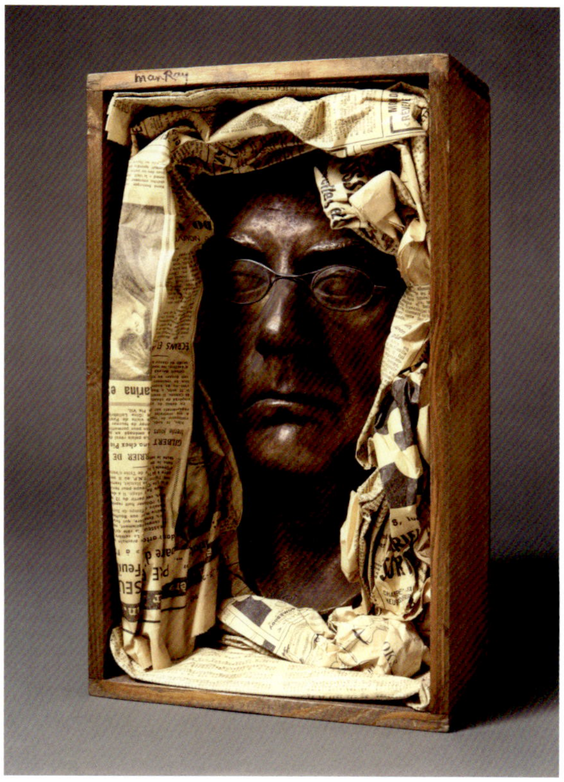

42
MAN RAY
SELF-PORTRAIT, 1933
Smithsonian American Art Museum, Washington, DC; gift of Juliet Man Ray

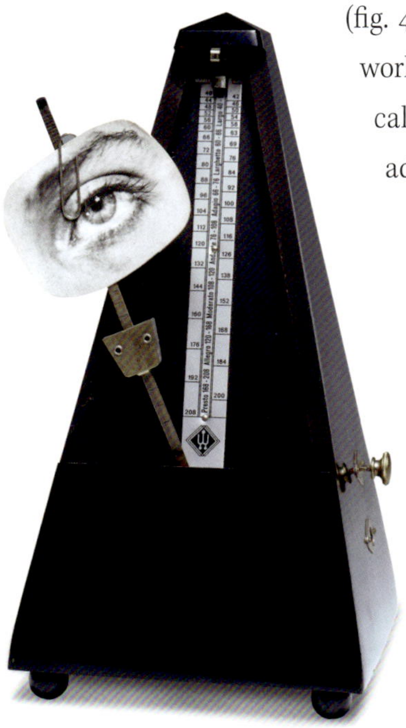

43
MAN RAY
OBJECT TO BE DESTROYED, 1932
Smithsonian American Art Museum, Washington, DC; gift of Samuel M. Greenbaum and Helen Mark families in memory of Helen Mark Greenbaum

The variety of subjects, methods, and materials in the 1933 exhibition was mind-boggling. Several, such as Dalí's *Retrospective Bust of a Woman* and Ray's *Self-Portrait* (fig. 42), were representational, albeit in different ways. Among Giacometti's six works was *Table*, a kind of sculpture-as-furniture innovation, and an installation called *Mannequin*, which did not, in fact, incorporate a store model; he merely added a cello neck and other objects to the plaster figure of a female nude.

Some exhibited works fulfilled the definition of an object functioning symbolically: things assembled into meaningful kinetic or interactive constructions. Ray's *Object to Be Destroyed*, 1932 (originally called *Eye-Metronome;* fig. 43), shows a photo of a human eye perilously attached to the inverse pendulum of a metronome, which can be wound up and set in motion. At top speed the eye appears frenetic and risks being cast off, and then gradually the mechanism slows and stops, a process accentuated by its ticking sound. Although the artist created this sculpture in a specific context—his affair with a talented and beautiful woman

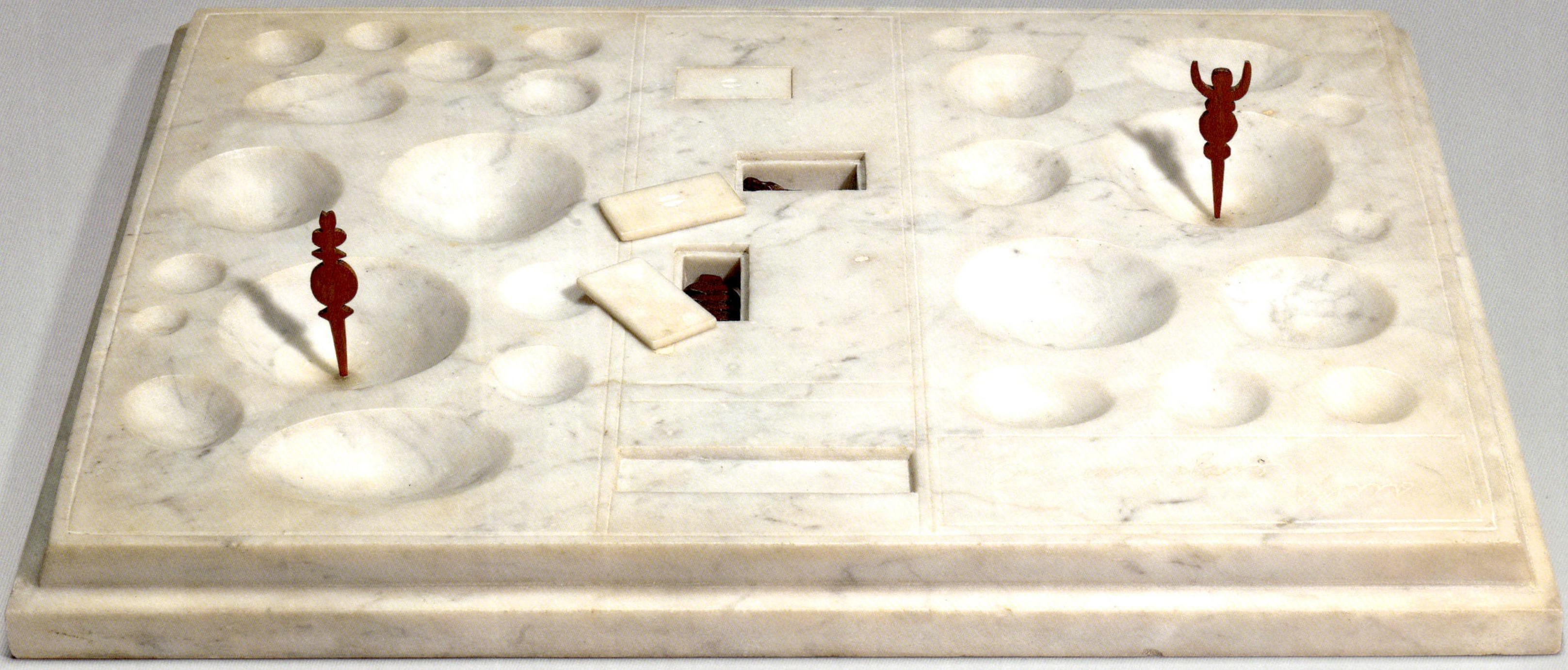

44

ALBERTO GIACOMETTI, *NO MORE PLAY*, 1931–32

National Gallery of Art, Washington, DC; gift of the Patsy R. and Raymond D. Nasher Collection, Dallas, in honor of the 50th Anniversary of the National Gallery of Art

had just ended—we are free to interpret the assemblage as a reminder of the passage of time in general, as a metaphor for humanity living at the mercy of machines, or as any idea or memory associated with seeing.[27] Arp's *Head with Annoying Objects*, 1930 (originally called *Head Covered with Three Disagreeable Objects: a Fly, a Mandolin, and a Pair of Mustaches*; fig. 45), also qualifies as an interactive game. Three abstract biomorphs are not secured in place so that viewers can rearrange them randomly in infinitely variable compositions. Giacometti's *No More Play*, 1931–32 (fig. 44), was more restricted and more symbolic. Two tiny figures—one raising its arms as if in supplication—stand in a miniature white landscape patterned with circular recesses that evoke associations with lunar, volcanic, and battlefield craters. Other entities repose inside graves with removable covers. We can infer that life is a perilous game that inevitably ends in death—quite a grim theme when compared to Arp's playful approach.

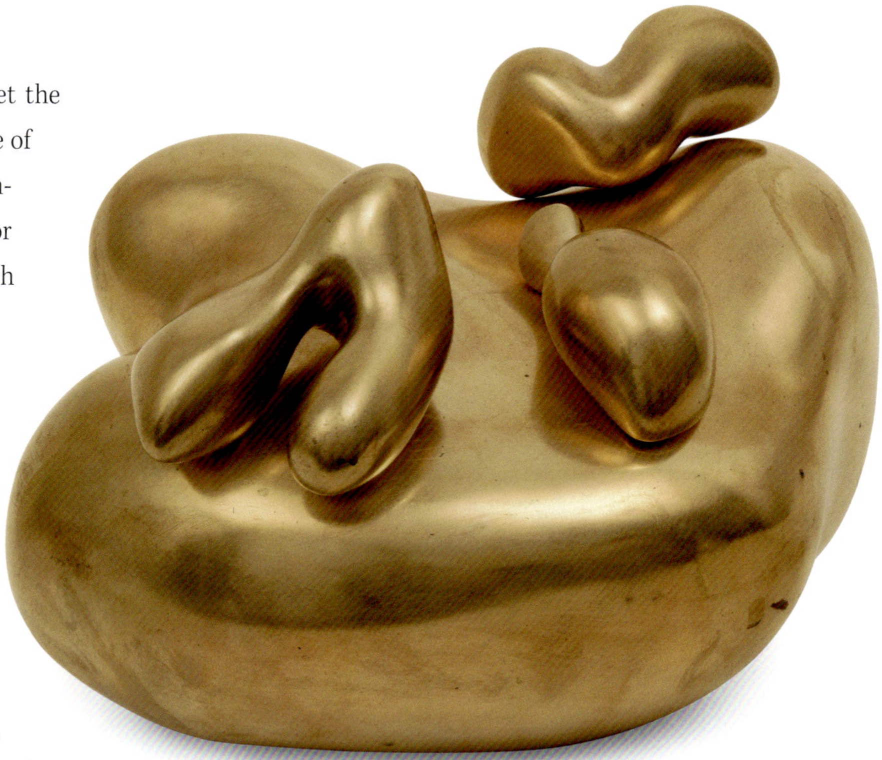

45
JEAN ARP
HEAD WITH ANNOYING OBJECTS (MUSTACHE, MANDOLIN, AND FLY), 1930
Private collection

After the plethora of objects in the 1933 exhibition, Giacometti's *Invisible Object*, 1934 (fig. 47), seems to offer a challenge to the Surrealists' new fad. A female nude rests her derriere on a plinth, as if momentarily paused in thought or frozen in shock. Her head leans forward, and her expression is a starry-eyed gaze at something not visible to us. She holds out her hands as if grasping something, but there is clearly nothing there, a witty criticism of the Surrealists' fascination with tangible things. The word "invisible" in the title may imply that theirs is an empty or pointless quest, or it might suggest that Giacometti seeks something else that cannot be seen or defined.[28] He abandoned Surrealism a few months later, despite the movement's increasing success and geographic expansion to northern and eastern Europe, Britain, the United States, Mexico, Peru, and Japan. The clarion call to liberate one's self from within appealed to many artists who felt stymied economically and

46
OSCAR DOMINGUEZ
THE WANDERINGS OF GEORGES HUGNET, 1935
Museo Nacional Centro de Arte Reina Sofía, Madrid

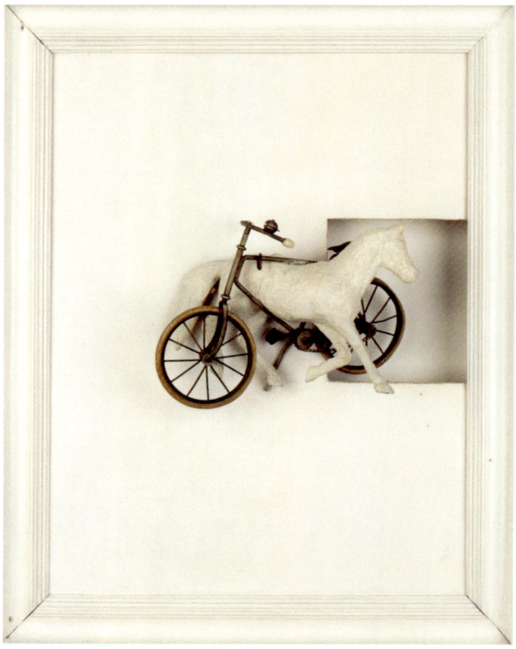

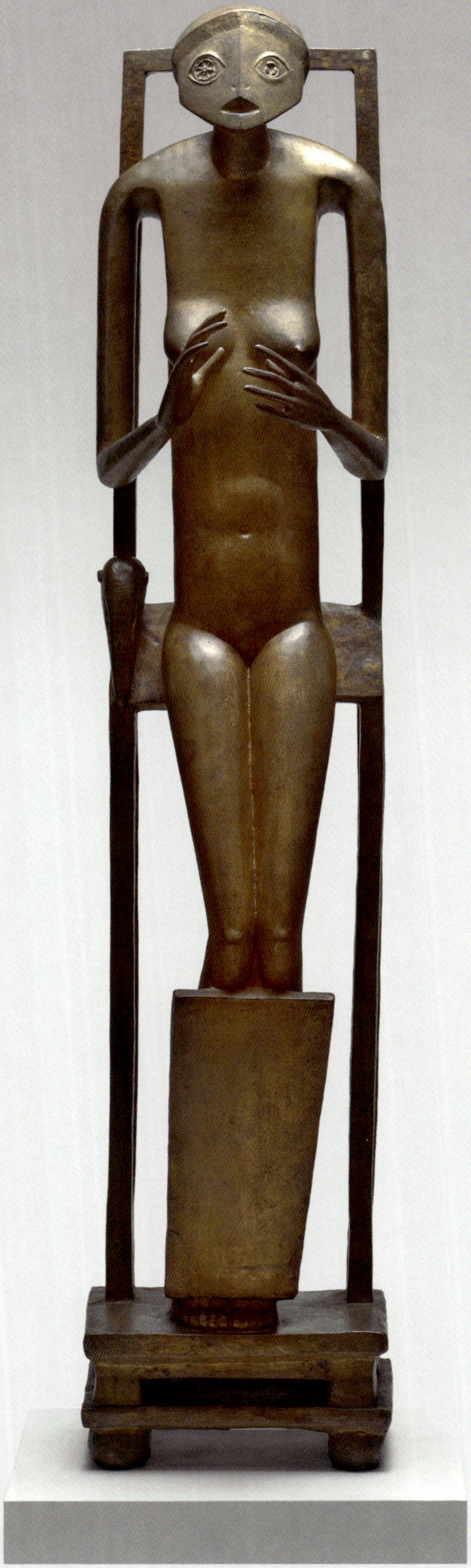

47
ALBERTO GIACOMETTI
THE INVISIBLE OBJECT
(HANDS HOLDING THE VOID), 1934
National Gallery of Art, Washington, DC;
Ailsa Mellon Bruce Fund

creatively by the Great Depression. Many Surrealist exhibitions were presented, including an international trifecta in 1936 in Paris, London, and New York.

The *Surrealist Exhibition of Objects*, which opened in May 1936 at the Galerie Charles Ratton, was packed to the rafters with object assemblages by progenitors and newcomers (fig. 50). The works were arranged into categories such as "found objects from nature," "objects for everyday use," and "interpreted objects." Duchamp's *Bottle Rack* and *Why Not Sneeze?* shared a vitrine with found objects and a biomorphic plaster by Ernst. The Spanish artist Oscar Dominguez contributed *The Wanderings of Georges Hugnet*, 1935 (fig. 46), which features a toy-sized horse entangled with a bicycle. Did he mean to imply that his fellow Surrealist Hugnet was accident-prone or perhaps overly cautious about venturing afar in body or mind? We could be satisfied by whatever first interpretation springs to mind, but Surrealist art urges us to dig deeper to find or invent something more. Although not in the exhibition, Miró's *Object* (fig. 48) dates from 1936. His most intricate and complex assemblage comprises a stuffed parrot perched on a branch above a hanging doll's leg, a map, and sundry other items. Might the lifeless bird allude to the outbreak of civil war in Spain, where freedom was dying? Could the little leg dangling from a string refer to the civilian victims of that conflict? Perhaps, but the sculpture as a whole does not exude an aura of terror or violence; rather, it might be something constructed by a child from cast-off things in an attic.

Dalí's *Aphrodisiac Jacket* (fig. 49), on one wall in the 1936 exhibition, could be classified as an object functioning alcoholically. A man's jacket, over a white shirt and bra, is adorned with several dozen shot glasses containing peppermint liqueur, one of the artist's favorite aphrodisiacs. He inserted a small straw in each glass, inviting viewers to drink. This hilariously interactive garment was dismantled after the exhibition but was immortalized in photographs of the installation.[29] Dalí made a replica for his department-store window display *She Was a Surrealist Woman, She Was Like a Figure in a Dream*, 1936 (fig. 51), in New York, and he created another for his *Dream of Venus* pavilion at the World's Fair in 1939.

Like the *Aphrodisiac Jacket*, many object-based sculptures of the 1930s did not survive and are known today through documentary photographs and later refabrications. Some, such as Duchamp's Assisted Readymades, faithfully reproduce the originals. Others were modified in ways that ensure their preservation, sometimes affecting how we perceive and interpret them today. Ray's *What We All Lack*, 1935 (fig. 53), a marvelous metaphor for the ephemerality of our desires and aspirations, originally consisted of a pipe blowing

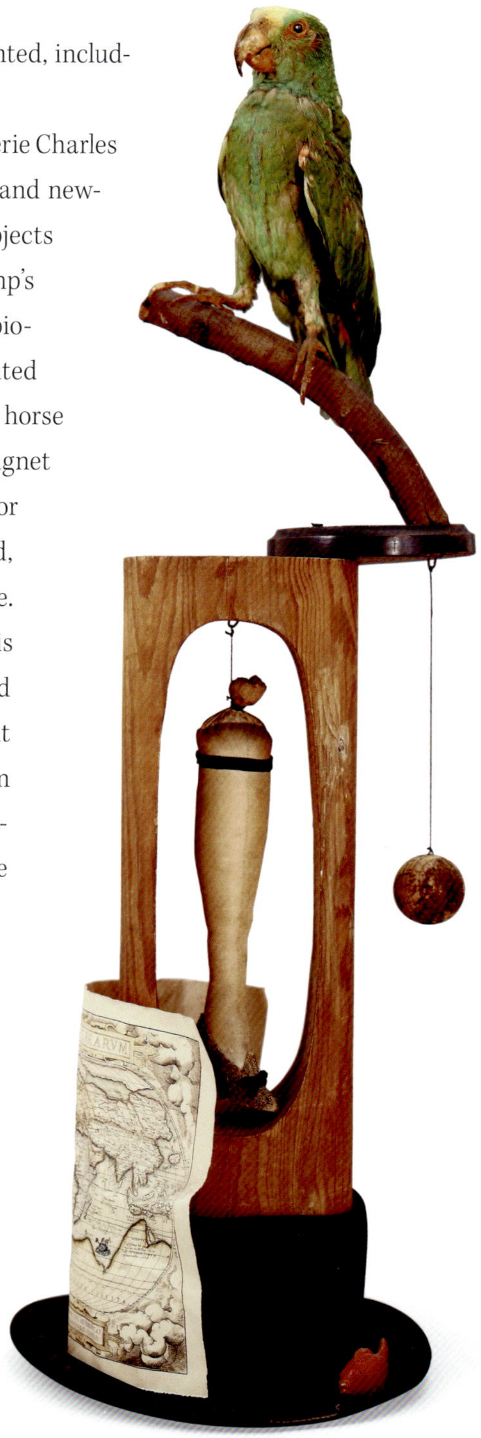

48
JOAN MIRÓ
OBJECT, 1936
The Museum of Modern Art, New York; gift of Mr. and Mrs. Pierre Matisse

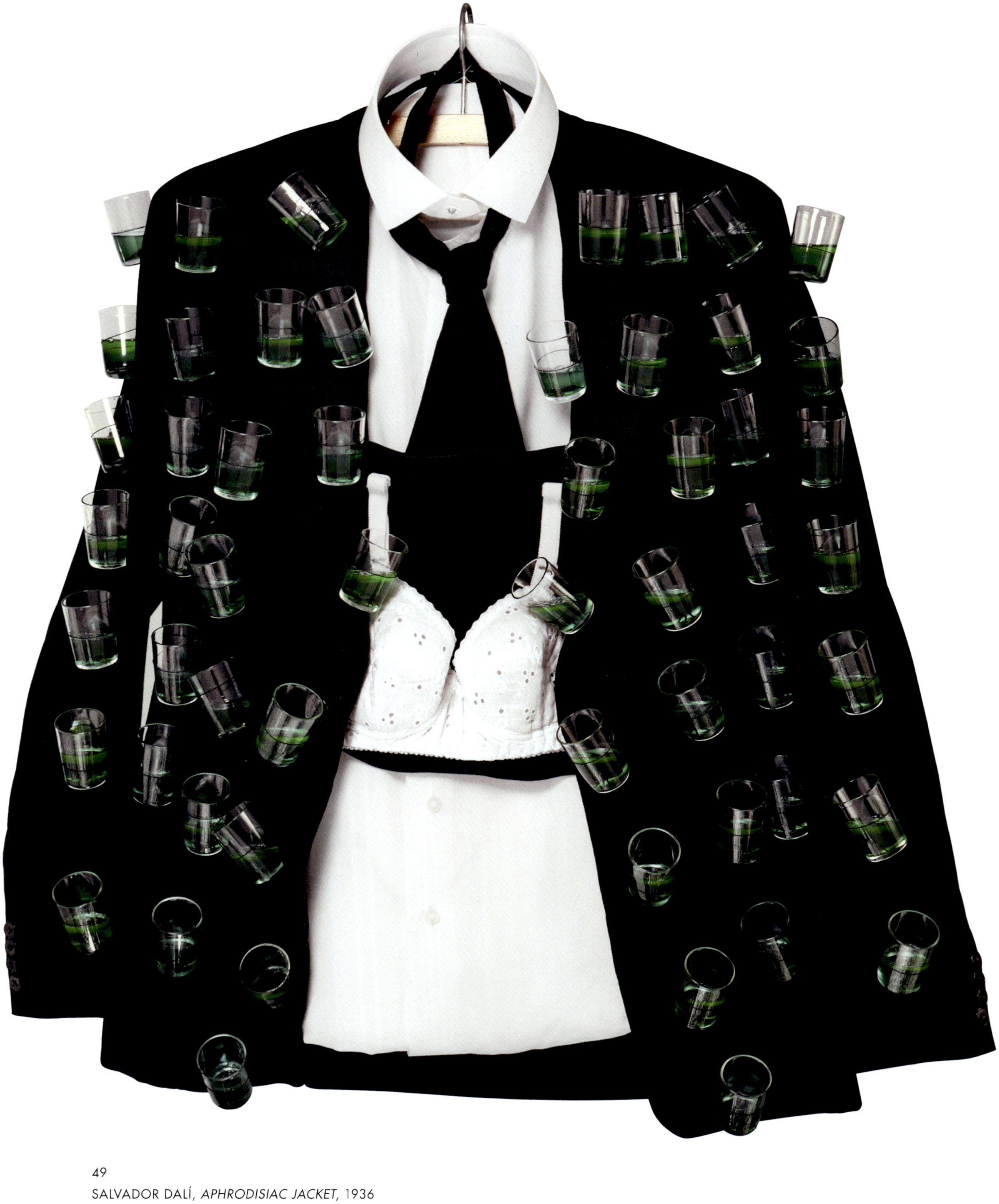

49

SALVADOR DALÍ, *APHRODISIAC JACKET*, 1936

Salvador Dalí Museum, Inc., St. Petersburg, Florida

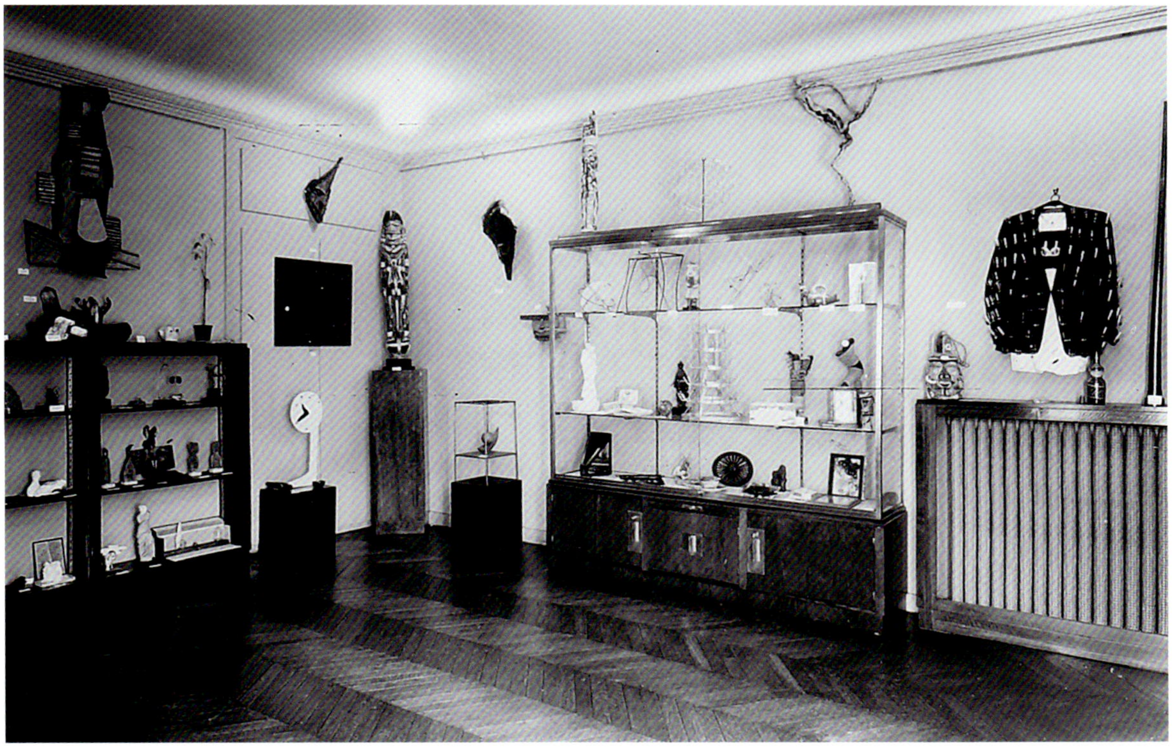

50
MAN RAY
SURREALIST EXHIBITION OF OBJECTS,
GALERIE RATTON, PARIS, 1936
Birger Raben-Skov Collection,
Copenhagen

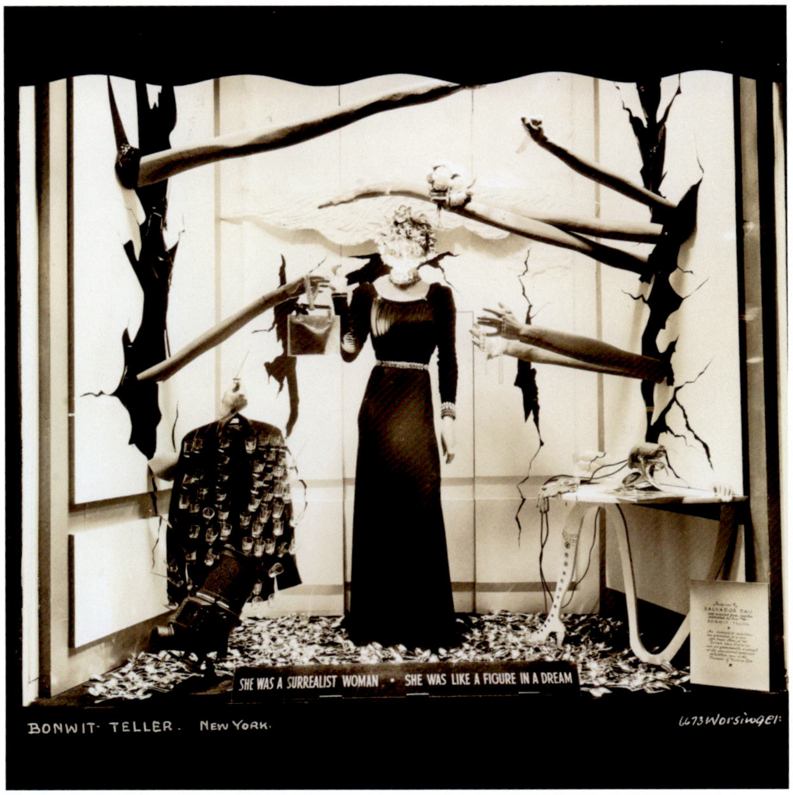

51
SALVADOR DALÍ
SHE WAS A SURREALIST WOMAN, SHE WAS LIKE A FIGURE IN A DREAM, 1936
Museum of the City of New York

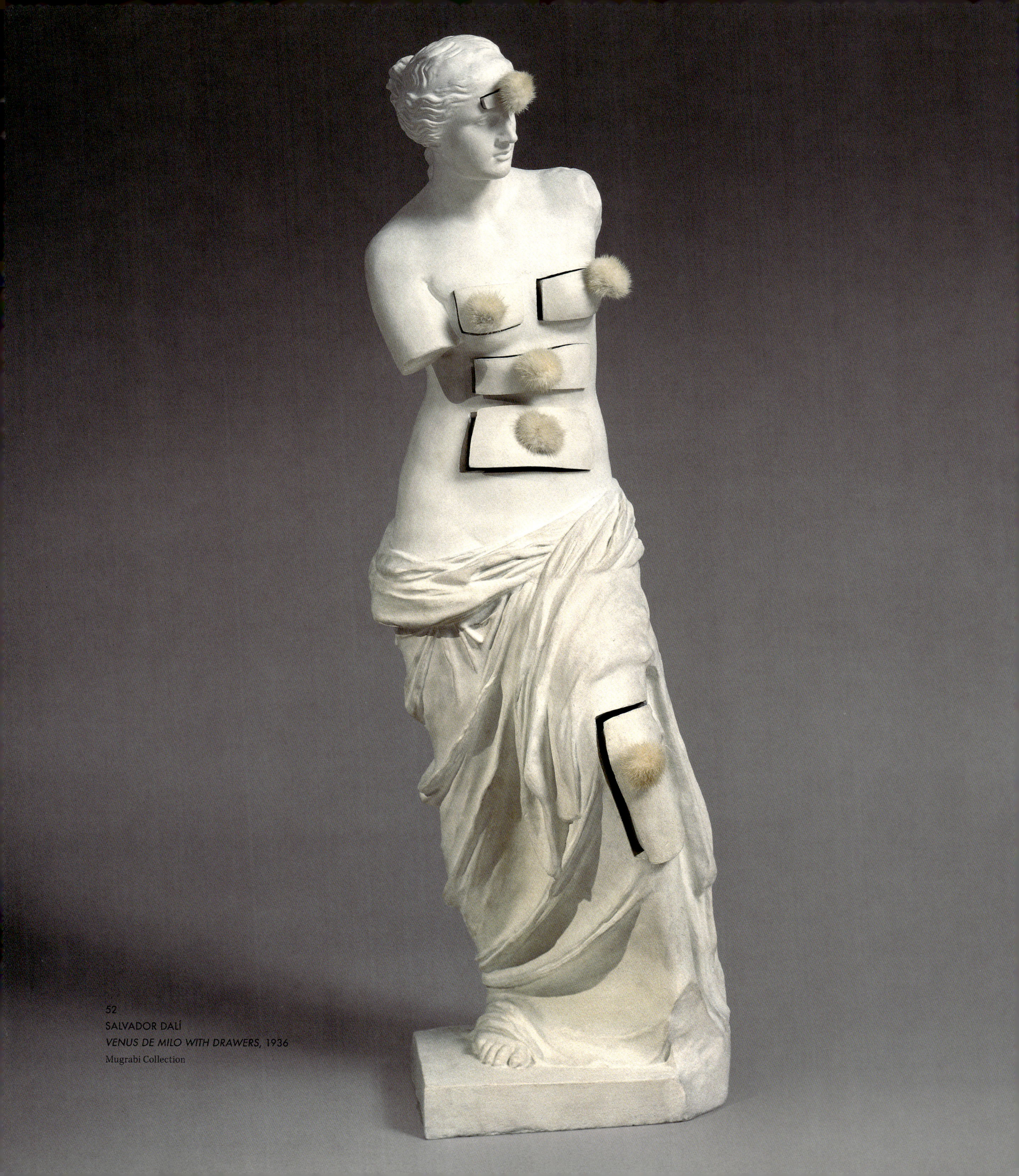

52
SALVADOR DALÍ
VENUS DE MILO WITH DRAWERS, 1936
Mugrabi Collection

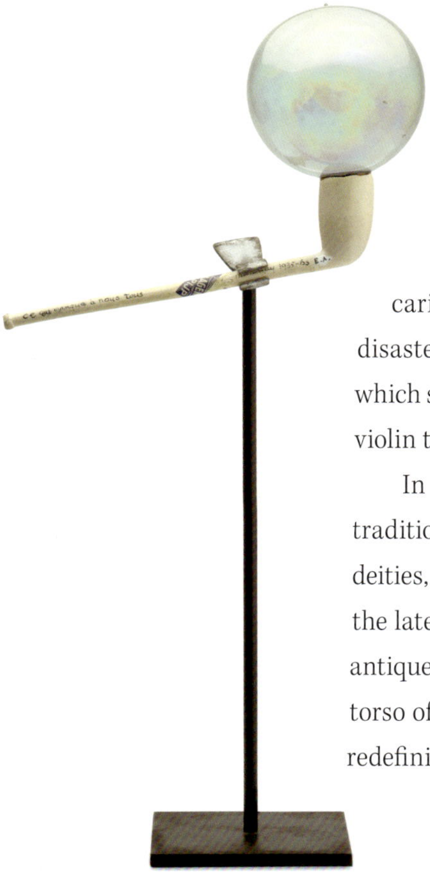

53
MAN RAY
WHAT WE ALL LACK, 1935
The Art Institute of Chicago; gift of Mary P. Hines in memory of her mother, Frances W. Pick

an exquisitely delicate glass bubble. When plunked directly on a table, it had the casualness of a chance encounter, but it was at constant risk. The later versions are mounted on a metal clamp or nestled in a satin-lined box, with connotations of laboratory specimens and precious gifts. For *Homage to Paganini*, 1936 (fig. 54), Maurice Henry wrapped a violin in gauze bandages as if it were the victim of an accident and exhibited it precariously balanced on its narrow side-rim at the edge of a glass shelf, as if inviting disaster. In the replica edition, the violin rests flat inside a glass-fronted wood box, which significantly diminishes the original aura of potential catastrophe and likens the violin to a carefully preserved museum artifact.[30]

In the mid-1930s several Surrealists expressed their disdain for the long-dominant traditions of classical art by modifying inexpensive replicas of Greco-Roman statues of deities, particularly Venus. Plaster casts of originals in the Louvre had proliferated in the late nineteenth century, and by the 1920s they could be found in art-supply stores, antique shops, and the showrooms of interior decorators. In *Venus Restored*, Ray tied a torso of the goddess of love with coarse rope, symbolically rendering her powerless and redefining her as a submissive practitioner of sadomasochistic bondage. Elsewhere he mounted a cast of *The Three Graces*—the muses of art, literature, and music—on a backboard, and by titling it *Universal Target*, he invited viewers to take potshots at them. Dominguez went further: he took a plaster cast of a Roman statue of a boy pulling a thorn from his foot, painted it black, and then cut off its head with a jagged shard of glass in the manner of a guillotine (fig. 55). While working in London, Magritte made *The Future of Statues*, 1937 (fig. 1), starting with a plaster death mask of Napoleon, which he transformed by painting on a blue sky and puffy clouds. Dalí took a cast of the famed

54
MAURICE HENRY
HOMAGE TO PAGANINI, 1936
Private collection, Ubu Gallery, New York

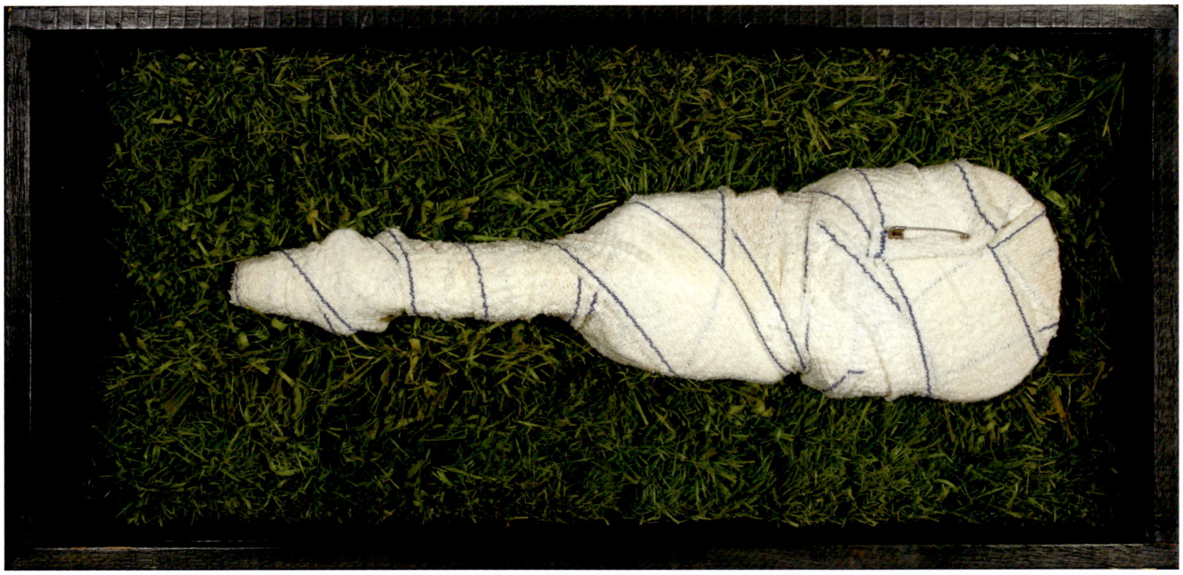

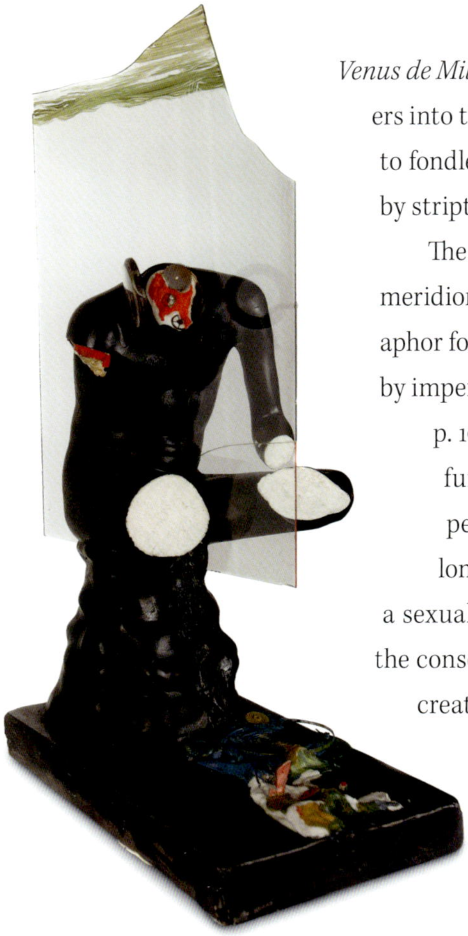

Venus de Milo (fig. 52) and reduced it to the status of mere furniture by inserting drawers into the figure. Adding insult to injury, the drawer handles of white fur invite us to fondle them; those on the breasts have obvious affinities with the pasties worn by striptease dancers.[31]

The British Surrealist Roland Penrose encased a torso of Venus in a metal meridional globe and called it *The Last Voyage of Captain Cook*, 1936 (fig. 56), a metaphor for the forced imposition of Western culture on territories around the world by imperialist Europeans. His other major assemblage, *The Dew Machine*, 1937 (see p. 191), was not so high-minded. It certainly fulfilled the criteria for an object functioning symbolically, but Penrose outdid even Dalí's predilection for perverse sexual innuendo. A mannequin's head hangs upside down, trailing long blond hair, inside a wire structure on which a clear liquid (presumably a sexual product best left unspecified) flowed down onto the head. A director of the conservative Tate Gallery contemptuously alluded to such displays as "objects created by those who flounder in . . . 'sewer-realism.'"[32]

After his summer vacation with Giacometti in Switzerland in 1934 or 1935, Ernst began to make biomorphic sculptures. He collected heavy stones smoothed by centuries of flowing water and painted their surfaces with colorful curvilinear shapes.[33] He also learned to mix and manipulate plaster, a medium that enabled him to model forms and make casts of objects. *Habakuk*, for example, consists of a segmented body cast from upturned flowerpots topped by an Arpian head. Ernst's *The Beautiful German Girl* (originally *Round Head*), 1935, used knitting needles for legs and a scallop shell for her pert derriere. The life-size plaster *Lunar Asparagus*, 1935 (fig. 57), was installed on the grassy lawn outside the 1936 exhibition at the Galerie Ratton. The composition may have been inspired by Giacometti's plaster *Three Figures*, 1934–35, a sculpture briefly installed on a hillside in Switzerland. Ernst's ghostly white asparagus stalks, presumably grown huge in the moon's low gravity, invoke fantasies of humongous plants such as the one in the tale of *Jack and the Beanstalk*. But Ernst's asparagus stalks are hybrid entities: their tips are also oddly shaped heads with bulging eyes.[34]

55
OSCAR DOMINGUEZ
THORN PULLER, 1934
Museo Nacional Centro de Arte Reina Sofía, Madrid

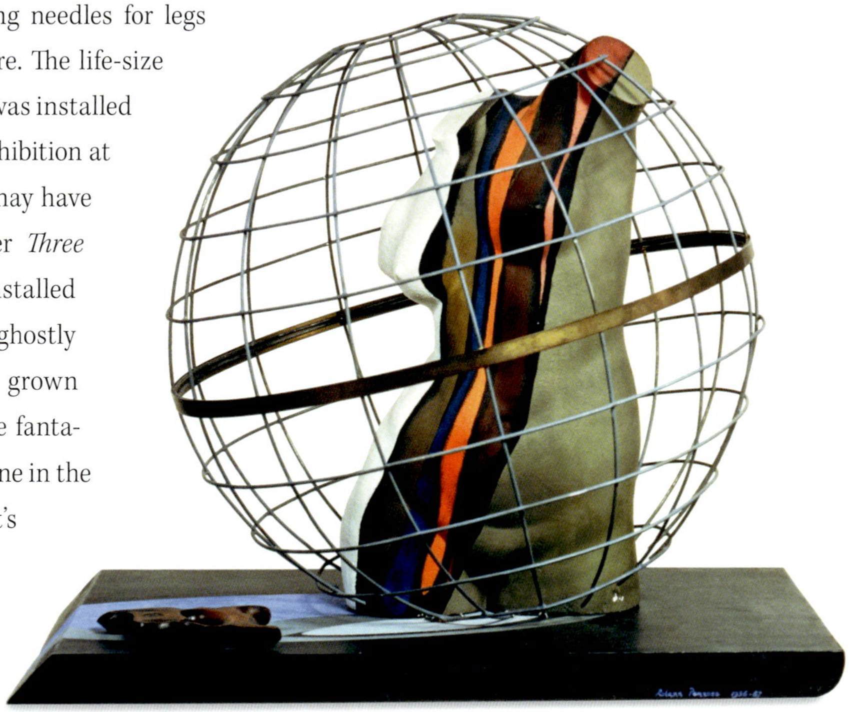

56
ROLAND PENROSE
THE LAST VOYAGE OF CAPTAIN COOK, 1936
Tate Gallery, London; presented by Mrs. Gabrielle Keiller through the Friends of the Tate Gallery

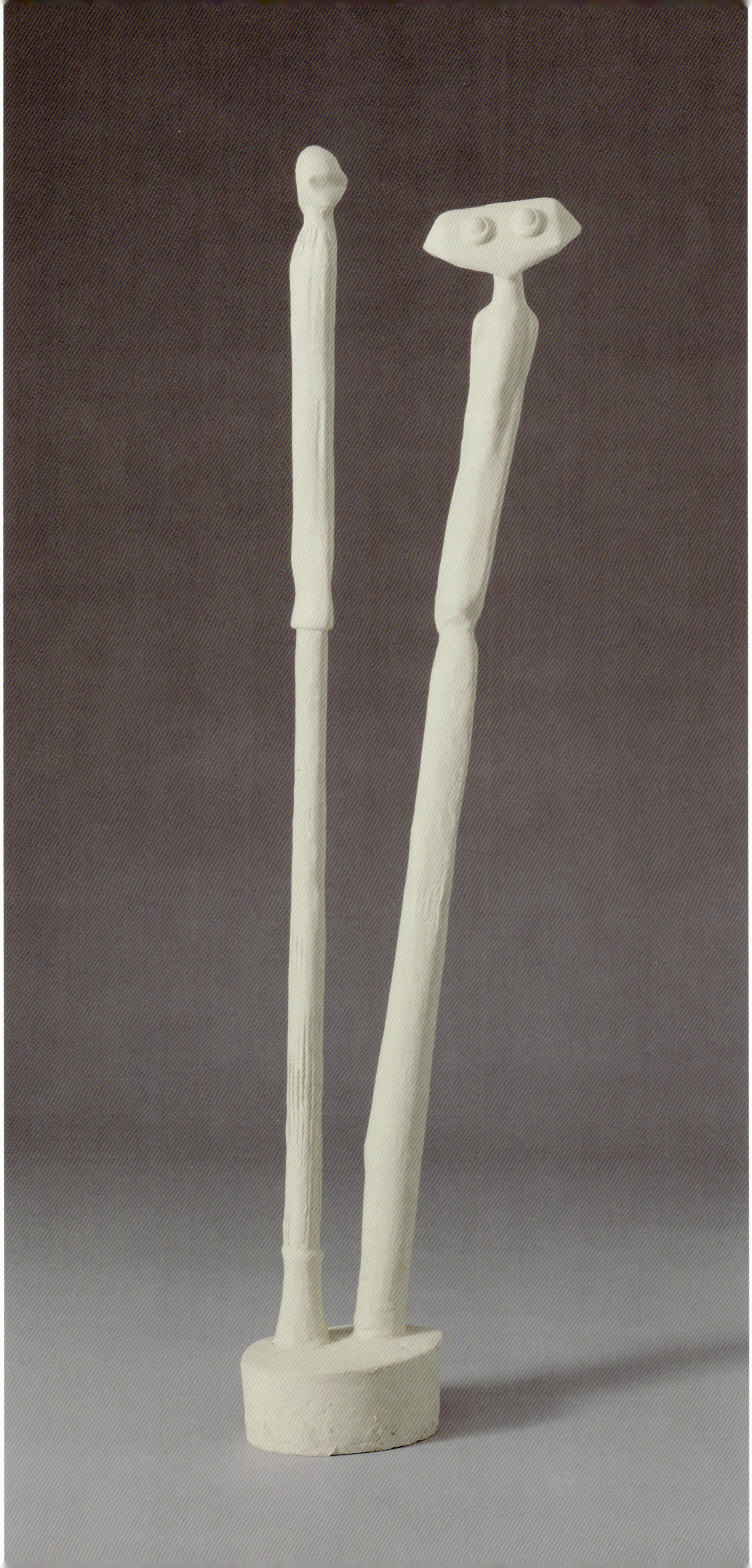

57
MAX ERNST
LUNAR ASPARAGUS, 1935
The Museum of Modern Art,
New York; purchase

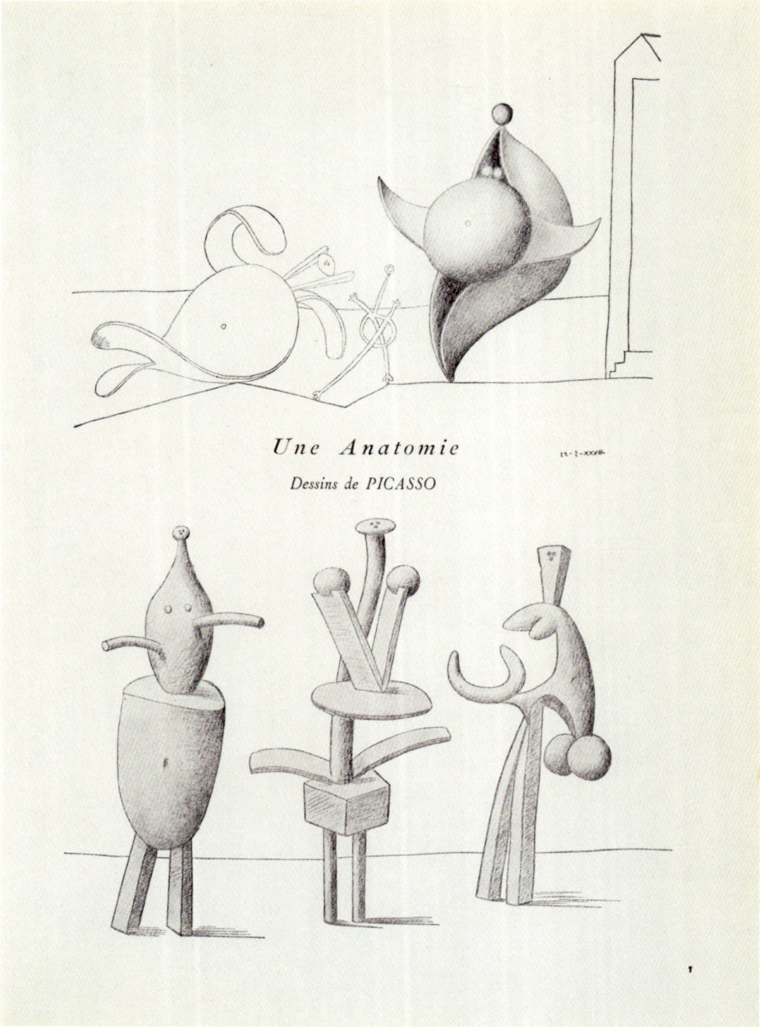

Une Anatomie

Dessins de PICASSO

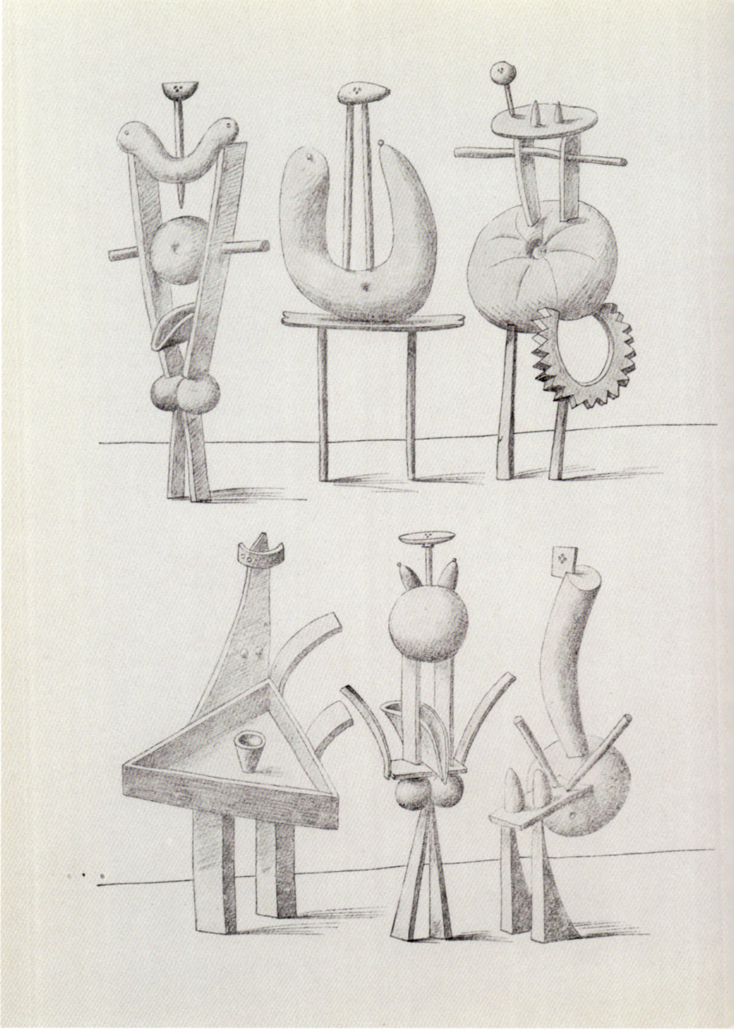

58

PABLO PICASSO, *ANATOMY*, 1933

Reproduced in *Minotaure*, no. 1 (1933)

By the time Arp had his second exhibition in Paris in November 1929, his aesthetics had been espoused by several painters. Pablo Picasso abandoned late Cubism for a style of emphatically rounded contours in drawings and paintings of *Bathers*, 1926–29, and *Projects for a Monument*, 1928–29. In *Anatomy*, he delineated sculptural open-form biomorphs that would become tremendously influential after they were published in *Minotaure* in 1933 (fig. 58). Yves Tanguy adapted biomorphic forms for his illusionistic paintings in 1927, and two years later biomorphism enabled Dalí to formulate his representations of bloated body parts and melted watches. Art historian Jennifer Mundy has remarked on this rapid assimilation of Arpian abstraction and the lack of critical discourse on it at the time: "At best, the presence of curvilinear and organic shapes in their works was alluded to only insofar as these forms suggested the capacity of desire, or hallucination, to transform, deform, or obliterate the identity of the object represented."[35] This initial oversight persisted for many decades, seriously diminishing our cognizance today of Arp's influential role in Surrealist art.

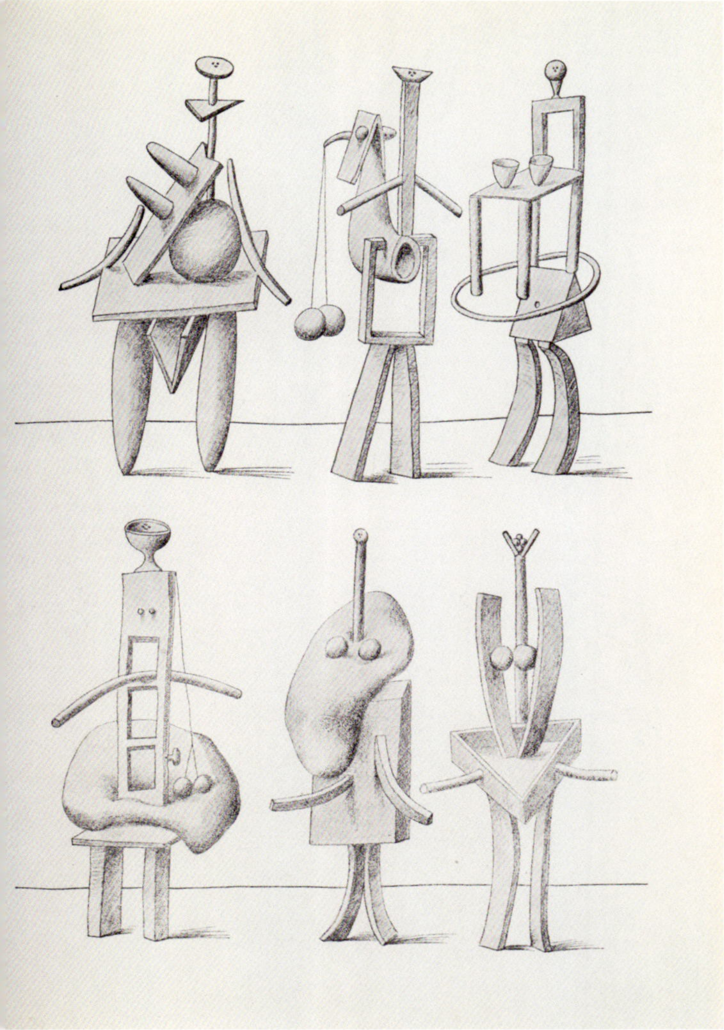

Arp continued to create whimsical reliefs exuding the naiveté and joy of children's drawings, such as *Torso, Navel, Mustache-Flower*, 1930 (fig. 59). The headless torso on the left conveys an impression of leaping upward and has a small "innie" belly button. Adjacent to it is a larger "outie" that resembles an inflated tire or other circular object. The red form on the right has the contour of a tulip, but it sports a goofy mustache, thereby changing the flower into a figure. Around 1930 Arp began to favor more abstract and less specific subjects, as seen in *Configuration with Two Dangerous Points* (fig. 23), where none of the protoplasmic forms can be identified as specifically animal, vegetable, or mineral. More amoebic than representational, these entities invite broader philosophical and conceptual interpretations. The "two dangerous points" occur where the flat black contours nudge up against the raised white ones; the reason why their contact is dangerous remains for us to imagine. Good against evil? Bacteria jostling under a microscope? Perhaps the upper form with two eyes indicates a watchful leader shepherding an unruly flock of sheep, or children, or ideas?

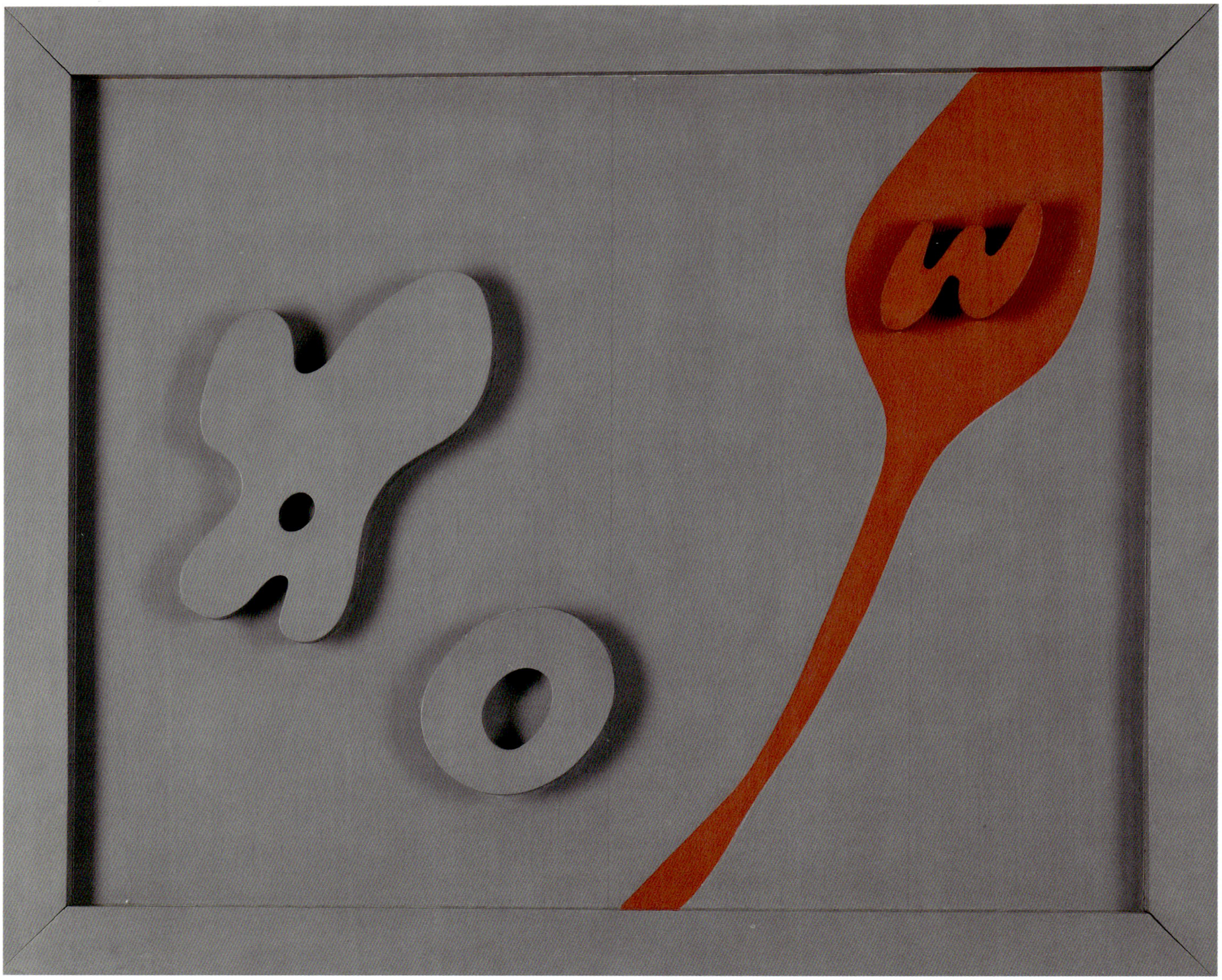

59

JEAN ARP, *TORSO, NAVEL, MUSTACHE-FLOWER*, 1930

The Metropolitan Museum of Art, New York; the Muriel Kallis Steinberg Newman Collection, gift of Muriel Kallis Newman

POIDS ET COULEURS

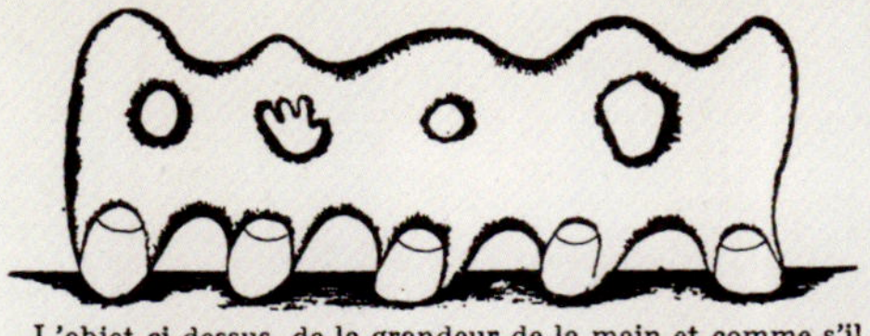

L'objet ci-dessus, de la grandeur de la main et comme s'il était pétri par elle, est en peluche rose. Les cinq terminaisons du bas qui se replient sur l'objet sont en celluloïd transparent et nacré. Les quatre trous dans le corps de l'objet permettent d'y passer les quatre grands doigts de la main.

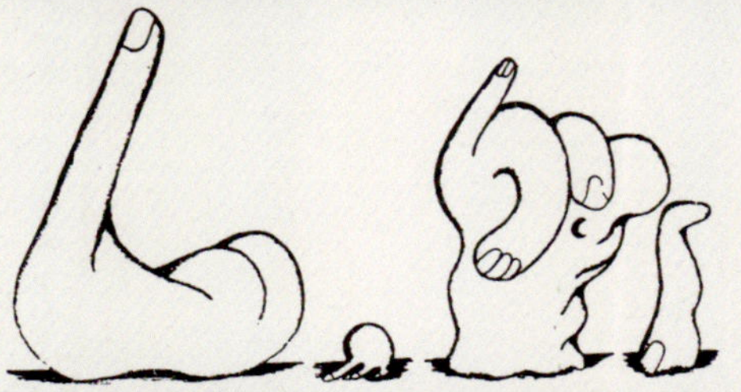

Dans l'ensemble ci-dessus, l'objet de gauche est en plâtre peint de couleur zinzoline et l'ongle rose. Il est lesté dans le bas par une boule de plomb qui, permettant des oscillations, le ramène toujours à la même position.

Le très petit objet du milieu, plein de mercure, est recouvert de paille tressée rouge vif afin de paraître extrêmement léger. Le gros objet de droite est en coton moulé vert pâle, les ongles en celluloïd rose. Le dernier objet de droite est en plâtre couvert d'encre noire, l'ongle est rose.

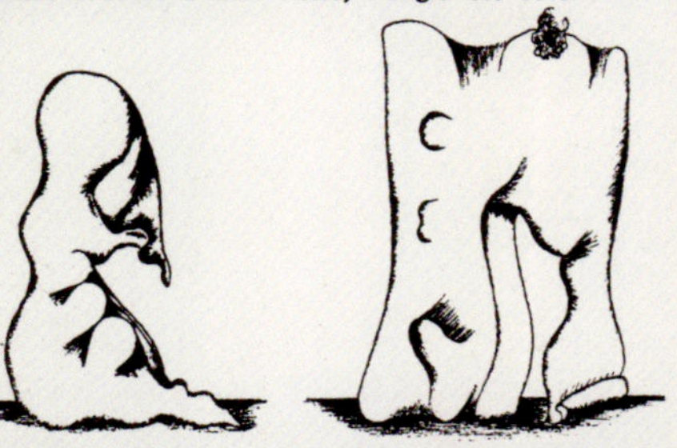

L'objet de gauche est en cire molle imitation chair. L'appendice du haut est flottant et d'une couleur plus brune. Les trois formes arrondies du centre sont en matière dure, d'un blanc mat.

L'objet de droite est en craie bleu ciel. Dans le haut, des poils. Cet objet doit servir à écrire sur un tableau noir. Il sera usé par la base, pour qu'il ne finisse par subsister que la touffe de poils du haut.

Yves TANGUY.

BOURGEOIS ET PROLÉTAIRES

« Il paraît que ce qui marche le mieux, en ce moment, c'est la fabrication et le commerce des coffres-forts ».

Clément VAUTEL.
(*Le Journal*, 29, 11, 1931).

« Lorsque nous aurons remporté la victoire à l'échelle mondiale, nous édifierons, je pense, dans les rues de quelques-unes des plus grandes villes du monde, des pissotières en or. »

LÉNINE.

★

DU GÉNÉRAL AU MARÉCHAL.

On n'a pas oublié la grande parade académique du printemps dernier, lorsque M. Paul Valéry reçut (et comment !) le maréchal Pétain.

La société des gens de lettres, la dame de l'hôtel Massa, la Masseuse, a massé, de son mieux, M. le général Weygand.

La parole fut donnée à M. Gaston Rageot.

Le *Journal* de s'extasier particulièrement sur ce passage du petit discours Rageoteur :

Cette simplicité et cette force d'âme, cette application à la vie, cette vigilance à la réalité, toutes ces qualités de notre nation que vous possédez à un degré si éminent, nous permettent aujourd'hui non seulement de saluer votre gloire dans le passé, mais de proclamer nos espérances de paix dans l'avenir, puisque nul n'est plus capable de défendre un pays que celui qui en résume toutes les qualités. Jusqu'à nouvel ordre, il faut que l'esprit soit défendu par la force : la France représente l'un et l'autre et elle a confiance en vous, mon général, parce qu'en vous elle se reconnaît toute entière.

Le scrognegneu à feuille de chêne, bien entendu, ne s'est pas fait prier pour répondre au provocateur civil

27

60
YVES TANGUY, *"POIDS ET COULEURS"* (WEIGHTS AND COLORS)
Le Surréalisme au service de la révolution, no. 3 (December 1931)

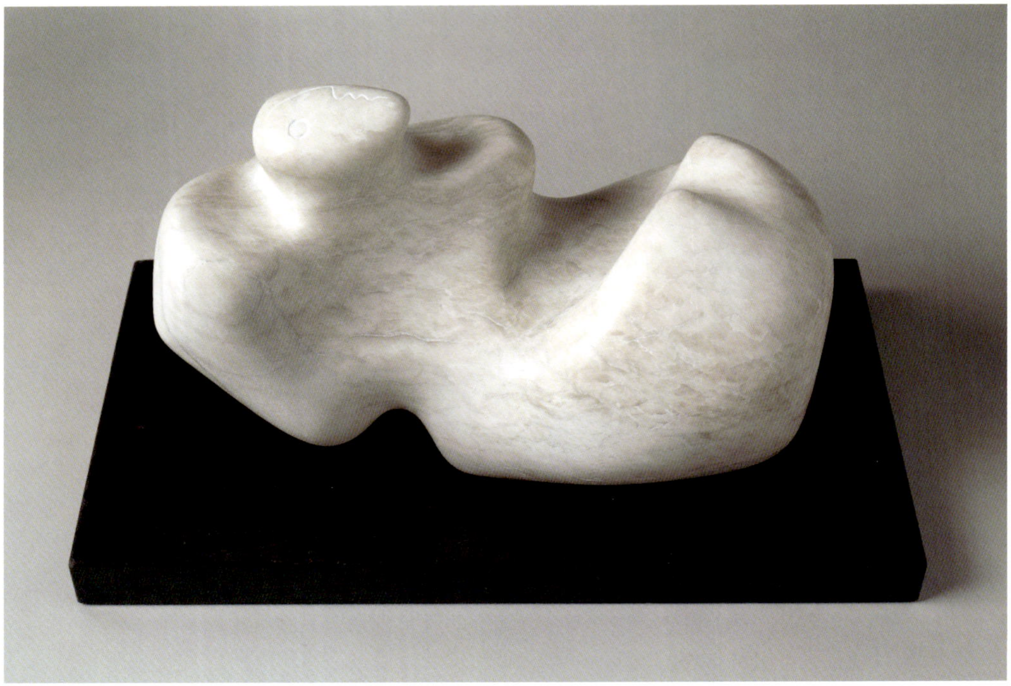

61
BARBARA HEPWORTH
RECLINING FIGURE, 1933
Hirshhorn Museum and
Sculpture Garden,
Washington, DC;
gift of Joseph H. Hirshhorn

During the 1930s Arp became increasingly interested in modeling and carving freestanding sculptures, which impressed other artists with their almost magical ability to morph as a viewer walks around them. Forms bulge and surge, at times even appear to breathe. This illusion of pulsing life within inert materials appealed to the British sculptors Henry Moore and Barbara Hepworth, who had previously specialized in carving wood and stone, often deriving their figural forms from the innate grain and texture of those materials. Between periodic trips to Paris, Moore and Hepworth learned about Surrealist art from magazines, and they must have seen illustrations of Arp's *Head with Annoying Objects* and Picasso's *Anatomy* drawings. After a visit to Arp's studio in 1932, Hepworth carved the undulating *Reclining Figure*, 1933 (fig. 61), in exquisite white alabaster. Her aesthetics emphasized the affinities between nature and sculpture, but she did not officially align herself with the Surrealist movement. Moore, on the other hand, chose to become actively involved with Surrealism, signing the British group's manifesto in 1935. His remarks at the time quietly reflect his new enthusiasm: "Abstract qualities of design are essential . . . but to me of equal importance is the psychological, human element." Each sculpture "takes on in my mind a human or occasionally animal character and personality."[36] Even decades later, Moore acknowledged that it was "the human figure which interests me deeply . . . natural

62
HENRY MOORE
FIGURE, 1935
Hirshhorn Museum and
Sculpture Garden, Washington,
DC; gift of Joseph H. Hirshhorn

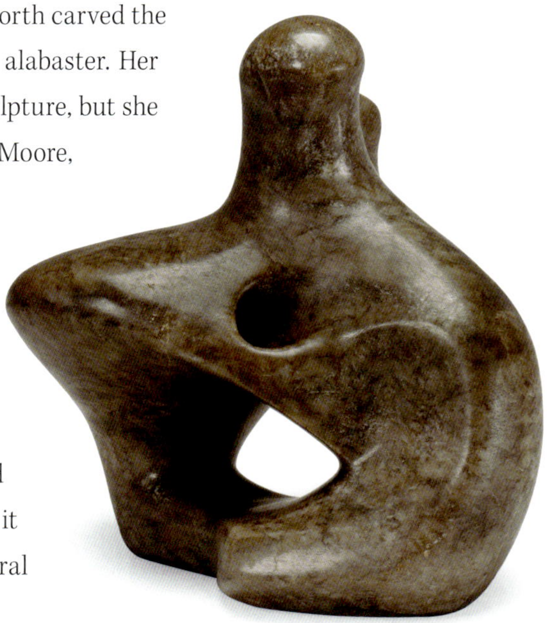

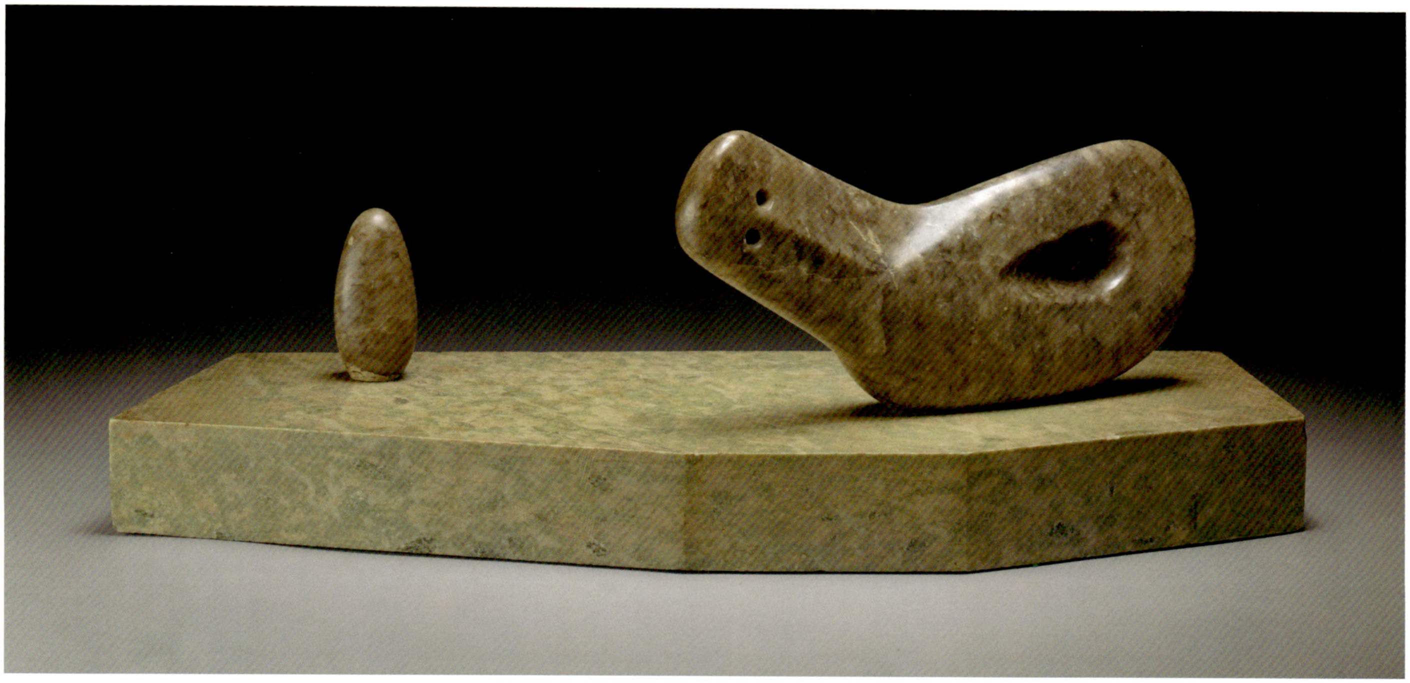

63
HENRY MOORE, *BIRD AND EGG*, 1934
Yale Center for British Art, New Haven; Paul Mellon Collection

64
HENRY MOORE, *RECLINING FIGURE*, 1931
The Henry Moore Foundation, Much Hadham, England; gift of the artist

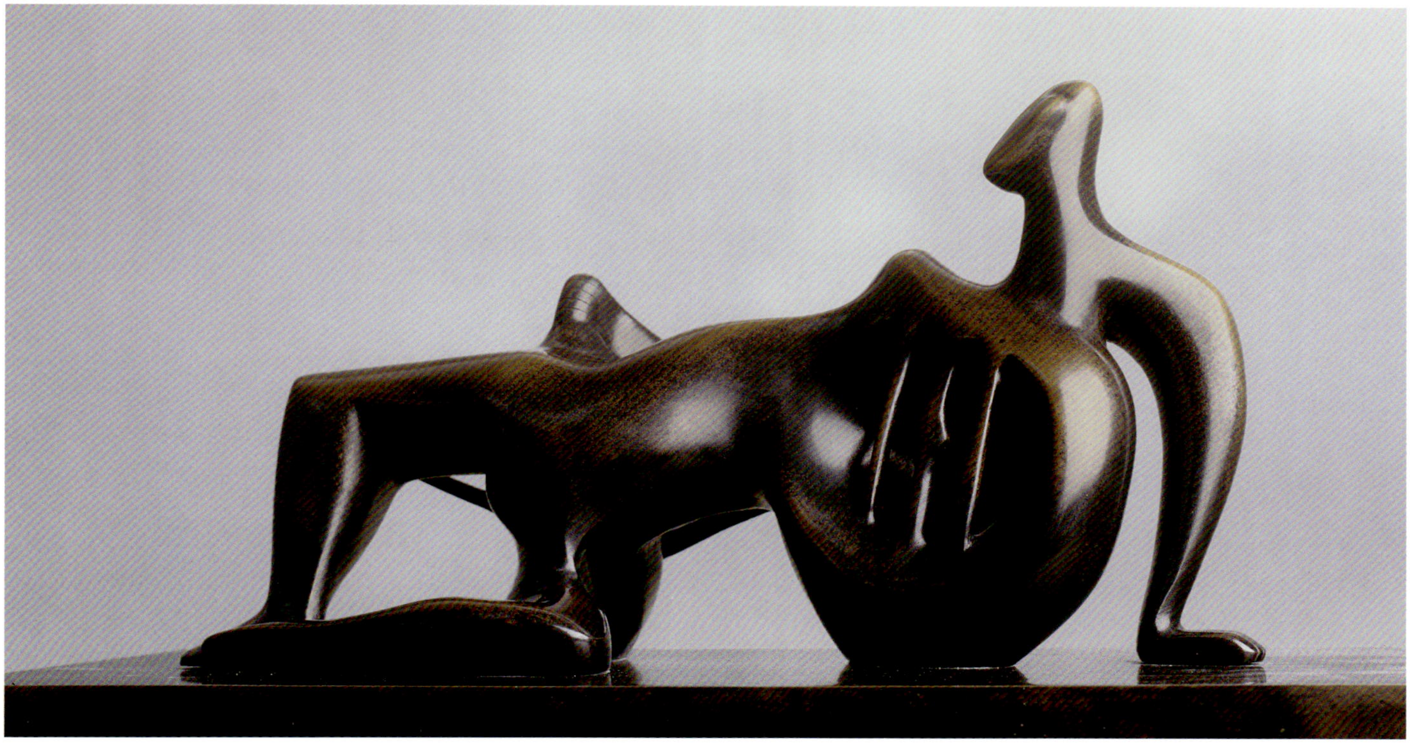

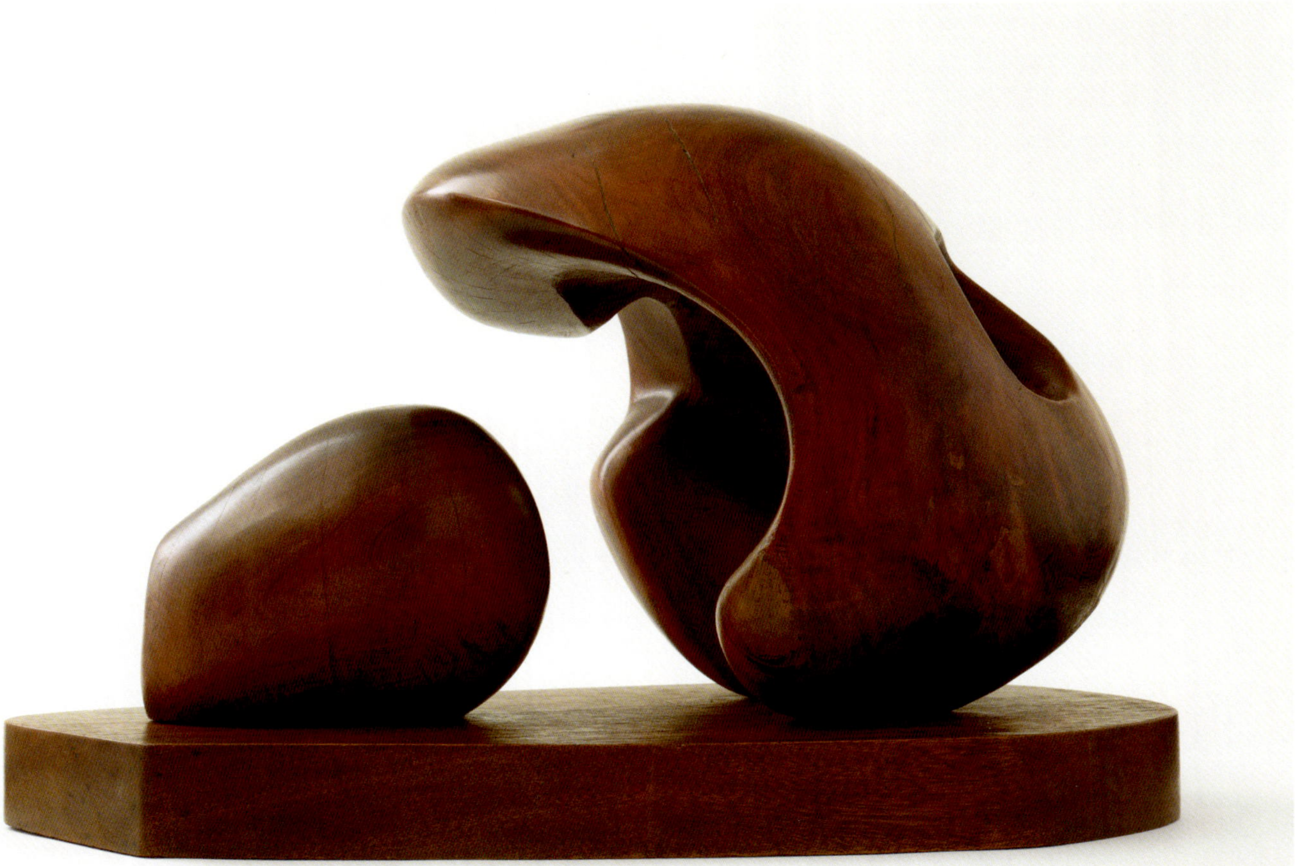

65

HENRY MOORE, *TWO FORMS*, 1934

The Museum of Modern Art, New York; Sir Michael Sadler Fund

forms such as bones, shells, pebbles, etc. . . . There are universal shapes to which everybody is subconsciously conditioned and to which they can respond if their conscious control does not shut them off."[37] Moore's exploration of organic forms, transformational metamorphosis, and expressive distortions resulted in a series of Surrealist sculptures, from several *Reclining Figures* in 1930–31 to the multicomponent *Bird and Egg* in 1934 (fig. 64 and fig. 63). Many are carved in stone but have the fluidity and malleability of soft clay, which has been pulled, polished, and even pierced, as it is in *Figure*, 1935 (fig. 62). When a viewer walks around *Two Forms*, 1934 (fig. 65), the visual associations change. The larger form at first suggests the ominous force of a tidal wave about to engulf its victim, but then from another angle it softens into a protective shelter. The small sphere is positioned opposite a similarly sized hole in the larger form, as if it has recently emerged from the opening or is contemplating escape through it.

The spread of biomorphic art had become so pervasive in England that the art critic Geoffrey Grigson complained about its prevalence in 1934. While not enthusiastic about works by Arp, he praised Moore's sculptures as existing "between the conscious and the unconscious and between what we perceive and what we project emotionally into the objects of our world." Grigson coined the word *biomorphism* (biological forms + metamorphosis), which he defined as being "either directly *derived from* natural forms (rocks, pebbles, bones, etc.) or *inspired* by memories of them."[38]

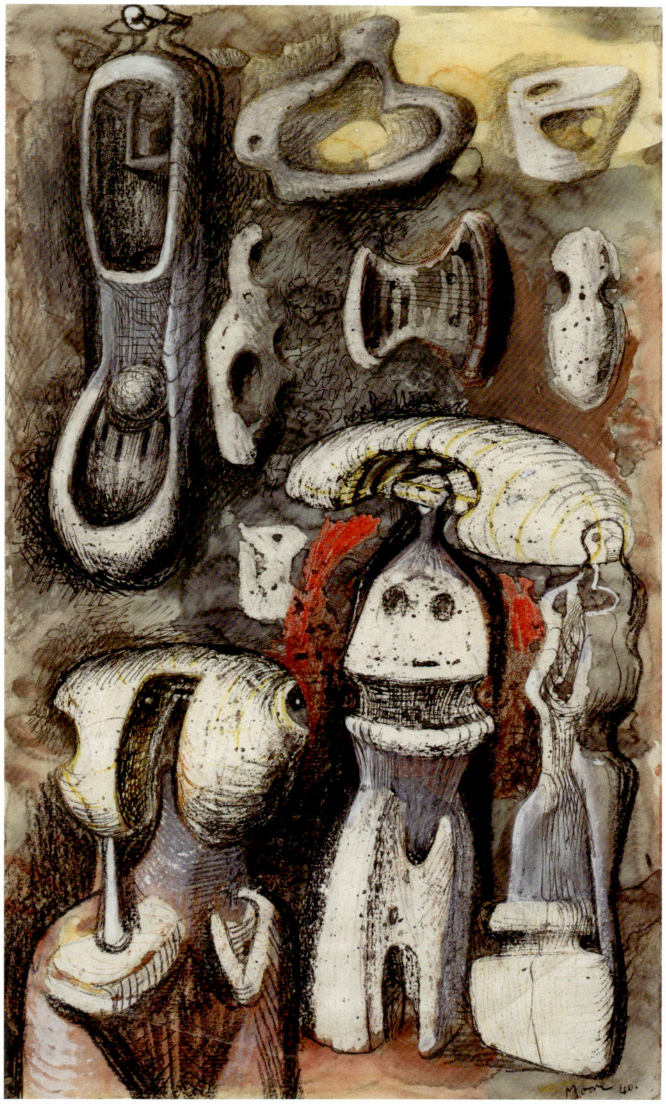

66
HENRY MOORE
IDEAS FOR SCULPTURE, 1940
Harvard Art Museums / Fogg Museum, Cambridge, Massachusetts; gift of Lois Orswell

One of the most innovative subsets of Surrealist sculptures is conceptualizing abstraction as landscape, and Moore defined early his particular propensity for associating a reclining figure with rolling hills and steep mountains. The elements in *Composition*, 1934, align like a ridge of boulders left behind by a glacier. In one drawing from 1939 (fig. 67) the forms are fluid, seeming to ebb and flow like a viscous or molten liquid. In his largest Surrealist sculpture, carved from a massive block of wood in 1939 (fig. 68), he likens the body to undulating peaks and valleys. The forms swell and dilate,

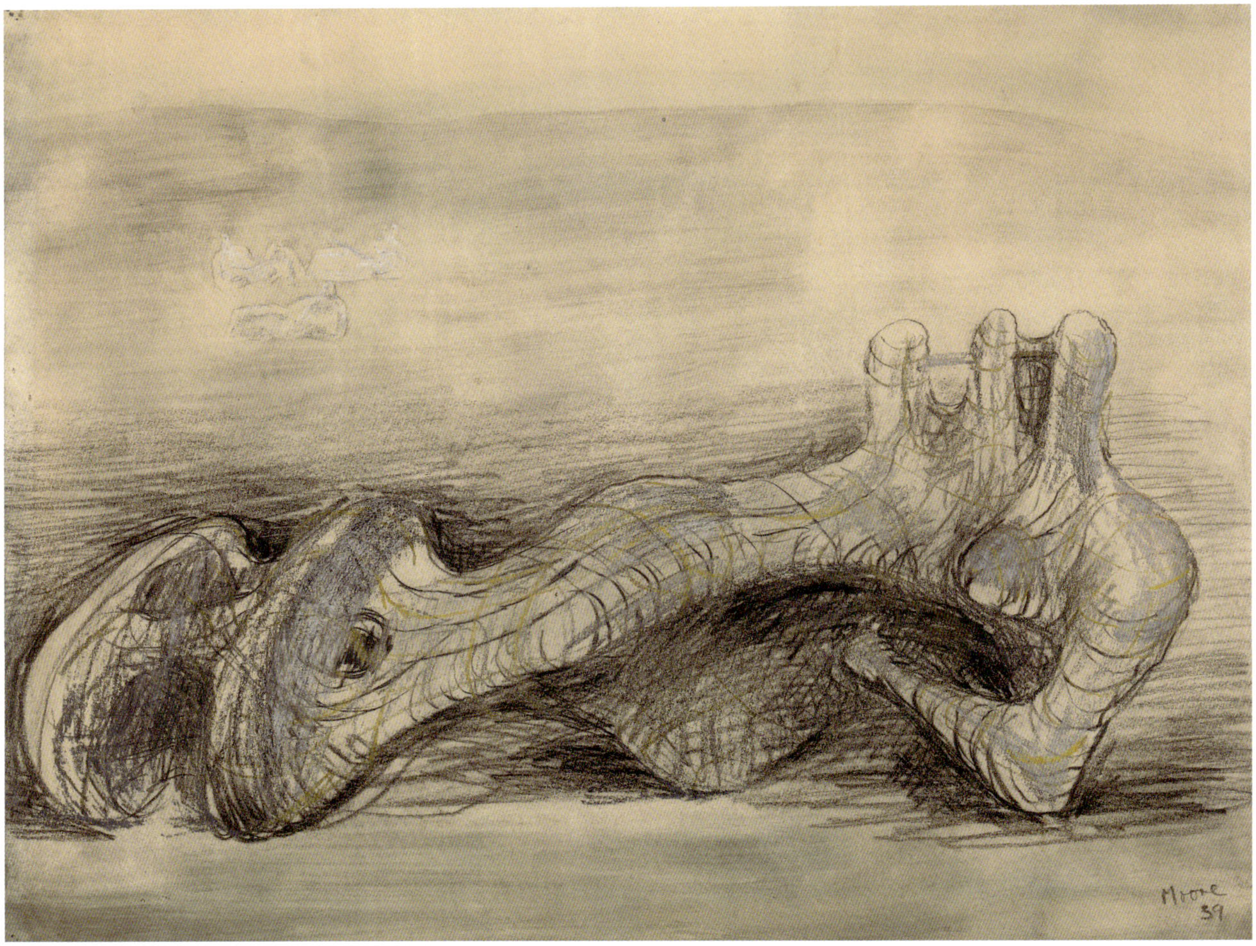

67

HENRY MOORE, *RECLINING FIGURE*, 1939

Yale Center for British Art, New Haven; gift of Jeffrey H. Loria, Yale B.A. 1962, in memory of Harriet Loria Popowitz

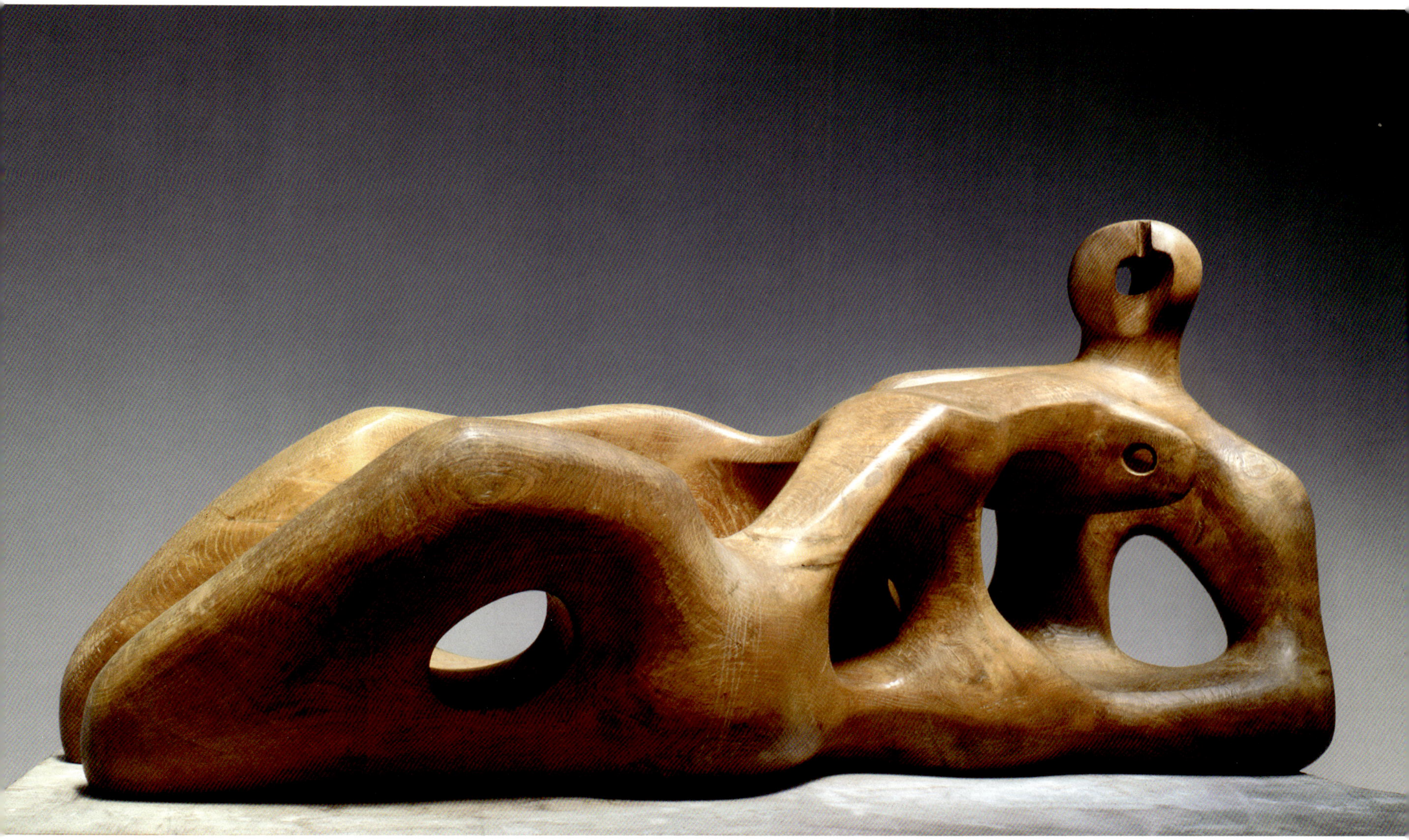

68
HENRY MOORE, *RECLINING FIGURE*, 1939
Detroit Institute of Arts; Founders Society Purchase

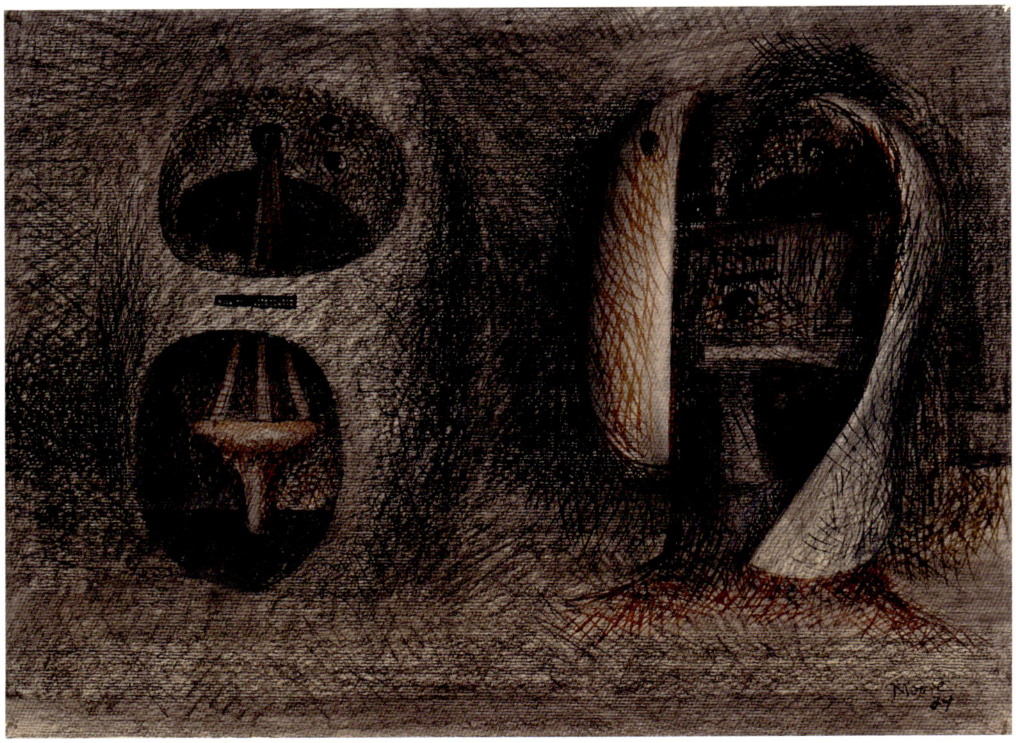

69
HENRY MOORE
TWO HEADS (DRAWING FOR METAL SCULPTURE), 1939
The Henry Moore Foundation, Much Hadham, England

surge and recede, rise and fall in intricate rhythms that can be discovered only by walking completely around the sculpture. Standing at the figure's feet, we discover that the legs are discreetly separated to allow intimate access. Viewing the composition frontally, we realize that one surging form morphs into a snake's or reptile's head lifting to bite the figure's breast. The subliminal sense of physical tension in this *Reclining Figure* would infuse many of Moore's later sculptures.

The extraordinary variety of Moore's Surrealist endeavors is revealed in certain drawings of the 1930s, ranging from automatist experiments in sketchbooks to highly finished compositions. *Ideas for Sculpture*, 1940 (fig. 66), is a worksheet of biomorphic figures and concepts. The standing figure in the center at bottom has Arpian legs and torso (where the breasts may be mistaken for eyes); a simpler form above has nothing in the middle, an expansion of the hole in the 1935 *Figure*. From 1937 until 1940, Moore depicted his visions of seemingly alive biomorphs situated in imaginary architecture and in nature. *Five Figures in a Setting*, 1937 (fig. 71), proffers a mysterious narrative or theatrical performance. *Sculptural Object in a Landscape*, 1939 (fig. 72), evokes an impression of massive dinosaur bones propped together like an antediluvian shrine. Moore considered these drawings of imagined sculptures so important that he showed more than thirty in his exhibition at the Mayor Gallery in February 1939.[39] Today, when we encounter Moore's monumental bronze sculptures in urban plazas, we can recognize the extent to which they originated in his Surrealist compositions of the 1930s.

As one of the co-organizers of the *International Exhibition of Surrealism* in London at the New Burlington Galleries in 1936, Moore contributed four sculptures and three drawings in

70
HENRY MOORE
STRINGED FIGURE NO. 1, 1937
Hirshhorn Museum and Sculpture Garden, Washington, DC; Joseph H. Hirshhorn Purchase Fund

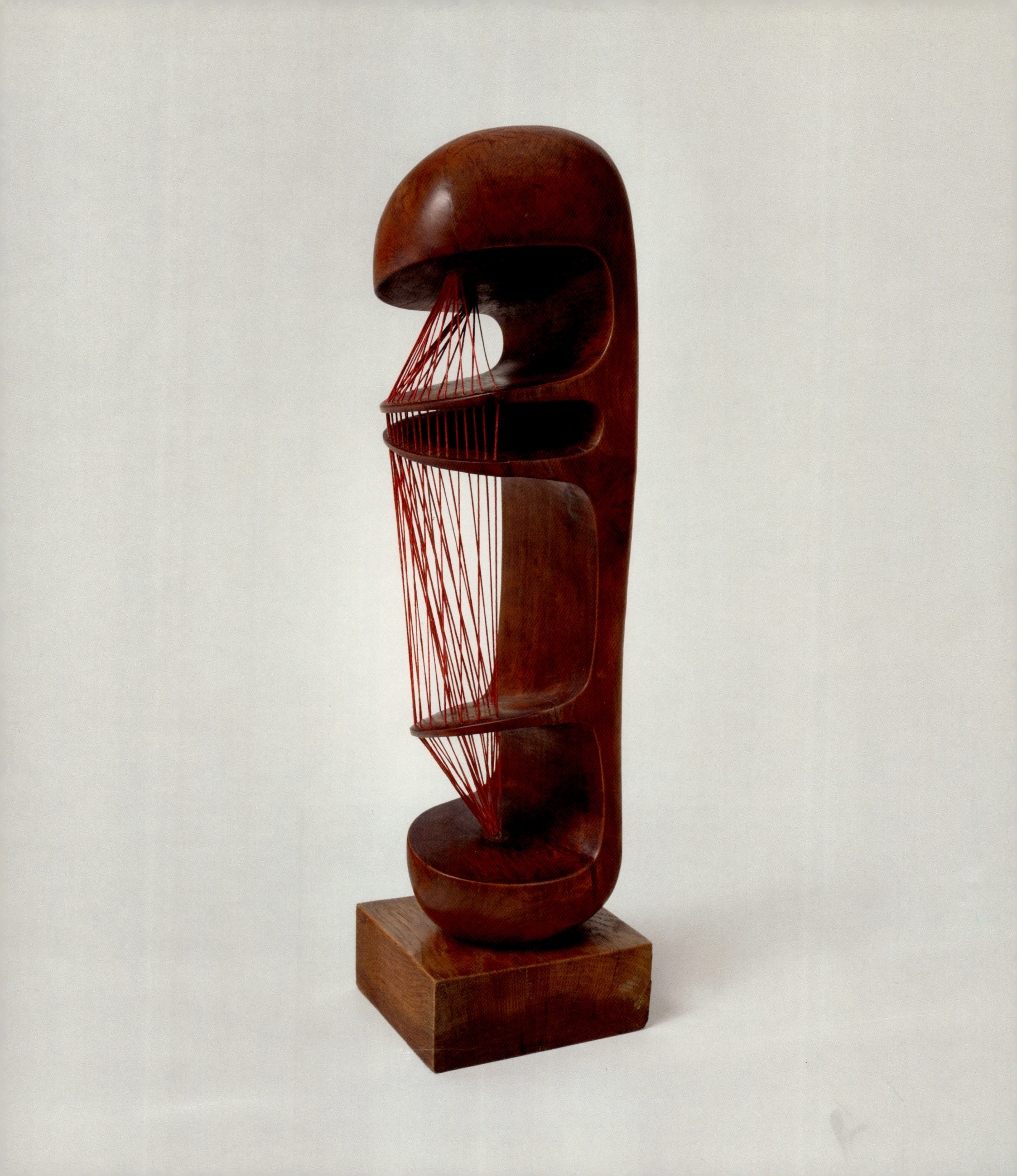

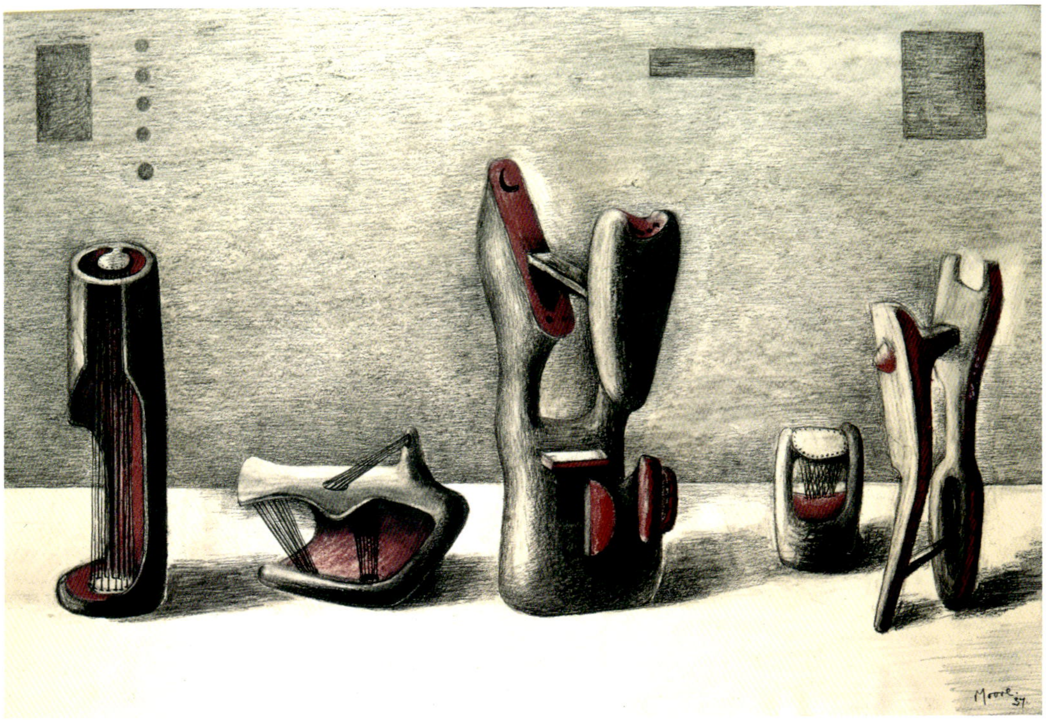

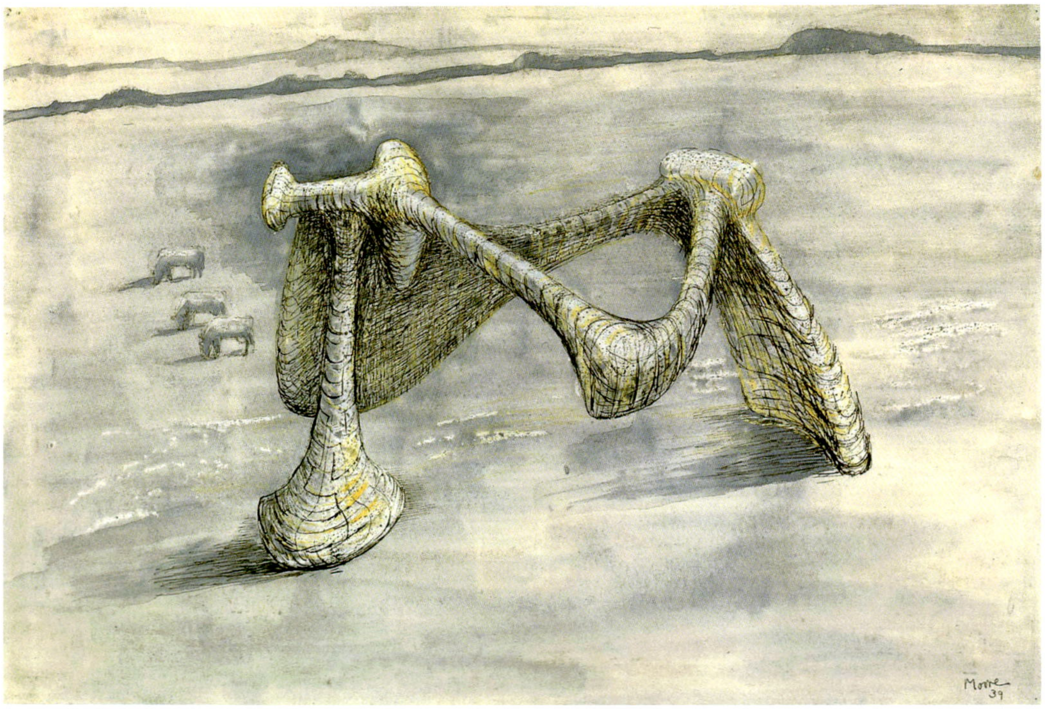

71

HENRY MOORE, *FIVE FIGURES IN A SETTING,* 1937

Private collection, London

72

HENRY MOORE, *SCULPTURAL OBJECT IN A LANDSCAPE,* 1939

Sainsbury Centre for Visual Arts, University of East Anglia, Norwich, England

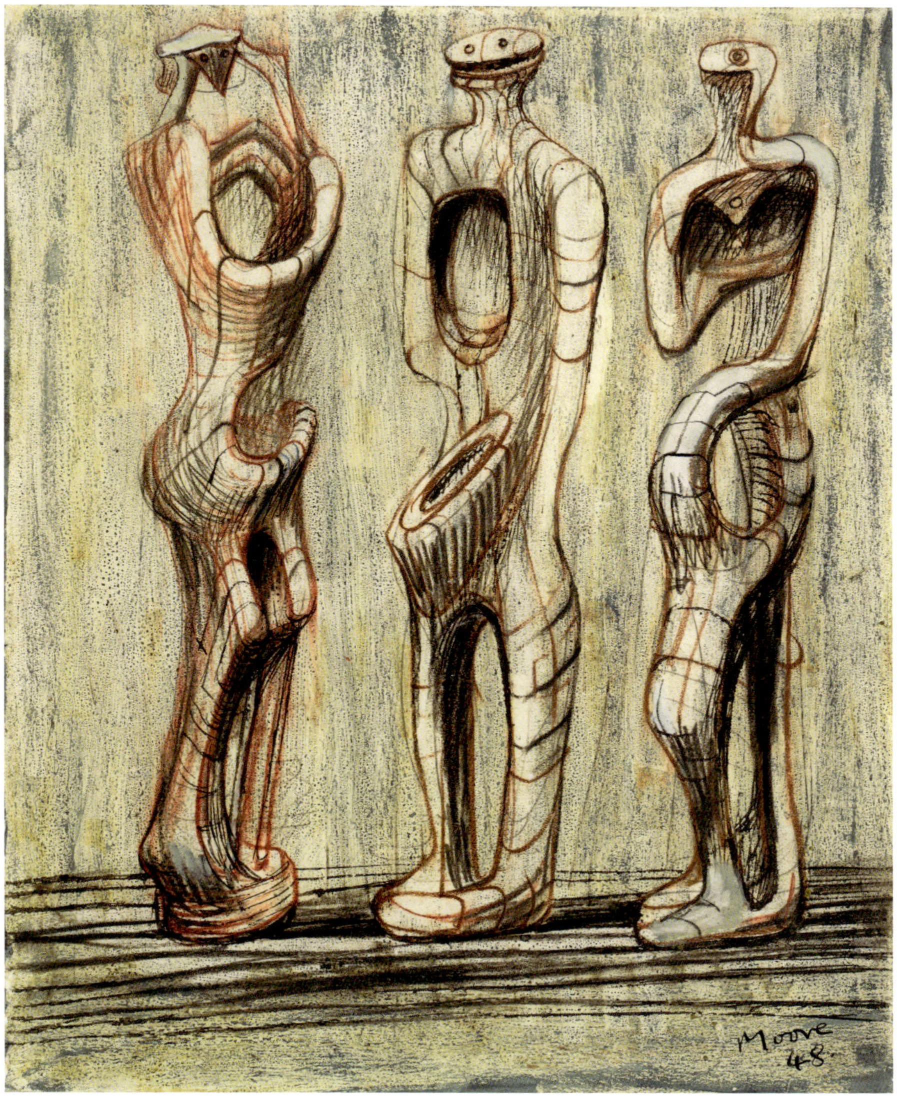

73

HENRY MOORE, *THREE STANDING FIGURES*, 1948

Harvard Art Museums / Fogg Museum, Cambridge, Massachusetts; bequest of Meta and Paul J. Sachs

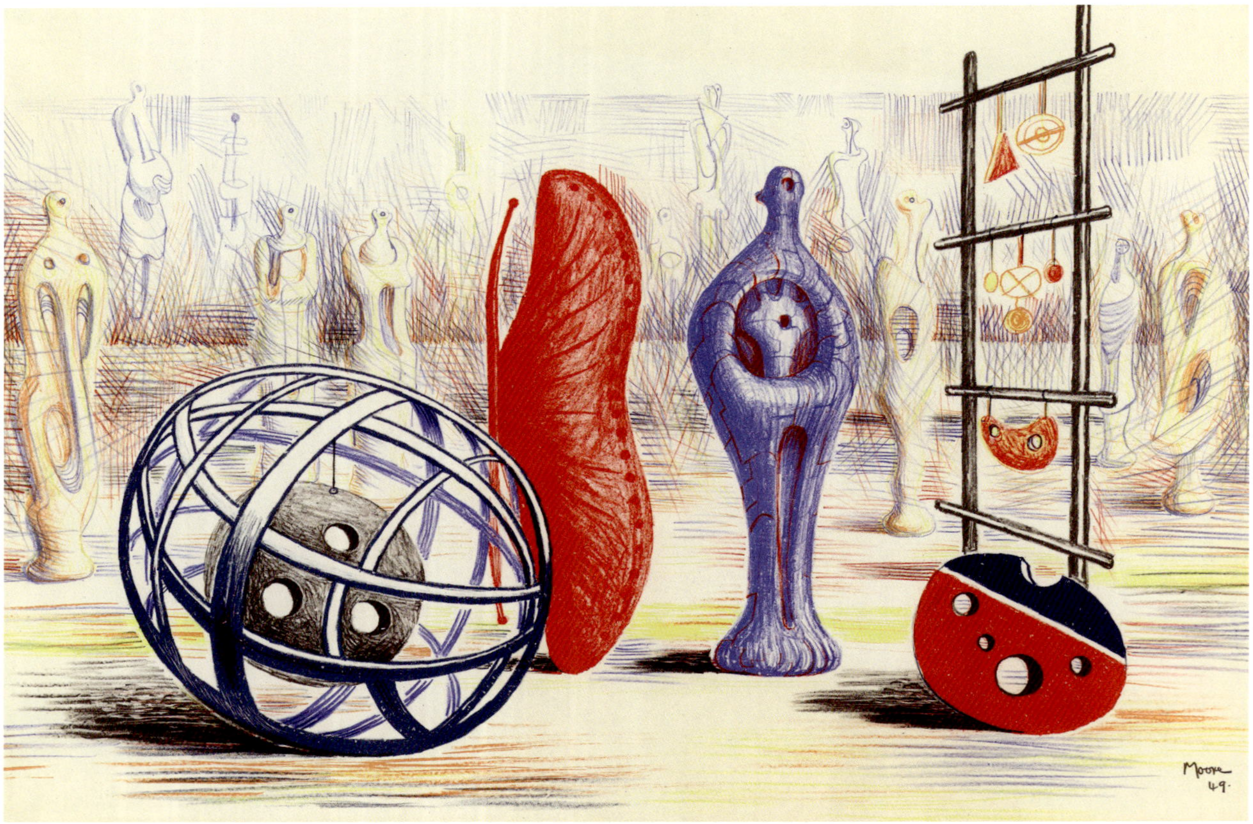

74

HENRY MOORE, *SCULPTURAL OBJECTS*, 1949

Museum of Fine Arts, Boston; gift of Edna and Matthew Brown in honor of the 100th anniversary of the Print Department

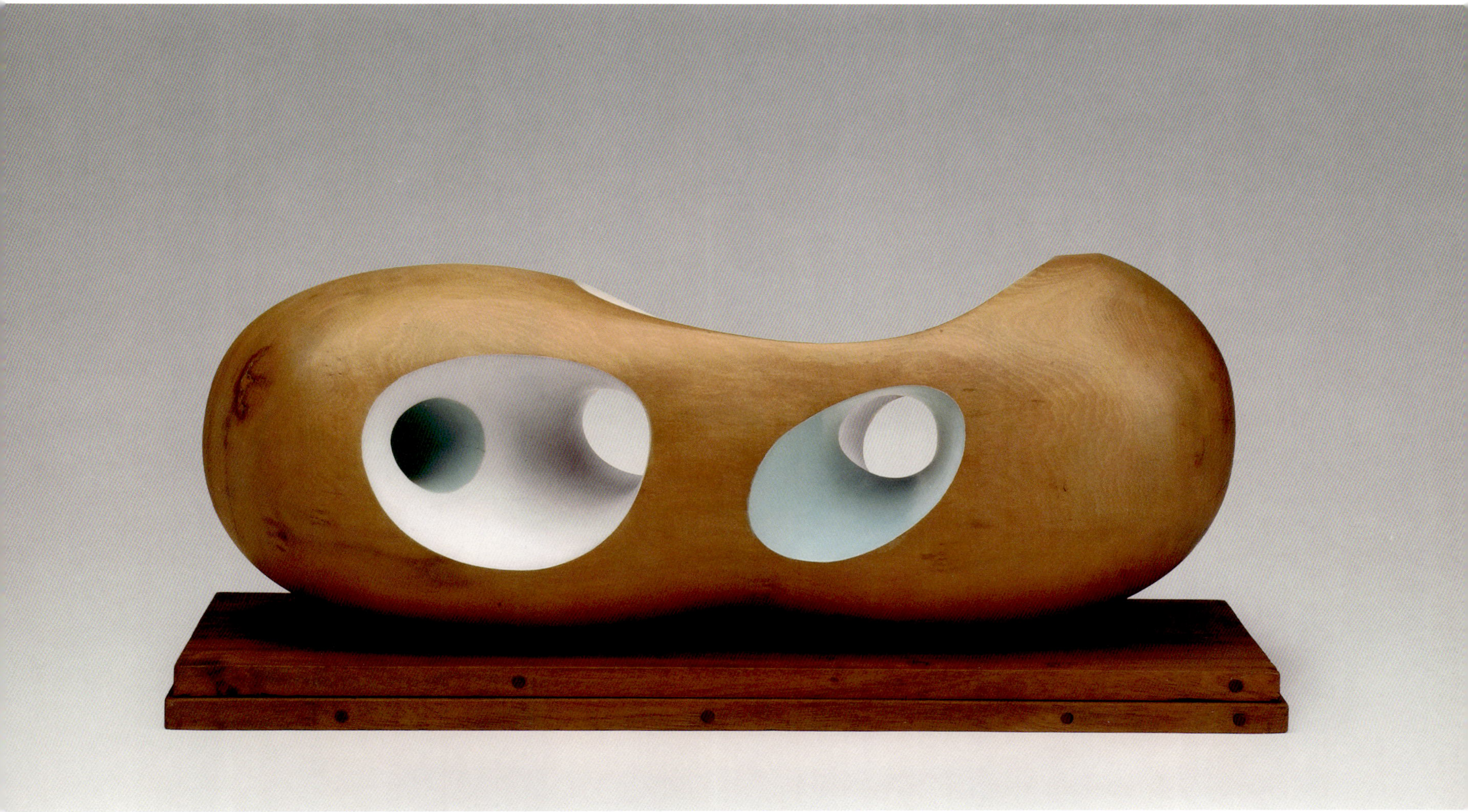

75
BARBARA HEPWORTH, *PENDOUR*, 1947–48
Hirshhorn Museum and Sculpture Garden, Washington, DC; gift of Joseph H. Hirshhorn

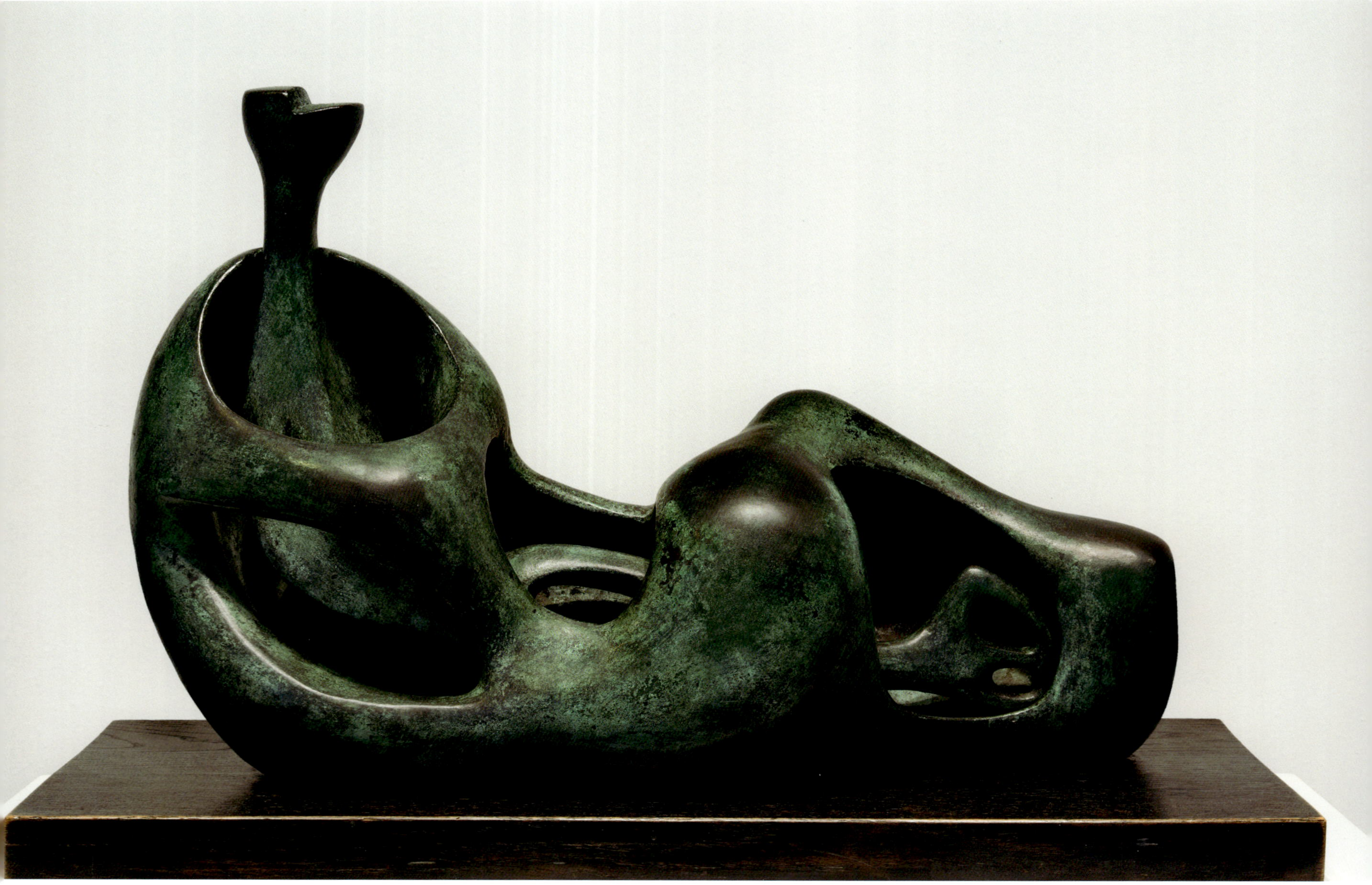

76
HENRY MOORE, *RECLINING FIGURE: INTERNAL AND EXTERNAL FORMS*, 1951
Hirshhorn Museum and Sculpture Garden, Washington, DC; gift of Joseph H. Hirshhorn

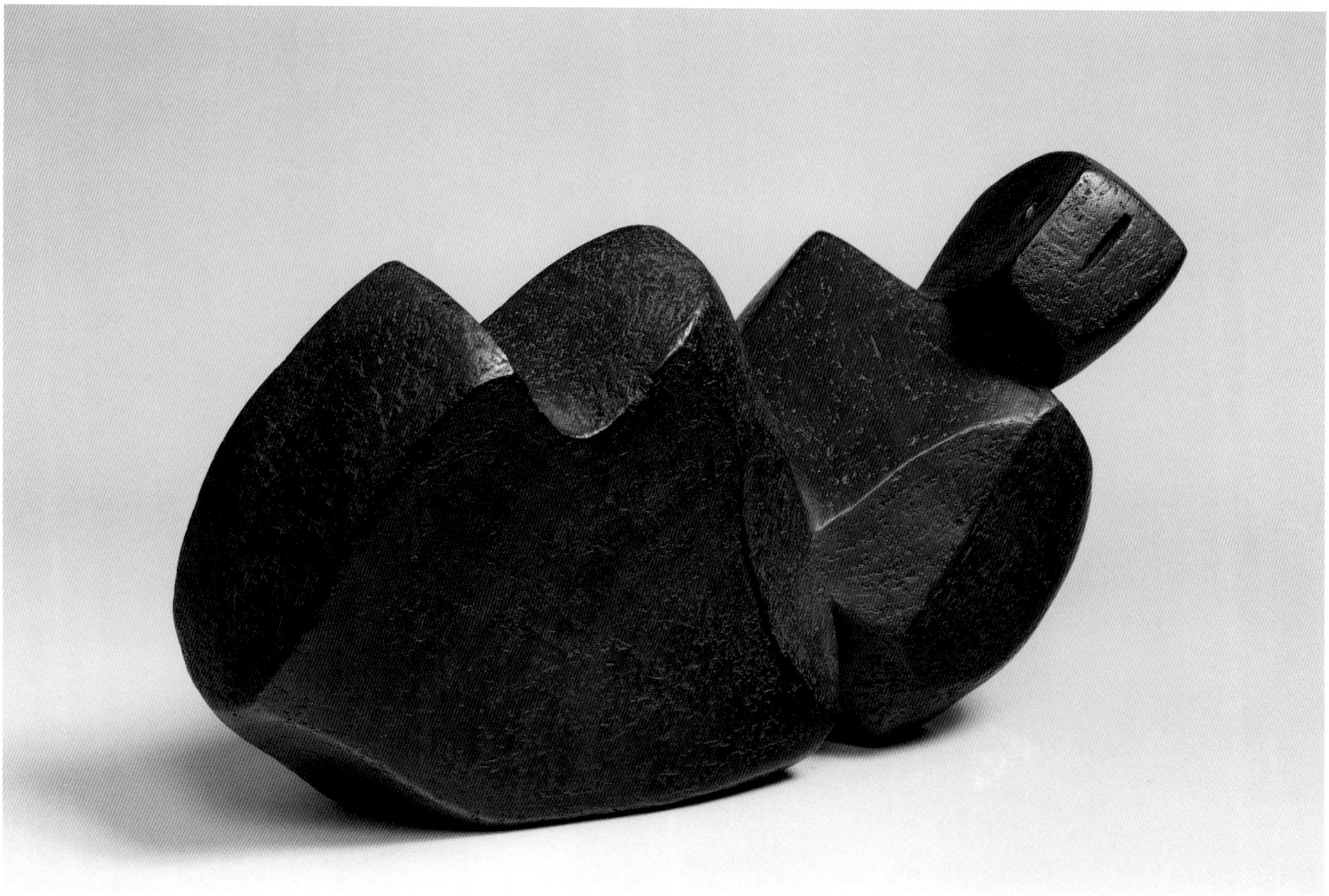

77
LOUISE NEVELSON, *MOUNTAIN WOMAN*, 1947
Hirshhorn Museum and Sculpture Garden, Washington, DC; gift of Joseph H. Hirshhorn

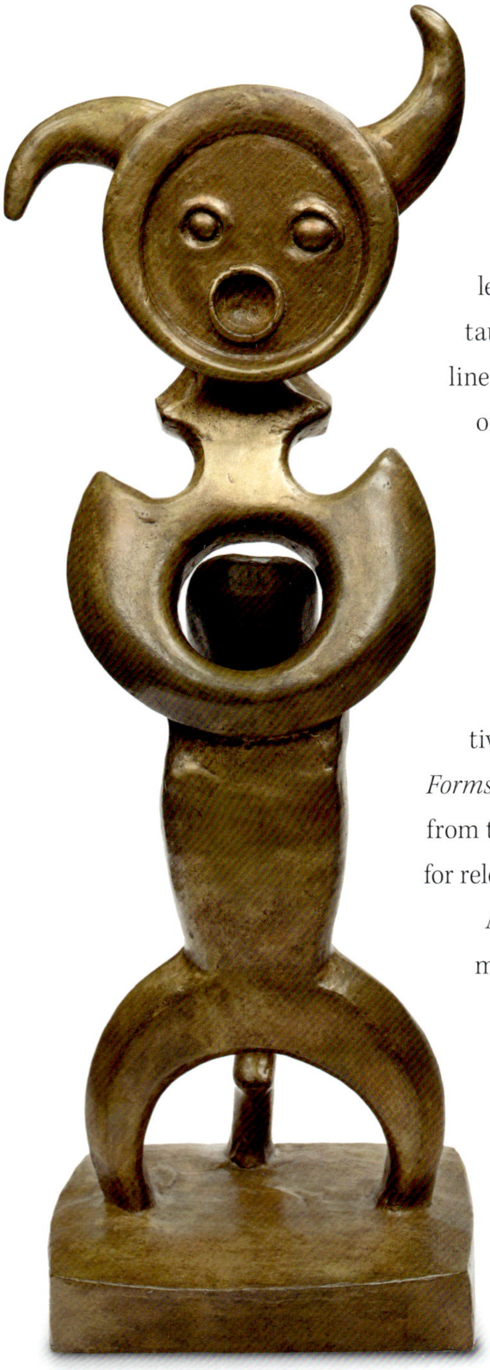

his new style. He also spent time with Breton, Arp, and other Paris-based Surrealists who had come to London. The next year Moore unleashed a flood of innovative sculptures and drawings. *Stringed Figure No. 1* (fig. 70) presents a dichotomous relationship between interior and exterior. The artist removed most of the wood log's interior, leaving the remaining mass on one side, and in the empty space he wove a taut yet delicate structure of string. The contrast between solid exterior and linear interior may be interpreted as the relationship between body and spirit or as an analogy for the persona we present to the world as a shield for the vulnerable within. He developed this concept in the drawing *Two Heads*, 1939 (fig. 69). This dualist concept would acquire greater significance just before and during World War II, when the British government hid from the real threat of German aggression and again when the British people took refuge in underground shelters during devastating bombardments. The ovoid hollow form in the upper left corner of *Ideas for Sculpture* protectively encloses an infant-like figure. In *Reclining Figure: Internal and External Forms*, 1951 (fig. 76), the inner person exists as its own entity, completely separate from the enclosing form, and lifts its face to the sky, as if looking for answers or for release.

As a response to the mechanistic and atomic destruction of World War II, many sculptors preferred organic forms to geometric ones. Moore picked up where he had left off, making small models and drawings of figures with intricate linear anatomies (fig. 74). The artist would draw upon these and earlier biomorphic Surrealist-inspired studies for many larger, later sculptures. The *Upright Motifs* series of 1955–56, for example, translates the elusive contours of *Three Standing Figures*, 1948 (fig. 73), into sturdy bronze, and *Vertebrae*, 1968, extrapolates from his 1934 *Composition*. Likewise, a seamless fusion of nature and sculpture provided the basis for nearly all Hepworth's mature sculptures. *Pendour*, 1947–48 (fig. 75), alludes to the Cornwall coast where the sea's relentless waves have carved caves in the stone cliffs, an association that the artist reinforced by painting the sculpture's interior blue and white. She implemented a similar approach for her *Figure for Landscape*, 1960, where the open interior is faintly tinted green in response to the verdant setting in which it stands. In Spain, Miró created *Solar Bird* and *Lunar Bird*, 1945–46, as small wood carvings that were later enlarged to monumental proportions (fig. 79). In New York, Ernst invented a cast of characters that includes *Young Man with a Beating Heart*, *An Anxious Friend*, and *Moonmad*, 1944 (fig. 78). Prior to making found-object sculptures in the 1950s, Louise Nevelson modeled *Mountain Woman*, 1947 (fig. 77).

78
MAX ERNST
MOONMAD, 1944
Hirshhorn Museum and Sculpture Garden, Washington, DC; gift of Joseph H. Hirshhorn

79
JOAN MIRÓ
LUNAR BIRD, 1945
Hirshhorn Museum and Sculpture Garden, Washington, DC; gift of Joseph H. Hirshhorn

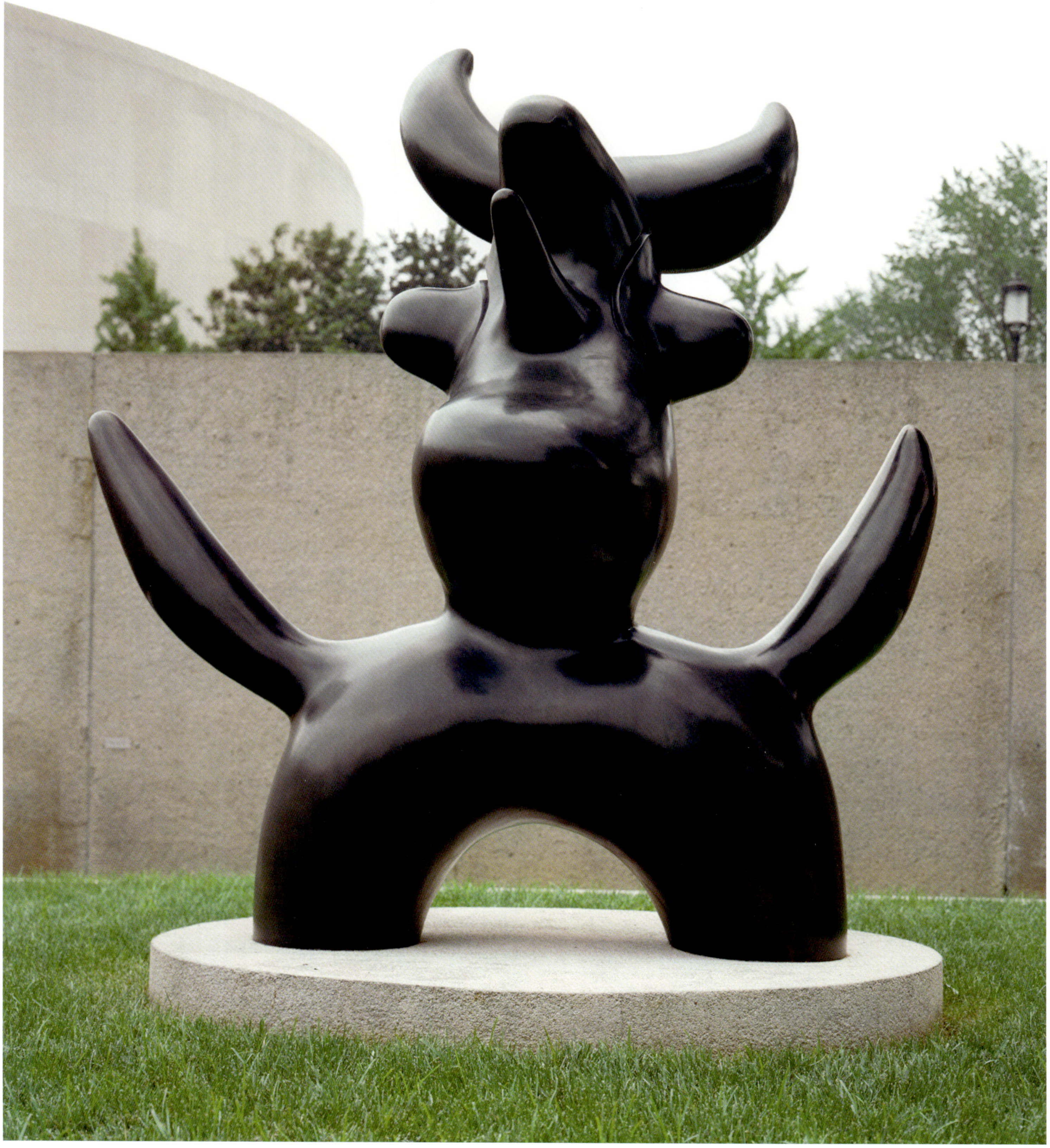

WOMEN AS OBJECTS AND EXHIBITIONS AS ENVIRONMENTS

Sex—or allusions to it—pervaded Surrealist art and literature from beginning to end, opening new paths of self-expression that are still hotly debated today. Scarcely two decades after the Victorian era had ended, male Surrealists made certain Freudian concepts, such as penis envy and fear of castration, their gospel, and the Marquis de Sade their hero. At best, women were divine muses and uninhibited lovers; at worst they were whores whose humanity could be ignored—a dichotomy of extremes that seems not only offensive but ridiculous today. When manifested in drawings and paintings, such images were disturbing enough, but in three dimensions they acquired an insistent physicality that was even more disconcerting.

Giacometti had established unforgettable precedents with the enlarged womb of *Spoon Woman*, the sensuous eroticism of *Reclining Woman Who Dreams*, the blatant aggression of *Man and Woman*, and the kinetic abstraction of *Suspended Ball*. But they pale when compared to *Woman with Her Throat Cut*, 1932 (fig. 80). A female figure with a bizarrely insectoid or crustacean anatomy sprawls on the floor. Her ribcage and spine are exposed as if violently eviscerated, and the splayed legs suggest dislocation and abuse from a vicious assault. Her neck is painfully arched and unnaturally elongated as if it has been forcefully pulled; a gash marks where the neck was cut by a blade. In the tiny head, the mouth opens as if screaming in pain, perhaps crying out at the moment of death. Giacometti readily acknowledged that *Woman with Her Throat Cut* was inspired by a recurrent daydream in which he rapes a mother and daughter before murdering them.[40] This sculpture instantly set a new standard for portrayals of women stripped of clothes, dominated, battered, and even killed. The original Surrealist goal of experiencing the marvelous as a joyful revelation comparable to childhood discoveries was supplanted by adult sexual fantasies. Yet *Woman with Her Throat Cut* manages to transcend the merely lascivious or horrific; it continues to intrigue viewers of both genders. We feel compelled to examine it like gawkers at a car crash, our repugnance battling with our curiosity. We become voyeurs of someone else's fantasy and are embarrassingly thrilled by it.

That disturbing ambivalence characterizes the works of the German artist Hans Bellmer. Partly inspired by the story of a doll who comes to life in Jacques Offenbach's *Tales of Hoffmann* opera, he modified plump baby dolls of the kind beloved by young girls, and he played with them, but not in a nice way (fig. 81). In a very early sculpture he cut off the lower arms and legs in order to insert ball bearings that permit a full range of movement. *The Doll: Ball-Joint*, 1934–36 (fig. 83), presents two of her dismembered limbs mounted on a lace-covered board. What might have once been a happy memory of childhood has become a disturbing trophy of arms akimbo, linked by a large artificial eye of the sort found in

80
ALBERTO GIACOMETTI
WOMAN WITH HER THROAT CUT, 1932
The Museum of Modern Art, New York; purchase

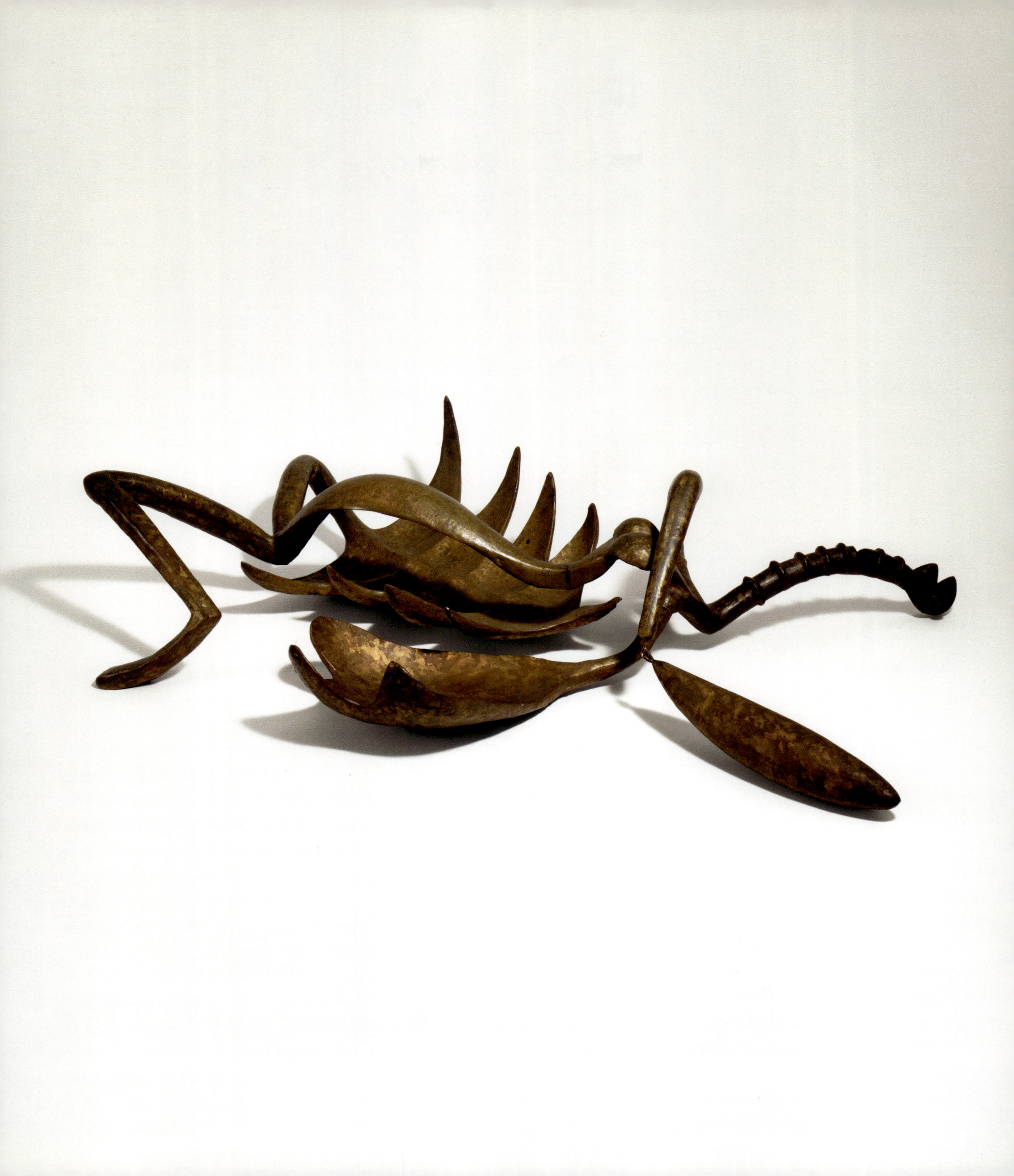

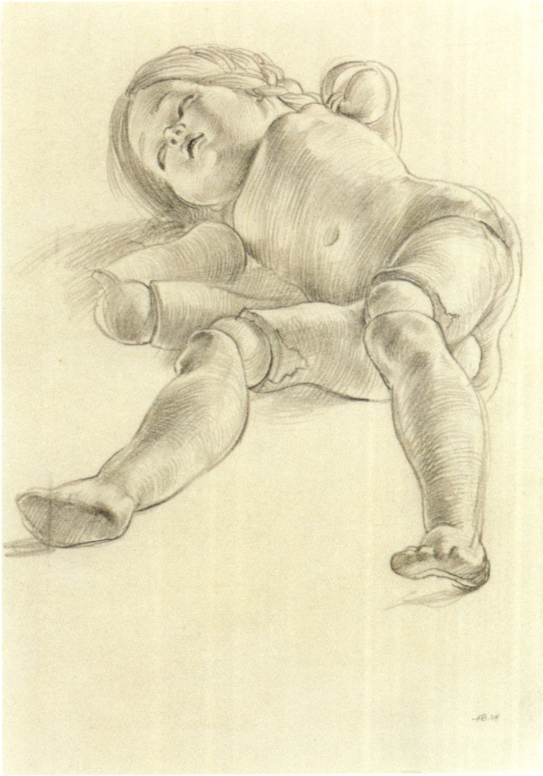

81
HANS BELLMER
UNTITLED (RECLINING DOLL), 1934
Pace Gallery, New York

very expensive dolls. The eye stares out directly at us, as if accusing us of complicity in the violence.

When Bellmer constructed a new, larger *Doll* in 1933–34, he incorporated prosthetic limbs of the kind manufactured for thousands of amputee war veterans. The artist stored the components on a wall in his room (fig. 82), where he could assemble and dismantle them at will; the doll's master had complete control. He photographed the doll in various poses, as if alive, sometimes wearing lingerie and a wig. When posed coquettishly, the plaster head with glass eyes, false eyelashes, and long hair acquired an aura of Lolita-like seduction (figs. 84–85). Even in a very small format, the image of the doll reclining on a mattress with no limbs and an apparently broken neck (figs. 87 and 92) conveys an inference of a misogynist attack very similar to what Giacometti achieved in *Woman with Her Throat Cut*. At one point Bellmer wanted to house in her stomach a miniature cinema showing the erotic fantasies of boys, but that was technologically unfeasible. Instead he devised *The Center of the Doll*, c. 1936 (fig. 86), by joining two pairs of buttocks linked by an internal ball-joint that enables viewers to reposition the upper and lower parts.

82
HANS BELLMER
THE DOLL, 1933–34
The Metropolitan Museum of Art, New York; Ford Motor Company Collection, gift of Ford Motor Company Collection and John C. Waddell

When Bellmer published a small book of his photographs in 1934, the introductory text proclaimed that *The Doll* was "an artificial girl with anatomical possibilities capable of recreating the heights of passion [and] inventing new desires." He rhapsodized about adolescent sexual imaginings and his desire to achieve "erotic liberation" through fantasies that transcend the physically possible. His *Doll* was a means of experiencing "the joy, the ecstasy, and the fear" that male imaginations seek. Viewers can "adjust [her] joints one to the other, arrange childlike poses … follow very gently the contours of the hollows, taste the pleasure of the curves, wandering the labyrinths of the ears, make everything pretty, and ruthlessly spill the salt of deformation." He recommended that we "coax the limbs, head, and torso into winsome poses, then run the eye and hand over these softly dipping vales, relish the pleasure of the shapely curves, give them a pretty turn or with blood-rousing gusto wrench them out of shape."[41]

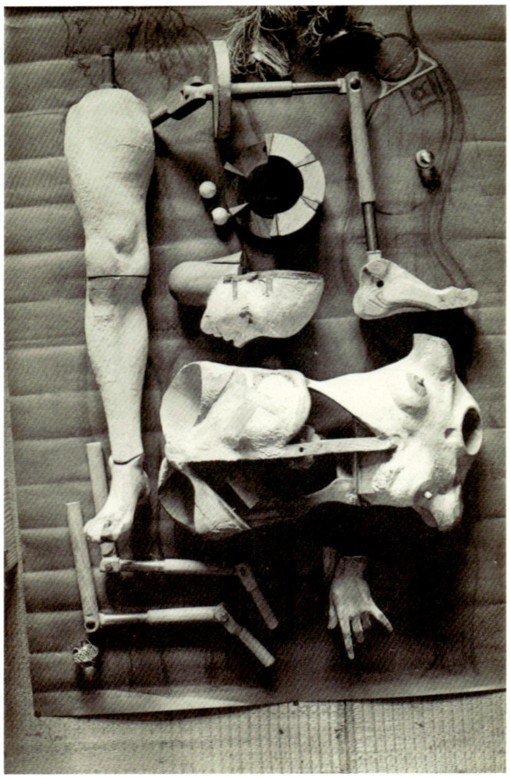

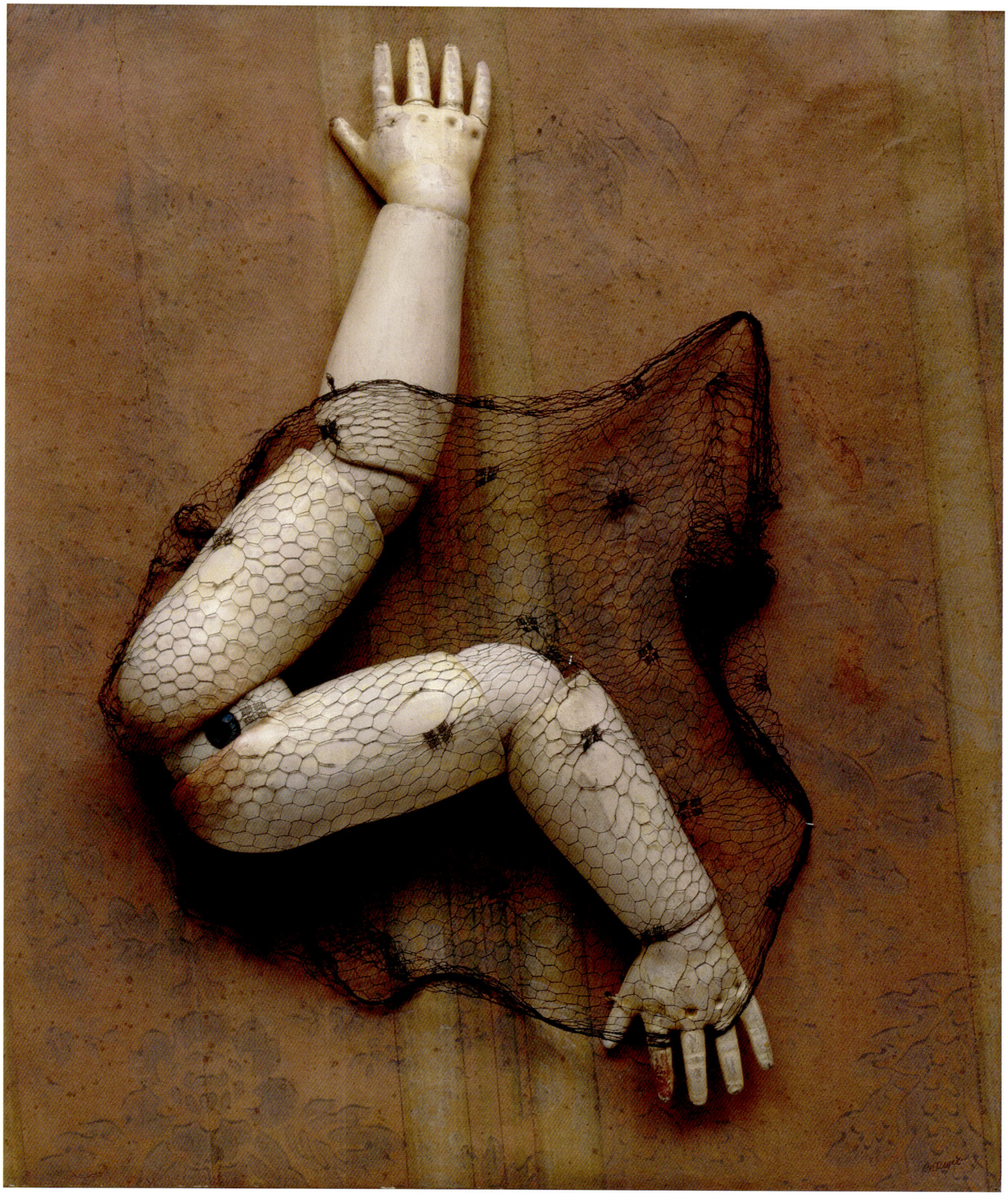

83
HANS BELLMER, *THE DOLL: BALL-JOINT*, 1934–36
Herbert Lust / Greenwich Fine Arts

After seeing Bellmer's photographs the Surrealists welcomed him into the fold by publishing eighteen of his images in the winter 1935 issue of *Minotaure* as *The Doll—Variations on the Assemblage of an Articulated Minor.* Usually small and slightly tinted with watercolors, the photographs have an uncomfortable similarity to contemporaneous pornographic pictures. But for a book called *The Doll's Games*, 1939, the writer Paul Eluard wrote evocative texts that provided more poignant associations. For the photograph of a one-legged doll at the bottom of a barren staircase and tied to its railing (fig. 88), he described a non-sexual context: "The winter at five in the morning. She gets up and, barely dressed, goes to pick up some dead wood. She could have died from the pity she felt for herself."[42]

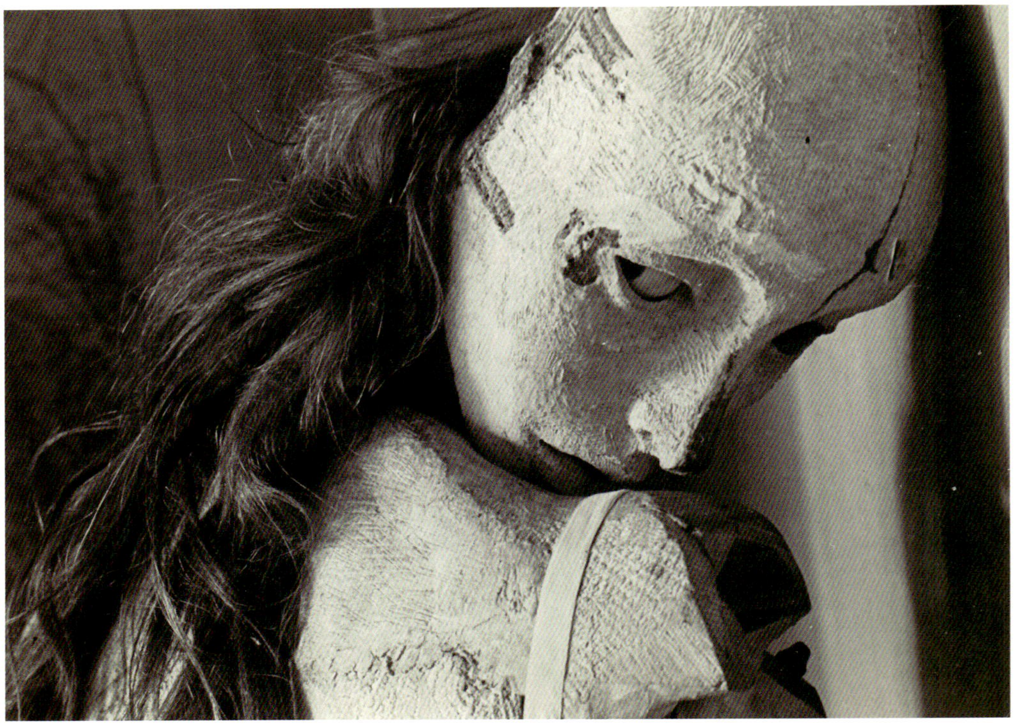

84
HANS BELLMER
THE DOLL, c.1934
The Metropolitan Museum of Art, New York; Ford Motor Company Collection, gift of Ford Motor Company Collection and John C. Waddell

Bellmer's second *Doll* construction was larger and more anatomically correct; she had two sets of adult breasts and two pairs of long shapely legs ending in a schoolgirl's shoes and white ankle socks. In determining which parts to pose in which locations, Bellmer often chose to compress the body, eliminate the head, drape the legs across a chair or hang them awkwardly from doorways and trees (figs. 89–91). Without portraying any actual violence, some images evoke comparisons with mutilated victims. Without depicting any sexual act, other compositions make us feel uncomfortable, as if we are seeing pornography. Even if intended as a metaphor for the modern psyche damaged by the pressures of life in difficult times, Bellmer's *Doll* is a helpless, female victim of male desire and control. By the time the artist moved to Paris in 1938, the Surrealists had enthusiastically appropriated his concept of a female figure as something to be manhandled, manipulated, and observed at will.

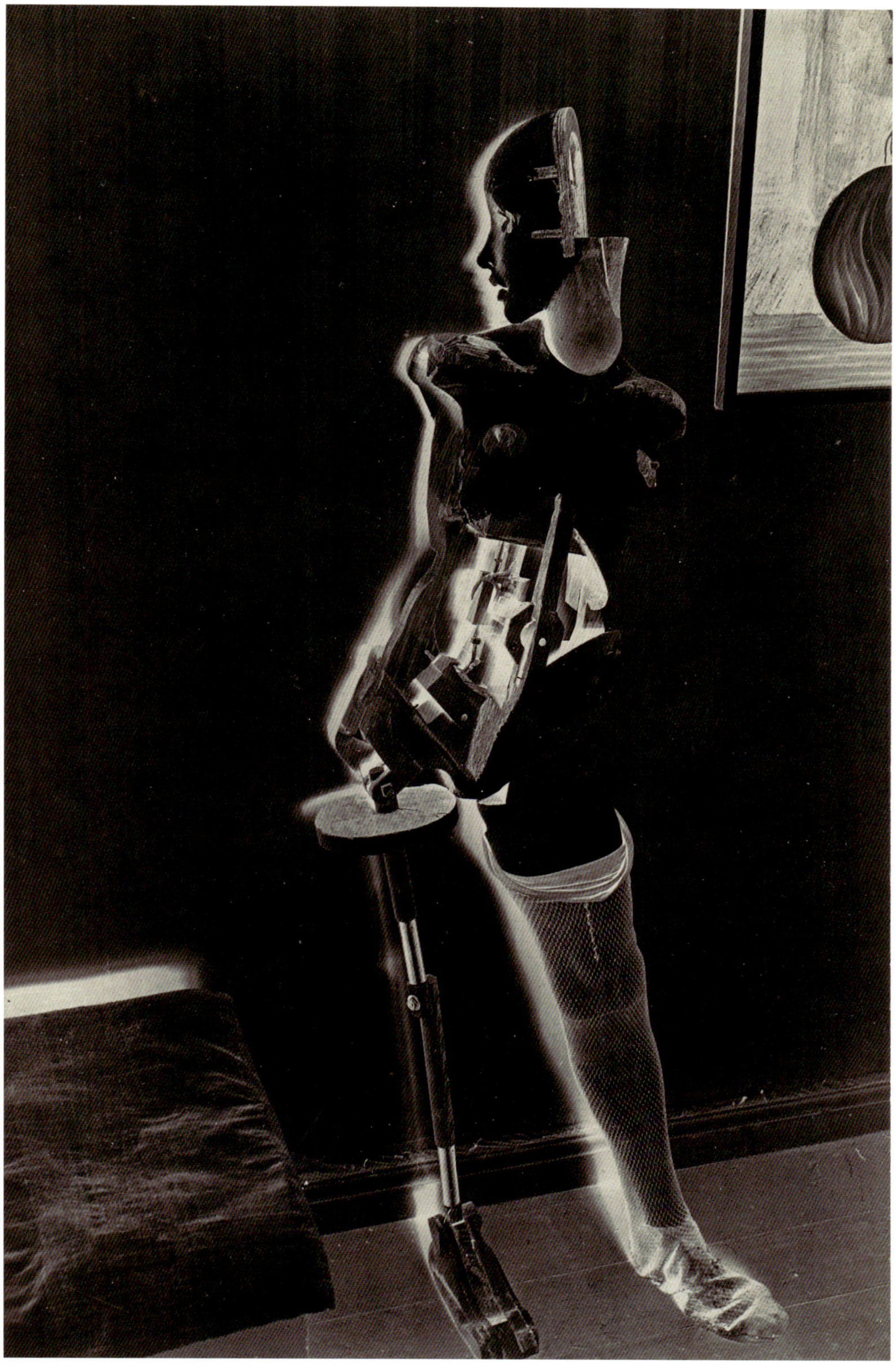

85
HANS BELLMER, *THE DOLL*, 1934–35
The Metropolitan Museum of Art, New York; Ford Motor Company Collection, gift of Ford Motor Company Collection and John C. Waddell

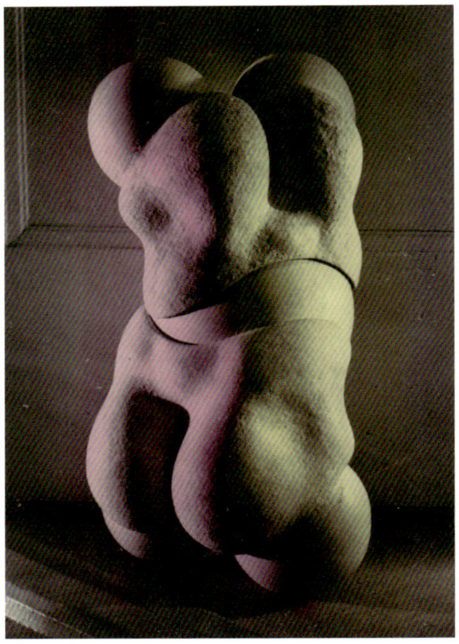

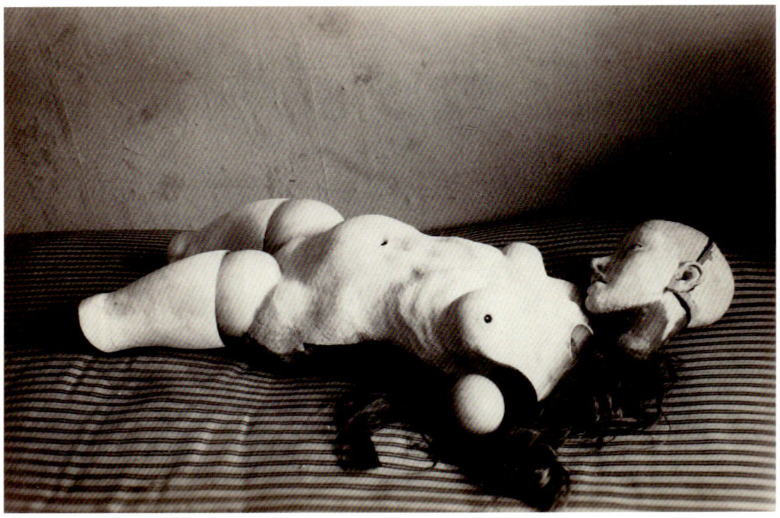

86
HANS BELLMER, *THE CENTER OF THE DOLL*, c.1936
The Metropolitan Museum of Art, New York; Ford Motor Company Collection, gift of Ford Motor Company Collection and John C. Waddell

87
HANS BELLMER, *THE DOLL*, 1934
Ubu Gallery, New York & Galerie Berinson, Berlin

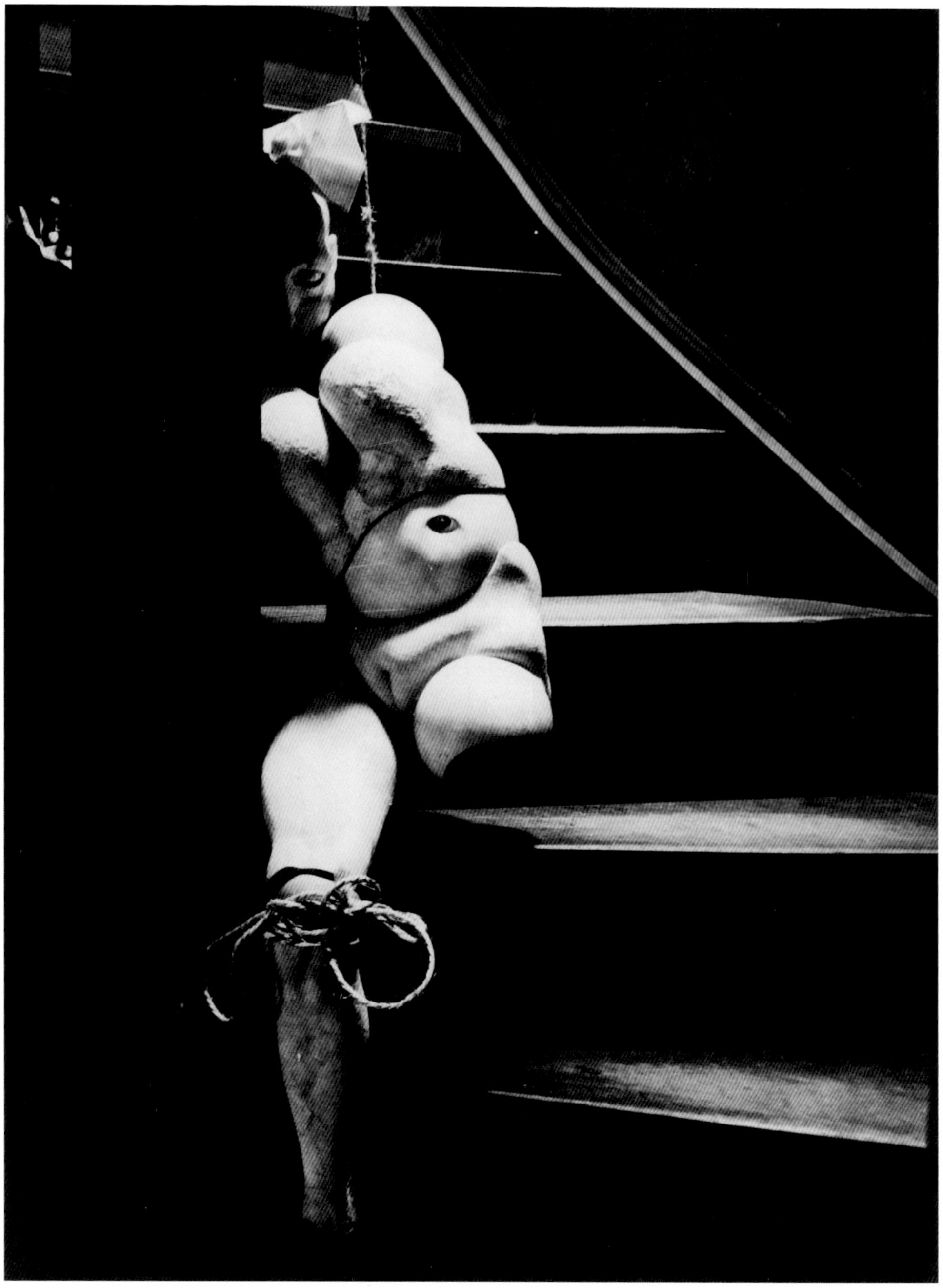

88
HANS BELLMER, *THE DOLL ON THE STAIRCASE*, 1935
Ubu Gallery, New York & Galerie Berinson, Berlin

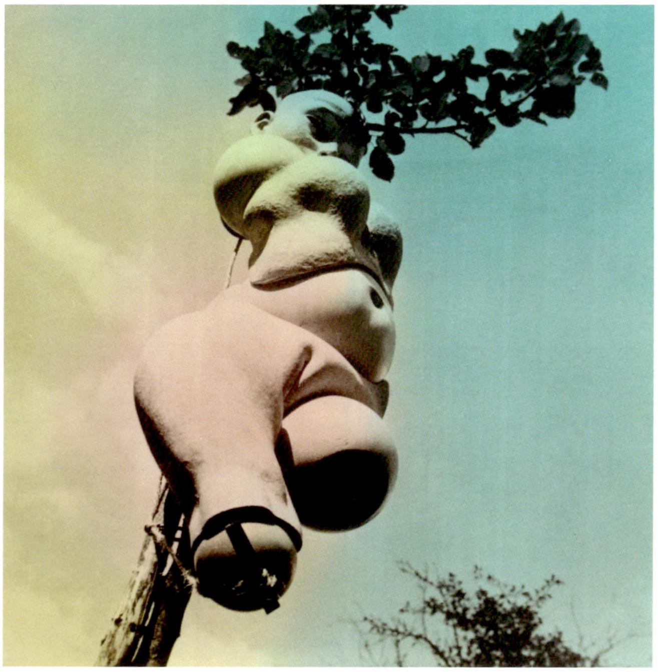

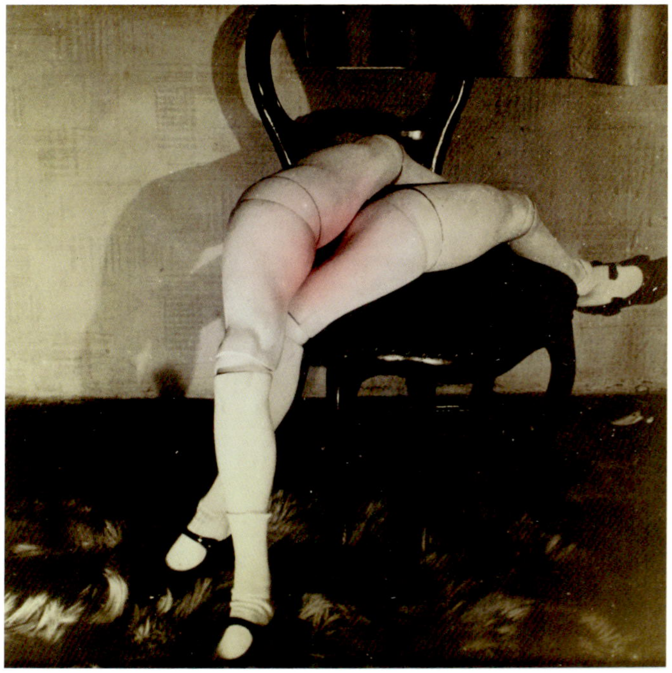

89
HANS BELLMER, *THE DOLL*, 1935
Ubu Gallery, New York & Galerie Berinson, Berlin

90
HANS BELLMER, *THE DOLL*, 1936
Ubu Gallery, New York & Galerie Berinson, Berlin

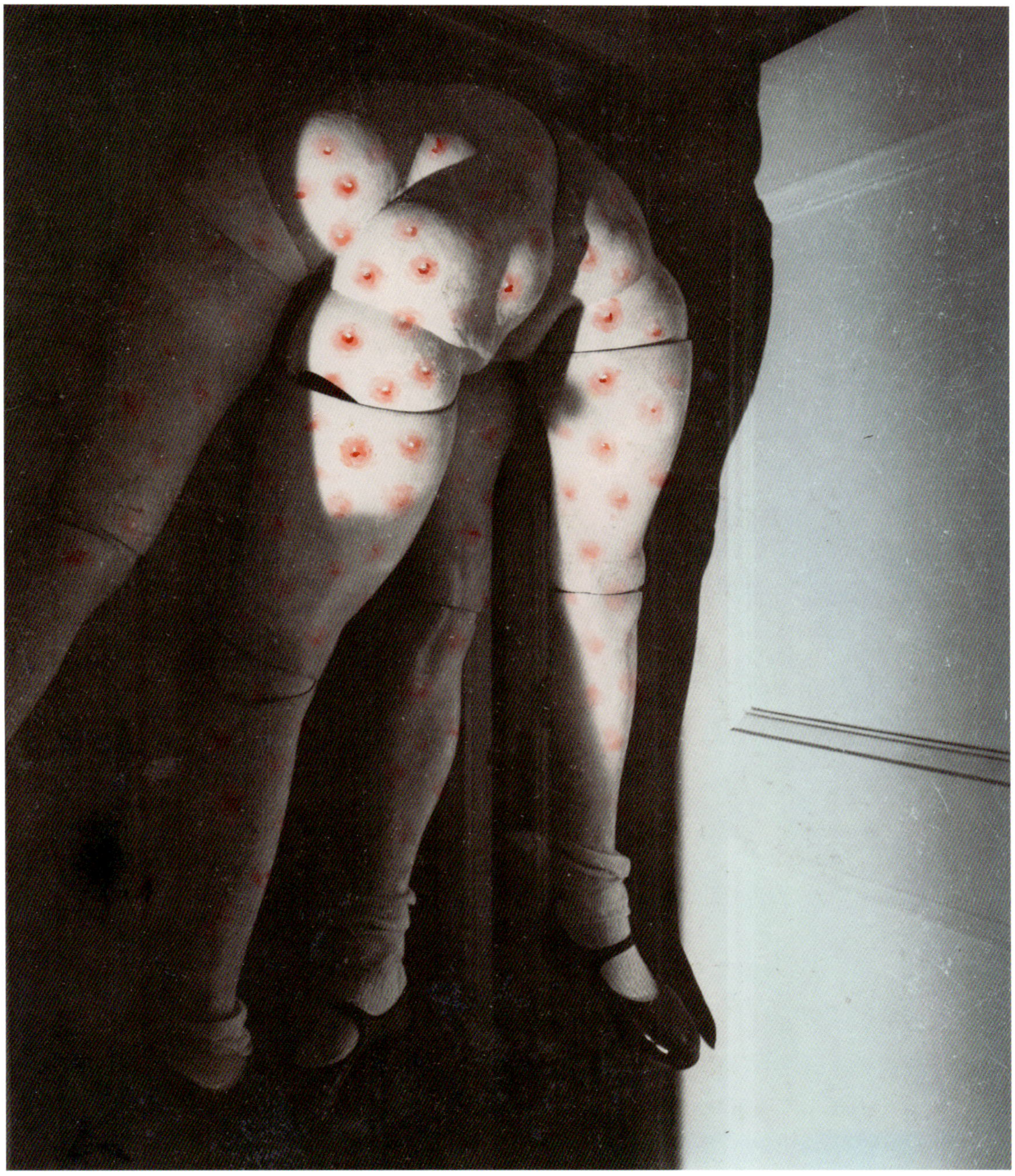

91

HANS BELLMER, *THE DOLL*, 1938

The Metropolitan Museum of Art, New York; Gilman Collection, purchase, Warner Communications Inc. Purchase Fund, by exchange

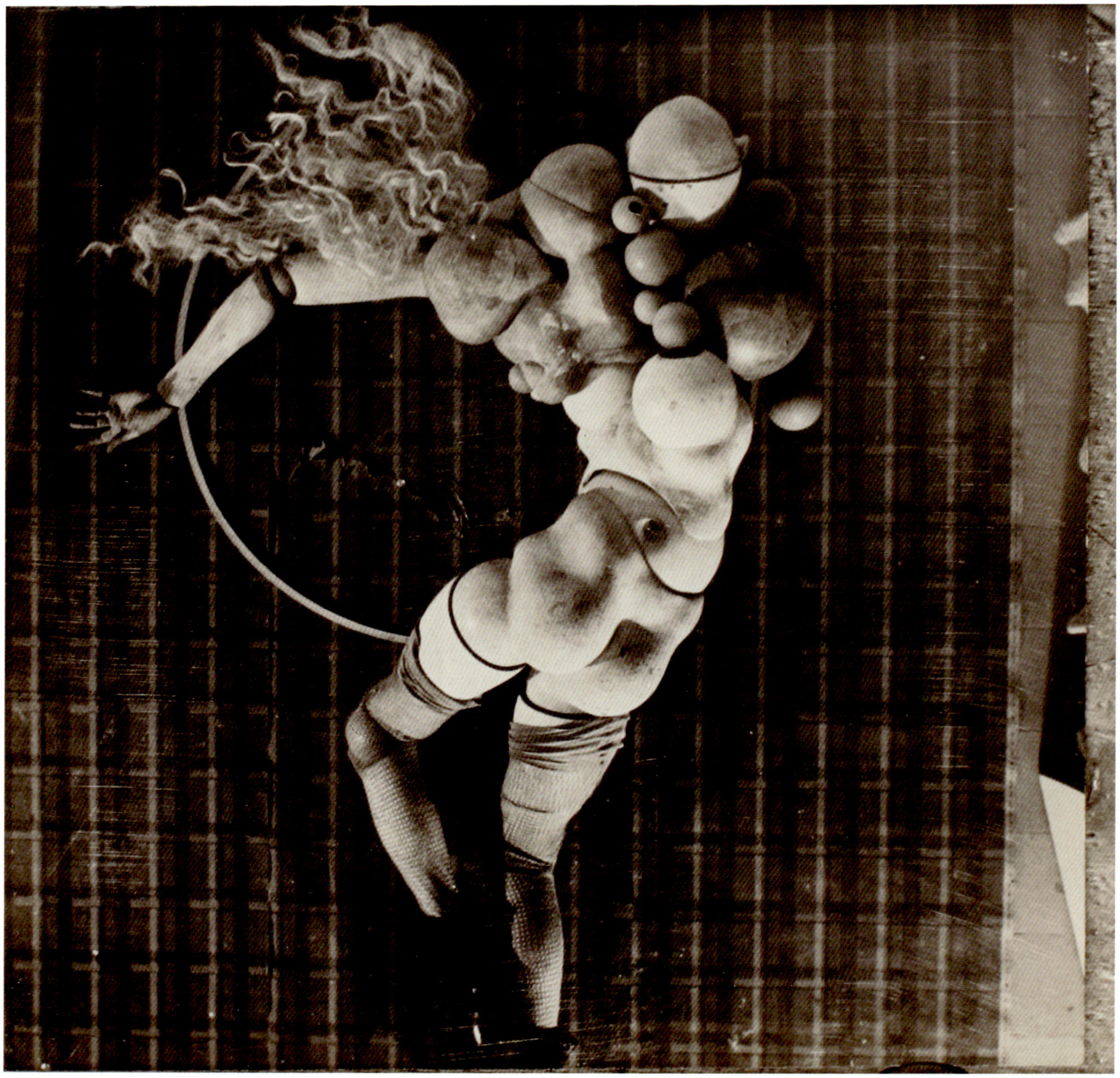

92
HANS BELLMER, *THE DOLL*, 1935
Ubu Gallery, New York & Galerie Berinson, Berlin

In early 1938, figures of women posed and clothed by men dominated the *International Exhibition of Surrealism* at the Galerie des Beaux-Arts. Outside the gallery's entrance stood Dalí's *Rainy Taxi* (fig. 93) containing a nearly naked, life-size wax figure as its passenger. She smiled perkily and stared blankly as water showered her from pipes above and live snails (one of the artist's preferred aphrodisiacs) crawled on her head and body. Her identity as domestic servant was signaled by a sewing machine beside her and the omelet in her lap. When visitors entered the first gallery, they traversed a narrow space lined on both sides with female mannequins of the type used to display haute couture; they were exceptionally realistic with articulated joints, luxuriant wigs, long eyelashes, and red lips.[43] Conceived as a cohesive theatrical installation, *The Surrealist Street* presented each mannequin under a street sign and illuminated from above as if to identify the figures as prostitutes awaiting customers.

The mannequins ranged from nearly naked to entirely clothed, and most were adorned with unexpected objects (figs. 94–100). Arp enveloped his figure in a bag emblazoned with the word *papillon* (butterfly), an allusion to the promise of transformational metamorphosis. Kurt Seligmann swathed his mannequin in a voluminous white robe, tied her hands, and crowned her with laurel leaves and an ostrich egg fixed in place by a large dagger (fig. 99). Wolfgang Paalen covered his figure with moss and mushrooms and placed a giant bat on her head, perhaps in reference to vampires or a particularly bizarre extravaganza at the Folies Bergère (fig. 100). In keeping with his alter ego Rose Sélavy, Duchamp partially

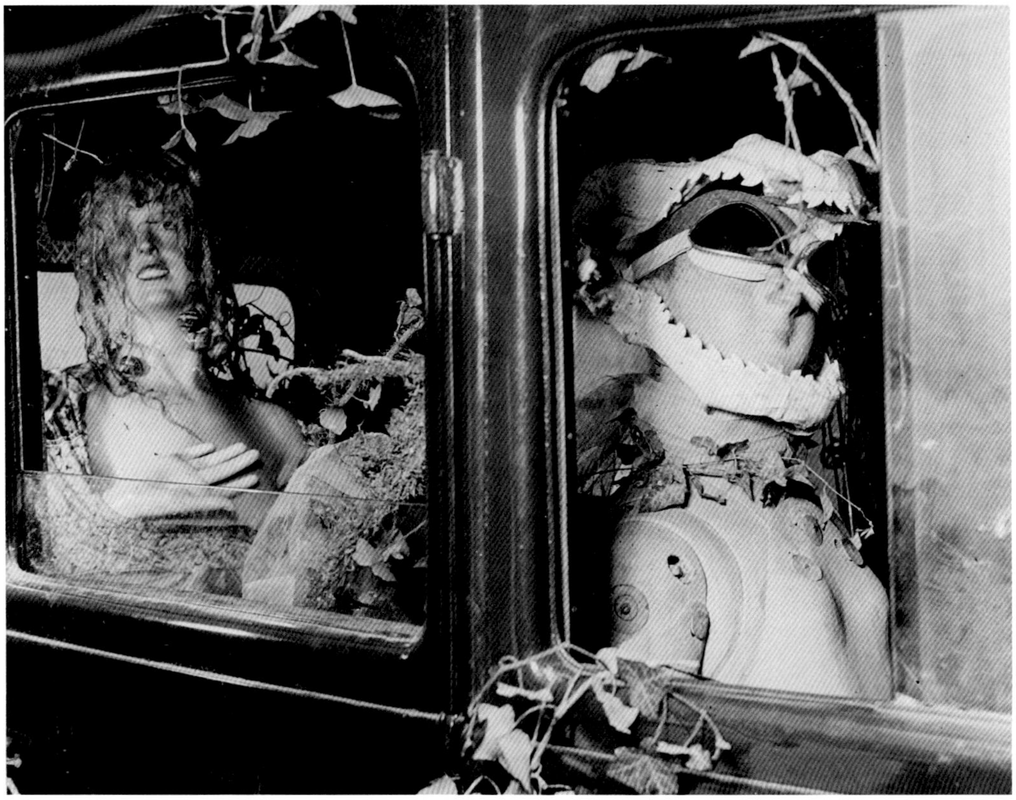

93
RAOUL UBAC
DALÍ'S "RAINY TAXI" AT THE INTERNATIONAL EXHIBITION OF SURREALISM, PARIS, 1938 (detail)
Collection Timothy Baum, New York

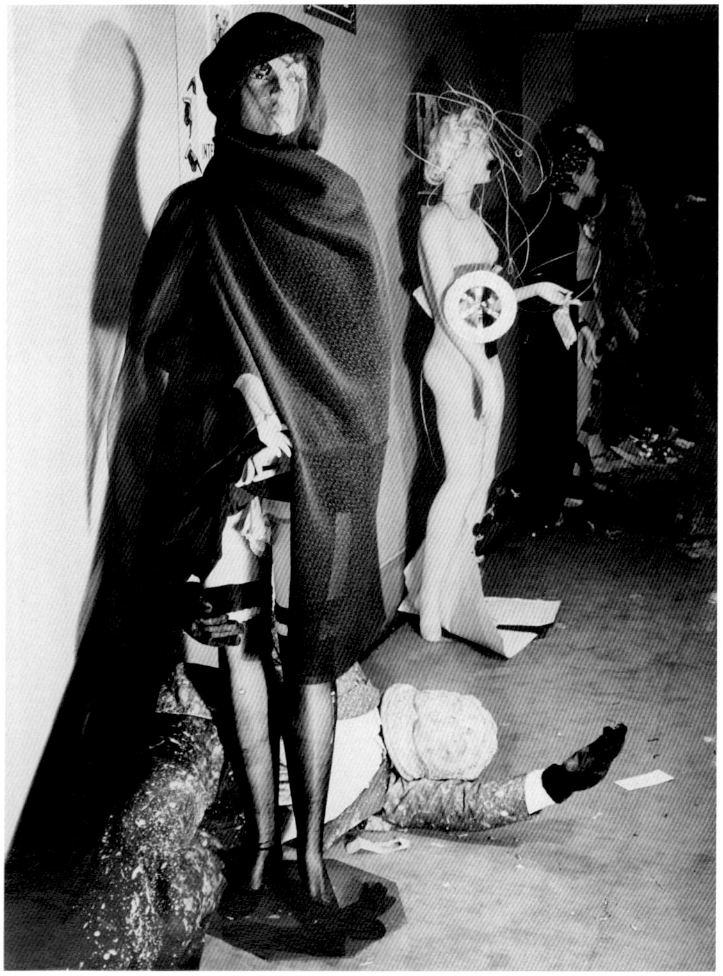

94
RAOUL UBAC
ERNST'S AND MIRÓ'S MANNEQUINS IN THE INTERNATIONAL EXHIBITION OF SURREALISM, PARIS, 1938
Collection Timothy Baum, New York

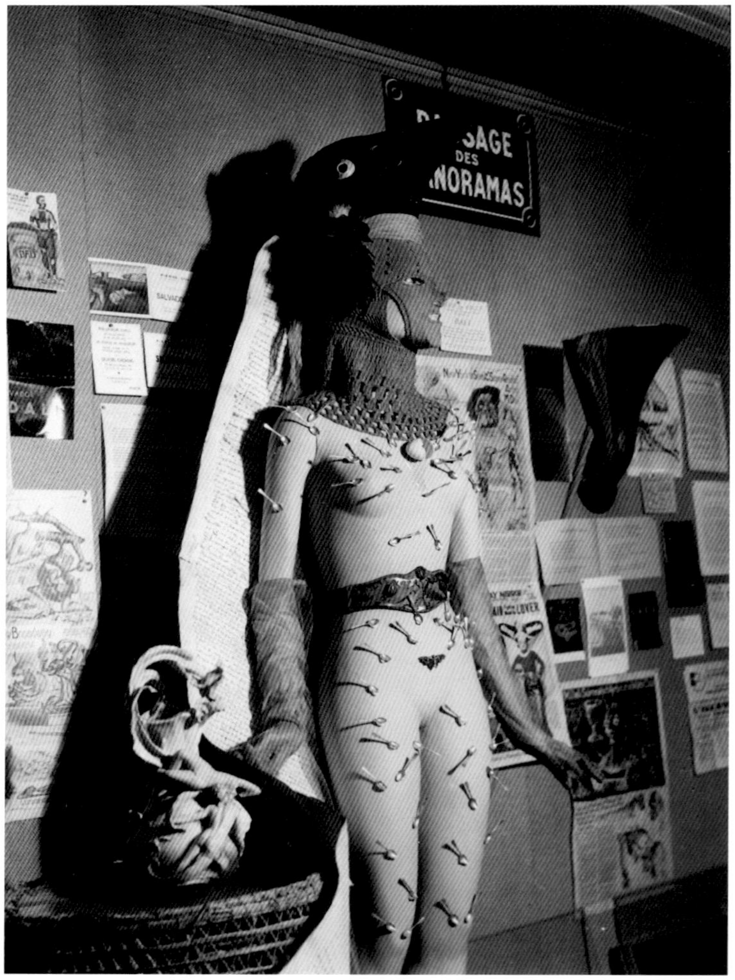

95
MAN RAY
DALÍ'S MANNEQUIN IN THE INTERNATIONAL EXHIBITION OF SURREALISM, PARIS, 1938
The J. Paul Getty Museum, Los Angeles

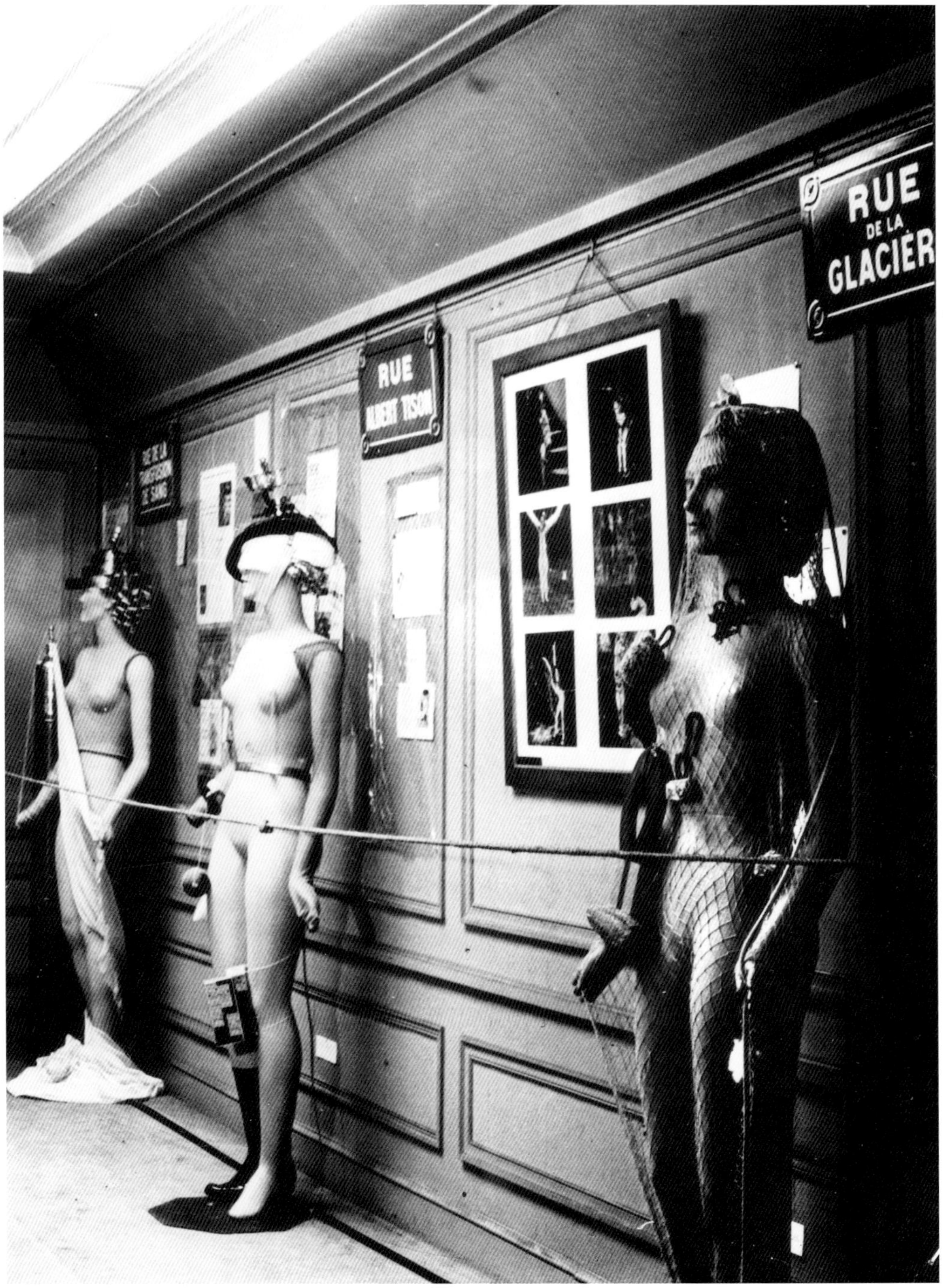

96
JOSEF BREITENBACH
"THE SURREALIST STREET" INSTALLATION IN THE INTERNATIONAL EXHIBITION OF SURREALISM, PARIS, 1938
The Getty Research Institute, Los Angeles

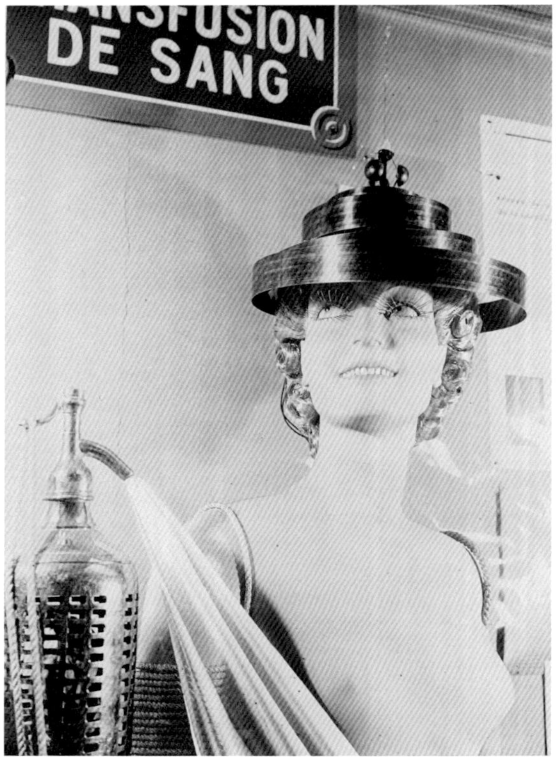

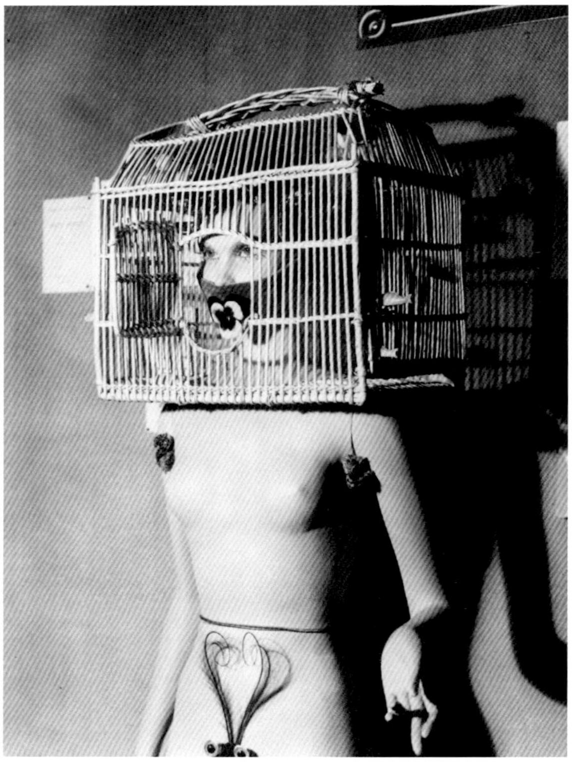

97
RAOUL UBAC
DOMINGUEZ'S MANNEQUIN IN THE INTERNATIONAL EXHIBITION OF SURREALISM,
PARIS, 1938
Collection Timothy Baum, New York

98
MAN RAY
MASSON'S MANNEQUIN IN THE INTERNATIONAL EXHIBITION OF SURREALISM,
PARIS, 1938
The J. Paul Getty Museum, Los Angeles

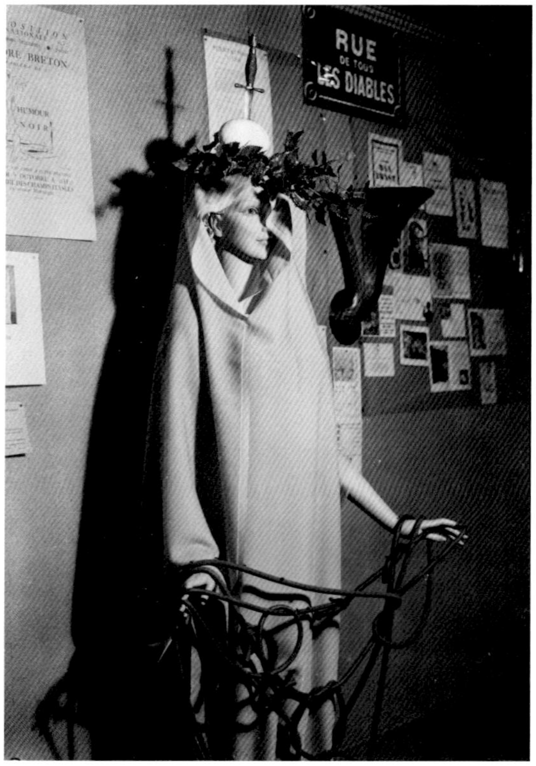

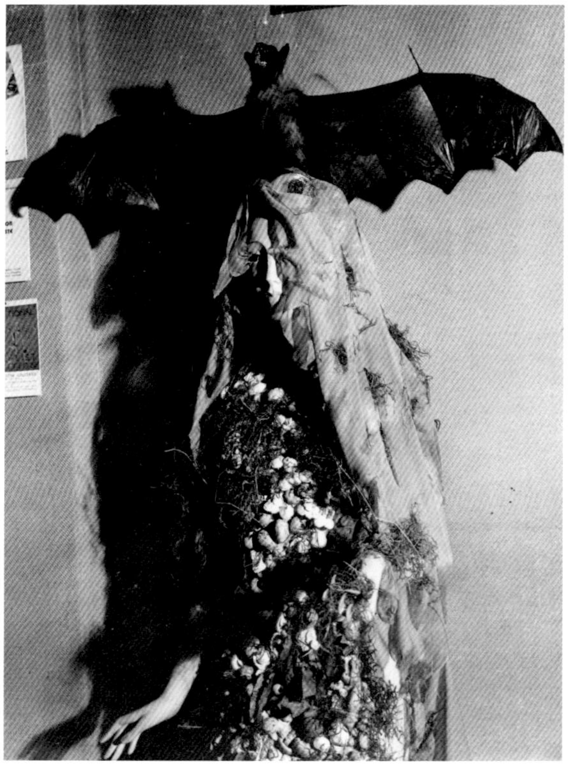

99
MAN RAY
SELIGMANN'S MANNEQUIN IN THE INTERNATIONAL EXHIBITION OF SURREALISM,
PARIS, 1938
The J. Paul Getty Museum, Los Angeles

100
MAN RAY
PAALEN'S MANNEQUIN IN THE INTERNATIONAL EXHIBITION OF SURREALISM, PARIS, 1938
The J. Paul Getty Museum, Los Angeles

dressed a mannequin in his own clothes but left the lower body naked. Might this convey the idea that women may dress like men and act like men, but are still valued primarily for their sexual availability?

The most popular mannequin was André Masson's *Green Gag in the Mouth of Thought*, naked except for the large birdcage enclosing her head (fig. 98). Through its open door, viewers could see that she had a fake flower stuck in her mouth like a baby's pacifier. Masson may have been inspired by a newspaper photo of a woman wearing a canary cage over her head at

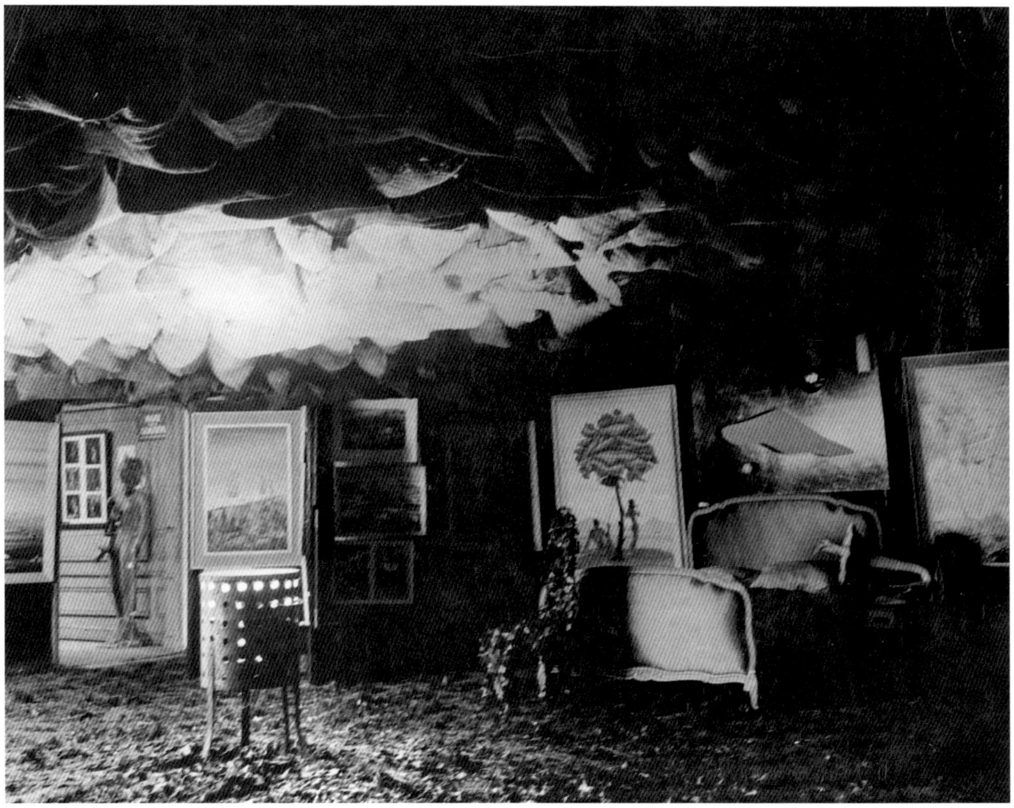

101
JOSEF BREITENBACH
DUCHAMP'S "1,200 COAL SACKS" INSTALLATION IN THE INTERNATIONAL EXHIBITION OF SURREALISM, PARIS, 1938
The Getty Research Institute, Los Angeles

a party for Dalí in New York in 1935, but he created a more unsettling image of imprisonment. Are we to infer that the voice and intellect of this ersatz woman must be firmly controlled by someone else? Marcel Jean enveloped his naked mannequin in a fishing net, like a recently caught nymphet awaiting a man's pleasure. Leo Malet put a blindfold over the eyes of his figure and tied a glass bowl containing goldfish to her nipples, though Breton removed the latter as offensive (a rather arbitrary judgment given the context). Ernst offered a different impression in his two-figure tableau of a widow clad in mourning (fig. 94). Independent and in control, she ignores her recently deceased, stuffed-dummy husband sprawled on the floor, who clutches at her thigh with one hand—perhaps the artist's tongue-in-cheek critique of the adjacent mannequins defined as sexually and intellectually submissive.

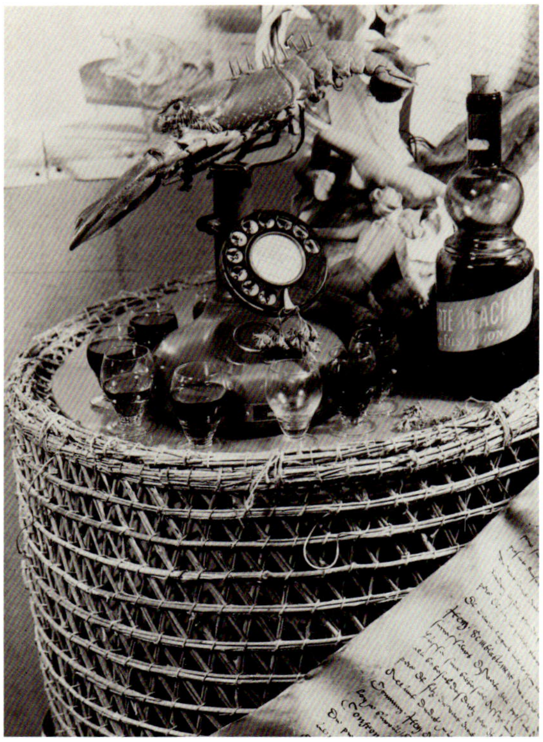

102
RAOUL UBAC
DALÍ'S "APHRODISIAC TABLE" IN THE INTERNATIONAL EXHIBITION OF SURREALISM, PARIS, 1938
Collection Timothy Baum, New York

Dalí's mannequin had dozens of small spoons glued on her skin and stood next to the *Aphrodisiac Table* (fig. 102), where glasses containing peppermint liqueur encircled a telephone with a real lobster substituted for the handset. The adjacent female nude becomes no more than the object of a man's sexual appetite. But, as explained in *The Abridged Dictionary of Surrealism*—the book published instead of a catalogue for the 1938 exhibition—Dalí planned an olfactory component: the lobster would gradually decay and smell, changing desire to disgust and reminding us of our own inevitable descent into death. After the exhibition ended, Dalí's British patron, Edward James, had an edition of the *Lobster Telephone* made; for obvious practical reasons he replaced the real lobster with a facsimile (fig. 103). Lacking the original context of the spoon-covered mannequin and the seductive liqueur, the *Lobster Telephone* now prompts us to laugh delightedly at its silliness and perhaps wonder if it is a visual analogy for phone sex.

Although highly entertaining, *The Surrealist Street* posed an awkward situation for women visitors, and the main gallery beyond offered some relief (fig. 101). Duchamp devised an immersive environment dominated by a low-hanging ceiling of dingy old coal sacks. By obscuring the gallery's skylight, he shut out the ordinary world and created a grim and claustrophobic penumbra. A metal brazier containing an artificial fire provided reddish illumination and exuded an odor of roasting coffee. The coal sacks and brazier might be interpreted as an allusion to the many workers and families rendered impoverished and homeless during the Great Depression. But even the collapse of capitalism could be mitigated by sex: the gallery contained four double beds, complete with sheets and pillows, ready for use by visitors.

Throughout the galleries there was no escape from female body parts taken from dolls, puppets, or mannequins and incorporated into furniture. Seligmann's hassock was supported by bestockinged legs and

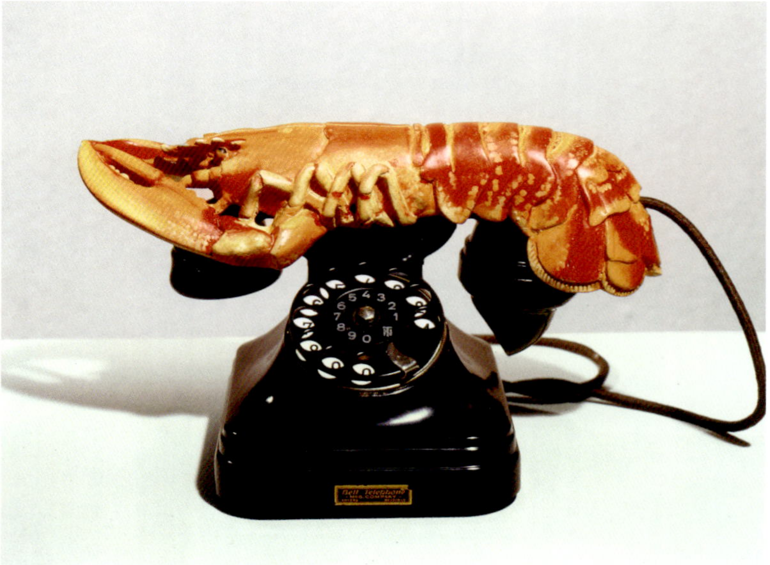

103
SALVADOR DALÍ
LOBSTER TELEPHONE, 1938
Edward James Foundation, West Dean, England (exhibited work). Photo of alternate version courtesy Tate Gallery, London

high-heeled shoes. Hugnet, whose family owned a furniture business, entrapped an artificial woman with long blond tresses in a kitchen table. Wilhelm Freddie used a stuffed dressmaker's dummy for *Zola's Desk*. A plaster phonograph by Dominguez featured a woman's forearm and hand as the tone-arm, and her leg was jammed into the loudspeaker. Such assemblages hammered home the idea of woman-as-domestic-object, usually attractive but mindless, and sometimes useful around the house as a servant or a source of comfort.

Not surprisingly, some women Surrealists pushed back, at least a little, against the pervasive male bias of the movement. As early as 1924, Breton's wife Simone wryly acknowledged the situation: "You wish my breast to be a snowball. Very well." But she also asserted that women should be entitled to their own fantasies; she, for example, wanted her lover to have five sexes.[44] Valentine Hugo's *Object* relief, 1931 (fig. 105), presents a sensuous metaphor for sexual desire, as described by a colleague:

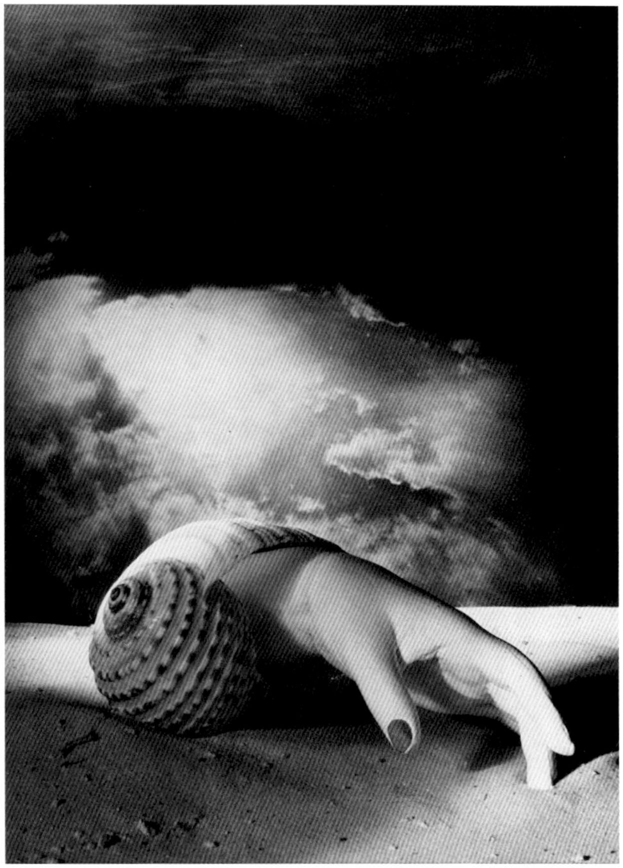

104
DORA MAAR
UNTITLED (HAND-SHELL),
1934
Musée national d'art moderne, Centre Georges Pompidou, Paris

> Two hands, one white-gloved, the other red, and both having ermine cuffs, are placed on a black roulette board from which the last four numbers have been removed. The [uppermost] hand ... holds between thumb and forefinger (its only movable fingers) a die. All the fingers on the red hand are movable ... its forefinger being put inside the [white] glove's opening.... The two hands are enmeshed in white threads like gossamer.[45]

Although it was not prominently placed in the Surrealist exhibition of 1933, her work impressed a critic who praised Hugo for achieving something more subtle and sensuous than the usual Surrealist predilection for psychological and sexual provocations: her "mysterious object ... a troubling evocation of love" surpasses the other works with its "magic language."[46]

Meret Oppenheim proclaimed her identity as female in *Object* (fig. 106), a fur-covered cup, saucer, and spoon shown in the 1936 Surrealist exhibitions in Paris, London, and New York. The assemblage of domestic items evokes associations with meals, which are usually prepared and served by wives and maids ("a woman's place is in the kitchen"). By lining the crockery and spoon with fur, Oppenheim transformed them into useless but sensual objects to be caressed. Alternatively, the thought of drinking from a hair-covered cup is repugnant, so we may interpret it as an oblique protest against the domestic role women were expected

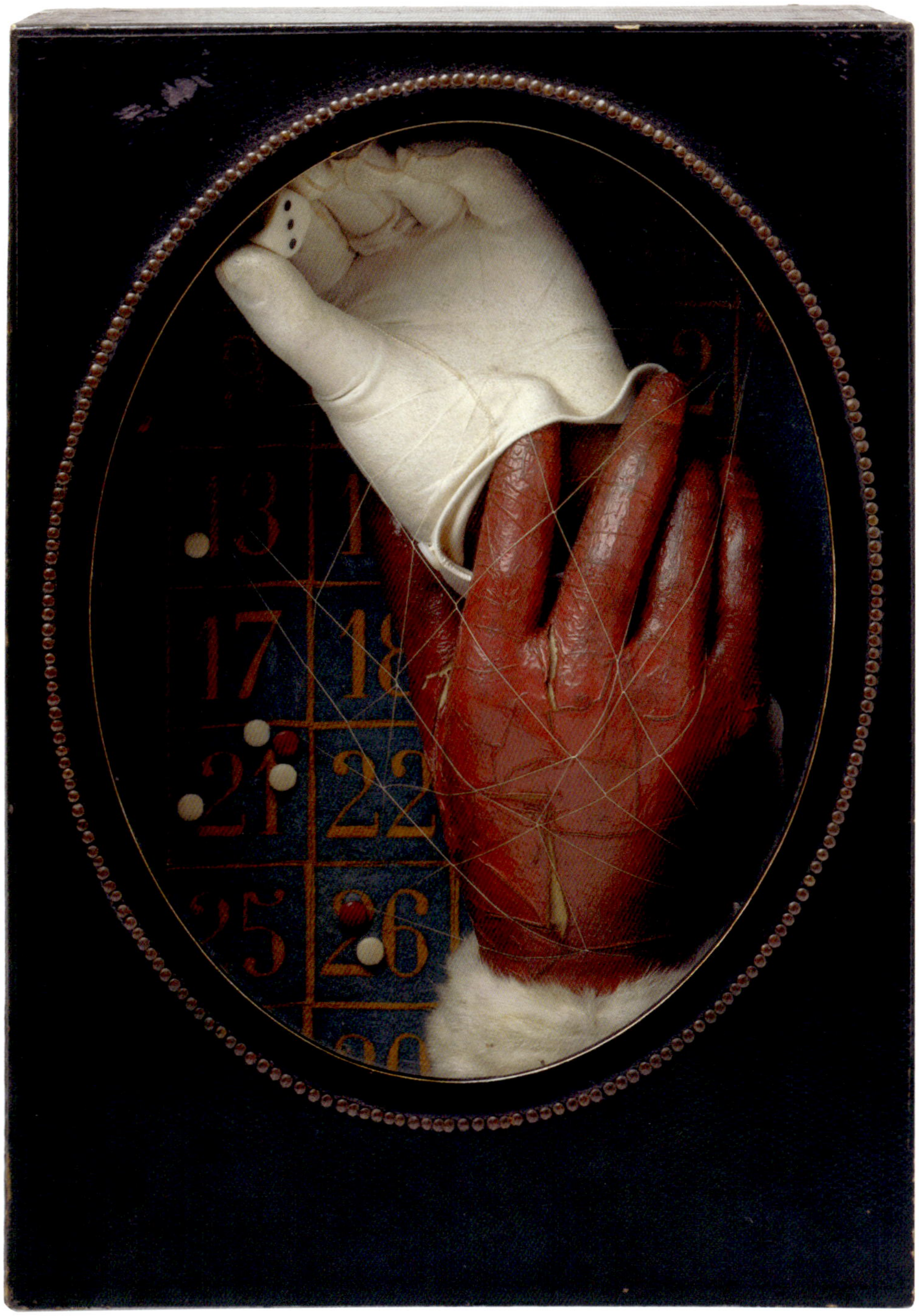

105
VALENTINE HUGO, *OBJECT*, 1931
Musée national d'art moderne, Centre Georges Pompidou, Paris

to fulfill. In *My Governess*, 1936 (fig. 107), Oppenheim placed her nanny's shoes, trussed up like a chicken, on a silver platter, as if the servant were no more than food for her employer's sexual appetites.

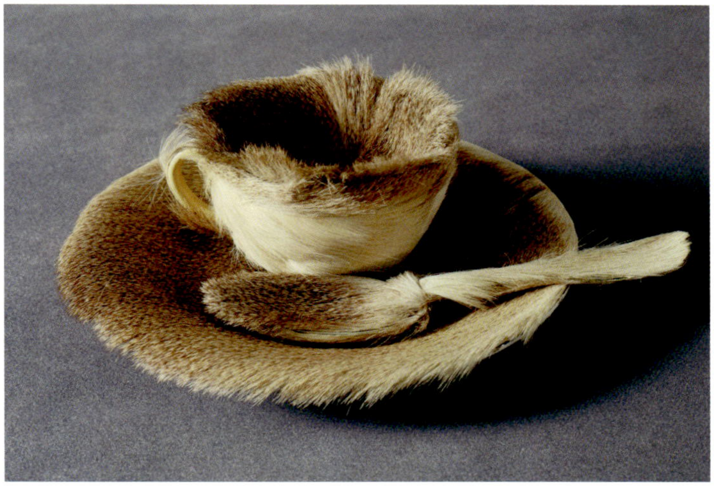

106
MERET OPPENHEIM
OBJECT, 1936
The Museum of Modern Art, New York; purchase

Claude Cahun, who is best known for her photographic self-portraits, also composed tableaux of objects. In *The Hour of Flowers*, 1936 (fig. 108), a little doll sits on a chair next to fluttering butterflies. Compared to Bellmer's images, Cahun's illustrations for *The Woodpecker's Heart* (*Le Coeur de Pic)*, 1937, a children's book by Lise Deharme, might be described as fond reminiscences of childhood games. Whereas Bellmer posed his damaged one-legged *Doll* tied to a newel post (fig. 88), Cahun scattered dainty doll shoes on a similar staircase (fig. 109). Another image presents a miniature bridal bed, perhaps from a dollhouse, which she exhibited in the 1936 exhibition at the Galerie Ratton. In a little-known series of photographs once owned by Breton (fig. 110), Cahun posed a small, gender-neutral, articulated wood figure of the kind often found in art classes; in other words, an asexual individual who operates freely within the clearly demarcated restrictions imposed by society.

Dora Maar—usually remembered only as Picasso's mistress—photographed a doll's hand emerging from a seashell in a vast empty landscape, 1934 (fig. 104). In New York, Ruth Bernhard depicted dolls and fragments of dolls as symbols of female identity, as in *Puppet Hand and Foot*, 1938 (fig. 114). The title of *Quicksand*, 1938 (fig. 113), could suggest that girls' youthful preoccupation with dolls is a trap from which there is no escape—a thought also expressed in Cahun's text "Beware of Domestic Objects." In *Creation*, 1936 (fig. 112), a doll's head, which appears to have been forcibly ripped from its body, rests gently in a wooden hand, perhaps an allusion to maternal care. *Broken Doll*, 1938 (fig. 111), depicts a much-used plaything on a shelf and may be interpreted both as a nostalgic reminiscence of childhood and as a metaphor for a woman's sense of having been badly used and abandoned.

107
MERET OPPENHEIM
MY GOVERNESS, 1936
Moderna Museet, Stockholm

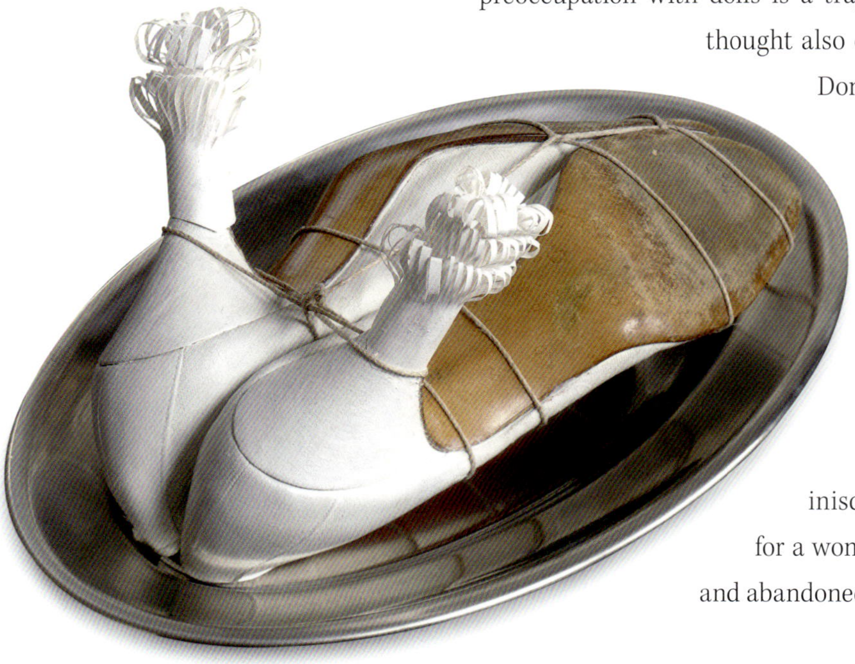

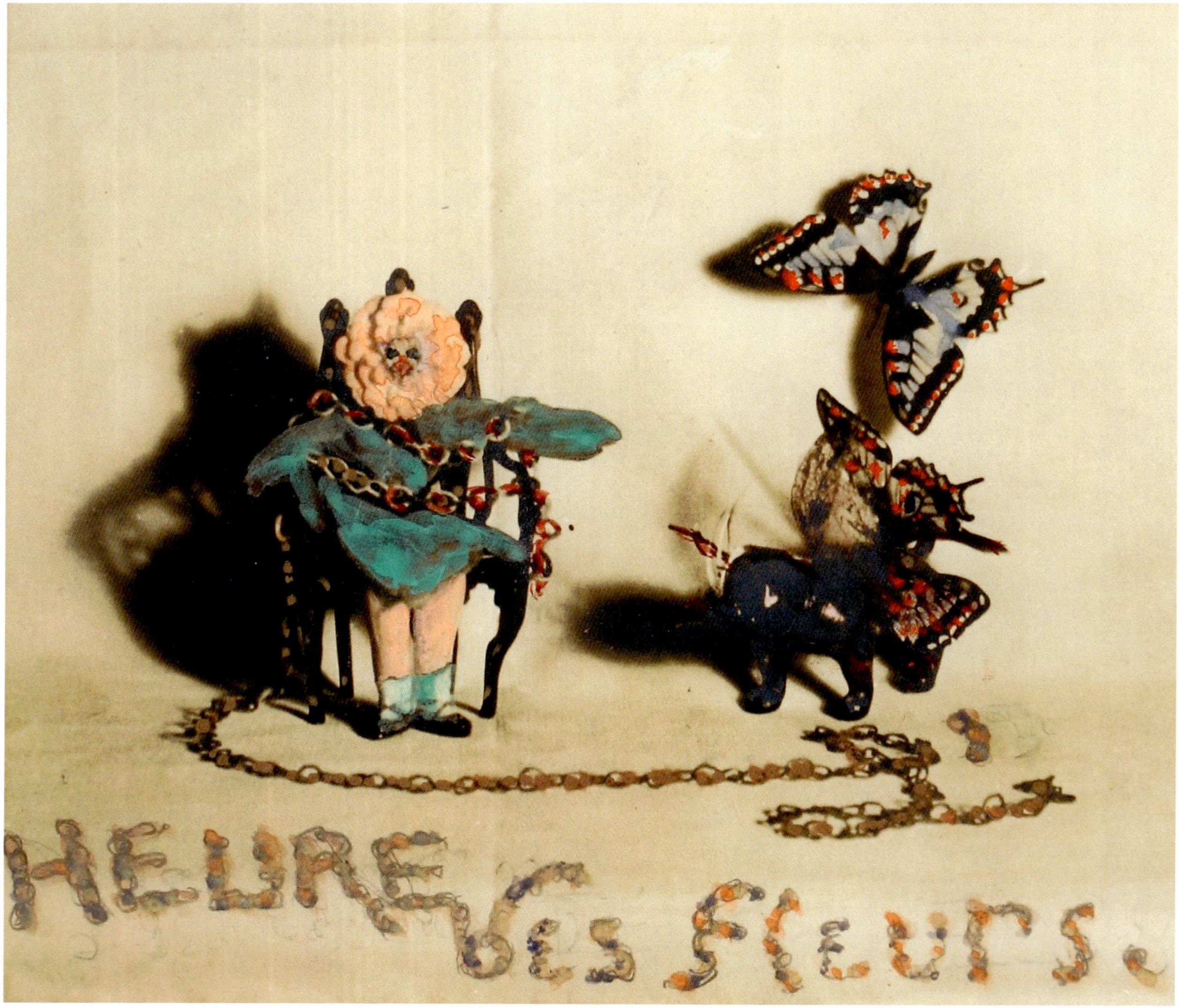

108
CLAUDE CAHUN, *THE HOUR OF FLOWERS*, 1936
Ubu Gallery, New York & Galerie Berinson, Berlin

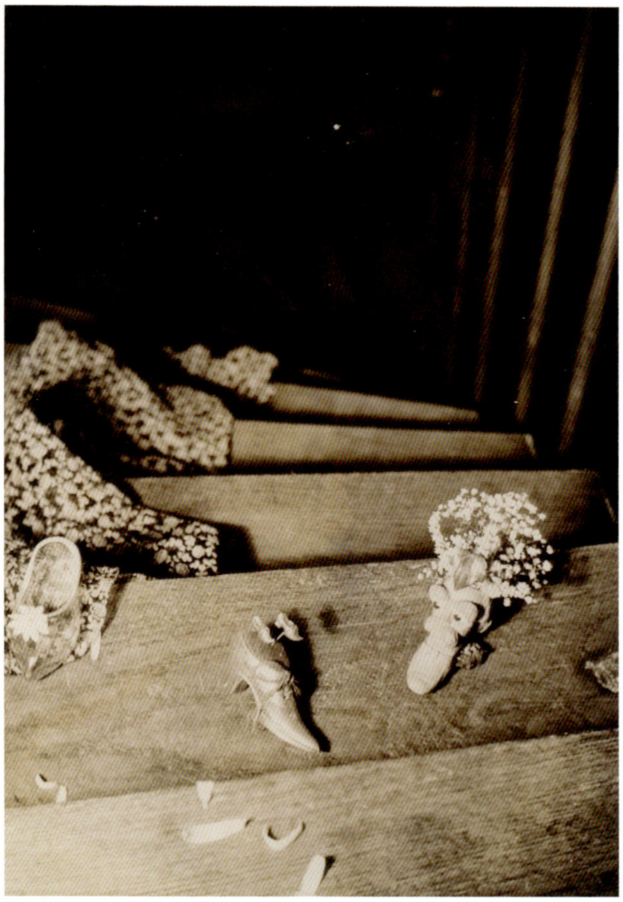

109
CLAUDE CAHUN, *UNTITLED*, 1936
Tate Gallery, London; museum purchase

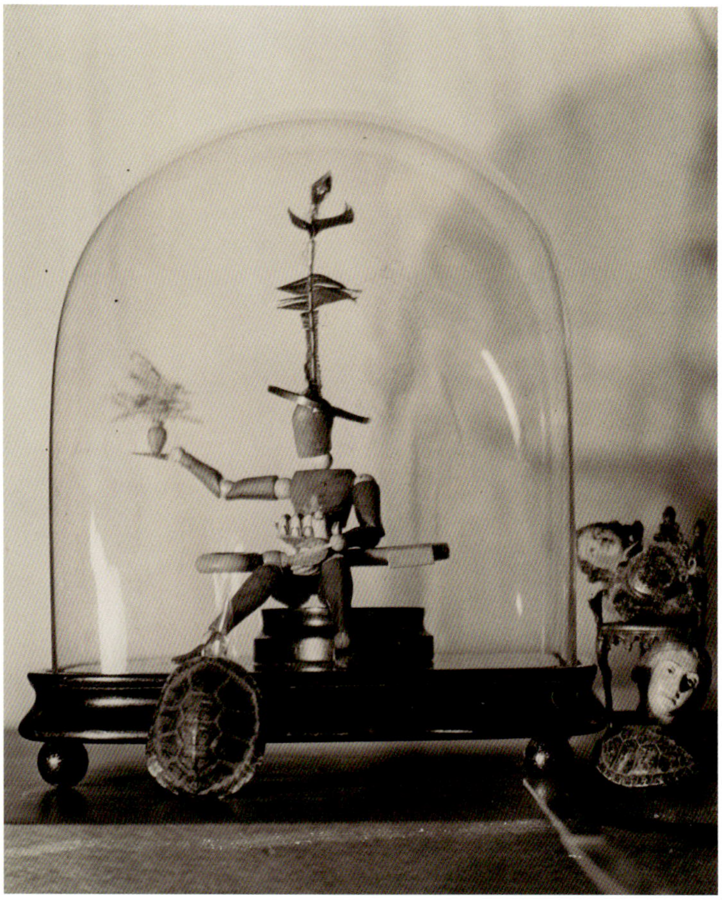

110
CLAUDE CAHUN, *UNTITLED*, 1936
Tate Gallery, London; museum purchase

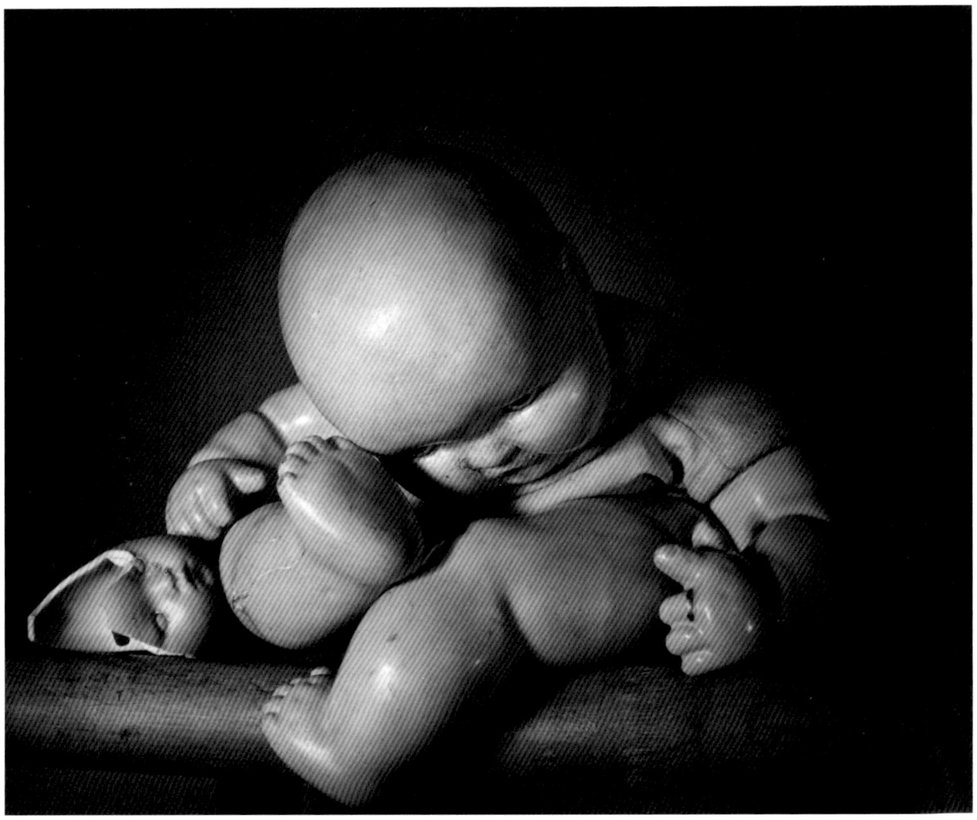

111
RUTH BERNHARD
BROKEN DOLL, 1938
Princeton University Art
Museum; bequest of
Ruth Bernhard

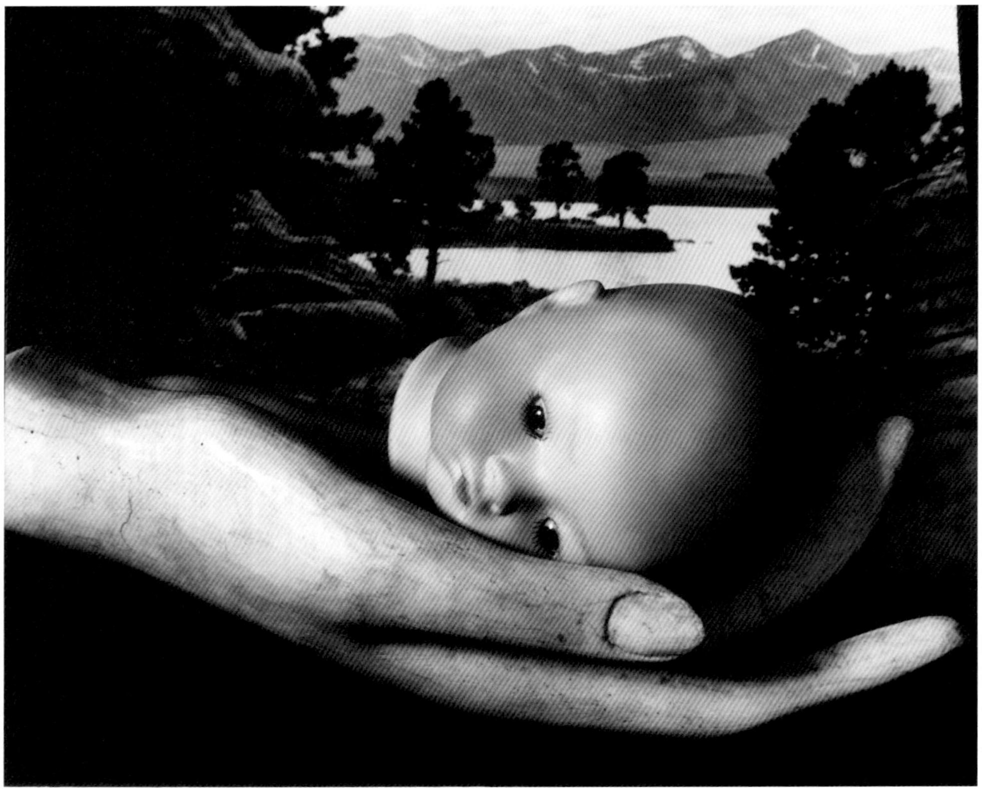

112
RUTH BERNHARD
CREATION, 1936
Princeton University Art
Museum; bequest of
Ruth Bernhard

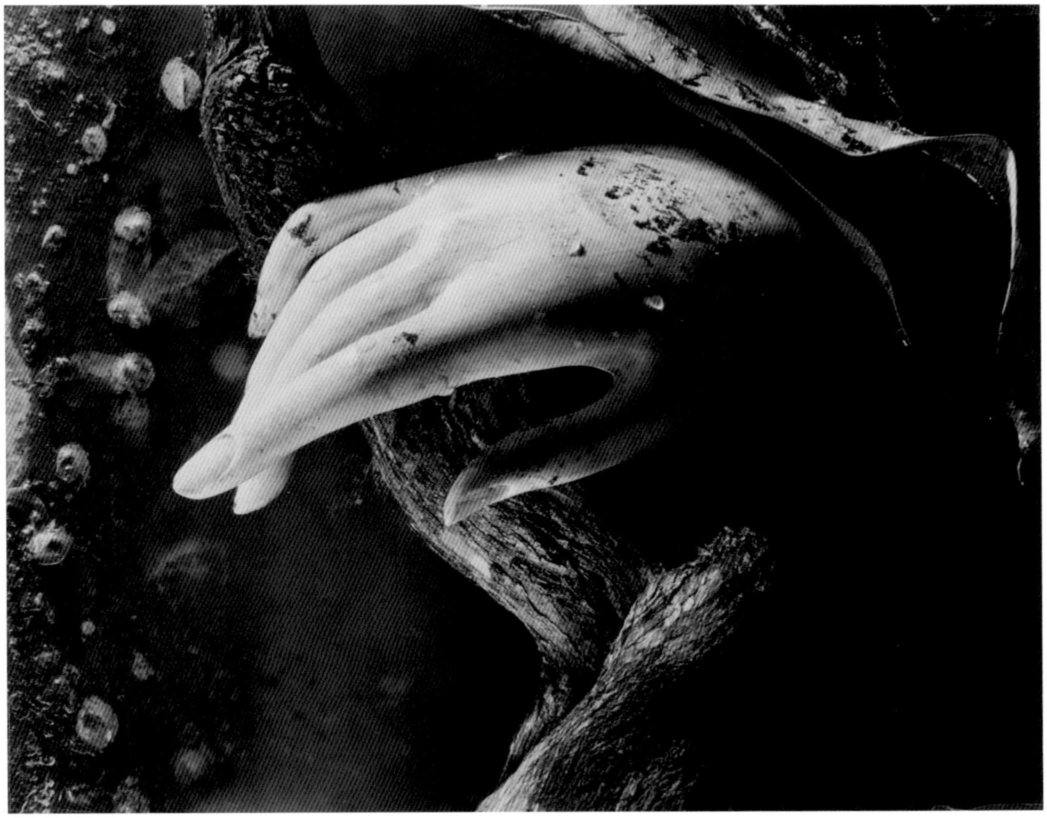

113
RUTH BERNHARD
QUICKSAND, 1938
Princeton University Art Museum; bequest of Ruth Bernhard

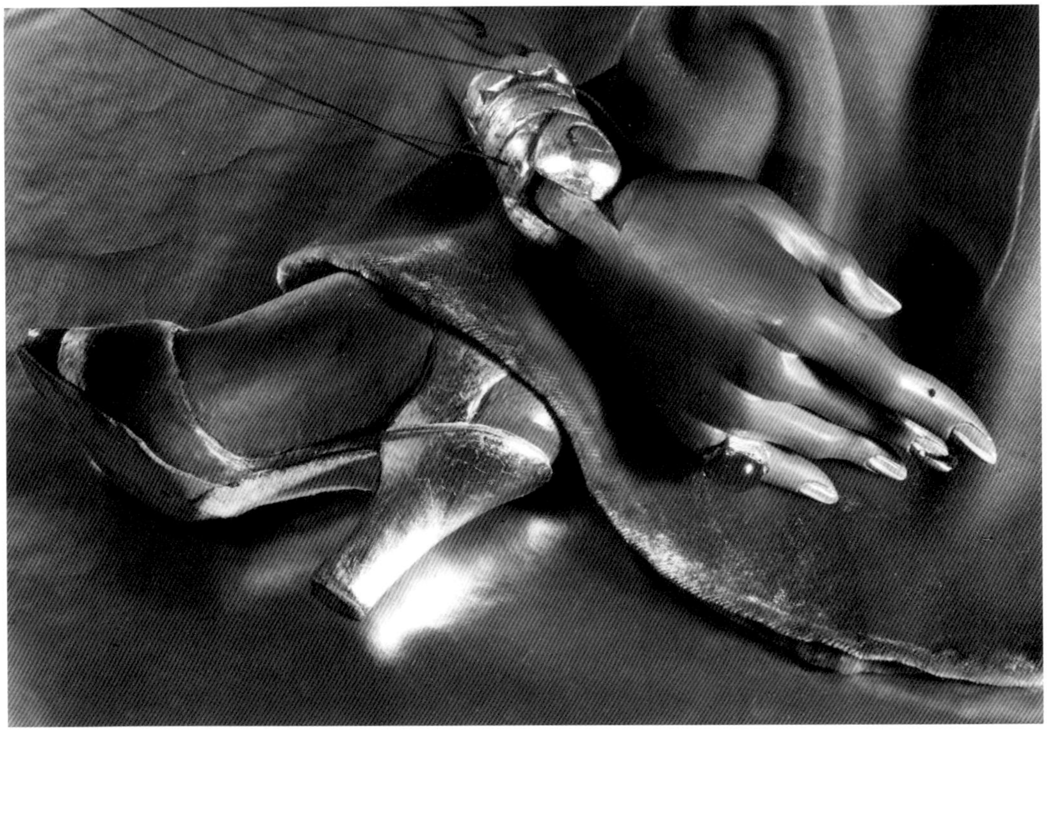

114
RUTH BERNHARD
PUPPET HAND AND FOOT, 1938
Princeton University Art Museum; bequest of Ruth Bernhard

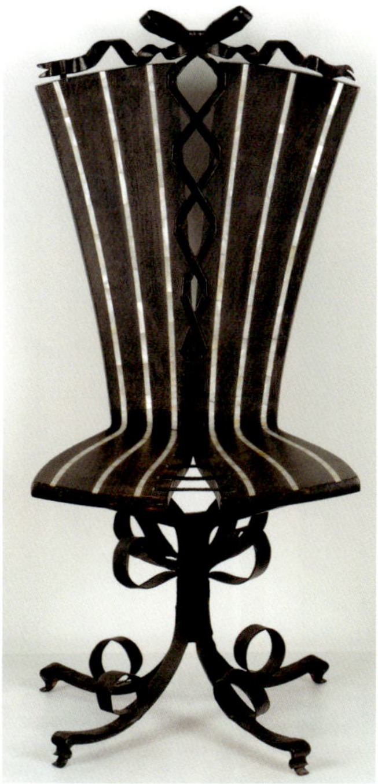

115
LEONOR FINI
CORSET CHAIR, 1939
Bauer Collection

In 1939 the painter Leonor Fini designed a feminist response to the woman-as-furniture works in the 1938 exhibition. Made of ebony and mother-of-pearl, *Corset Chair*, 1939 (fig. 115), mimics the shape of an old-fashioned laced-up whalebone corset, a symbol of antiquated notions of submission and unreasonable standards of beauty. When a man sits in *Corset Chair*, he is enfolded in lavish lingerie, a potentially uncomfortable intimation of transvestism.

NEW LIFE IN THE NEW WORLD

From the mid-1930s through the late 1940s, biomorphic abstraction and found-object assemblages were infused with new life and redirected by American sculptors. Joseph Cornell, Isamu Noguchi, Alexander Calder, and David Smith absorbed and adapted from Surrealism without joining a group or adhering to a communal doctrine. Prior to 1936, few Surrealist sculptures were exhibited in New York, so artists tended to learn about them through illustrations in international art magazines, notably *Cahiers d'art* and *Minotaure*. Direct contact with European Surrealists and their works ranged from episodic to in-depth. Cornell never traveled to Europe. Noguchi studied modern sculpture during four months in Paris in 1927. When Smith first visited Paris in 1935, he saw as much vanguard art as possible, but the city was only one stop on an international journey. Calder, however, spent long periods between 1926 and 1933, and again in 1937, working in Paris, where he saw key exhibitions of Surrealist art and knew many Surrealists. Nevertheless, he steadfastly pursued his own interests in abstract constructions.

In New York, Surrealist sculptures were first shown in the *Surréalisme* exhibition at the Julien Levy Gallery in early 1932. By titling the show in French, Levy acknowledged the movement's headquarters in Paris, but he deliberately included works by Americans, thus appropriating the foreign movement's cachet without being encumbered by its ideological dogmas. A champion of Surrealist art, Levy also organized the first American exhibition of Dalí's paintings and another of Giacometti's Surrealist sculptures in late 1934.[47] The other place where Surrealist art could be seen in New York was the Pierre Matisse Gallery, which presented annual shows of Miró's paintings and drawings and Calder's sculptures. Arp's compositions, including *Configuration with Two Dangerous Points*, could be seen at A. E. Gallatin's Gallery of Living Art and in the Société Anonyme collection.

The Museum of Modern Art's *Fantastic Art, Dada, Surrealism* exhibition, originally called *Art of the Marvelous and Anti-Rational*, provided a historical overview of seven hundred works from medieval times to the present. Despite one critic's assertion that *Fantastic Art* served only the dying gasp of an outmoded movement, the show was eagerly anticipated in the months before it opened in December 1936.[48] Galleries vied with each other to show works by Miró, Dalí, Ernst, and Calder; Levy published a book on Surrealism.[49] *Fantastic Art* was so popular it traveled to six additional venues, and the show's selection of Surrealist sculptures established the canon for generations to come. Both organic abstractions and object assemblages were included, along with works that fit neither category: reliefs and freestanding sculptures by Arp, Moore's *Two Forms*, Ernst's *Lunar Asparagus*, Giacometti's *No More Play* and *The Palace at 4 a.m.*, and Miró's *Object*, 1936 (fig. 48).

Then, from September 1939 through 1941, when World War II began and escalated, many artists fled from Europe to the United States. Two new art journals, *VVV* and *View*, promoted Surrealism and devoted issues to individual artists.[50] In the fall of 1942 two exhibitions attracted widespread attention: *Artists in Exile* and the *First Papers of Surrealism*. Europeans mingled with American artists at Peggy Guggenheim's Art of This Century gallery and at the studio of Chilean-born Roberto Matta, who unlike Breton was fluent in English and expounded passionately on automatist methods, metamorphic organic forms, and the creative possibilities of the subconscious. His paintings and drawings of turbulent organic landscapes, with titles like *Inscape* and *Psychological Morphology*, stimulated interest in Freudian and Jungian theories and encouraged some, particularly Noguchi and Smith, to express the darker recesses of their subconscious minds in sculpture.

DREAM WORLD IN A BOX

A self-taught artist living in his family's house in Queens, Cornell paralleled the practices of the Parisian Surrealists years before he met any of them. During the late 1920s he foraged among the secondhand shops of Lower Manhattan, acquiring books, toys, and miscellaneous objects. By chance, he discovered Ernst's collages at Levy's gallery in late 1931 and started making his own, quickly followed by small assemblages that he pointedly titled *Objects*. He delighted in creating little surprises and discoveries and putting things in places where they couldn't be discovered. He secreted trivial things such as glass marbles, sequins, coral, and . . . in pill boxes, old watch cases, even wallets. In his first exhibition at the Levy Gallery in late 1932, he showed two glass domes, each containing a delicate assemblage. *Untitled (Glass Bell)* (fig. 116) featured a small doll's hand holding an engraved image of a rose— a nostalgic and somewhat feminine evocation of the innocent joys of childhood.[51]

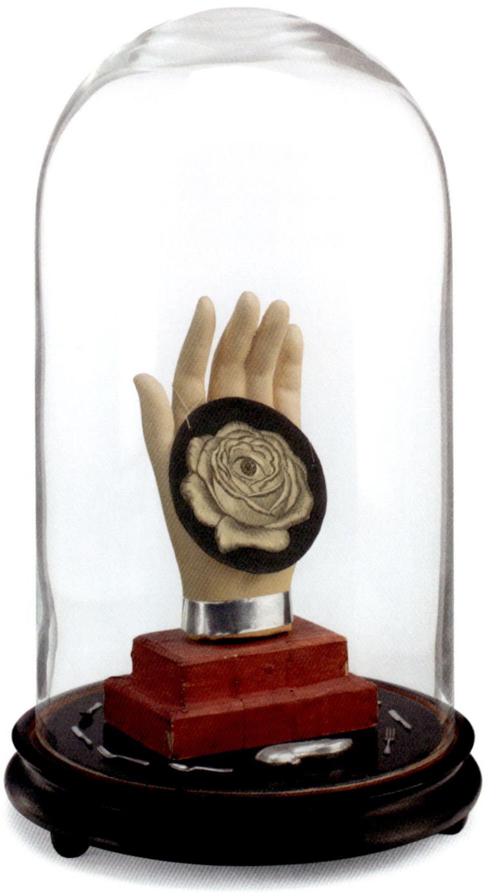

116
JOSEPH CORNELL
UNTITLED (GLASS BELL), 1932
Private collection

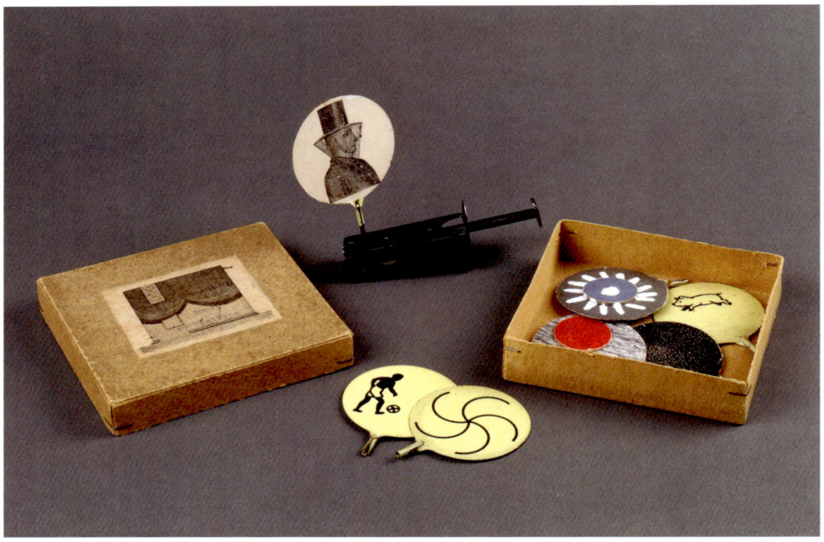

117
JOSEPH CORNELL
JOUET SURRÉALISTE (SURREALIST TOY), c.1932
Smithsonian American Art Museum, Washington, DC; gift of Mr. and Mrs. John A. Benton

In that sense Levy's oft-disputed assessment—that Cornell was "one of the few Americans who fully and creatively understands the Surrealist viewpoint"—was correct, although being labeled a Surrealist later annoyed the artist because he disliked having his art equated with the more outrageous and offensive proclivities of certain European artists, particularly Dalí. Cornell's letter to MoMA's director in November 1936 should be understood in that context: "I would appreciate your saying [in the catalogue of *Fantastic Art*] that I do not share in the subconscious and dream theories of the Surrealists. While fervently admiring much of their work, I have never been an official Surrealist, and I believe that Surrealism has healthier possibilities than have been developed."[52] While Surrealists in Paris enthused over Giacometti's *Suspended Ball* and Bellmer's photographs, and while Penrose constructed *The Dew Machine* in London, Cornell rejected offensive and discordant images of phalluses and women as sexual playthings. He preferred the evocative possibilities of children's toys, fairy tales, romantic novels, natural history, ballet, and Renaissance art; he remained faithful to the original Surrealist goal of experiencing the marvelous through the magic of everyday things.

118
JOSEPH CORNELL
UNTITLED (HARLEQUIN JUMPING JACK), c.1935–38
The Fralin Museum of Art at the University of Virginia, Charlottesville; gift of the Joseph and Robert Cornell Memorial Foundation

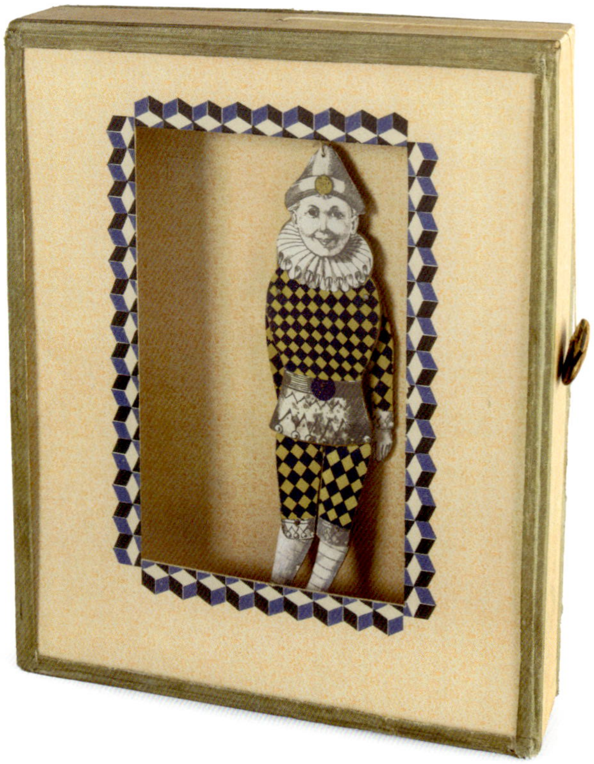

More than any other American sculptor, Cornell developed the idea of direct interaction between a work of art and its viewers. Several early objects were little more than actual toys that he modified only slightly: for *Jouet Surréaliste* (*Surrealist Toy*), c. 1932 (fig. 117), he merely changed the images on the rotating disk.

Untitled (Harlequin Jumping Jack), c. 1935–38 (fig. 118), emulates another kind of toy; when someone pulls the string dangling from one side of the box, it activates the marionette inside. Although the activity implies that the viewer has complete control of a helpless puppet, its jerking and flailing movements are amusing in an innocent way far removed from Bellmer's victimized *Doll*.

From the outside *Untitled* (fig. 119) at first appears to be no more than a round cardboard container, but when the cover is removed, one can see that the interior is filled with rolled-up excerpts from a French book. Although now the texts remain untouched in a museum, Cornell expected viewers to untie, unroll, and read them. In doing so he hoped they would discover not a continuous narrative but illogical sequences of phrases that could be interpreted in infinite ways. Inside *Bel Echo Gruyère*, c. 1939 (fig. 120), reposes a putative slice of cheese wrapped in aluminum foil. When someone picks it up, a toy hidden inside makes the "moo" sound of a cow.

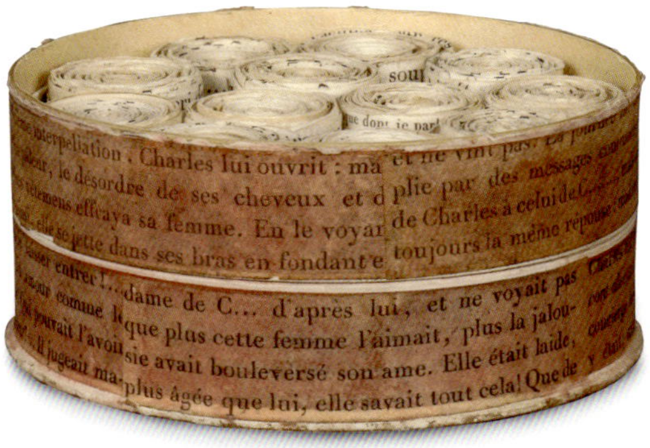

119
JOSEPH CORNELL
UNTITLED, not dated
Joseph Cornell Study Center, Smithsonian American Art Museum, Washington, DC

In 1934 Cornell dramatically expanded the complexity of his boxed assemblages, specifically in those he titled *Natural History*. Inside fine wood boxes formerly used as cigar humidors and jewelry cases, which open at the top, we discover a treasure trove of objects and images. Rows of small glass vials of the type found in pharmacies and laboratories are neatly aligned. Each one presents a different combination of ephemeral things, such as beads from costume jewelry, lace, colored sand, feathers, and fragments of maps that hint at mysterious underlying connections. The box's contents would fascinate a child, yet an adult's mind is needed to recognize (or invent) the conceptual linkages.

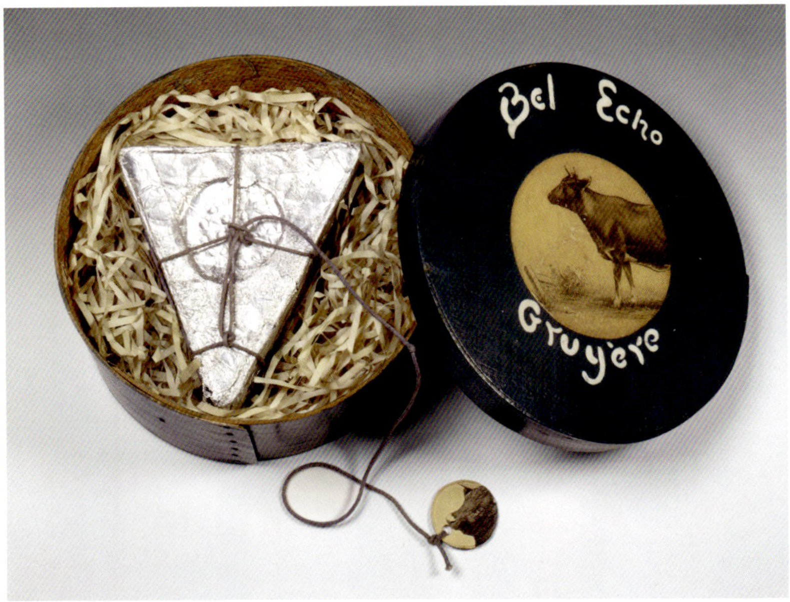

120
JOSEPH CORNELL
BEL ECHO GRUYÈRE, c.1939
Smithsonian American Art Museum, Washington, DC; gift of the Joseph and Robert Cornell Memorial Foundation

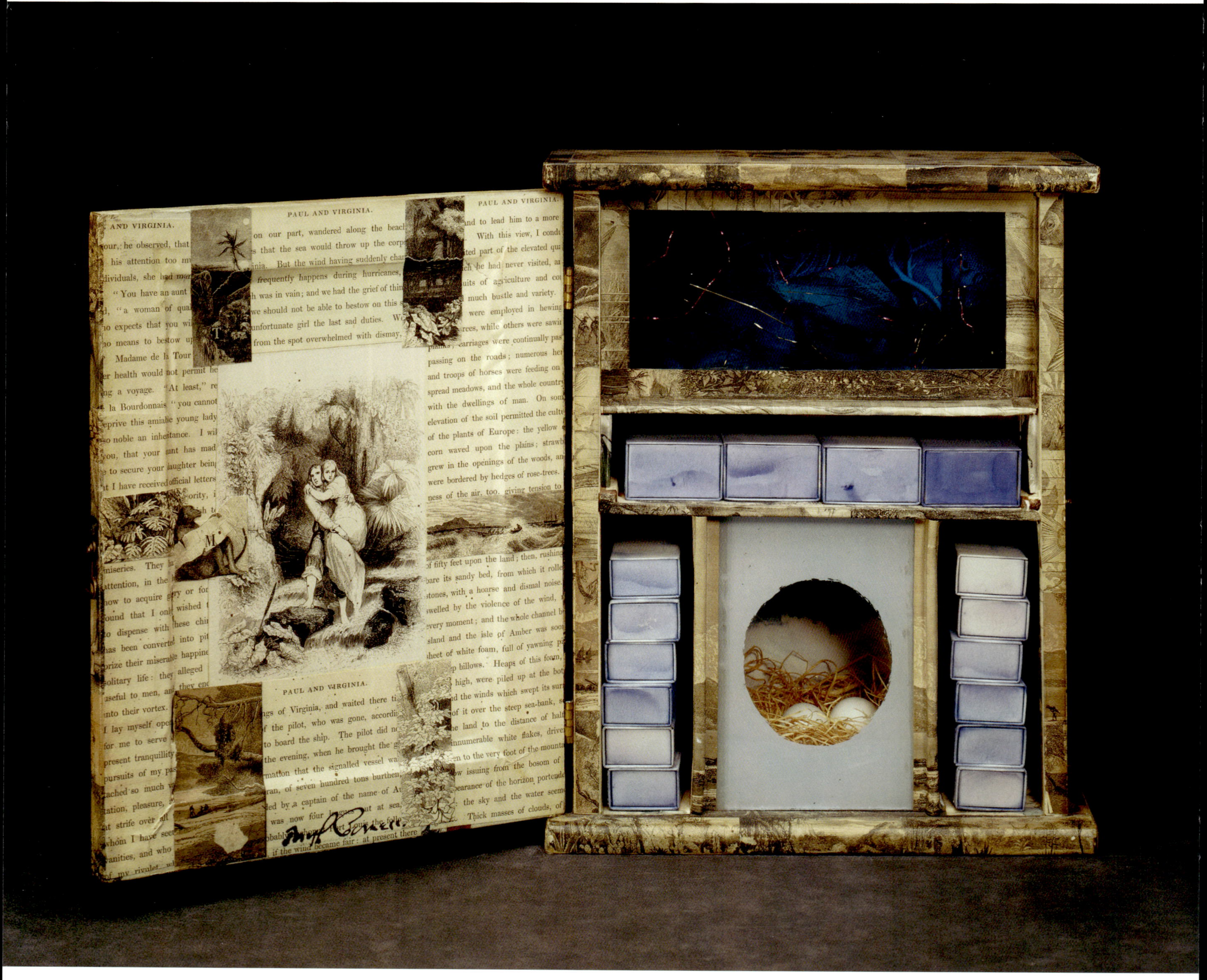

121
JOSEPH CORNELL, *UNTITLED (PAUL AND VIRGINIA)*, c.1946–48
The Robert Lehrman Art Trust, courtesy of Aimee and Robert Lehrman, Washington, DC

Cornell returned to the subject of natural history in one of his most complex creations, *Untitled (Paul and Virginia)*, c. 1946–48 (fig. 121). The container has architectural features, such as a foundation, a roof cornice, and a door that swings open on hinges, but it is also a three-dimensional book. The exterior and interior are covered with pages from the novel *Paul and Virginia* by Jacques-Henri Bernardin de Saint-Pierre, first published in 1788. The protagonists (seen in the illustration inside the door) are childhood friends, raised on the tropical island of Mauritius, where they fall in love and live in harmony with nature. The texts selected by Cornell describe their desperate attempts to escape the censure of a class-conscious and hypocritical society. But the story itself is not the focus; rather, the texts are tantalizingly incomplete and evocative. One section reads:

> ... wandered along the beach ... that the sea would throw up the corpse ... But the wind having suddenly changed ... frequently happens during hurricanes ... was in vain; and we had the grief of thinking ... we should not be able to bestow on this unfortunate girl the last sad duties. We ... from the spot overwhelmed with dismay ...

These fragments express so much: the power of nature, tragedy, and loss. The interior of Cornell's house-book-box reverberates with those themes. The upper part is a miniature "aquarium" containing motifs and objects pertaining to the sea (fish, coral, reeds); the blue

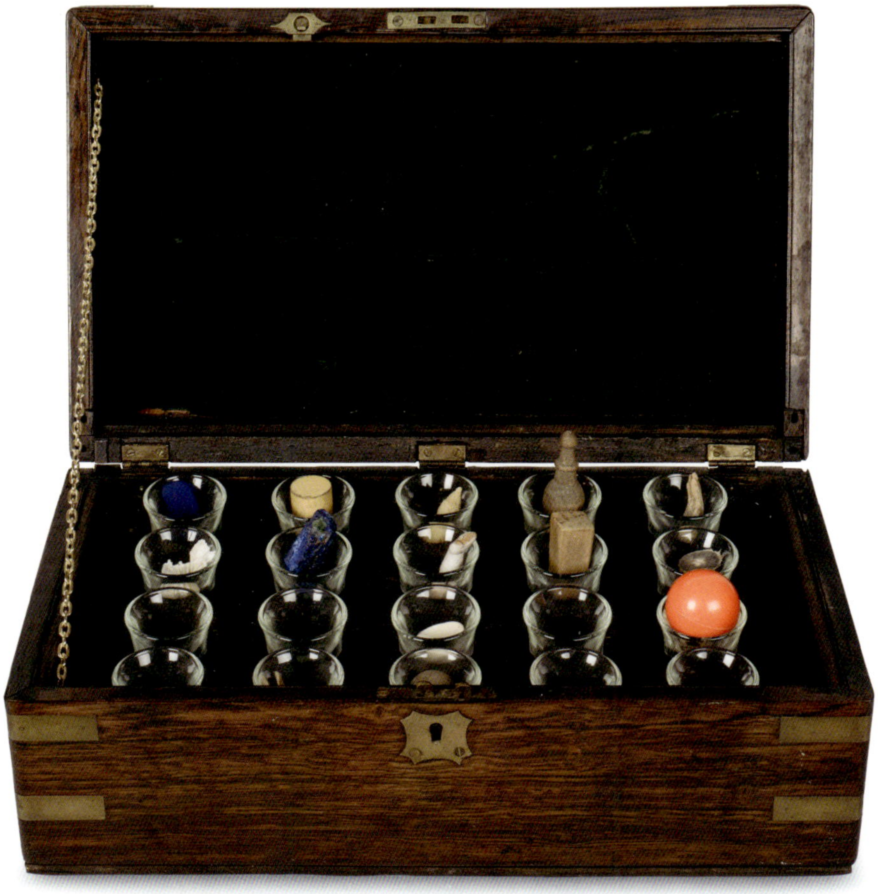

122
JOSEPH CORNELL
UNTITLED (MUSEUM BOX),
early 1940s
Wadsworth Atheneum Museum of Art, Hartford; gift of the Joseph and Robert Cornell Memorial Foundation

glass adds to the illusion of water and marine life. Below is the round opening of a birdhouse, through which we see an actual nest with fragile eggs. The matchboxes stacked on either side are empty but colored like a blue sky with ephemeral white clouds. The text opposite the little boxes refers to the lovers having just missed their escape vessel, a commercial ship that had left without them. Perhaps the matchbooks could be used to build a raft on which they could still escape? Cornell teasingly invites us to enter a world of literature, nature, and sentimental romance.

In addition to resembling a child's collection of mementoes, Cornell's meticulous arrangements bring to mind the specimen trays used by scientists for collections of minerals, insects, invertebrates, and other items from nature, organized by species and subspecies using the

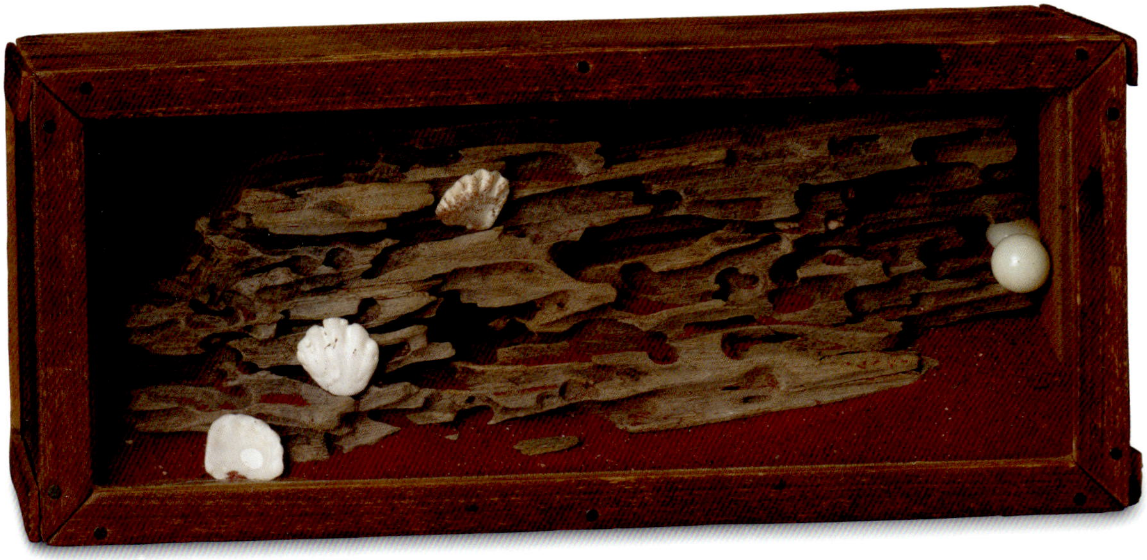

123
JOSEPH CORNELL
UNTITLED (RED SAND BOX), c.1940
Collection of Robert Lehrman, courtesy of Aimee and Robert Lehrman, Washington, DC

system introduced by Carl Linnaeus in the eighteenth century. This association becomes explicit in the series of *Museum* boxes in which items are presented like artifacts. One holds plastic ice cubes; another displays memorabilia of a nineteenth-century ballerina. *Untitled (Museum Box)*, early 1940s (fig. 122), contains twenty shot glasses of the kind used in cafés and bars everywhere. Each one features a single object, ranging from natural items (driftwood, copper, lapis lazuli) to children's toys (glass marbles, a leg from a small doll). The common link is childhood, its playful activities, and the sense of discovering everything as new.

The exterior and interior of *Untitled*, 1940s (fig. 124), are unprepossessing until a viewer takes out the twenty-eight glass vials and examines their contents. The unifying theme is travel to the cultural capitals of Europe; most vials house fragments of maps cut out of old guidebooks. Floorplans of the Louvre in Paris and the Uffizi in Florence express Cornell's yearning to visit these distant places, but even when he could afford to go in later years, he did not, preferring instead to be an armchair traveler.

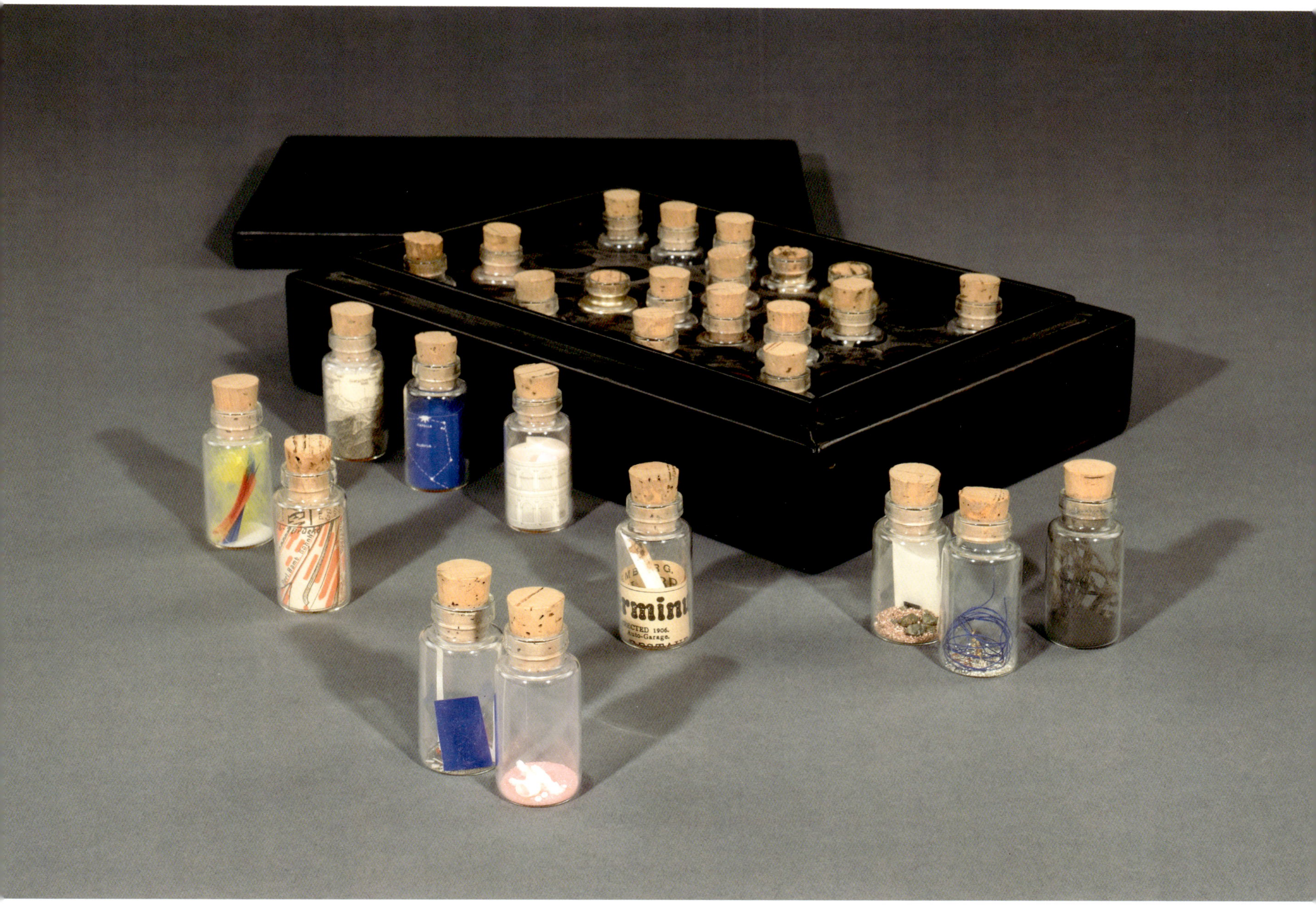

124
JOSEPH CORNELL, *UNTITLED*, 1940s
Smithsonian American Art Museum, Washington, DC; gift of the Joseph and Robert Cornell Memorial Foundation

For decades Cornell meticulously crafted boxes containing colored sand and other oceanic items, all intended as playthings. *Untitled (Red Sand Box)*, c. 1940 (fig. 123), features a wonderfully eroded piece of driftwood, red sand, and white seashells. When the box is picked up, the sand flows like water, fast and unpredictable. *The Seaside*, 1952–54 (fig. 130), contains a white starfish, a piece of coral, and layers of pink and blue sand between panes of glass. When the box is tilted, the contents slide around at different speeds (sand being the fastest), producing ever-different compositions and an analogy for the ebb and flow of waves on a shore—always moving and never the same.

Cornell was a stargazer, literally in life and figuratively in art. Fascinated with discoveries of new planets and stars, he read scientific magazines. *Soap Bubble Set*, 1949–50 (fig. 126), features a map of the moon, and the seven cylinders across the top bear astrological signs. Flanking the lunar map are meerschaum pipes made in the Netherlands, the country of Cornell's ancestors. He undoubtedly knew the painting *Soap Bubbles* by Jean-Baptiste-Siméon Chardin and its traditional interpretation as an allegory for the brevity of life. Many viewers remember happily blowing soap bubbles as children.

Starting with his first *Soap Bubble Set*, Cornell often crafted his own glass-fronted wood boxes. The glass pane distances observers from the contents inside, which can no longer be handled. Like a child peering into a shop window, we remain outside looking in at Cornell's miniature world of dreams and memories, where logic does not apply and where anything is possible. As the artist once noted in his journal: "Complete happiness [is] quickly being

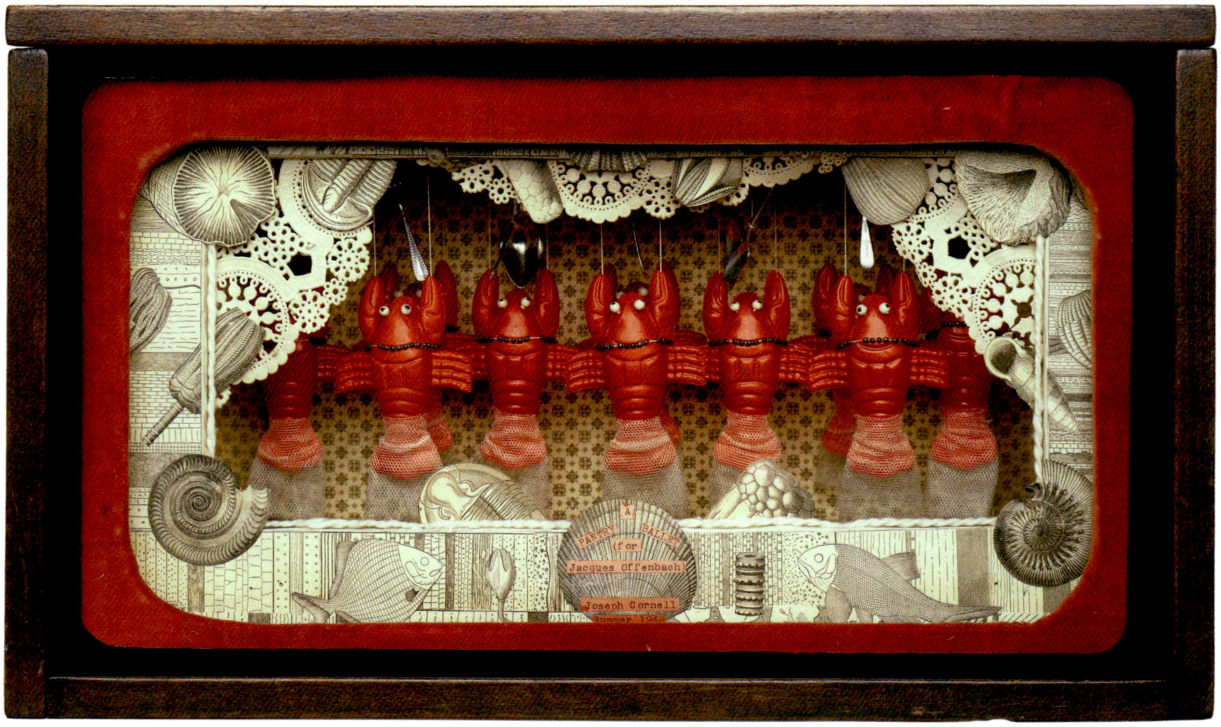

125
JOSEPH CORNELL
A PANTRY BALLET (FOR JACQUES OFFENBACH), 1942
The Nelson-Atkins Museum of Art, Kansas City; gift of the Friends of Art

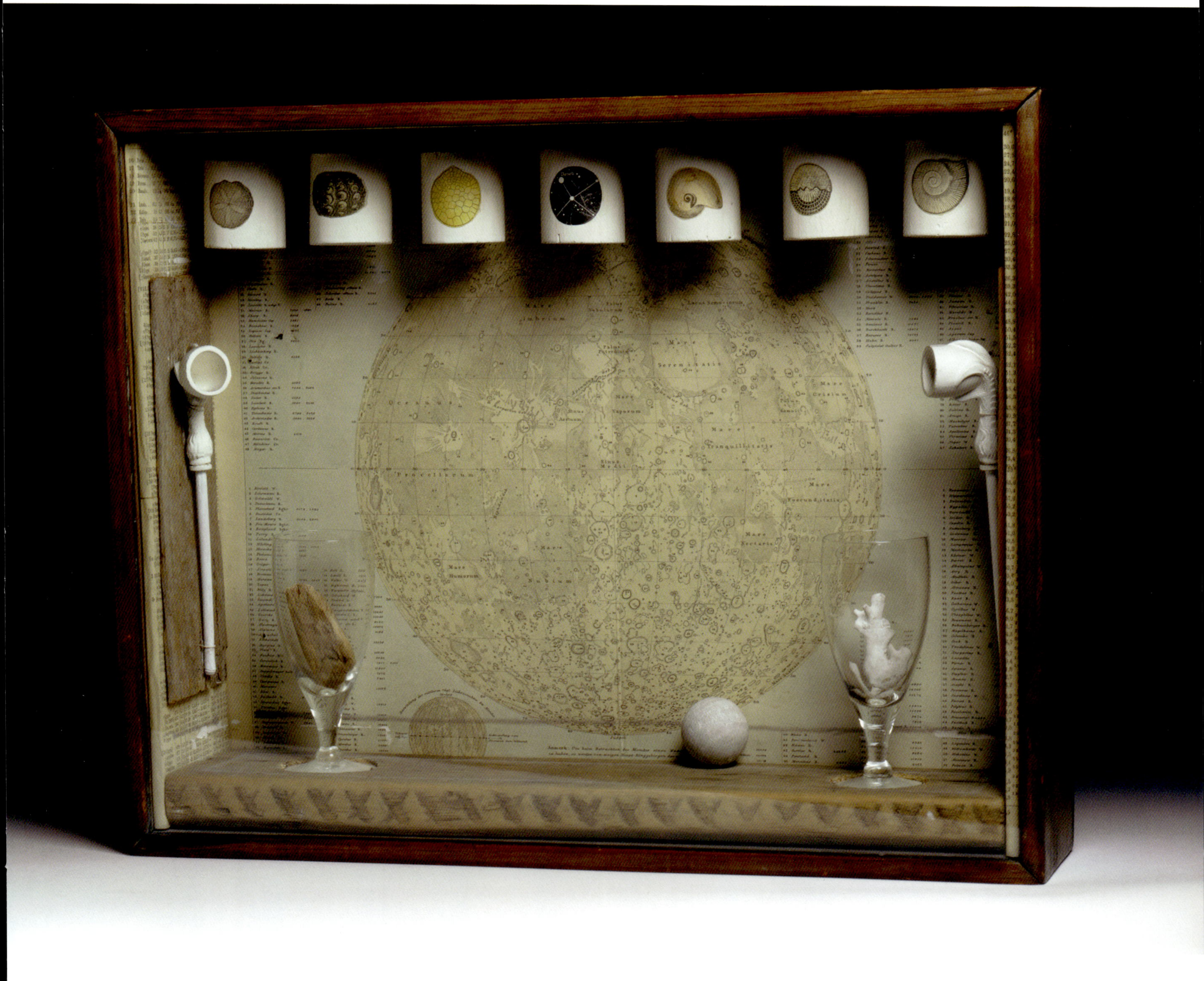

126
JOSEPH CORNELL, *SOAP BUBBLE SET*, 1949–50
Smithsonian American Art Museum, Washington, DC; museum purchase made possible by the American Art Forum

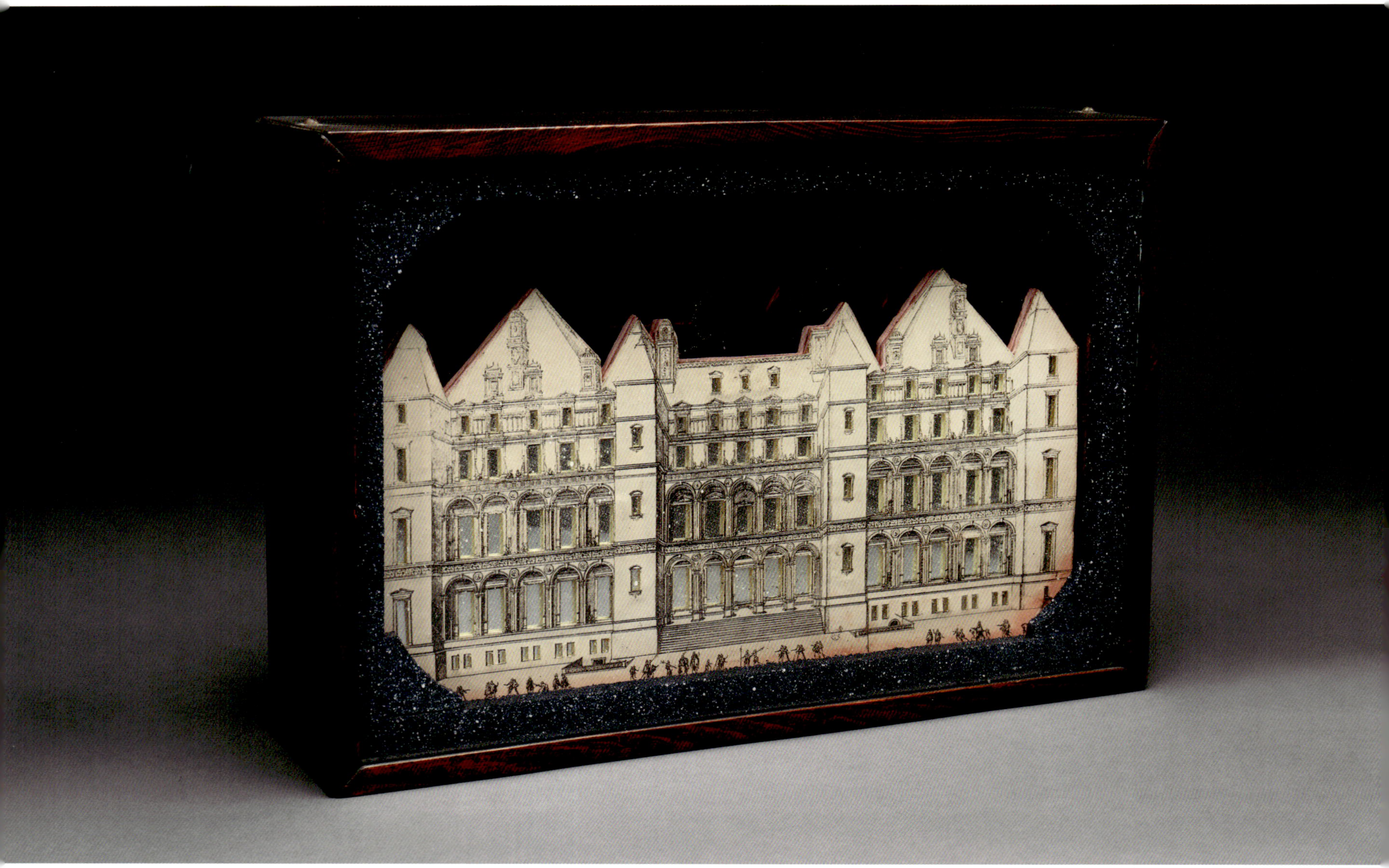

127
JOSEPH CORNELL, *UNTITLED (PINK PALACE)*, 1946
Smithsonian American Art Museum, Washington, DC; gift of Donald Windham

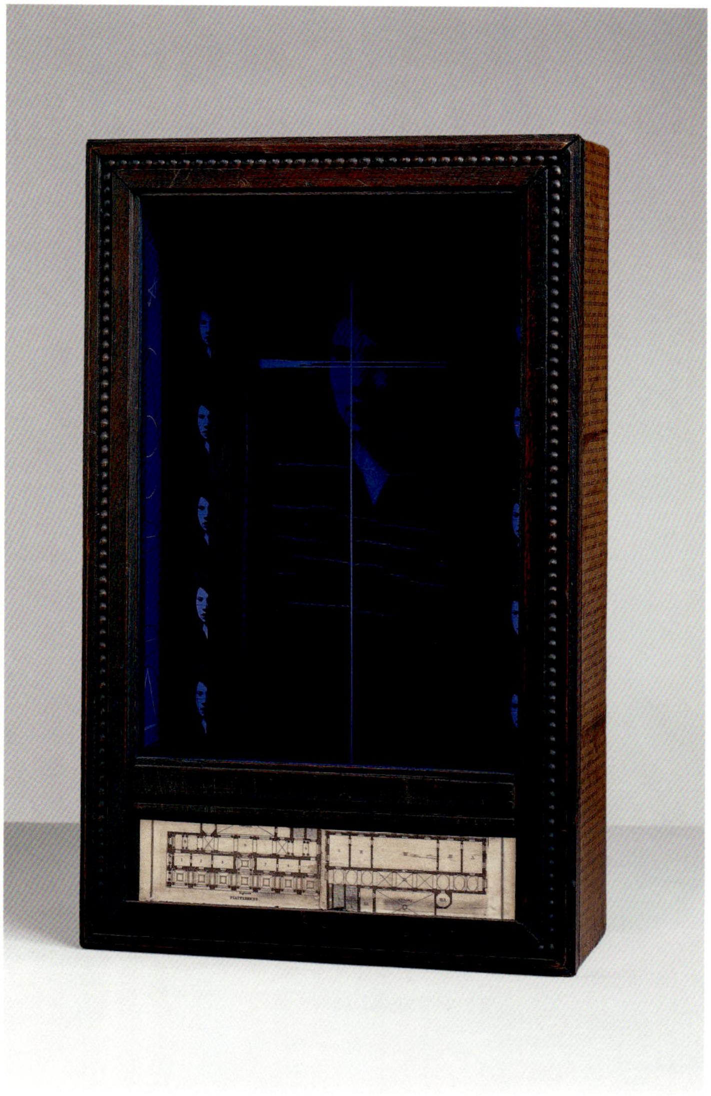

128
JOSEPH CORNELL
CARAVAGGIO PRINCE (MEDICI SLOT MACHINE VARIANT), c.1950
National Gallery of Art, Washington, DC; Corcoran Collection, gift of the Friends of the Corcoran Gallery of Art

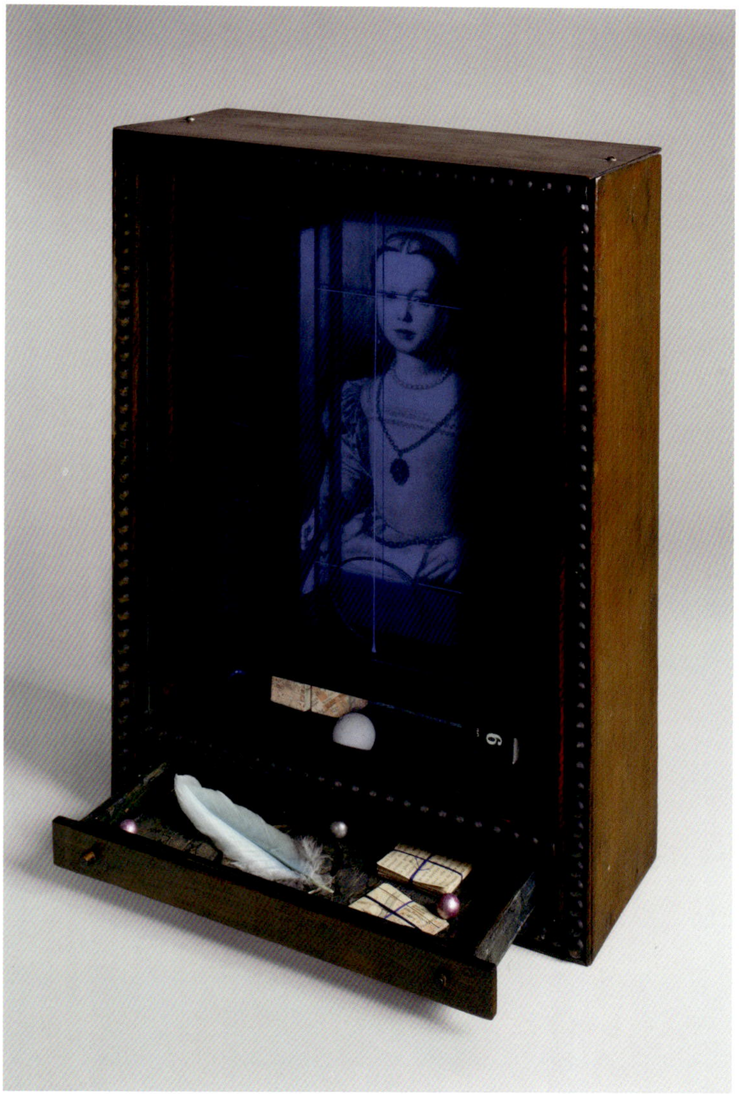

129
JOSEPH CORNELL
MEDICI PRINCESS, c.1948–52
Hirshhorn Museum and Sculpture Garden, Washington, DC; museum purchase

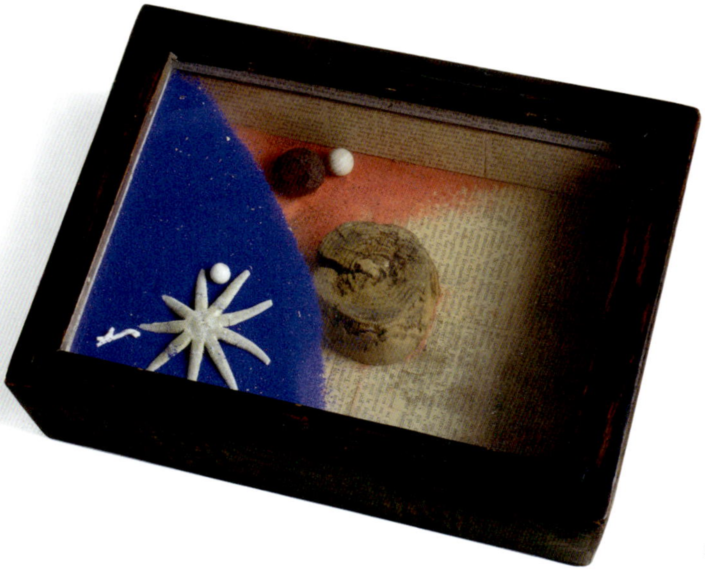

plunged into a world in which every triviality becomes imbued with significance."[53]

As part of his fascination with times and places far removed from his own, Cornell devoted a series of boxes to Renaissance portraits of children, such as *Caravaggio Prince*, c. 1950 (fig. 128). *Medici Princess*, c. 1948–52 (fig. 129), features Agnolo Bronzino's portrait of Bia, an illegitimate daughter of a duke in the powerful Florentine dynasty whose wealth and influence could not prevent her death at an early age. The blue glass adds a celestial note, and the drawer below contains faux pearls and sections of a map of Florence. Cornell drew upon memories of fairy tales like *Sleeping Beauty* for *Untitled (Pink Palace)*, 1946 (fig. 127), presented in the format of a miniature theater. The setting is the façade of a grand building surrounded by twigs representing a forest; silvery glitter is everywhere. A viewer peering into the box will see her own reflection in the mirrored windows, bringing her into this imaginary and magical realm.

130
JOSEPH CORNELL
THE SEASIDE, 1952–54
Hirshhorn Museum and Sculpture Garden, Washington, DC; the Joseph H. Hirshhorn Bequest

Although it is rarely noticed, some of Cornell's assemblages allude to works by Surrealist artists he knew, especially Duchamp (whom he admired) and Dalí (whom he detested). Dalí's largest work was the *Dream of Venus* pavilion at the 1939 World's Fair.[54] Its exterior was crudely biomorphic on the outside, with gnarly details and a ticket booth in the shape of a fish head. The interior offered a succession of environments, starting with a tableau of the goddess of love (in the form of a semi-nude live model sleeping in red satin sheets). The main room represented a gigantic aquarium furnished with a grand piano and fireplace; scantily clad young women would periodically dive in. Publicity photos featured a nude model wearing and holding lobsters. In other words, Dalí produced a sensational plethora of nearly naked young women with allusions to sexual desire. In that context Cornell's

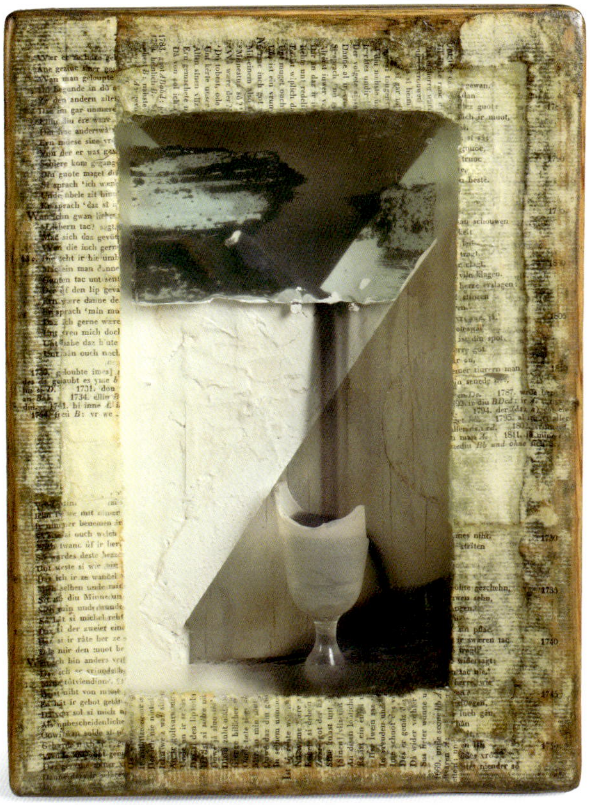

131
JOSEPH CORNELL
SAND FOUNTAIN, c.1955–57
Hirshhorn Museum and Sculpture Garden, Washington, DC; gift of Joseph H. Hirshhorn

exhibition at the Levy Gallery in December 1939 takes on a new resonance. The artist created an immersive environment: a large baby doll occupied the center of a darkened room. She was showered with confetti and surrounded by objects and shadow boxes containing birds, books, pipes, thimbles, bottles, and artificial foliage. The overall effect was magical and intimate, quite the opposite of the *Dream of Venus*. Lest anyone miss the point, Cornell dedicated this tableau as an "Offering for Salvador Dalí." In ensuing years he constructed several boxes containing red plastic lobsters. In *A Pantry Ballet (for Jacques Offenbach)*, 1942 (fig. 125), the setting is a theater stage, where a row of crustaceans suspended by threads look like performers in a corps de ballet or a Broadway burlesque. Any motion of the box sets the little critters to jiggling and swaying in a comedic and uncoordinated chorus line—an indirect and funny rebuttal of Dalí's obsession with aphrodisiac foods.

In the early and mid-1950s Cornell's compositions became simpler and more abstractly composed. Some perpetuated the themes and formats devised during the Surrealist years, such as *Suite de la Longitude*, 1955–57, with its schematic of the earth's longitudinal arcs. The cordial glasses contain blue marbles, reminders of childhood games that visually resonate with the cosmic map. *Sand Fountain*, c. 1955–57 (fig. 131), no longer refers to the seashore; it contains a lone broken glass and charcoal-gray sand. Turning the box upside down causes the sand to move into an upper compartment, and when the box is returned to its original upright position, the sand flows down, filling the glass and ultimately half-burying it, reminding us that *tempus fugit*.

LANDSCAPES OF THE MIND

At about the time Cornell made his first assemblages, biomorphism and its potential for free association had entered American art, initially in paintings and drawings. The Armenian-born artist Arshile Gorky embraced the Surrealist automatist methods and the evocative power of organic forms in the early 1930s, using them to express the turmoil and darkness of his soul. He repeatedly tried to convert his friend the Japanese-American sculptor Isamu Noguchi to Surrealism, but to no avail because Noguchi preferred the refined aesthetics of Constantin Brancusi and the utopian philosophy of Buckminster Fuller. Still, Noguchi did experiment with organic forms and fantastic metamorphosis in his proposal for the *United Hosiery Workers' Memorial*, 1933–34 (fig. 132). Instead of a heroic laborer of the kind portrayed in Social Realist art, Noguchi presented an object in the spirit of Dalí's melting watches: a sewing machine (identifiable by its needle, spool, and thread) that sprouts an arm and hand that reach over to cut the thread with scissors. Nothing similar ensued.

The Japanese attack on Pearl Harbor in December 1941 provided a traumatic catalyst for Noguchi's aesthetics. Although not required to join other American citizens of Japanese

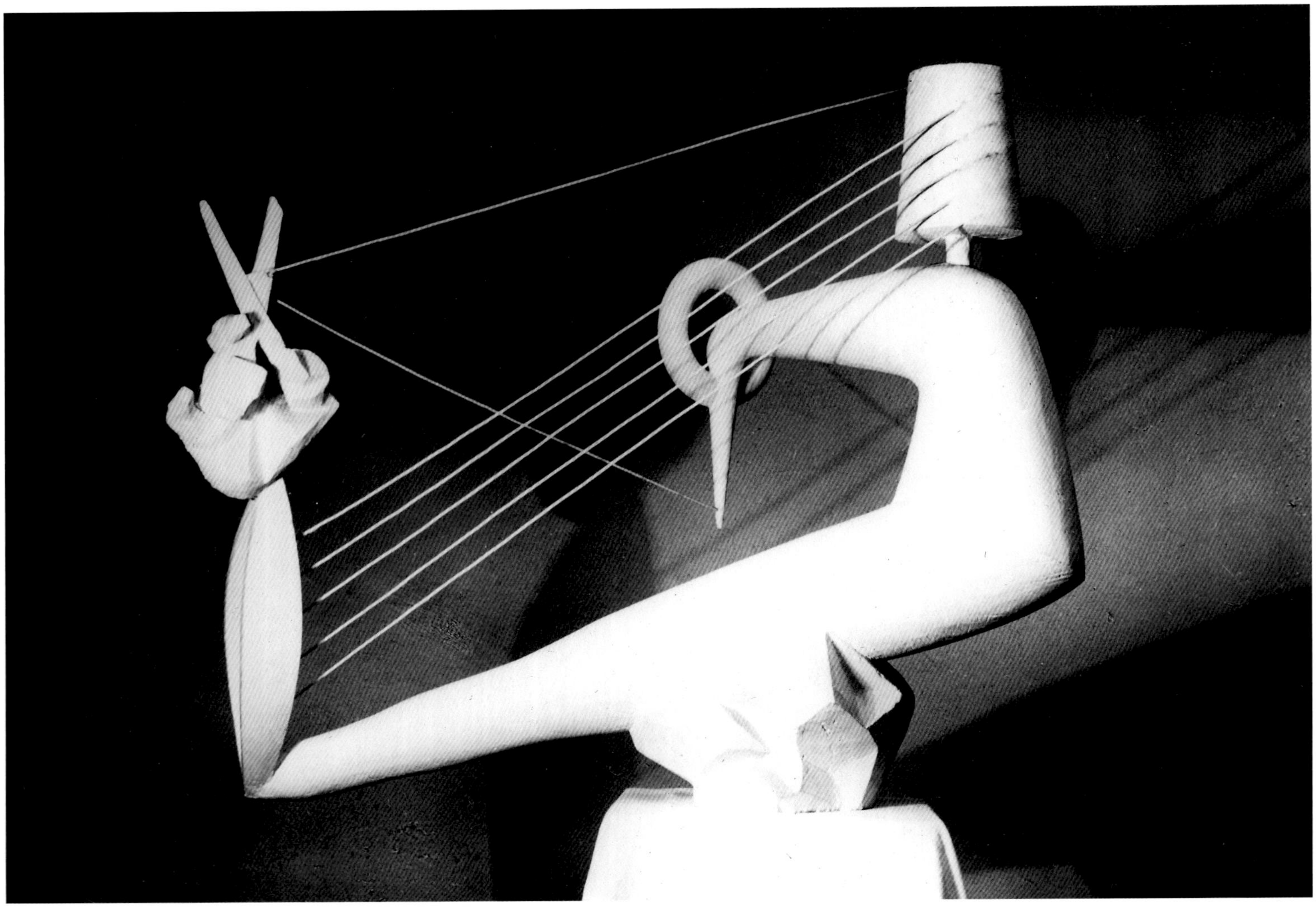

132
PHOTOGRAPH OF ISAMU NOGUCHI, *UNITED HOSIERY WORKERS' MEMORIAL,* 1933–34
Courtesy the Noguchi Museum, New York

descent in prison camps in the Southwest deserts, he opted to enter one voluntarily in May 1942, idealistically hoping to improve living conditions by applying his design experience to the buildings and their environs. After four months of frustration he returned to New York. The emotional and psychological impact of his experience profoundly affected Noguchi, who was shaken by the realization that his mixed parentage nearly classified him as an enemy alien. He was left bitterly disillusioned and depressed, susceptible to the inner-directed art of Surrealism that encouraged exploring one's own psyche as a defense against a difficult and dangerous world.

133
YVES TANGUY
NAKED WATER, 1942
Hirshhorn Museum and Sculpture Garden, Washington, DC; gift of Joseph H. Hirshhorn

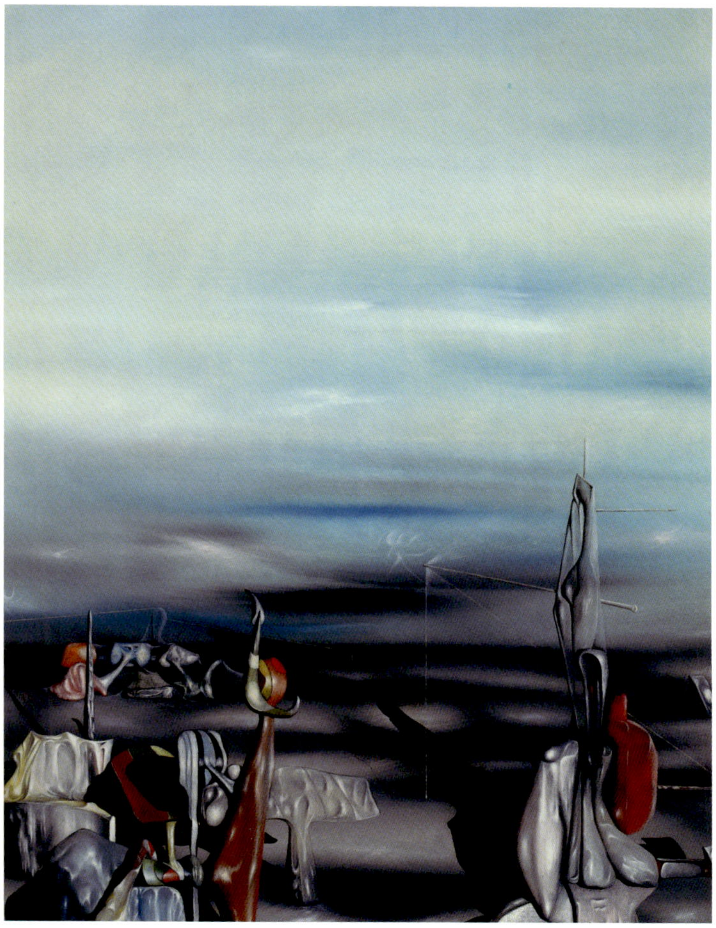

The presence of émigré Surrealists in New York meant that Noguchi had ready access to Matta's studio soirées, where the "psychological morphology" paintings and drawings were on display. Given his recent placement in Arizona, Tanguy's illusionistic images of biomorphs in deserted landscapes may have also provided a starting point for Noguchi. Since coming to the United States, Tanguy had modified his style, making his biomorphs more intricate and more sculptural, often with overlapping and interpenetrating forms, as seen in paintings like *Naked Water* (fig. 133) and his landscape drawing on the cover of *View* magazine in 1942.[55]

Noguchi's personal adaptation of biomorphism in 1943 is characterized by pessimism and despair. The black cardboard tube of *Monument to Heroes* (fig. 135) houses blade-like wood elements and an animal bone dangling from strings. In a bitterly ironic mimicry of ancient monuments erected in honor of military triumphs and heroic actions, such as *Trajan's Column* in Rome, Noguchi confronts us with the gruesomeness of war. The forms in *Untitled* (fig. 134) invite us to see victims of torture, their dismembered body parts skewered on a metal spike like a barbaric trophy. The cratered topography of *This Tortured Earth* (fig. 137) may reflect Noguchi's awareness of Giacometti's *No More Play* in Levy's collection but was actually inspired by an aerial reconnaissance photograph of a North African desert after

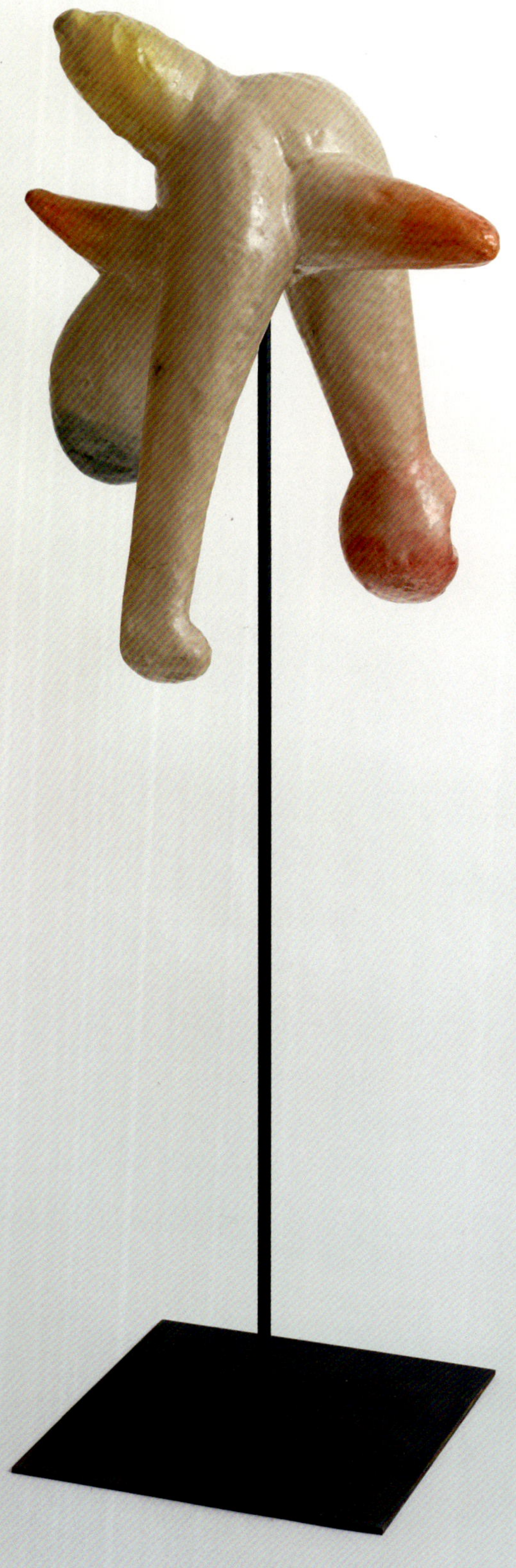

134
ISAMU NOGUCHI, *UNTITLED*, 1943
Noguchi Museum, New York

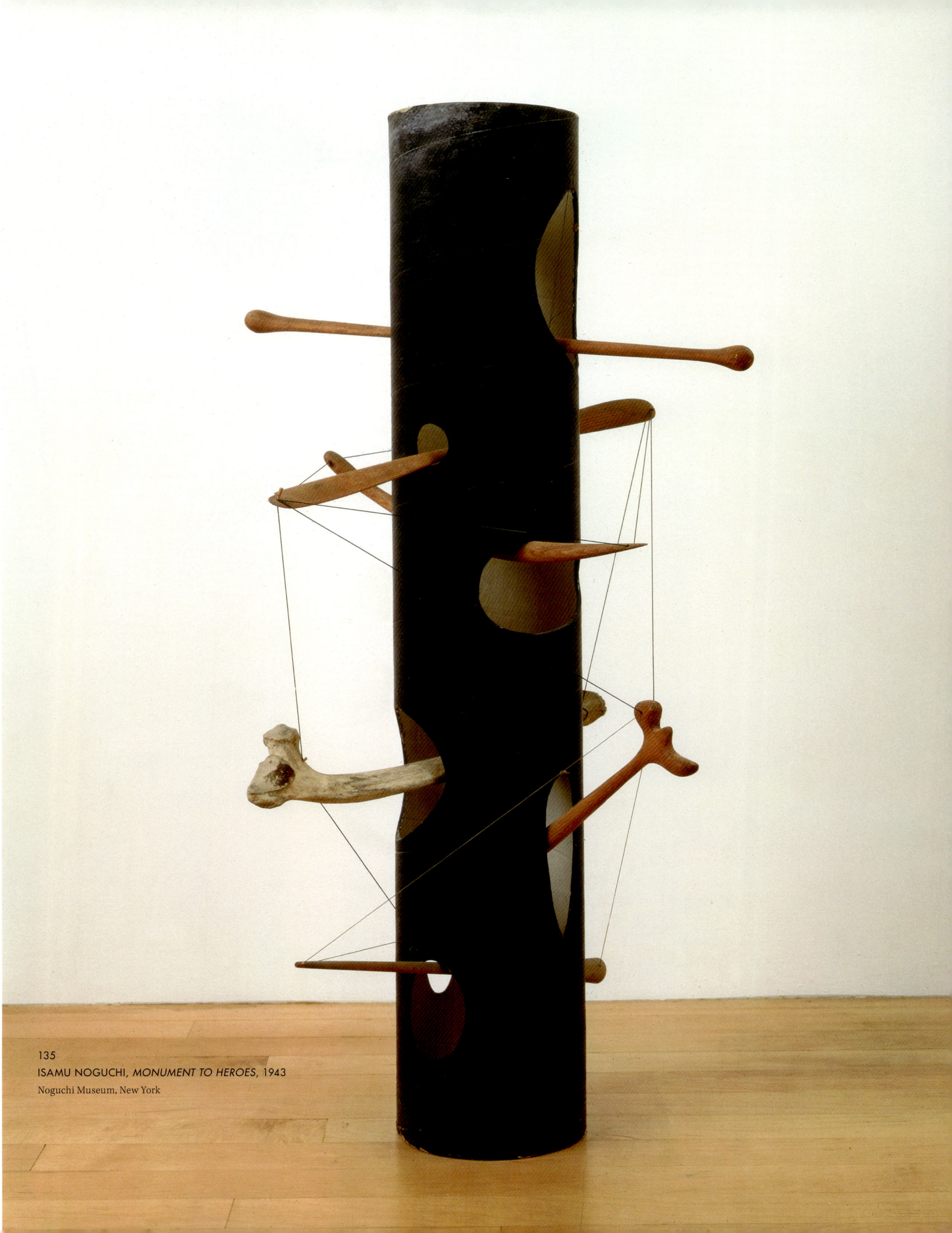

135
ISAMU NOGUCHI, *MONUMENT TO HEROES*, 1943
Noguchi Museum, New York

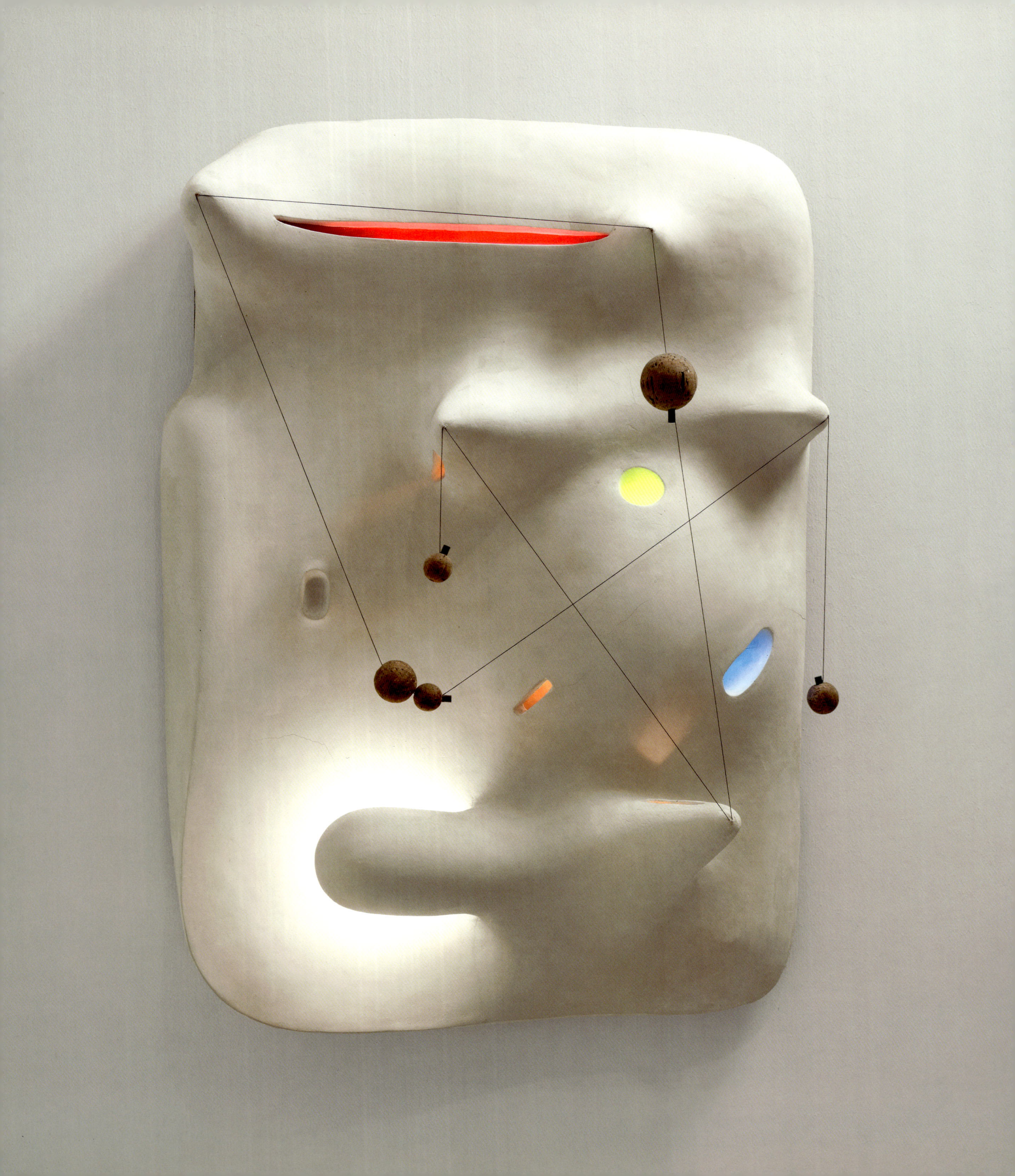

heavy bombing. Decades later, in connection with the war in Vietnam, Noguchi would propose enlarging the concept of *This Tortured Earth* as a public monument consisting of acres of ground reshaped entirely by bombing—a savagely morbid earthwork.

Noguchi countered these horrific compositions with biomorphic sculptures illuminated by internal electric lights, which he called *Lunars*. Instead of the dark vision of *This Tortured Earth*, the surging forms in *Lunar Landscape*, 1943–44 (fig. 136), are bathed in eerily glowing areas of colored light. Over the moonscape the sculptor suspended cork fishing-floats that may be paradoxically interpreted as either cosmic satellites or as bombshells poised over a burning terrain. In the 1970s, Noguchi recalled that this work arose from a specific recollection:

136
ISAMU NOGUCHI
LUNAR LANDSCAPE,
1943–44
Hirshhorn Museum and Sculpture Garden, Washington, DC; gift of Joseph H. Hirshhorn

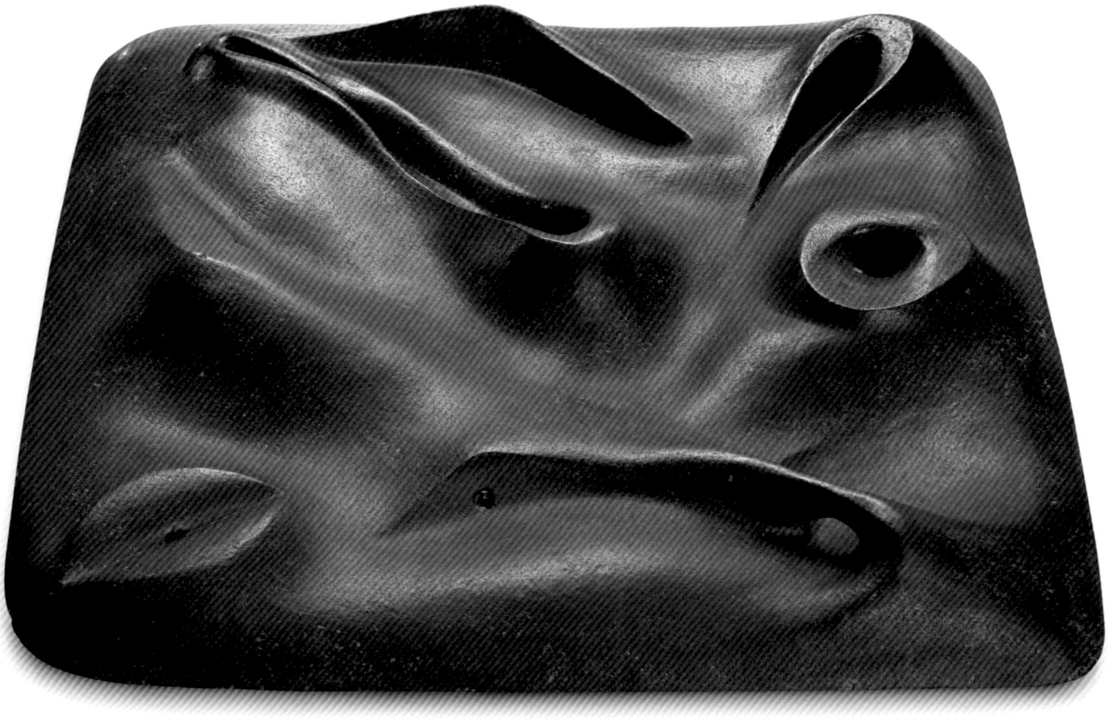

137
ISAMU NOGUCHI
THIS TORTURED EARTH,
1943
Noguchi Museum, New York

> The memory of Arizona was like that of the moon, a moonscape of the mind.... Not given the actual space of freedom, one makes its equivalent—an illusion within the confines of a room or a box—where the imagination may roam to the further limits of possibilities, to the moon and beyond.[56]

Other works in the series expressed the artist's anger at being marginalized because of his parentage. The jagged crystalline shafts of *Red Lunar Fist*, 1943–44 (fig. 139), aggressively jut out of a blood-colored clenched hand with bulging knuckles. *Lunar Infant*, 1944 (fig. 138), presents a white biomorph hanging inside an open cage (similar to the one in Giacometti's

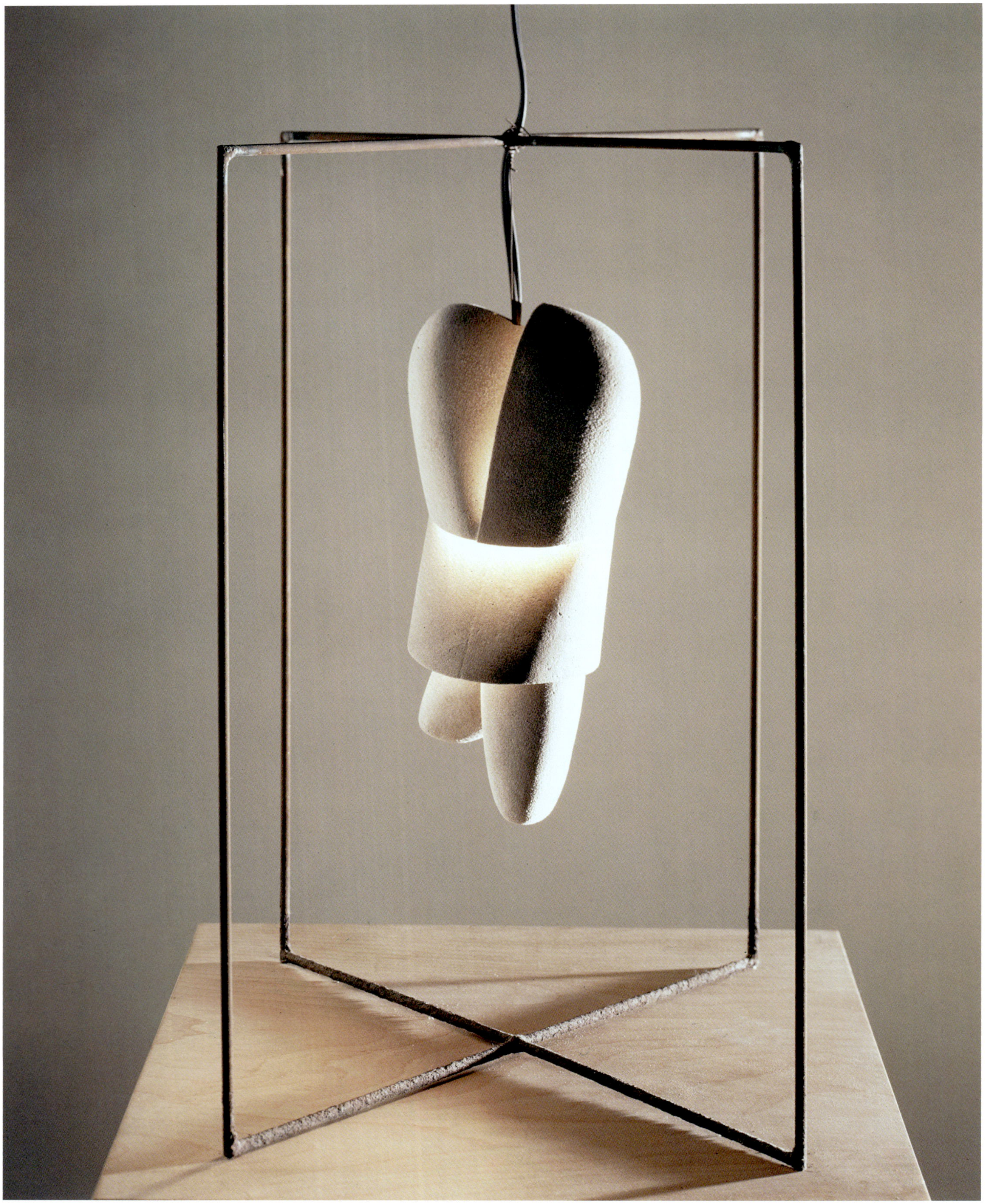

Suspended Ball), which may be interpreted as either a devastated corpse or an embryo promising a new birth. The white light emanating from within tilts the balance in favor of hope.

From 1945 through 1948 Noguchi created a series of imagined hybrid figures assembled like three-dimensional jigsaw puzzles (figs. 140–43). He described these compositions as memories of humanity, "transfigurations, archetypes, and magical distillations."

> A purely cold abstraction doesn't interest me much. Art has to have some kind of a humanly touching ... quality. It has to recall something which moves a person—a recollection, a recognition of his loneliness or tragedy or whatever ... things that happen at night, somber things.[57]

The anthropomorphic creatures stand on slender legs that have minimal purchase on the ground. Using no dowels or glue, Noguchi assembled the interpenetrating components in a delicate, often precarious balance—an analogy for the vulnerability of the human psyche. "The very fragility gives a thrill.... It's like life—you can lose it at any moment."[58]

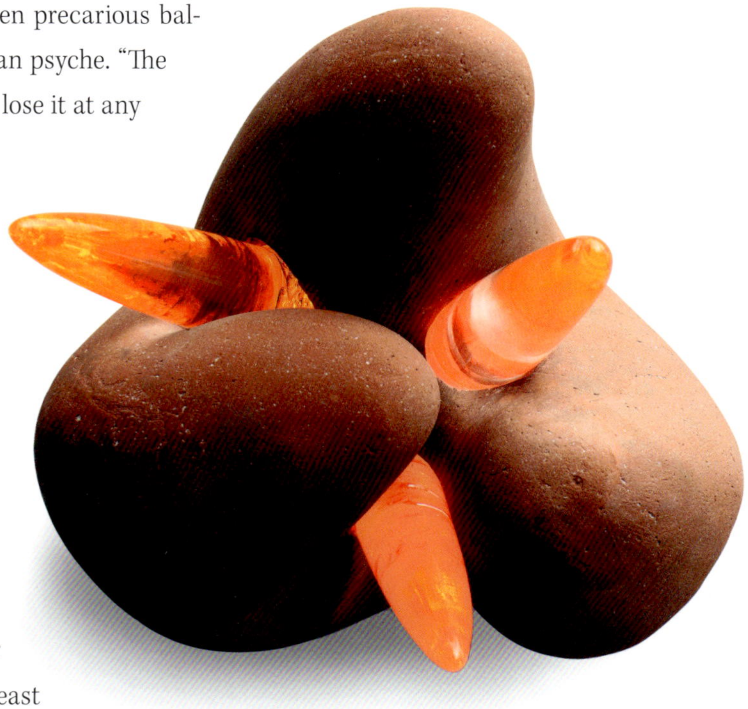

Strange Bird (To the Sunflower), 1945, was inspired by a sense of longing expressed in a poem by William Blake, though viewers need not be familiar with the specific verse to formulate their own interpretations. With the title as guide, we may interpret the creature as a bird, the universal symbol of freedom and escape, but it resembles a flightless emu or ostrich with long fragile bones. The small slanting element may be its head, or (as suggested by the alternate title) a downward tilted sunflower blossom, a tall gawky plant that gently turns from east to west every day, seeking always to face the sun and drooping when it cannot—another metaphor for spiritual or emotional yearning.

Whereas the Surrealists relished the disturbing depths of their own psyches, Noguchi sometimes expressed his emotions through literary references. The title of *Gregory*, 1946, alludes to the protagonist in Franz Kafka's 1915 novella *The Metamorphosis* (translated into English in 1930). After awaking one morning to find himself transformed into a giant insect, Gregor Samsa is treated as an outcast (as Noguchi felt himself to be during the war years spent mostly within the confines of his studio). When Gregor finally comes out of his room, his father throws rotten apples at him; one lodges deep in Gregor's body and kills him. The rectangular torso of Noguchi's sculpture can be interpreted as the carapace of a beetle or cockroach painfully pierced by hooked forms. The sculpture's alternate title, *Effigy*, recharaterizes

139
ISAMU NOGUCHI
RED LUNAR FIST, 1943–44
Noguchi Museum, New York

138
ISAMU NOGUCHI
LUNAR INFANT, 1944
Noguchi Museum, New York

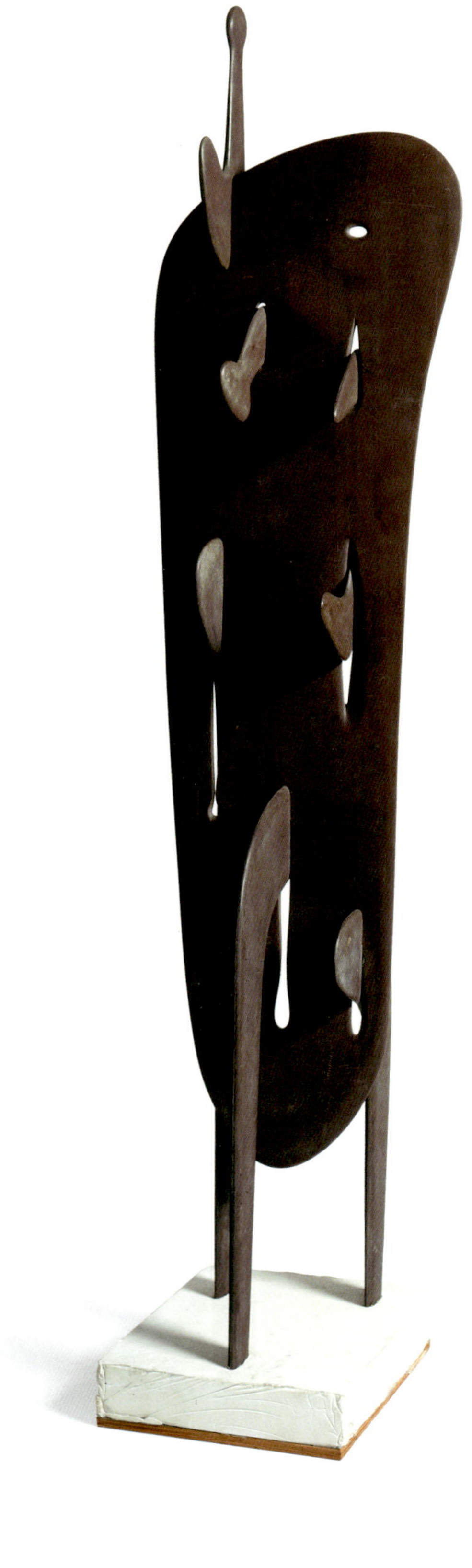

140
ISAMU NOGUCHI, *GREGORY (EFFIGY)*, 1946
Noguchi Museum, New York

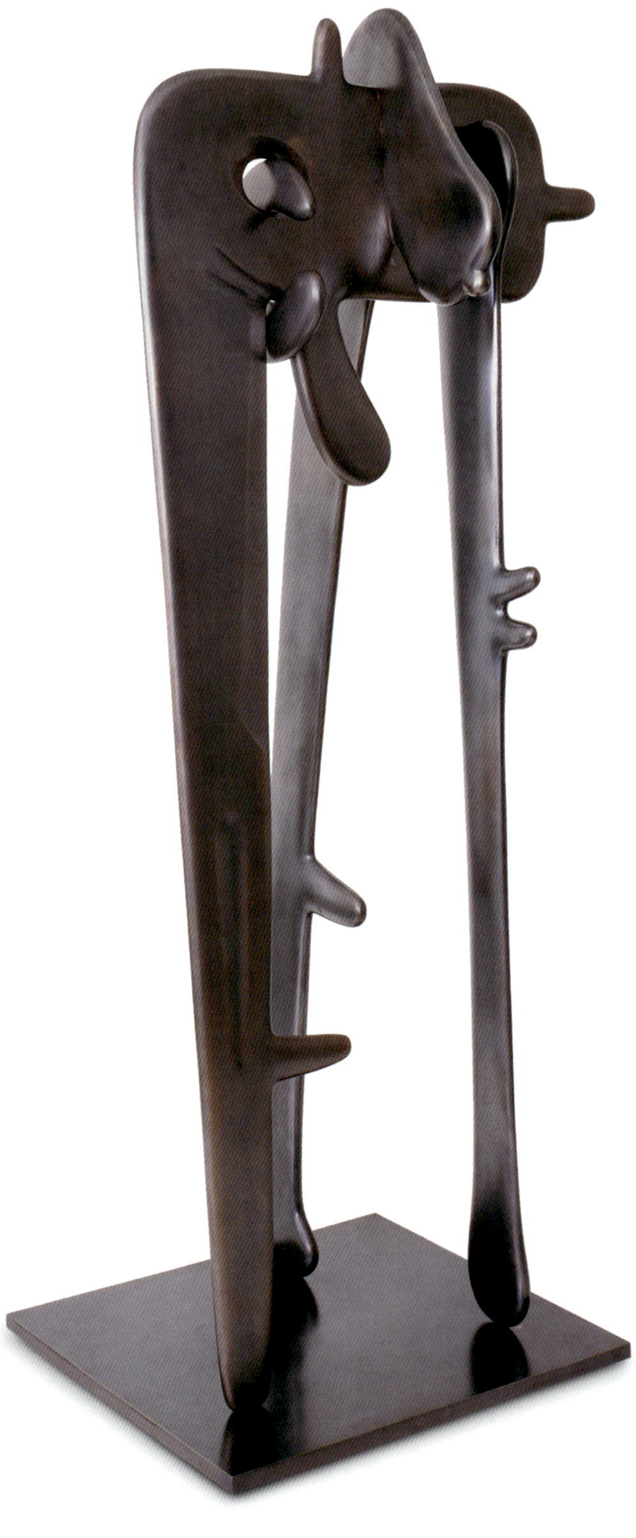

141
ISAMU NOGUCHI, *AVATAR*, 1947
Private collection, courtesy Pace Gallery, New York

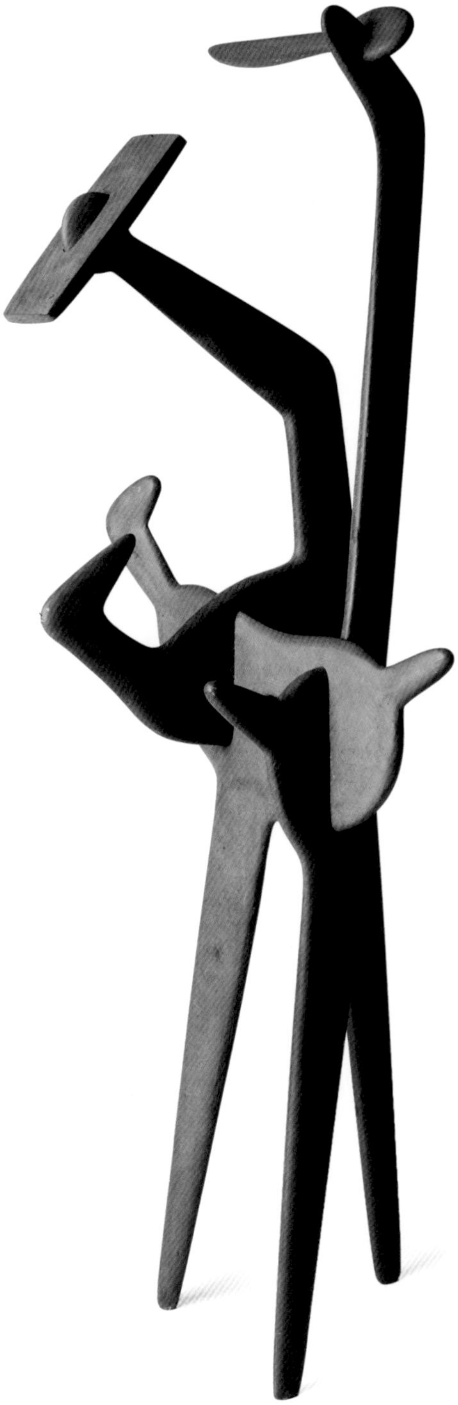

142
ISAMU NOGUCHI, *STRANGE BIRD (TO THE SUNFLOWER)*, 1945
Noguchi Museum, New York

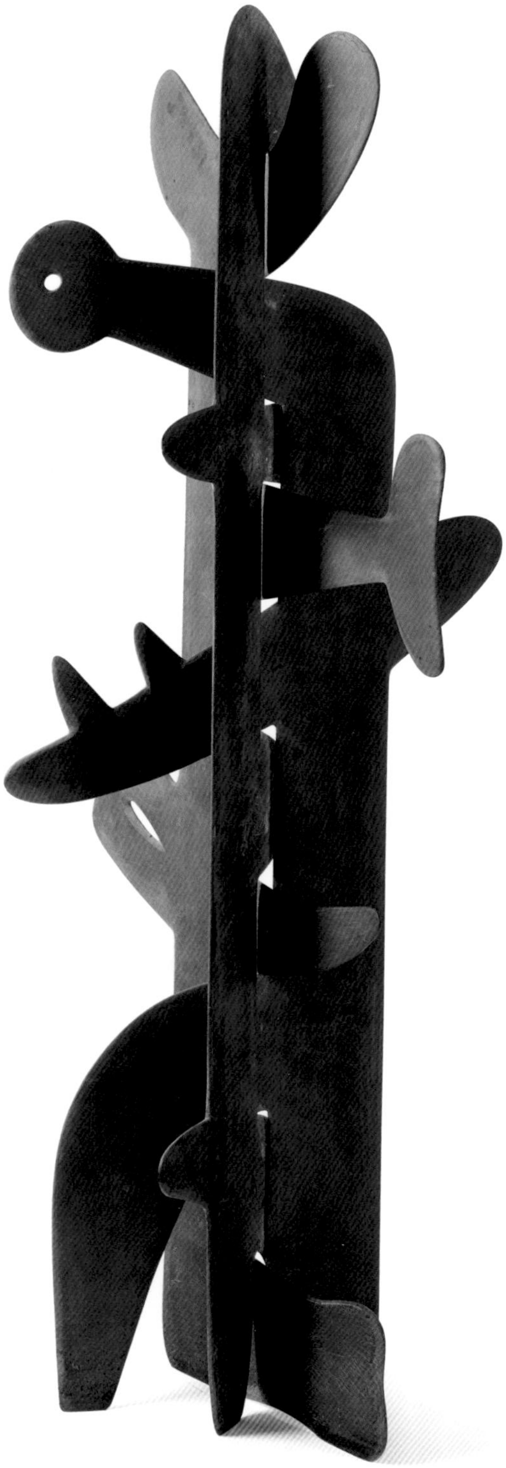

143
ISAMU NOGUCHI, *TRINITY*, 1945
Noguchi Museum, New York

the work as an anonymous figure of the kind paraded by a mob and eventually dismembered or torched—a symbolic death that can be enacted over and over again.

Trinity, 1945, has three clearly demarcated sides, so that when we look at one, we cannot see the other two. The three identities are bound together and share interlocking parts in an enforced coexistence, a metaphor for an individual psyche that struggles to integrate conflicting aspects, or for diverse societies that thrive only when disparate elements unite and support one another. The title also invokes the religious concept of triadic divinity in Christianity (Father, Son, Holy Spirit), Hinduism (Brahma, Vishnu, Shiva), and other creeds. That the three identities of Noguchi's sculpture are not a compatible trio is made clear in the individual motifs: bony shapes, a club with spikes (or phallus with thorns), a one-eyed profile head protruding as if trying to escape. At the level of the figures' chest a large scissors-like shape pierces the body.

INDUSTRIAL-STRENGTH SURREALISM

Working independently of each other, Smith and Calder transformed Surrealist sculptures of the 1930s and 1940s into sophisticated abstractions that provided the foundation for the geometric steel that typified American sculpture in the 1950s and beyond. Both artists had direct experience working with metal: Calder trained as an engineer, and Smith worked as a welder in factories. But they differed in their intersections with Surrealist art. Between mid-1926 and mid-1933, and again in 1937, Calder spent long periods in Paris, where he knew many of the Surrealists. Smith, on the other hand, did not go to Europe until 1935; his prior sources were limited to illustrations in art magazines and gallery exhibitions of Surrealist art in New York.

Despite his early contacts with Surrealism in Paris, Calder dedicated his efforts to constructing geometric abstractions, usually linear in style. Some were kinetic, powered by hand-cranks and motors, which Duchamp christened *mobiles* in 1931. Arp named the stationary ones *stabiles* a few months later. Although he never officially joined the movement and was temperamentally unsuited to Breton's intellectual dogmatism and political affiliations, Calder's periods in Paris coincided with the first exhibitions of Surrealist sculptures in 1931–32. He knew Arp, was a close friend of Miró, and probably visited the studios of other artists.

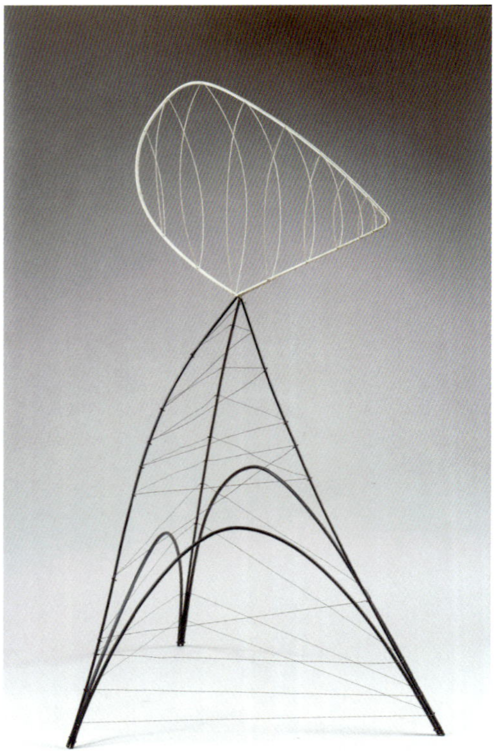

144
ALEXANDER CALDER
HOLLOW EGG, 1939
The Phillips Collection, Washington, DC; partial and promised gift in memory of Betty Milton, a close friend of Louisa Calder

In early 1933 Calder had begun to use organic forms episodically and participated in a six-artist show with Arp and Miró at the Galerie Pierre Loeb. Before his departure for New York in June, he may have had the opportunity to see the *Surrealist Exhibition: Sculptures, Objects, Paintings, Drawings* at the Galerie Pierre Colle. When Calder returned to live in the US, he brought along a major painting by Miró and a relief by Arp, which he kept for the rest of his life.

In 1936, in anticipation of MoMA's *Fantastic Art* exhibition, Calder moved decisively into a Surrealist mode that was both biomorphic and constructivist. *Cello on a Spindle*, 1936, consists of a shaped surface of sheet metal on which perches a small Arpian biomorph. Having bought a farm in rural Connecticut, Calder made good use of useless things from nature. The body of *Apple Monster*, 1938 (fig. 147), is a branch that had fallen off an apple tree, and the white head atop the wood body of *Untitled*, 1938 (fig. 146), is a vertebra from a cow's spine. The latter creature balances on three long metal-rod legs, a structural format that characterizes many of Calder's Surrealist critters, including the 1936 *Mantis* shown in *Fantastic Art*. Another exhibited work, *Gibraltar*, 1936 (fig. 145), was quite different: a chunk of solid wood represents the famous promontory rising from the sea. The range of Calder's subjects and materials from 1936 through 1944 was as varied and innovative as Giacometti's had been in the early 1930s.

The change in Calder's aesthetics in 1936 occurred after his *Mobiles and Objects* exhibition at the Matisse Gallery in February, where he presented linear geometric abstractions with mobile components. The transition was complete by the time of the next exhibition at the same gallery in February 1937, when he revealed a veritable menagerie in metal. Leaving behind the delicate materials and small size of most Surrealist sculptures up to that time, Calder chose to work with sheet metal joined by welds or bolts. *Big Bird*, 1937 (fig. 148), elegantly combines two painted-metal components, one red and one black. Viewers who walk around the sculpture discover that the black arc appears to morph from a rooster-like tail to a boomerang piercing its avian prey. Originally, the creature

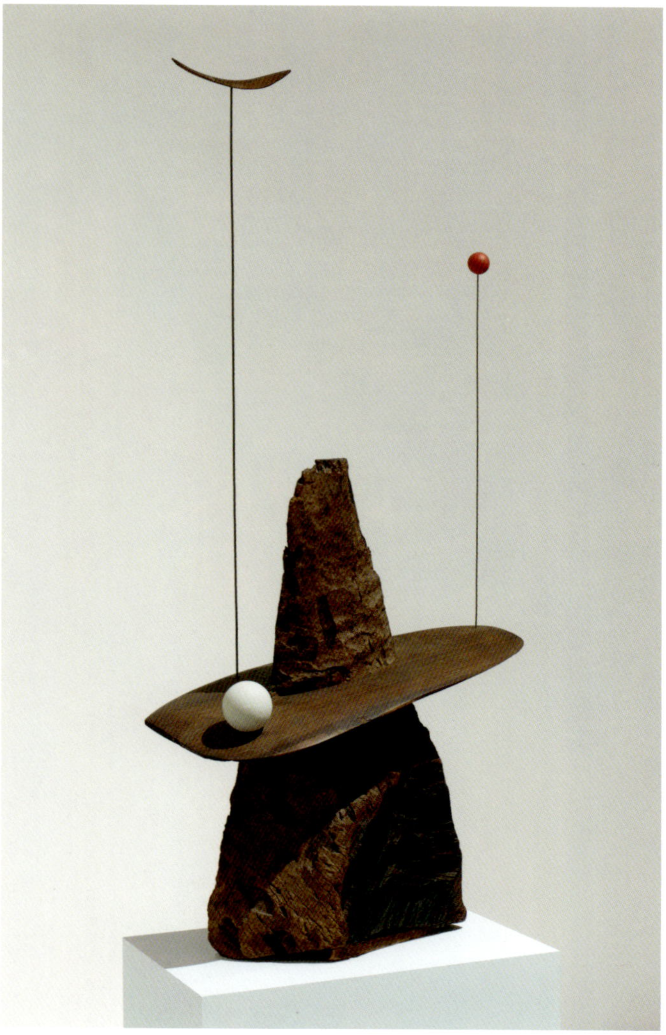

145
ALEXANDER CALDER
GIBRALTAR, 1936
The Museum of Modern Art, New York; gift of the artist

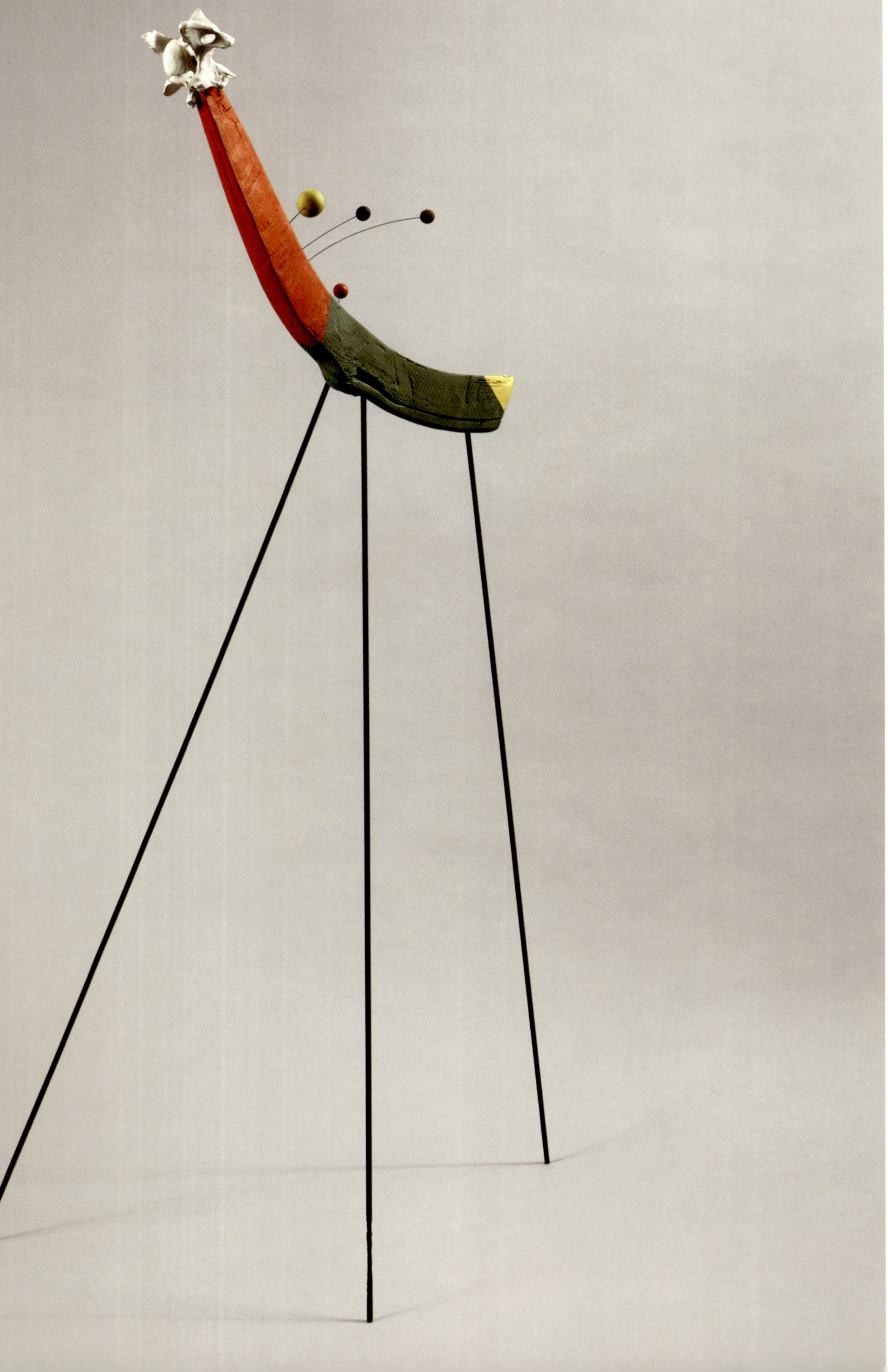

146
ALEXANDER CALDER
UNTITLED, 1938
Calder Foundation, New York;
gift of Holton Rower, 2014

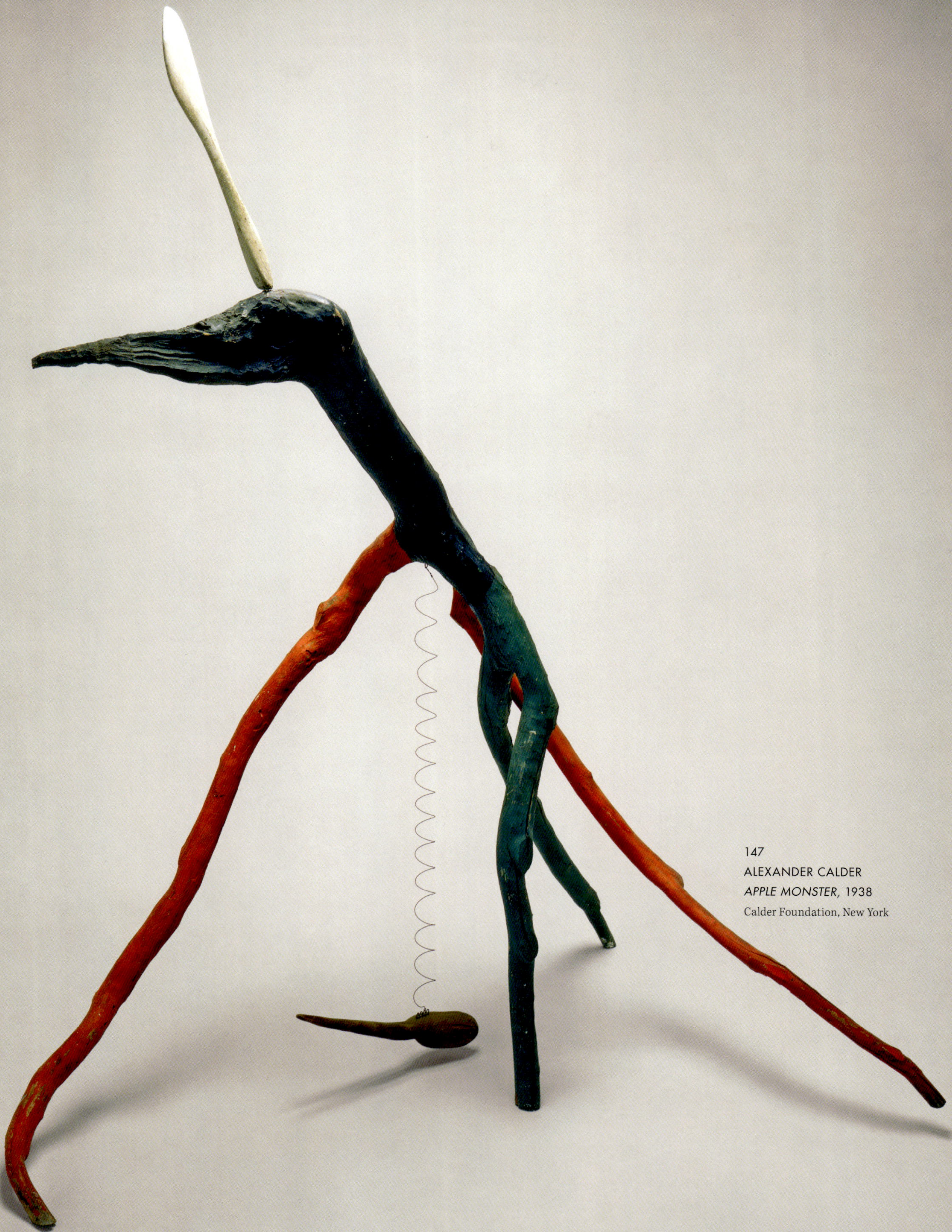

147
ALEXANDER CALDER
APPLE MONSTER, 1938
Calder Foundation, New York

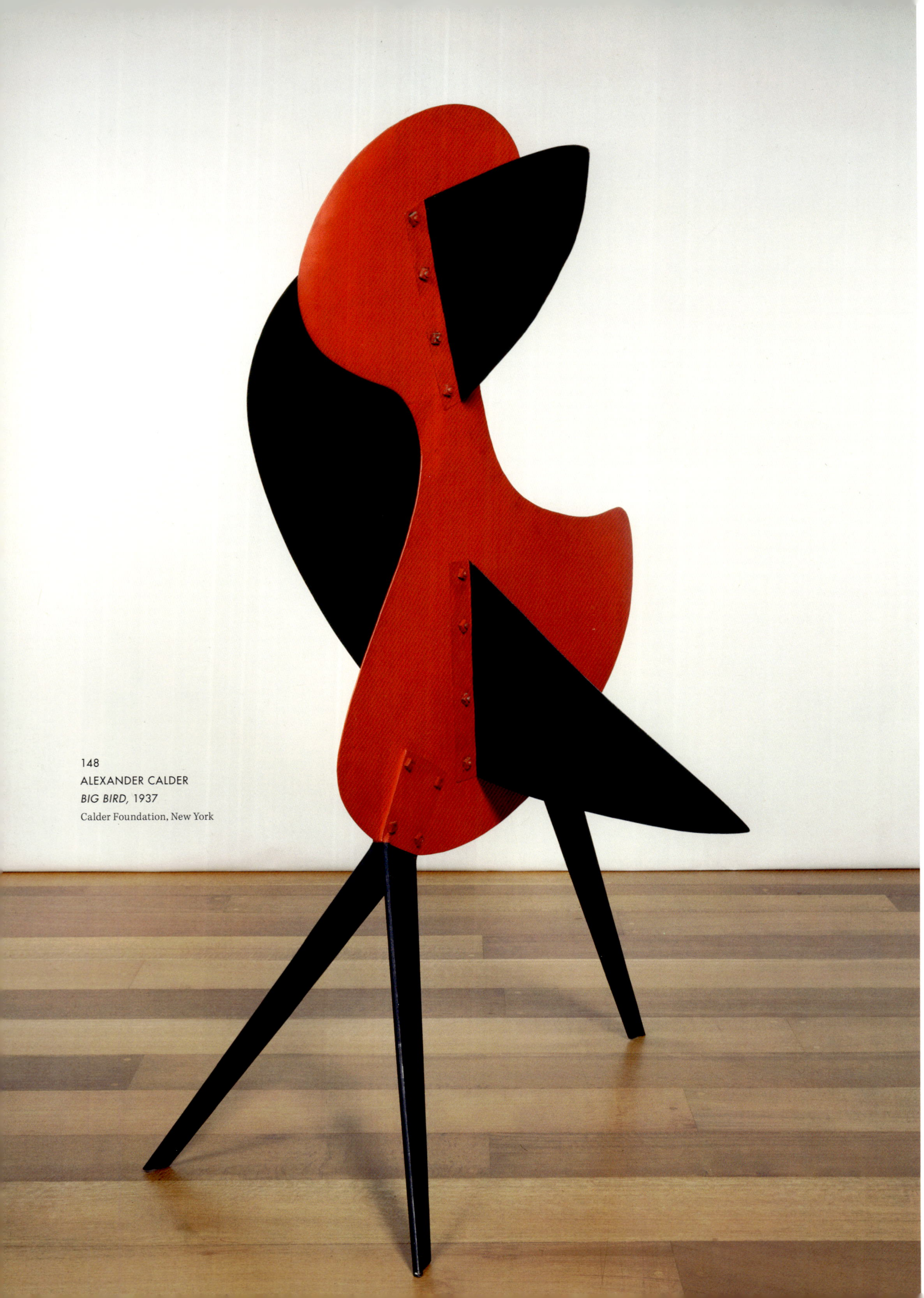

148
ALEXANDER CALDER
BIG BIRD, 1937
Calder Foundation, New York

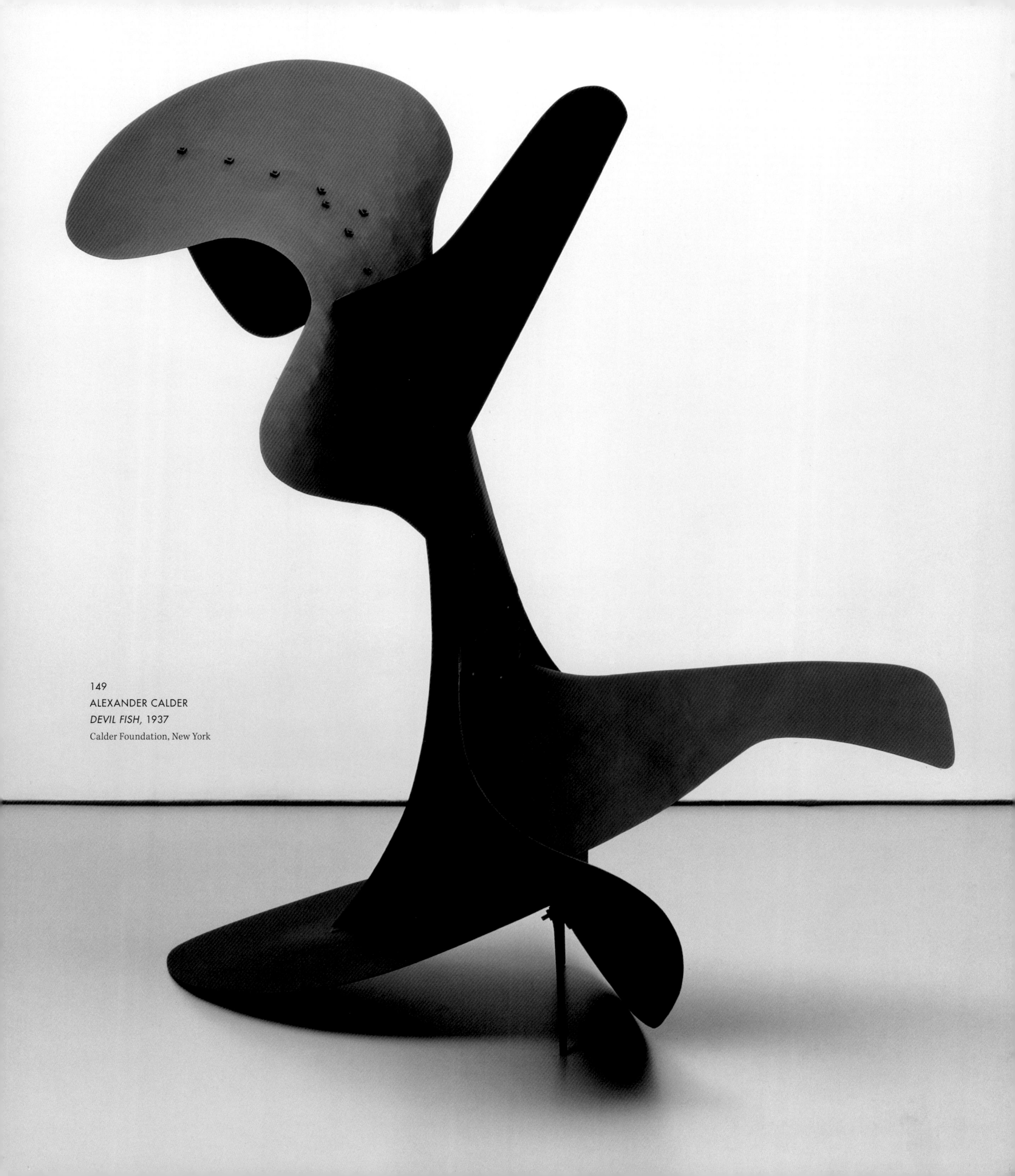

149
ALEXANDER CALDER
DEVIL FISH, 1937
Calder Foundation, New York

stood on longer legs so its head touched the gallery's ceiling and loomed over viewers. With typical Calderian humor, he posed several small birds (possibly studies for *Big Bird*) underneath, like ducklings or chicks sheltering under their powerful mommy.

Devil Fish, 1937 (fig. 149), translates Arpian whimsy into a more muscular mode. The sculpture is large and impressively strong, its thick steel plates held together with industrial bolts. *Devil Fish* presents a striking metamorphosis when circumambulated: from a relatively benign fish, it changes into an aggressive orca-like one, and from another angle, it resembles a portly and ponderous figure. Calder's imposing upright fish had come a long way from Arp's early biomorphs, such as the squid walking on floppy limbs in *Man-Mustaches*. When *Devil Fish* was featured in Calder's exhibition at the Mayor Gallery in London (where the artist spent several months, with ample access to the Surrealist works of Moore and others), one review noted that "the most startling object in his present show is an eight-foot monster, a cross between a ship's propeller and a shark's fin."[59] In materials, method, and fanciful subject, *Devil Fish* laid the groundwork for many of Calder's later sculptures, such as the monumental *Stegosaurus*, 1973 (fig. 151).

150
ALEXANDER CALDER
LA DEMOISELLE (YOUNG LADY), 1939
Glenstone

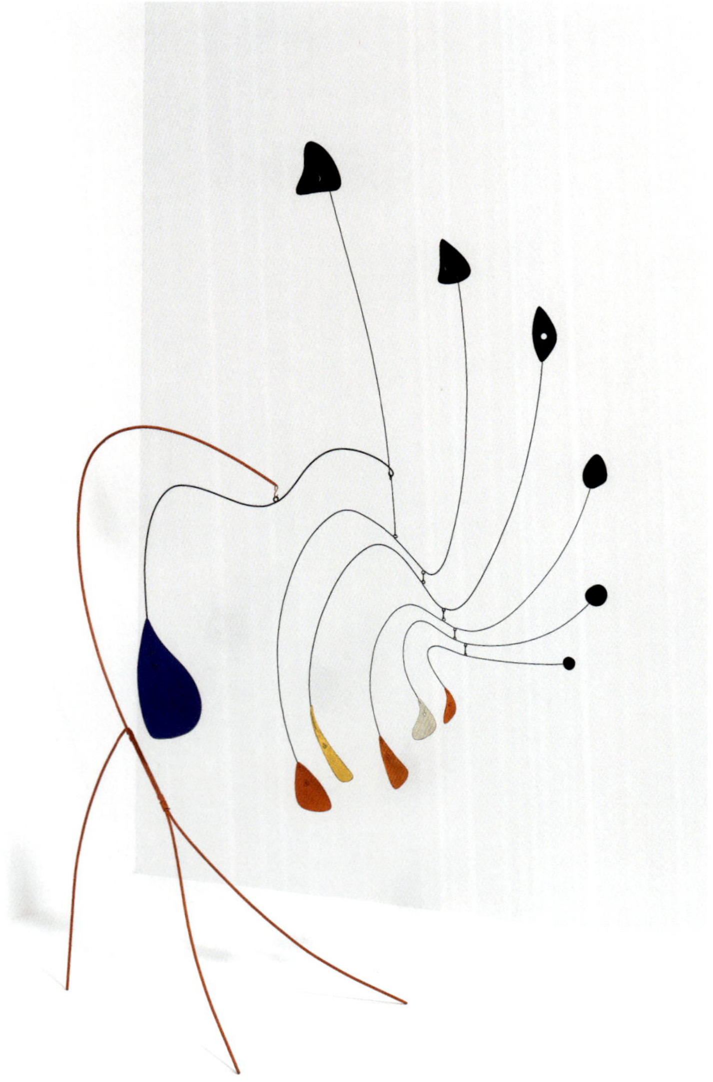

After returning to Connecticut in February 1938, Calder fabricated an extensive menagerie of fantastic creatures that continued through the mid-1940s. In contrast to *Devil Fish*, many have no central mass at all, only thin contours of curving wire that convey an impression of lightness and fragility. Balancing precariously on three skinny legs, the egg (a traditional symbol of new life) in *Hollow Egg*, 1939 (fig. 144), becomes a figure with a humorously empty head. The title of *La Demoiselle*, 1939 (fig. 150), invites us to see the composition as a young girl making a dainty curtsy. Raised on three curved legs, the "figure" consists of round pieces of painted

151
ALEXANDER CALDER
STEGOSAURUS, 1973
Ella Burr McManus Trust, Hartford

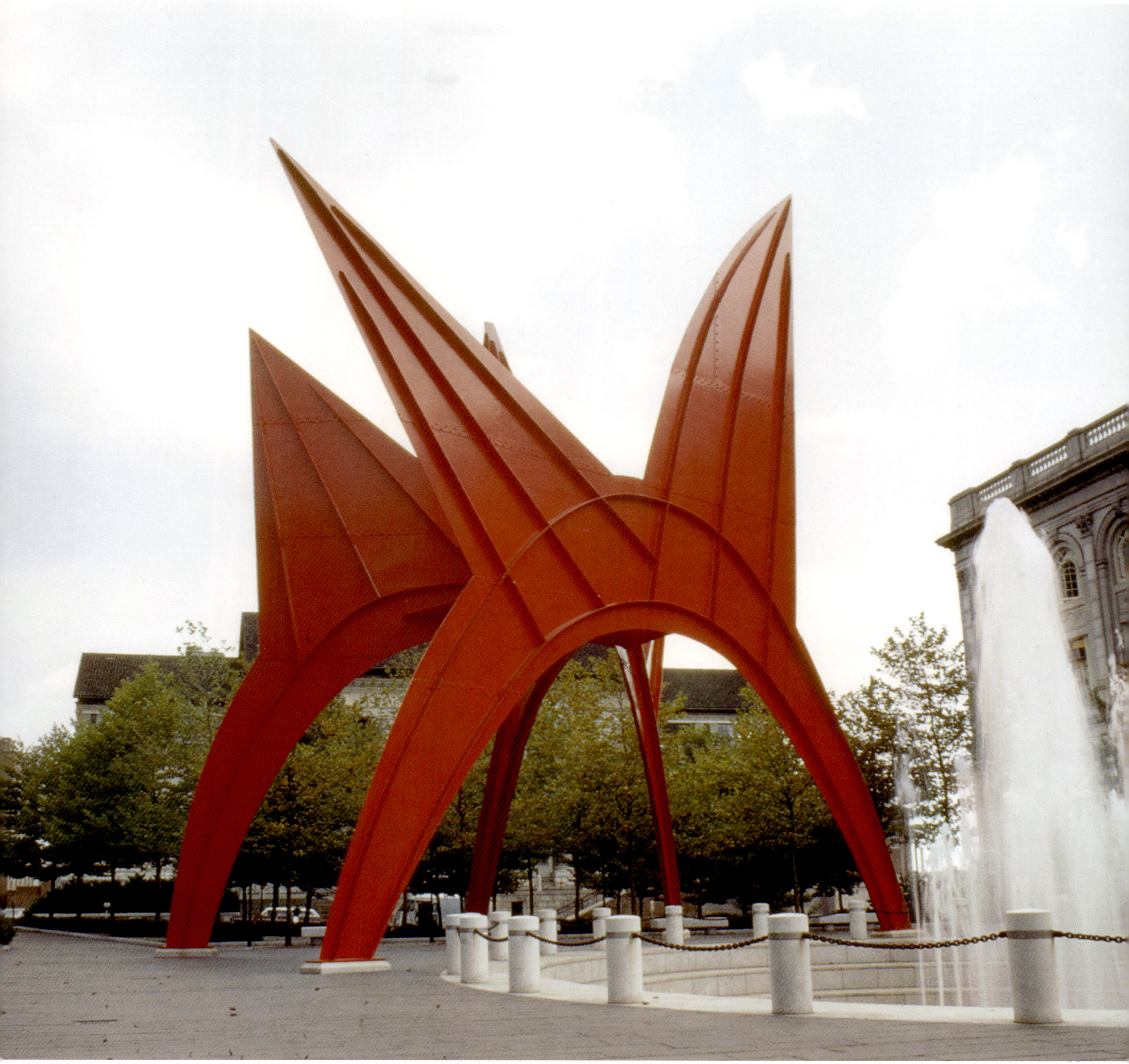

metal dangling from metal rods. The slightest wisp of air can set them in motion, sometimes swinging back and forth, sometimes bobbling like a dashboard toy. Physical movement brings the sculpture to life. A seven-foot tall *Giraffe*, 1941, features a long neck bending in the act of eating foliage from a tree; the animal itself is stationary, while the leaves are mobile. During World War II, when metal was rationed, Calder turned to found objects, using old license plates for a *Peacock* mobile and broken bits of glass and ceramic for the scales of *Fish*, 1944 (fig. 154). When displayed in a strong light, the red, yellow, and blue pieces appear to glow and cast multicolored shadows evocative of brilliantly colored fish darting through clear water.

Calder's repertoire of animals, insects, and plants fascinate and sometimes entertain viewers, and that aspect was appreciated in the context of global war, particularly during his retrospective at MoMA in late 1943. But a surprising number of his works convey a subliminal aura of menace that is not usually associated with his aesthetics. When its suspended black elements move, the enormous *Spider*, 1940 (fig. 153), can be surprisingly intimidating.

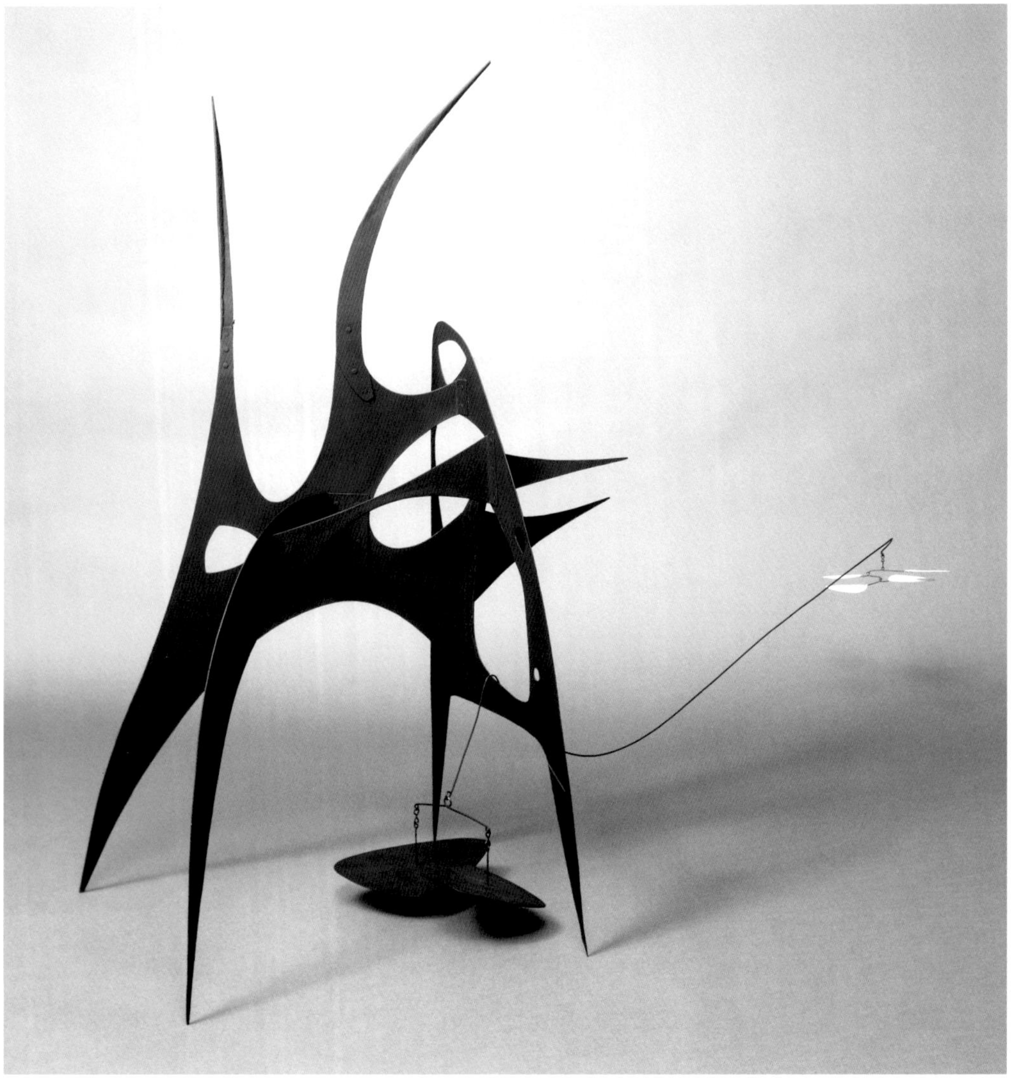

152
ALEXANDER CALDER
BAYONETS MENACING A FLOWER, 1945
Mildred Lane Kemper Art Museum, Washington University in St. Louis; University purchase, McMillan Fund

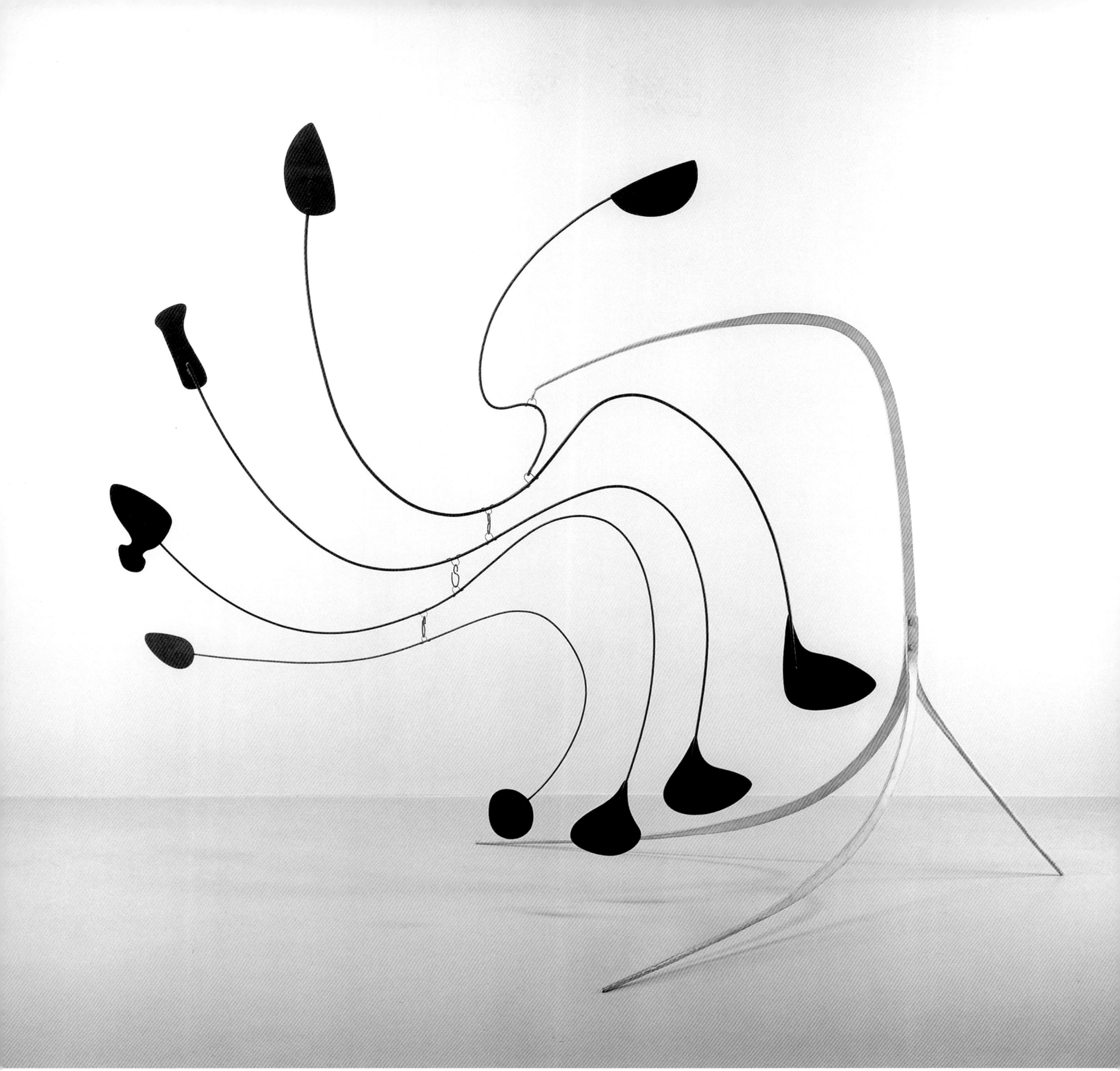

153
ALEXANDER CALDER, *THE SPIDER*, 1940
Raymond and Patsy Nasher Collection, Nasher Sculpture Center, Dallas

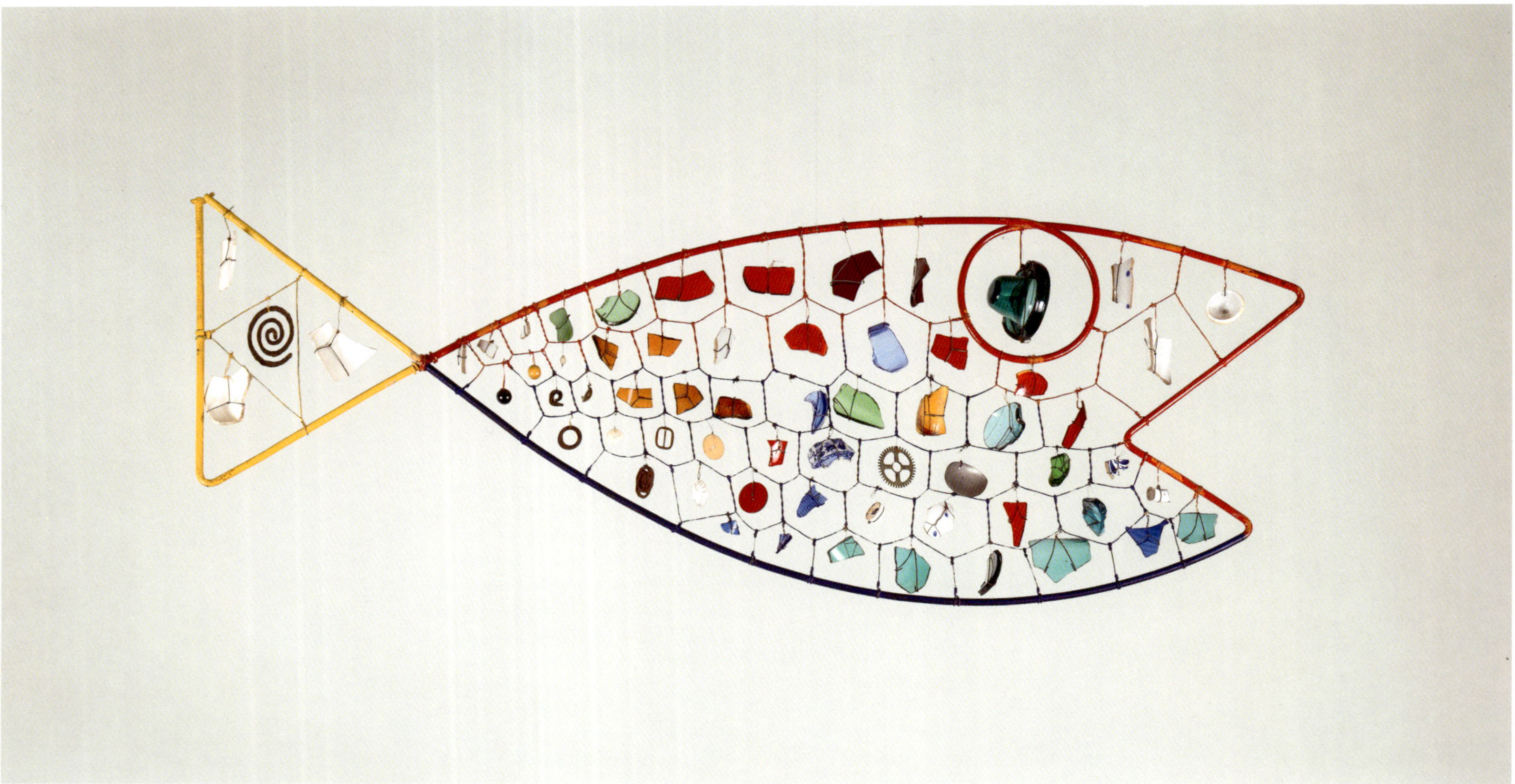

154
ALEXANDER CALDER, *FISH*, 1944
Hirshhorn Museum and Sculpture Garden, Washington, DC; gift of Joseph H. Hirshhorn

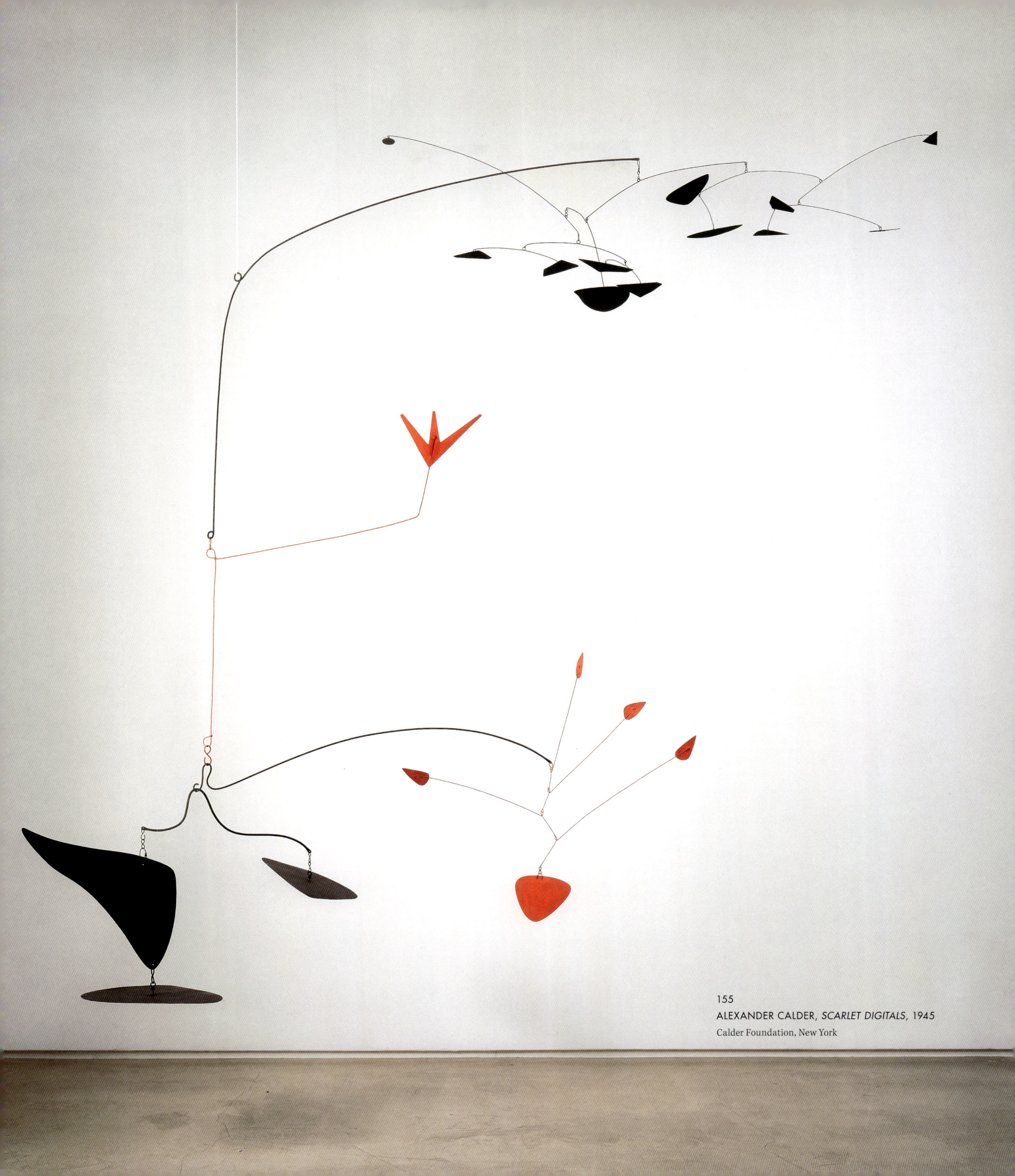

155
ALEXANDER CALDER, *SCARLET DIGITALS*, 1945
Calder Foundation, New York

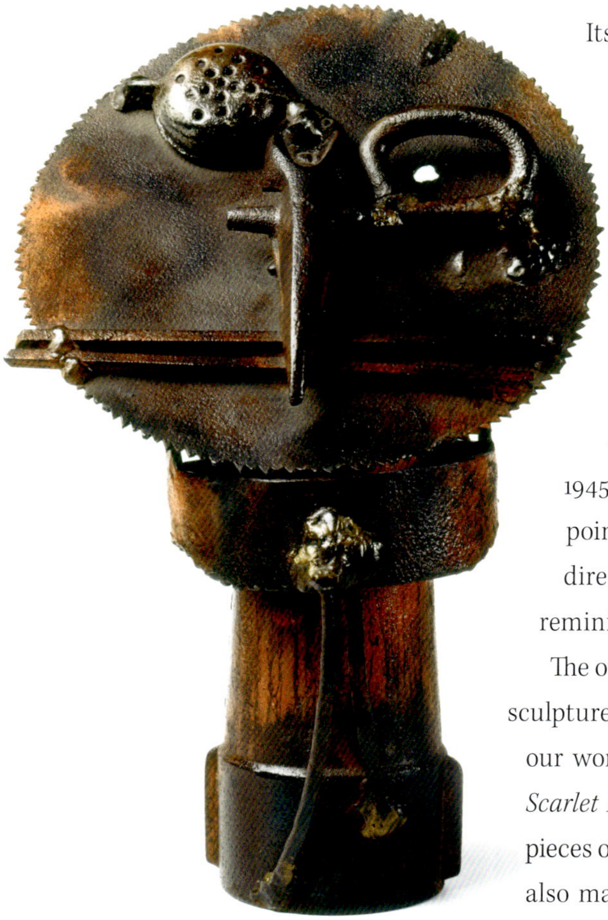

Its elements can shift unpredictably and even threaten to strike a too-curious viewer who steps within their orbit.[60] In his exhibition at the Matisse Gallery in May 1940, *Black Beast* filled one room from side to side and top to bottom; although stationary, its physical presence was almost oppressively claustrophobic. One of Calder's largest sculptures is titled *Man-Eater with Pennants*, 1945; when displayed in MoMA's garden, the staff deemed it wise to encircle the sculpture with a low perimeter marker to keep visitors from coming too close to its heavy, mobile elements. *Bayonets Menacing a Flower*, 1945 (fig. 152), is much smaller but is succinctly threatening: the sharp points of the black stabile form almost bristle with hostile energy directed at a very small white entity dangling out in space, an effect reminiscent of Giacometti's *Flower in Danger*.

The overall impression conveyed by most of Calder's Surrealist-related sculptures is playfulness, even delight at the unpredictable changes of our world and our lives. His mobiles suspended from the ceiling, like *Scarlet Digitals*, 1945 (fig. 155), have almost no mass, just small shaped pieces of painted metal, and therefore embody a physical buoyancy. They also manifest the forces of nature, notably gravity (which the mobiles seem to defy) and propulsion. Wind and drafts of air set the components in motion (Calder designed several indoor works to hang from the vents in walls). Their varied sizes and shapes entail different amounts of resistance, resulting in seemingly random speeds and orbits—an excellent visual analogy for the dynamism of nature, from fragile flower petals to tempestuous storms, from the inner workings of our busy minds to the vast paths of stars and planets in the outer cosmos. Calder's fusion of form and meaning, abstraction and representation, philosophy and humor, is perhaps his greatest legacy to the history of modern sculpture.

156
DAVID SMITH
SAW HEAD, 1933
The Estate of David Smith, New York

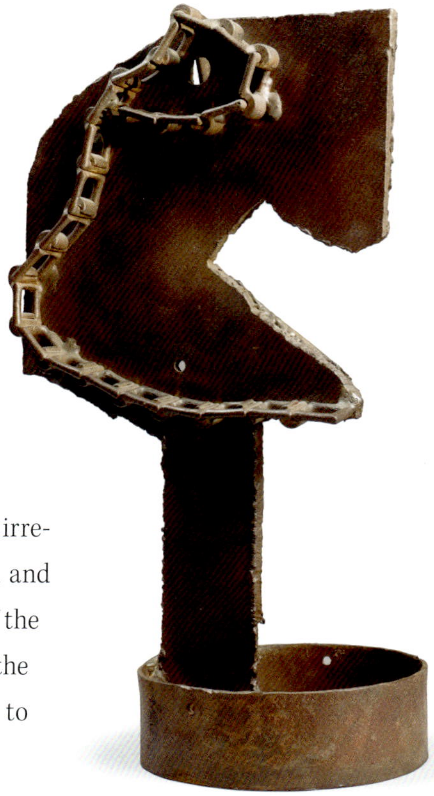

157
DAVID SMITH
CHAIN HEAD, 1933
The Estate of David Smith, New York

Meanwhile, during the same period of time from 1932 through the late 1940s, Smith pursued his independent, and often solitary, exploration of Surrealist ideas, methods, and styles. Unlike the irrepressibly humorous Calder, Smith's personality was more introverted and intellectual. The Surrealist fascination with the mysterious recesses of the unconscious appealed to his analytical mind. Yet Smith was among the first of his generation to use found objects and to expand selections to

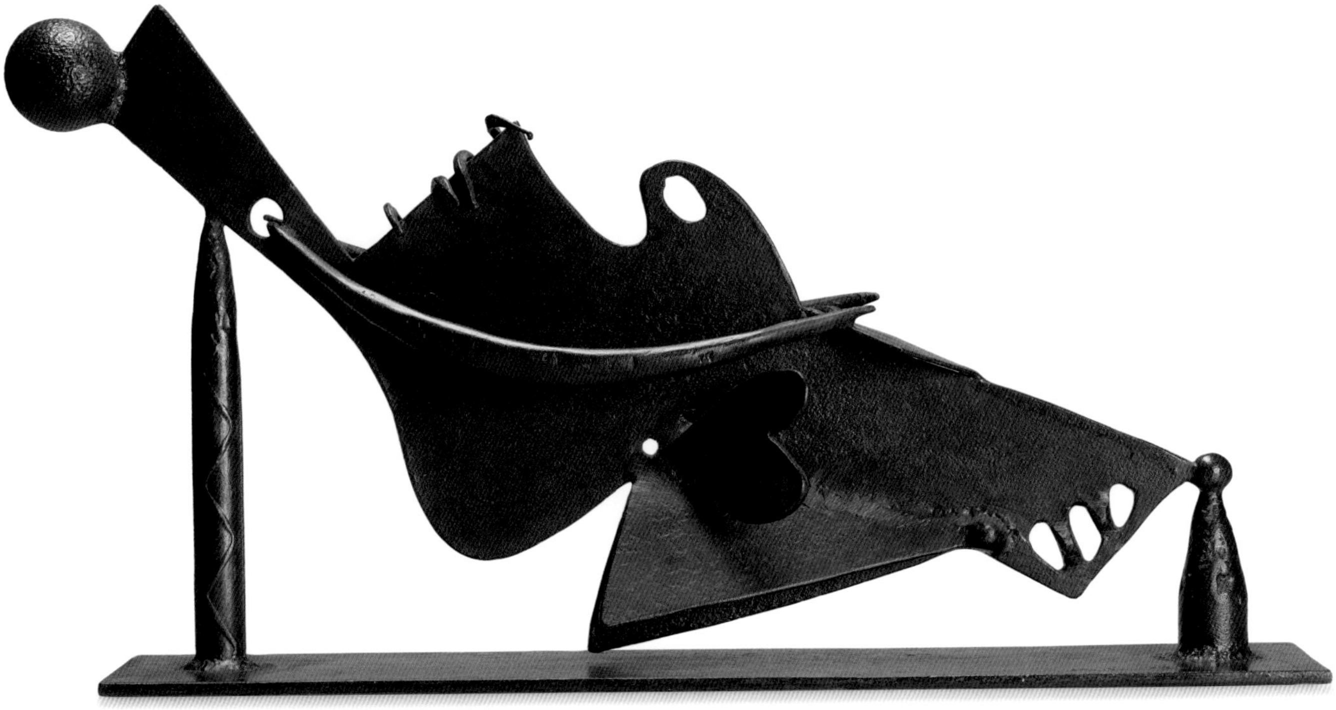

include industrial items, particularly those related to his professional work as a welder. That experience imbued the artist with an awareness of his country's role as the global leader of manufacturing, which depended on the hard physical labor of thousands of men. Smith appreciated the strength of iron and steel, and knew how to use them as the structural skeletons of his sculptures from the mid-1930s to the 1960s. The catalyst for him to apply these thoughts and methods to art were illustrations of post-Cubist welded metal constructions by Picasso and Julio González, which were illustrated in art periodicals in the early 1930s. Picasso incorporated metal utensils in some works, such as a colander to represent a figure's head, while González had the technical skill to assemble more abstract and minimalist compositions. Smith proclaimed his affinity for this new direction by incorporating tools and metal remnants into three works in 1933: *Agricola Head*, *Saw Head*, and *Chain Head* (figs. 156–157). The sculptor wrote in his notebook several years later: "the objects I had worked with in the factory [gears, cross-members, brackets] were abstract. They were always functional pieces, having relationships, but were not objects of realism."[61]

158
DAVID SMITH
RECLINING CONSTRUCTION, 1936
Yale University Art Gallery, New Haven; gift of Caral and M. J. Lebworth, B.A. 1948

Picasso's biomorphic paintings and drawings from 1926 through 1932 also intrigued Smith, particularly sketches related to the series of *Projects for a Monument*, 1928–29 (which Smith knew from photographs in *Cahiers d'art*).[62] Their puffy yet bony forms, surging with an Arpian sense of vitality, appear to rise, fall, and twist in a shallow space. Smith experimented with biomorphic forms in combination with open metal structures in a series of *Reclining Figure* sculptures from 1931 through 1937. An early one is rugged and raw in appearance; the iron elements have rough edges and are twisted as much as welded.

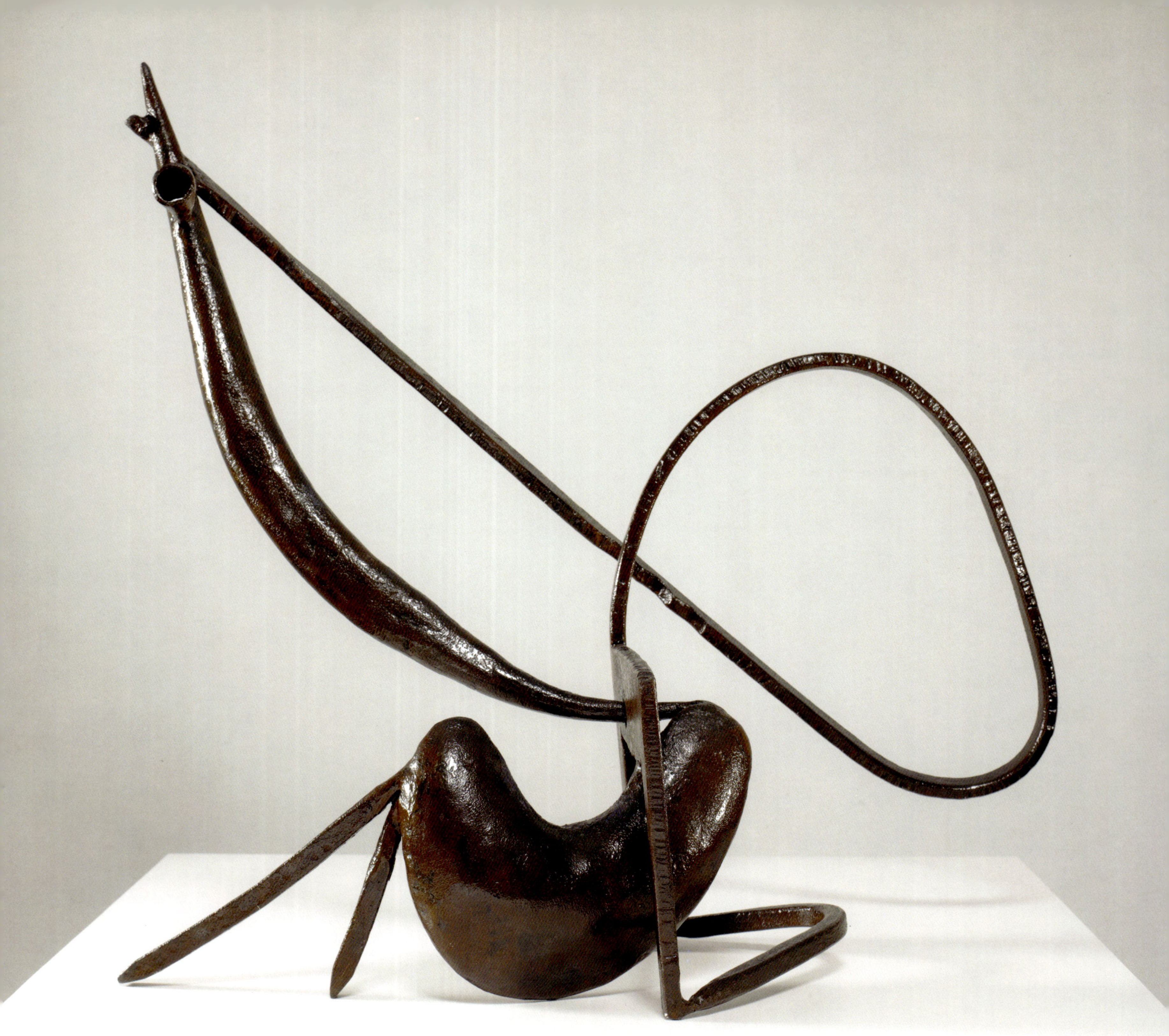

159
DAVID SMITH, *SWUNG FORMS*, 1937
The Estate of David Smith, New York

By 1935–36, the sculptor had developed a more integrated and intricate style. The sinuous linear components of *Suspended Figure*, 1935, define a figure with almost no mass. Although the pose refers to Giacometti's *Woman with Her Throat Cut*, the overall impression is one of dynamic elegance. *Reclining Construction*, 1936 (fig. 158), has it all. The recognizable figure is defined in purely abstract terms; the body's organic planar forms originate in the raised spherical head and flow downward in waves, like water over unseen boulders. The energy is akin to the works of Arp and Moore, but in Smith's own idiom. It is tempting to consider his *Swung Forms*, 1937 (fig. 159), as a virtuosic riposte to Moore's *Two Forms*, which was shown in the *Fantastic Art* exhibition in late 1936 and then acquired for MoMA's collection. As a viewer walks around *Swung Forms*, the kidney-shaped mass resembles a reclining figure leaning on one elbow, then an amorphous infant resting comfortably in a sling, and finally, a taut form caught in the middle of three precariously tilted rods. The metamorphoses are visually sophisticated and subliminally suggestive. In that sense the sculpture parallels the biomorphic paintings of contemporaneous Americans like Gorky and Mark Rothko.

Smith, who read about the theories postulated by Freud and Carl Jung, wanted to portray the mind's hidden recesses in his sculptures from 1944 through the mid-1950s. He recognized the potential of certain Surrealist innovations, particularly sculptures as conceptual landscape and as metaphors for memories and emotions. As World War II came to an end and Smith no longer needed to work in a locomotive factory, he suddenly produced more works

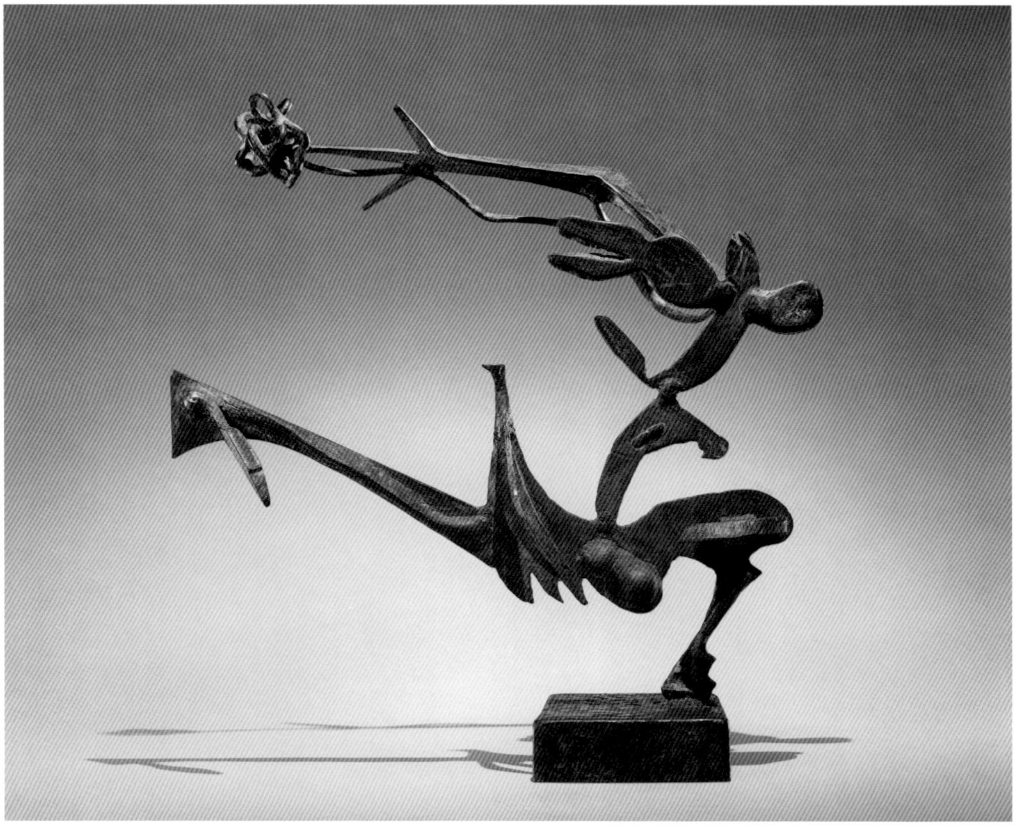

160
DAVID SMITH
SPECTRE RIDING A HEADLESS HORSE, 1951–52
Hirshhorn Museum and Sculpture Garden, Washington, DC; gift of Joseph H. Hirshhorn

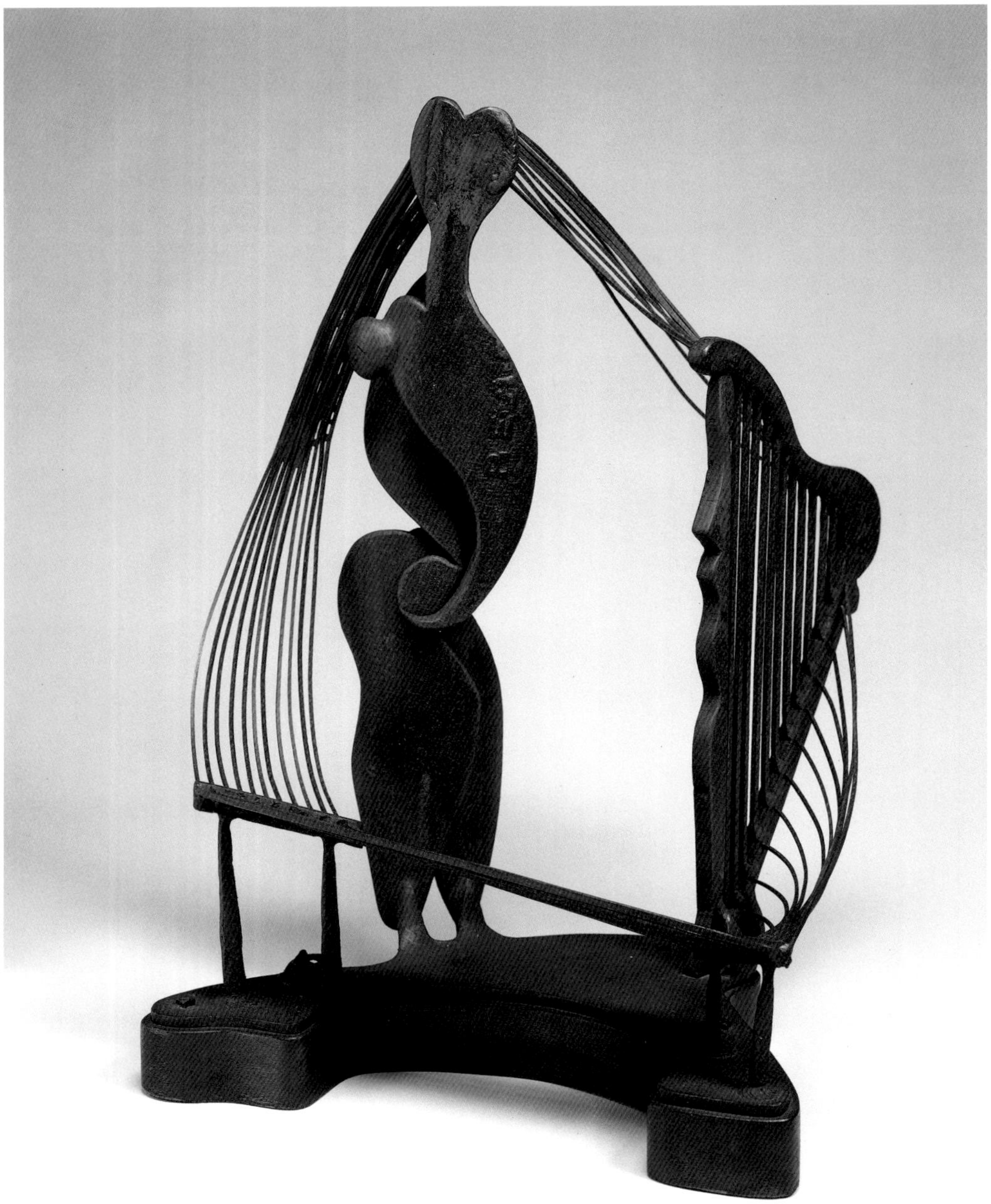

161
DAVID SMITH, *ANCIENT HOUSEHOLD*, 1945
Hirshhorn Museum and Sculpture Garden, Washington, DC; gift of the Joseph H. Hirshhorn Foundation and Lily Harmon

162
DAVID SMITH, *AGRICOLA I*, 1951–52
Hirshhorn Museum and Sculpture Garden, Washington, DC; gift of Joseph H. Hirshhorn

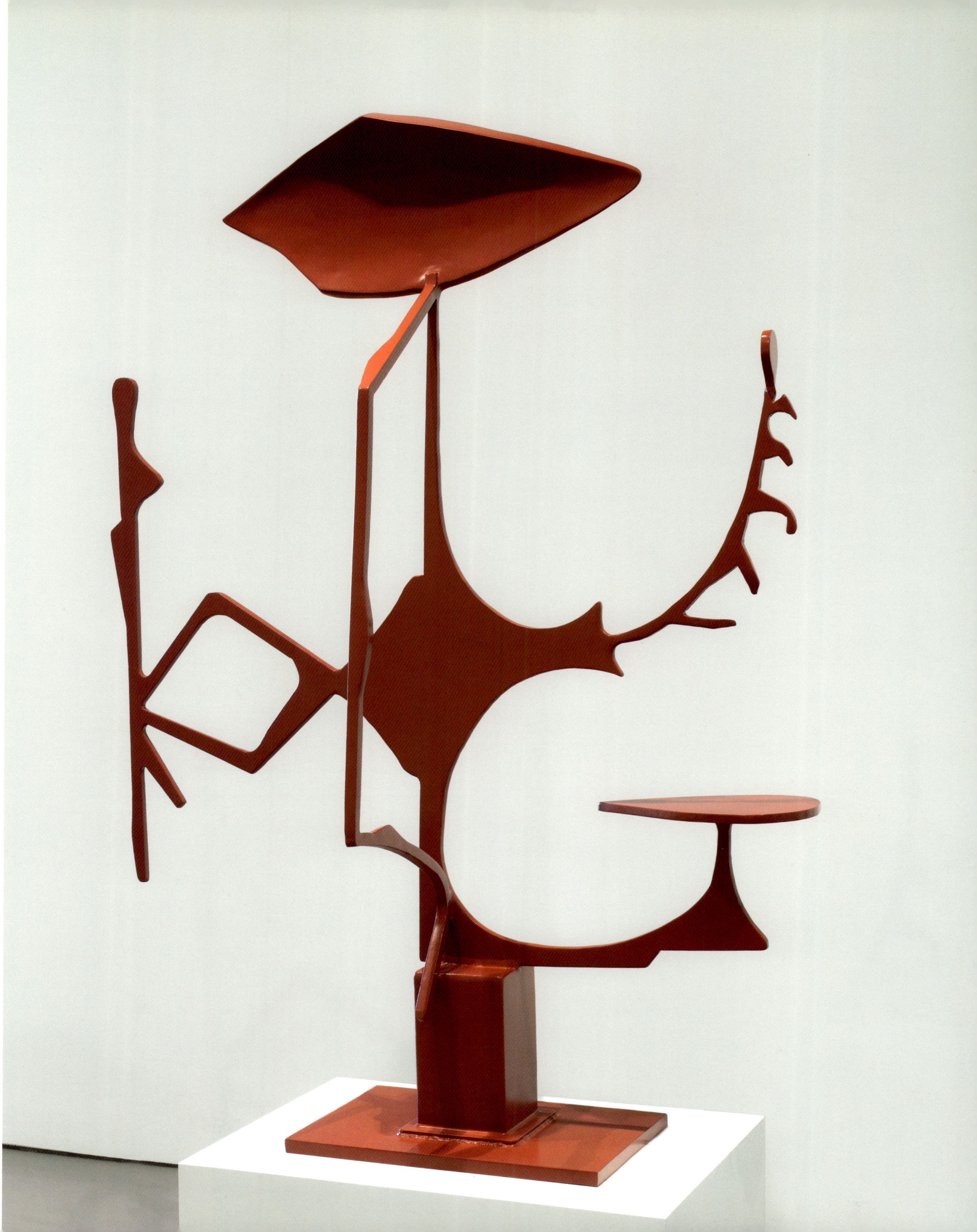

in 1945 than in any other year of his life. Biomorphism melded with mythic and nightmarish subjects. The head of *Ring-Toothed Woman* is a large mouth opened to reveal a circle of sharp teeth—defining her as a dangerous and powerful threat. The motif also refers to the Freudian "vagina dentata" that threatens to castrate and emasculate. All that in a figure less than eight inches tall.

Many of Smith's compositions of the late 1940s express his sense of self and his emotions, from a barely suppressed fury to occasional whimsy. In the spirit of Giacometti's architectonic and autobiographical *The Palace at 4 a.m.* (which was often on view at MoMA), Smith created personal metaphors in *Objects Left at the Terminal Iron Works*, 1940, and *Home of the Welder*, 1945. Whereas Giacometti's *Cage* represents an internalized conflict, Smith externalized it in the pointed, thorny body of *Aggressive Character*, 1947. *Family Decision*, 1951–52, made while Smith and his wife, the sculptor Dorothy Dehner, separated and divorced, presents an internal landscape where the small components have a niggling or chattering repetition equivalent to the artist's description of the biomorphic forms in his drawings, such as *Study for "Question and Answer,"* 1951: "Sometimes [drawings] are atmospheres from which sculptural form is unconsciously selected.... Then again, they may be amorphous floating direct statements in which I am the subject."[63]

Birds serve as metaphors for escape, freedom, and even aggression in sculptures such as *Pillar of Sunday*, 1945, and *Cockfight*, 1945. Smith ventured into the realm of ancient prehistory and mythic ancestry in *Jurassic Bird*, 1945, and *Royal Bird*, 1947–48. The surprising athleticism of his birds would re-emerge and become more geometric and abstract in the *Raven* series of 1955–60. In a series of landscape sculptures begun in 1946, the artist used organic shapes (both linear and solid) to refer to nature. *Hudson River Landscape*, 1951, depicts a scene viewed through a window, a vista of syncopated hills across the river from Smith's home. Even the cosmos was not beyond his reach, as he demonstrated in the vectors of *Star Cage*, 1950.

Ancient Household, 1945 (fig. 161), conveys an impression of grandeur despite the genre subject of a woman with a harp. The figure's curvaceous body is a metal remnant from a factory's trash; vestiges of raised lettering cover her torso like clothing. Her flowing tresses morph into the harp's strings; the industrial strength of the iron rods—shaped through heat and force—express power. Female presence and feminine wiles, mythic narrative, music, aesthetic beauty, and industrial might all co-exist in one sculpture. This multiplicity of meanings and visual sophistication are the hallmarks of Smith's greatest sculptures of the postwar years.

The Surrealist enthusiasm for dreams, especially nightmares, echoed faintly in Smith's series of six sculptures called *Spectres*, 1944–46, and in another series made five years later. *Spectre Riding a Headless Horse*, 1951–52 (fig. 160), draws upon the American mythic folk tale of the headless horseman of Sleepy Hollow. The artist used exaggerated asymmetry and forms to depict conceptual speed and frenetic movement, rather than the story itself. In fact, the

163
SEYMOUR LIPTON
IMPRISONED FIGURE, 1948
The Museum of Modern Art, New York; gift of the artist

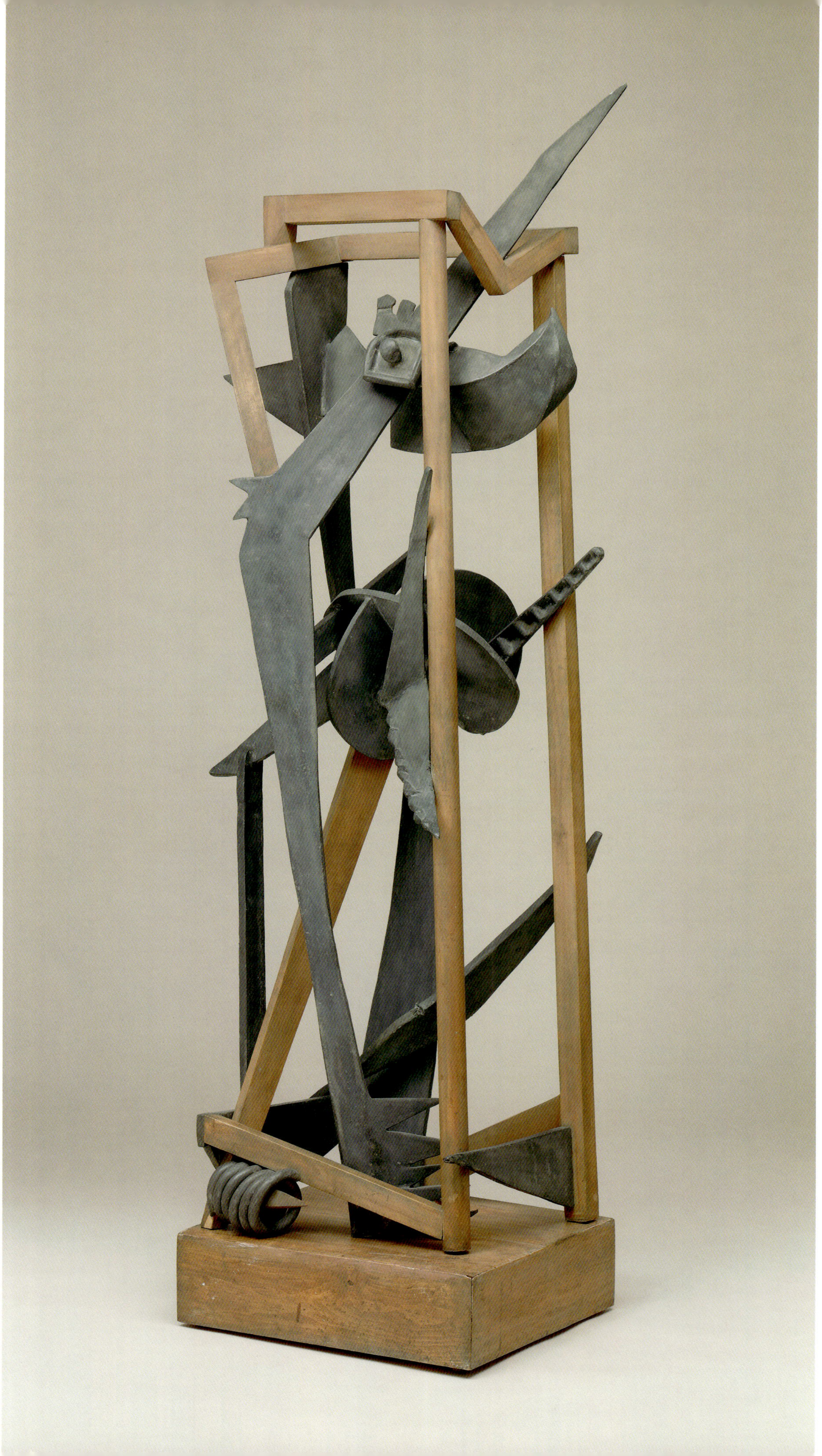

ghost in Smith's sculpture faces one way while the head (which is also partly decapitated) rushes in the opposite direction, perhaps an analogy for the artist's state of mind or an ironic criticism of contemporary political events.

Smith made the transition to larger scale and greater abstraction in totemic figures alluding to Freudian and Jungian archetypes in 1951–52, notably *The Hero* and the first of the *Agricola* series (fig. 162). He chose the title—*agricola* is the Latin word for farmer—because he was inspired by dismantled machine parts from local farms. In *Agricola I* the figure appears to stand above the horizontal seat of his tractor while also holding an implement of some sort. Smith described the components as "machine parts, dismantled tools, and forged steel rod" and wrote this thought on a preliminary drawing: "With time and the passing of their function and a separation of their parts, a metamorphic change can take place, permitting a new unity."[64] By using found objects, Smith incorporated the mundane world into his sculpture, yet ultimately he transformed his sources into a new artistic reality, where memories of labor, functionality, and purpose underlie the formal beauty.

EPILOGUE

Having risen phoenix-like from the ashes of World War I, Surrealism declined and expired in the aftermath of World War II. The refugees returned to Paris, where Breton and Duchamp organized the *Surrealism in 1947* exhibition at the Galerie Maeght. This remarkable show featured assemblages by new recruits, notably Victor Brauner's *Wolf-Table* and Wifredo Lam's altar for *Falmer's Hair*. The installation was once again conceived as an immersive environment with dramatic lighting, and Frederick Kiesler illusionistically transformed the staircase into a giant stack of books. But no revolutionary movement can remain vital forever.

The postwar generation of sculptors in the United States drew upon Surrealist precedents as they established a new aesthetic of constructed metal sculptures. Arp's lighthearted biomorphs gave birth to Theodore Roszak's creepy *Spectre of Kitty Hawk*, 1946–47. Giacometti's *Cage* gave rise to Seymour Lipton's *Imprisoned Figure*, 1948 (fig. 163), where the internal forms are larger, bolder, and more aggressive.

During the 1960s biological and morphing forms grew to monumental proportions, from Lee Bontecou's mysteriously intimidating reliefs to Magdalena Abakanowicz's woven bulbous shapes, which silently voiced her resistance to the rigid regimentation of the Soviet regime in Poland. More recently, Ernesto Neto has presented bulging and swooping fabric forms that fill large galleries and envelop viewers in a womb-like setting. Mona Hatoum's *Entrails Carpet*, 1995, has come a long way from the tumescent penis in Arp's *Clock* and the poop in Dalí's *Object Functioning Symbolically*. Angelika Arendt and Julie Brookner continue to push organic forms and living transformations in new directions.

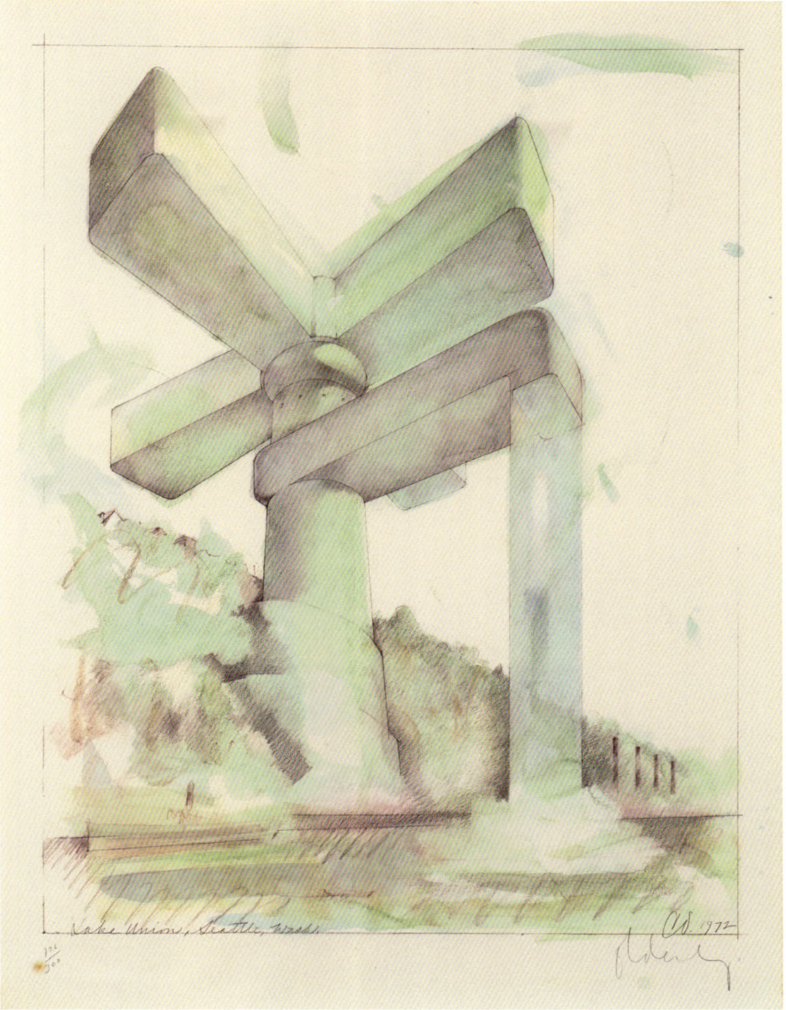

164
CLAES OLDENBURG
PROPOSAL FOR A CATHEDRAL IN THE FORM OF A COLOSSAL FAUCET, 1972
Hirshhorn Museum and Sculpture Garden, Washington, DC; the Joseph H. Hirshhorn Bequest

The Surrealists' fascination with ordinary objects as a means of accessing the marvelous has too many progeny to list. Notable examples from the era of Pop art in the 1960s and 1970s include Claes Oldenburg's melting *7-Up* and droopy *Soft Bathtub*, and especially his visionary conceptions for fantastic monuments, from the straightforward *Clothespin* to the *Proposal for a Cathedral in the Form of a Colossal Faucet*, 1972 (fig. 164). Henry's wrapped violin reverberates in Arman's burnt one in *To Hell with Paganini*, 1966. Juxtaposition became the principle underlying Arman's *Accumulations* and Robert Rauschenberg's *Combines.* In a more serious tone than Dalí's *Venus de Milo with Drawers*, Michelangelo Pistoletto's *Venus of the Rags*, 1967, juxtaposes a white plaster cast of the goddess of love with dirty old clothes as a metaphor for high art in a low art reality, for wealthy culture up against a wall of poverty. The cars buried nose-first into the ground in *Cadillac Ranch*, 1974, in Texas recall Dalí's suggestion in 1931: "Let some huge motorcars, three times as big as actual ones, be made in plaster or onyx with a thoroughness of detail . . . let them be wrapped in women's underwear and buried in a graveyard, the spot being indicated merely by a thin yellow-colored clock."

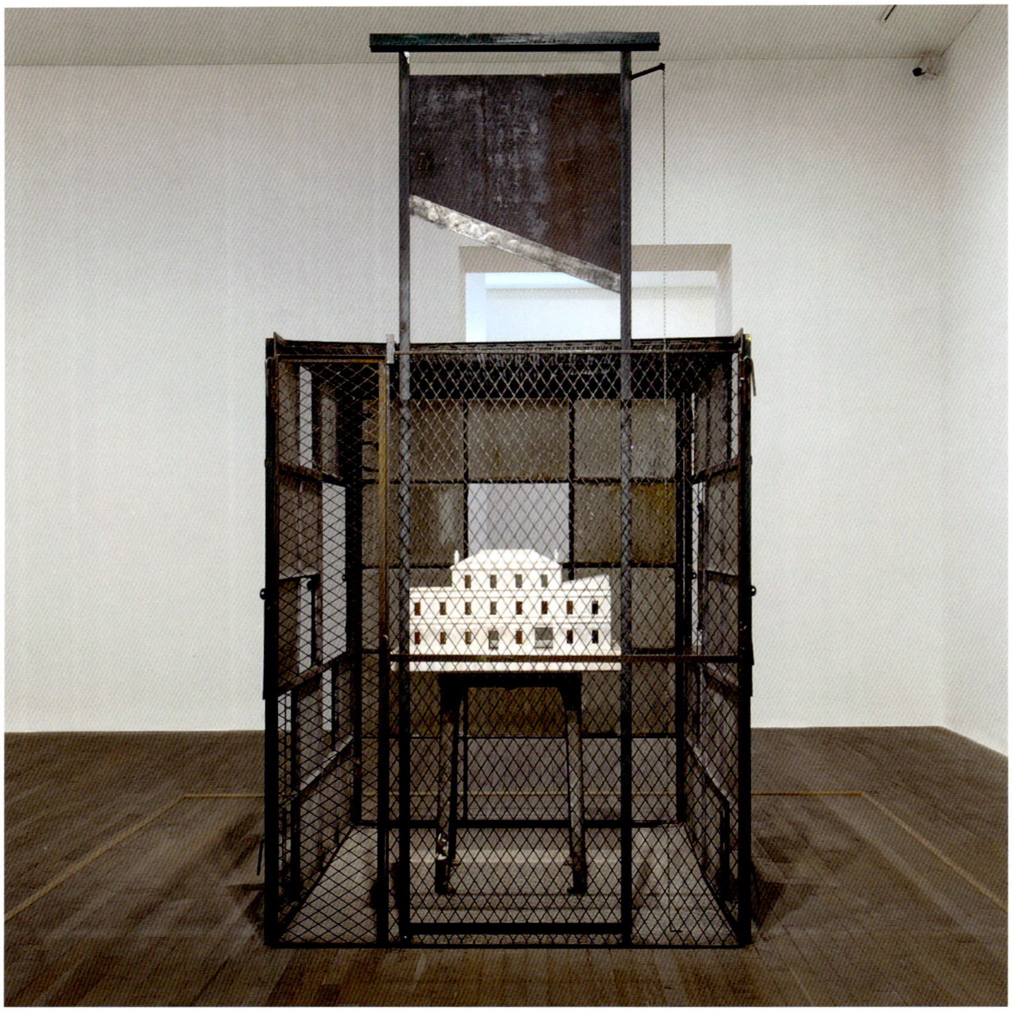

165
LOUISE BOURGEOIS
CELL (CHOISY), 1990–93
Courtesy the Easton Foundation, New York

Since the 1980s many artists have created object assemblages for loftier purposes; Yinka Shonibare, for example, repudiates the global dominance of European imperialist culture in his *Age of Enlightenment*, 2008. New generations of sculptors readily fabricate magical installations using almost anything. Tim Hawkinson assembled a chair, turntable, and an adding machine into a metaphor for the depersonalization of self. Cildo Meireles has used coins, lightbulbs, bullets, bones, and candles for his evocative installations. Do Ho Suh's *Karma*, 2003, shows dozens of tiny toy figures massed under a giant boot. Tara Donovan built a solid cube from thousands of straight pins that hold together without adhesives and a stunningly beautiful biomorphic ceiling from styrofoam coffee cups.

As for the chauvinistic attitude of Surrealist men and their obsession with genitalia, women responded with feminist critiques ranging from ironic humor to frustrated fury. During the 1960s Yayoi Kusama covered chairs, sofas, ironing boards, baby carriages, and even a rowboat, with hundreds of stuffed-fabric penises, often in shiny silver or girlish pink. Perhaps more than any other artist of the late twentieth century, Louise Bourgeois pursued psychoanalytic self-discovery and cathartic release from memories of her childhood by means of her darkly visionary sculptures. Before coming to New York in late 1938, she had lived in her family's chateau and then in Paris (above Breton's Gradiva bookshop, of all places), where she witnessed the Surrealists' exhibitions. Decades later she still simmered with resentment at the 1938 extravaganza of mannequins and female furniture. When she started making sculptures in the late 1940s, they bore titles like *Dagger Child*, *The Observer*, and *Persistent Antagonism*. In 1968 she impaled an enormous wax penis on a meat hook, calling it *Little Girl*, and she excoriated her domineering parent in *Destruction of the Father*, 1974. Her later series of room-sized *Cell* sculptures express her inner reality of feeling profoundly haunted by her life experiences and are nearly always centered on the idea of imprisonment. *Cell (Choisy)*, 1990–93 (fig. 165), centers on a model of her childhood home behind a full-sized guillotine, a powerful metaphor for the danger of revisiting the past.

Today, in the post-modern era of irony and cynicism, the Surrealists' desire for experiencing the marvelous has been dismissed as hopelessly naïve. But not so fast: every generation yearns to escape into another reality and to experience thrilling moments of surprise and discovery. Arp's anthropomorphic flowers, Dalí's fixation on aphrodisiacs, Giacometti's nightmares of rape and murder, Ernst's *Lunar Asparagus*, Cornell's imagined travels to the great cities of Europe, Noguchi's eerily glowing embryo in a cage—are they really so different in spirit from the fantasies of virtual reality?

NOTES

1 André Breton, *Manifesto of Surrealism* (Paris, 1924), in Breton, *Manifestoes of Surrealism,* trans. Richard Seaver and Helen R. Lane (Ann Arbor, 1969), 3, 15–16, 18, 39.

2 Experiencing the marvelous is stated as the Surrealists' ultimate goal in numerous publications of the time, including Nancy Cunard's "Beginning of the Surrealist Movement" in *Outlook* (May 1927), Breton's novel *Nadja* (1928), and Aragon's text for *Challenge to Painting* (1930). Alberto Giacometti wrote passionately: "I search, groping, to catch hold of the invisible white thread of the Marvelous that vibrates in the void; from it escape facts and dreams with the sound of a stream running over small, precious, living pebbles. It gives life to life.... All life [is] in the marvelous sphere that envelops us." Giacometti, "Charbon d'herbe," *Le Surréalisme au service de la révolution*, no. 5 (May 15, 1933): 15. Trans. by the author.

3 Breton, *Introduction to the Discourse on the Paucity of Reality* (Paris, 1924). Breton suggested that "one should manufacture some of the articles one meets only in dreams, articles which are as hard to justify on the grounds of utility as on that of pleasure." He envisioned a book with pages made of black wool and a cover bearing a statuette of a gnome with a white Assyrian beard. "I want to have a few articles of the same kind made, as their effect would be distinctly puzzling and disturbing."

4 Breton, *Manifesto of Surrealism*, 10.

5 Many of Sigmund Freud's writings from 1905 through 1918 were translated into French and published after the war, starting in 1920 with *Three Essays on the Theory of Sexuality*, followed by *Psychoanalysis*, *Introduction to Psychoanalysis*, and *Psychoanalysis and Occultism* in 1921. *The Psychoanalytic Method* and *Psychopathology in Daily Life* were published in 1922, followed by *Totem and Taboo* in 1923, *Collective Psychology and Self-Analysis* in 1924, and *The Interpretation of Dreams* in 1925.

6 Isidore Ducasse (a.k.a. the Count of Lautréamont), *Les Chants de Maldoror* (Paris, 1869).

7 Louis Aragon, "Manifesto of the Dada Movement," *Littérature* 2, no. 13 (May 1920): 1; trans. in Dawn Ades, ed., *The Dada Reader: A Critical Anthology* (Chicago, 2006), 181.

8 Max Ernst, "Beyond Painting," in *Max Ernst: Oeuvres de 1919 à 1936*, (Paris, 1937): 13–46. Trans. by the author.

9 When this work was published and exhibited in New York and Paris prior to 1945, the title was simply *Why Not Sneeze?* See catalogue for the 1936 show at Galerie Ratton and the 1938 *Abridged Dictionary of Surrealism*. *Why Not Sneeze?* was first exhibited at the Levy Gallery in 1932, four years before it was shown in Paris.

10 Breton, *Les Pas Perdus* (Paris, 1924), trans. as "Wandering Footsteps," *This Quarter* 5, no. 1 (September 1932); later retranslated as "The Lost Steps." See also Julien Levy, *Memoir of an Art Gallery* (New York, 1977), 83.

11 See Jean Arp, *On My Way* (New York, 1948). See also *Jean Arp, Arp on Arp: Poems, Essays, Memories*, ed. Marcel Jean (New York, 1972), 327; translation revised by the author.

12 Margherita Andreotti, *The Early Sculpture of Jean Arp* (Ann Arbor, 1989) has documented the earliest date for any reliefs as November 1916. Arp said his new style began in 1917, and several were shown in the 1918 exhibition *Die Neue Kunst* in September 1918. Bernd Rau, *Jean Arp: The Reliefs, Catalogue of Complete Works* (New York, 1981), provides data on which reliefs were exhibited during the 1920s and 1930s. More data, compiled largely by Greta Ströh and Walburga Krupp, remains unpublished in the archives of the Stiftung Arp in Berlin. Establishing precise dates for works is sometimes complicated because Arp later replicated some and repainted many.

13 Marcel Duchamp, "Jean (Hans) Arp," in *Collection of the Société Anonyme: Museum of Modern Art 1920* (New Haven, 1950), 69.

14 Arp, "It Will Turn into a Head," (1922); trans. in *Arp on Arp*, 12.

15 Arp, "The Navel Bottle," (1948); trans. in *Arp on Arp*, 239.

16 Ernst planned to incorporate sculptures into an inspirational *Monument to Birds*. He showed several studies for it in his exhibitions at the Galerie Van Leer in March 1926 and at the Galerie Georges Bernheim in December 1928.

17 At the time Arp's influence on Miró was taken for granted by such critics as Christian Zervos. Jacques Dupin (Miró's friend, biographer, and compiler of his catalogue raisonné), confirmed that Arp influenced Miró, rather than vice-versa as is usually assumed (conversation with the author, May 1989).

18 See "Second Manifesto of Surrealism" (1930); trans in Breton, *Manifestoes of Surrealism*, 112–94.

19 Although *Suspended Ball* has long been dated to 1930, most scholars now accept the date as 1930–31 (also for *The Cage* and *The Hour of Footprints*). *Miró–Arp–Giacometti* had no catalogue or surviving checklist (my thanks to Véronique Wiesinger, former director of the Fondation Alberto and Annette Giacometti, for this information). *Suspended Ball* was first illustrated as *Object* in *Le Surréalisme au service de la révolution*, no. 3 (December 1931): 39. In other publications of the early 1930s, the work was sometimes misidentified as *The Hour of Footprints*.

20 Salvador Dalí, "Objets Surréalistes" (Surrealist Objects), *Le Surréalisme au service de la révolution*, no. 3 (December 1931): 16–17; trans. in Haim Finkelstein, ed., *The Collected Writings of Salvador Dalí* (Cambridge, 1998), 231–32. Breton's assemblage still exists but is rarely seen; although its nuanced textures and colors are visually fascinating, the sequence of actions and their symbolic functions are impossible to understand without the explanation in Dalí's essay.

21 *Personage with Umbrella* was originally untitled; when illustrated in *Le Surréalisme au service de la révolution*, no. 3 (December 1931): 38, the caption was simply *Sculpture*.

22 Dalí, "The Object as Revealed in Surrealist Experiment," *This Quarter* 5, no. 1 (September 1932): 197–207. See also Dalí, "Surrealist Objects."

23 See Olivier Bernier, *Fireworks at Dusk: Paris in the Thirties* (New York, 1993). At the Bal Onirique bon voyage party for Dalí in New York prior to his departure for Paris in January 1935, guests came dressed as dreams. Dalí wore a glass window on his shirt, and Gala Eluard wore a red cellophane dress and a lobster-and-doll hat. Dickran Tashjian, *A Boatload of Madmen: Surrealism and the American Avant-Garde 1920–1950* (New York, 1995), 54.

24 A few weeks before the exhibition opened, there was a special issue of *Le Surréalisme au service de la révolution* (May 15, 1933). It includes Dalí's barely comprehensible essay "Psycho-Atmospheric-Anamorphic Objects" and a peculiar text "About the Experience Relevant to the Irrational Knowledge of Objects" by Maurice Henry. Even Giacometti, who was not much interested in found objects, accepted the term "object" as meaning "Surrealist sculpture." Referring to *The Palace at 4 a.m.* and *The Hour of Footprints,* he wrote in *Minotaure* (December 1933), "Once the object has been constructed, I tend to find in it, transformed and shifted, images and impressions and facts that have moved me deeply (often unknown to me)."

25 For information on the *Miró: Sculptures-Objects* exhibition, see *Cahiers d'art,* nos. 9–10. In the Galerie Ratton exhibition in 1936 Miró showed sculptures from 1932 because his most recent assemblages were still in Spain. *Object* was taken by Pierre Matisse and shown in MoMA's *Fantastic Art* exhibition. Breton acquired *L'Objet du Couchant* in late 1936 or early 1937; it was shown in the 1938 group exhibition at the Galerie des Beaux-Arts.

26 Miró, letter to Pierre Matisse, September 28, 1936, in Margit Rowell, ed., *Joan Miró: Selected Writings and Interviews* (Boston, 1986), 125.

27 Although a date of 1923 is sometimes given for the first version of this composition, it is very unlikely. The checklist for the group exhibition at Galerie Pierre Colle in 1933 lists the work as *Eye-Metronome,* 1932, which corresponds with the end of Man Ray's affair with photographer Lee Miller. When Ray recreated the work for an exhibition at the Levy Gallery in 1945, he called it *Object to Be Destroyed*; in another exhibition in Los Angeles in 1946 he called it *Last Object.* The two titles most often used now are *Object to Be Destroyed* and *Indestructible Object*, which are teasingly antithetical.

28 Giacometti added the subtitle *Hands Holding the Void* in the early 1950s, when his art was affiliated with the existentialist philosophy defined by Jean-Paul Sartre. "Void" was Sartre's term for the vast metaphysical abyss in which we exist and struggle to find meaning.

29 The jacket was illustrated and described in *Cahiers d'art,* nos. 1–2 (1936), a special issue published in conjunction with the exhibition at Galerie Ratton. The issue includes essays on "the object": Breton's "Crisis of the Object," Claude Cahun's "Beware of Domestic Objects," Dalí's "Honor to the Object!," and Zervos's "Mathematical, Natural, Savage, Found, Irrational, Readymade, Interpreted, Incorporated, Moving Objects." Illustrations include works by Hans Bellmer, Jacqueline Breton, Alexander Calder, Dalí, Oscar Dominguez, Ernst, Giacometti, Georges Hugnet, Miró, Meret Oppenheim, Wolfgang Paalen, Roland Penrose, and a now-lost installation *Stairway to Psyche's Love* by Gala Eluard.

30 See Adina Kamien-Kazhdan, "Duchamp, Man Ray, and Replication," in Germano Celant, ed., *The Small Utopia: Ars Multiplicata* (Milan, 2012), 97–113. Information on the refabrications of Surrealist sculptures is dispersed in monographs or remains unpublished, as is the case with Stephanie d'Alessandro's documentation on Dalí's *Venus de Milo with Drawers* at the Art Institute of Chicago.

31 According to Robert Descharnes in *The World of Salvador Dalí* (New York, 1962), the artist probably acquired the cast in November or December 1935, then in January 1936 marked it with a pencil to indicate where the drawers should go. He entrusted it to Duchamp, who took it to a plaster specialist for implementation. *Venus de Milo with Drawers* was not included in the Galerie Ratton exhibition in 1936, but it could be seen in Dalí's home from mid-June 1936 to February 1939, when he left for New York.

32 British object-oriented artists showed their mettle in the *Surrealist Objects and Poems* exhibition at the London Gallery in November 1937; very few works from the show survive. For illustrations and information, see Michel Remy, *Surrealism*

in Britain (London, 2001), Paul Ray, *The Surrealist Movement in England* (Ithaca and London, 1971), as well as *Britain* (London, 2001), as well as installation photographs by Penrose and others in the Tate Archive, London.

33 Photographs of Ernst's river stones were published in *Cahiers d'art* 11, nos. 6–7 (1936). During the 1930s Ernst was renowned for collecting and using objects, but most of those assemblages did not survive. An unsigned review of *Surrealist Paintings by Max Ernst,* an exhibition at the Mayor Gallery in London in 1937, noted that "in Paris, American art students [have] made pilgrimages to the Surrealist studios [and] found the terrace garden of Max Ernst's studio littered with seashells, objects in plaster and wood, bristled over with safety pins." The writer further stated that the artist was "famed for his objects," including one made for the front window of the Mayor Gallery in London: "a table laid with bottle, plate, knife, and fork" suspended from the ceiling because the two rear legs of the table had been cut off and attached to the top of the table. As "a supreme surrealist touch, the stool in front of the table was covered with bits of broken glass." Published in *Cavalcade*, June 12, 1937, clipping in Mayor Gallery archive, London. The review also mentions an assemblage that Ernst made during a recent trip to the United States: "a fantastic and useless group of cork legs, safety pins, and fishing flies."

34 A photo of Giacometti's *Three Figures in a Field* is published in *Minotaure* 1, nos. 3–4 (December 1933). See *L'Atelier d'Alberto Giacometti* (Paris, 2007), 101. In the early 1970s, when *Lunar Asparagus* was made into an edition of bronzes, only two were painted white to replicate the original's ghostly character; the others have a dark patina that lends a more ominous aura.

35 Jennifer Mundy, "Comment on England," in Christopher Stephens, ed., *Henry Moore* (London, 2010), 32.

36 Henry Moore, 1934, cited in Philip James, ed., *Henry Moore on Sculpture* (London, 1966), 72, and Moore, 1937, cited in Alan Wilkinson, ed., *Henry Moore: Writings and Conversations* (Aldershot, 2002), 197.

37 Moore, cited in Christa Lichtenstern, "Henry Moore and Surrealism," *The Burlington Magazine* 123, no. 944 (November 1981): 644–58.

38 Grigson, "Mysticism, Sculpture, and Machine Guns," *Bookman* (May 1934) and "Comment on England," *Axis* no. 1 (January 1935). Clippings in the Mayor Gallery and Tate Archive, London. Excerpts from the latter can be found in Mundy, "Comment on England," 22. The critic's interest was so piqued that he tried to visit Arp during a trip to Paris in 1934.

39 A critic disliked the undercurrent of unease in several drawings, remarking that "There is usually something indefinably sinister.... Sometimes, too, Mr. Moore invents figures that seem to be a monstrous progeny of a skeleton and a bidet." *New Statesman*, February 18, 1939; clipping in Mayor Gallery archive, London.

40 Giacometti, "Hier, Sables Mouvants" (Yesterday, Quicksand), *Le Surréalisme au service de la révolution*, no. 5 (May 15, 1933): 45.

41 Bellmer, *The Doll* (1934), trans. and cited in Peter Webb and Robert Short, *Hans Bellmer* (London, 1985), 29.

42 Herbert Lust, "For Women Are Endless Forms: Hans Bellmer's Dark Art," in *Hans Bellmer* (New York, 1990), 13–16, provides a compelling interpretation of Bellmer's *Doll* as an "anxiety object." Lust points out that Eluard persuaded the photographer to omit his most disturbingly sexualized images from the book: "Eluard's gentler, sunnier nature reined in Bellmer's violent despair, making [*The Doll's Games*] more balanced and universal."

43 For further information, see Lewis Kachur, *Displaying the Marvelous* (Cambridge, MA, 2001). Kachur's research showed that the Surrealists used a new, more realistic type of mannequin than had been previously available in Paris. Life-size male mannequins were available but not used; see photograph in *Documents* (1929).

44 Simone Breton, "Surrealist Text," *La Révolution surréaliste,* no. 1 (December 1, 1924): 14

45 Dalí, "Surrealist Objects," trans. and cited in Conroy Maddox, "The Object in Surrealism," *London Bulletin*, nos. 18–20 (June 1940): 43.

46 Raymond Cogniat, "Les Surréalistes exposent" (The Surrealists Exhibit), *Beaux Arts* (June 16, 1933).

47 The Giacometti exhibition attracted little critical or popular attention, and no works were sold, but Levy acquired *No More Play* for his personal collection.

48 A review in *Art Digest* (February 1, 1937) vehemently asserted that the "movement is absolutely finished in the lands of its origins" and accused MoMA's exhibition of trying to "help an outlived... movement...to perpetuate itself and to survive transplanted to another country."

49 Objects reproduced in the book include a relief and sculpture by Arp; Duchamp's *Why Not Sneeze?*; Giacometti's *Palace at 4 a.m.* and *No More Play*; Oppenheim's *Object*; Dalí's *Aphrodisiac Jacket*; a mobile by Calder; and Cornell's *Soap Bubble Set*.

50 Notably Tanguy in *View* (May 1942) and Ernst in *VVV* (June 1942).

51 An exhibition review in the *New York Sun* (December 3, 1932) described Cornell's simple assemblages in glass domes as having "a mesmeric air. They are almost perfect ornaments for a small table in the waiting-room of an astrologist, a palmist or a mind-reader." Cited in Deborah Solomon, *Utopia Parkway: The Life and Work of Joseph Cornell* (New York, 1997), 67–68.

52 Cornell, letter to Alfred Barr, November 13, 1936. Archives of the Museum of Modern Art, New York. Cited in Solomon, *Utopia Parkway*, 84. Levy voiced his opinion in *Memoirs of an Art Gallery*.

53 Cited in Solomon, *Utopia Parkway*, 92.

54 The *Dream of Venus* was one of many temporary structures in the 1939 World's Fair, where the theme was "The World of Tomorrow." Most pavilions offered optimistic promises of a better life to come, ranging from new domestic appliances to the concept model for an interstate highway system. See Eric Schaal's color photographs in Ingrid Schaffner, *Salvador Dalí's Dream of Venus: The Surrealist Funhouse from the 1939 World's Fair* (New York, 2002).

55 During his life, Noguchi acknowledged being inspired by Constantin Brancusi, Buckminster Fuller, Calder, and Gorky, but repudiated any affinities with Tanguy. The denial stemmed from the bitter humiliation he experienced in 1946 when the Museum of Modern Art refused to acquire *Kouros*—one of Noguchi's greatest biomorphic sculptures—because their curator considered it derivative of Tanguy's paintings. See Sam Hunter, *Noguchi* (New York, 1978), 83, and Dore Ashton, *Noguchi East and West* (New York, 1992), 71–73.

56 Noguchi, letter to the Hirshhorn Museum, August 1972. Archives of the Hirshhorn Museum and Sculpture Garden, Washington, DC.

57 Noguchi, "Interview with Katharine Kuh" (1962), cited in Diane Apostolos-Cappadona and Bruce Altshuler, eds., *Isamu Noguchi: Essays and Conversations* (New York, 1994), 131.

58 Ibid.

59 Unsigned, "Genius in Wire," *New Review*, December 1937; clipping in Mayor Gallery archive. An installation photograph shows the upper portion of *Devil Fish* and part of *Tightrope*.

60 *The Spider* was displayed in the *First Papers of Surrealism* exhibition in late 1942 as an alternative to Duchamp's original proposal to hang Calder's mobiles from the *Miles of String* installation. which Breton vetoed because it went too far with Duchamp's intention to frustrate visitors and to obscure the works of art.

61 Smith, c. 1938, Notebook 4 (Smith Papers, Archives of American Art); cited in Miranda McClintic, *David Smith: The Hirshhorn Museum and Sculpture Garden Collection* (Washington, DC, 1979), 22.

62 *Cahiers d'art* 4, nos. 8–9 (1929). Smith cut out these images to study them more closely over time; they remain among his papers in the Archives of American Art.

63 Smith, lecture in Portland, Oregon (March 23, 1953); transcription in Smith Papers IV, Archives of American Art, cited in McClintic, *David Smith*, 22.

64 Ibid.

it will turn into a head

the sphinxes carefully stick their noses out of the bark
for mister thread is bringing the rope
and mister rope is bringing the thread
to tie up the bag filled with obelisk butterflies

the bones in the stones grow faster and faster
in the foundation the kisses are festering
the sky revolves like an umbrella in the wind
the vases sigh like diamonds

if you sew a cackling bouquet on this happy holiday
it will turn into a head
that instantly looks at itself in a mirror
and wonders: is that me or isn't that me

the gloves ask themselves the very same thing
when their comfortable tongues recite the following litany
go up and push down
go down and push up
go forward and push back
go back and push forward
go right and push left
go left and push right

that's why it would be best to take down the mast-hats
the inner neckties
and the celibacy eggs from the thousandth floors
and to put them back on the table of creation
to ask the laurel-covered little quarter-hours to sit down on their
ephemeral chairs
to arrange the ephemeral chairs and the table of creation rigorously
in the shape of an interim pretzel
and then to discharge oneself of one's shoes as quickly as possible
and to leave the rest of the final eel that incorporates the gratis rural
policeman.

JEAN ARP

(1922)

U N T I T L E D

the medal rises while the sun after fifty years of service retires into the calcined wheels of the light.

it was a man who replaced alarm clocks with earthquakes, showers of rice with downpours of hail. the shadow of a man encountering the shadow of a fly causes a flood. and it was a man who taught the horses to embrace like presidents. with his eleven and a half tails man counts ten and a half objects in the furnished room of the universe: the scarecrows wearing volcanoes and geysers in their buttonholes, the show windows of eruptions, the displays of lava-string, the systems of solar currency, the labeled stomachs, the walls razed by poets, the palettes of the caesars, the stock-still lifes, the stables of the sphinxes, and the eye of the man who turned to stone while squinting at sodom.

enter the continents without knocking but with a filigree muzzle.

leaves never grow on trees, like a mountain in a bird's-eye view they have no perspective. the onlooker is always in the wrong vis-à-vis a leaf. as for branches trunks and roots i declare that they are bald men's lies. like a lion ferociously sniffing a succulent young married couple the lime tree grows docilely on the boarded plains. the start of the chestnut tree and the oak tree is signaled by the lowered flag. the cypress is not a shank of a eucharistic ballet.

harnessed four abreast before the four preceding ones, like cemeteries for ventriloquists or fields of honor, the insects come out. here is eve, the only one still left. she is the white accomplice of the newspaper robbers, here is the cuckoo, the origin of the clock, the noise of its jaws is like the noise of heavily falling hair. thus one includes among the insects vaccinated bread, the chorus of cells, the lightning under fourteen years of age, and your humble servant.

the sky of the seascapes was decorated by expressionist upholsterers who hung up a shawl of frost flowers. during the harvest of conjugal diamonds one meets on the seas immense mirrored wardrobes floating on their backs. the mirror is replaced by waxed floors and the wardrobe itself by castles in the air. these mirrored wardrobes hire themselves out as boxing rings to midwives and storks for their countless rounds or as stools to gigantic rusty feet which rest on them and sometimes take a few steps on them, pampam. that's why the seas are called pampas because pam means pace and two paces are pampam.

thus you see that one doesn't consume one's pater except slice by slice, it's impossible to do it in a single picnic and even the lemon falls to its knees before the beauty of nature.

(1925)

UNTITLED

but what will replace it

the wings drop from the summit of the table
like leaves of earth
before the lips
it is night in the wings
and between the wings the chanting chains are missing

the skeleton of the light empties the fruits

the body of the kisses will never awaken
it was never real
the sea of the wings cradles that tear
the bell speaks with the head
and the fingers lead us across the fields of the air
toward the nests of the eyes
there the names melt

but what will replace it
in the height of the skies
neither sleeping nor waking
for the tombs are brighter than the days

(1929)

UNTITLED

the kings groom the forests brandish the intoxicated birds and ride to
the thermal baths on their iron canes
the growing beasts dance on glass buskins
the tree trunks custom-make their own birds
the flagellated birds lose all their blood in the colonnade

the whips crack and the well-groomed shadows of the shepherds come
down from the mountains
the black eggs and the jesters' bells drop from the trees
the storms and the bass drums and the smaller drums gush out of the
donkeys' ears
the wings graze the flowers
the wells stir in the eyes of the boars

(1930)

From *Arp on Arp: Poems, Essays, Memories*, Marcel Jean, ed.; trans. Joachim Neugroschel (New York: Viking Press, 1972), 12–13; 23–24; 39; 43.

ANDRÉ BRETON

MANIFESTO OF SURREALISM

(excerpts)

So strong is the belief in life, in what is most fragile in life—*real* life, I mean—that in the end this belief is lost. Man, that inveterate dreamer, daily more discontent with his destiny, has trouble assessing the objects he has been led to use, objects that his nonchalance has brought his way, or that he has earned through his own efforts . . . all he can do is turn back toward his childhood which . . . still strikes him as somehow charming. There, the absence of any known restrictions allows him the perspective of several lives lived at once; this illusion becomes firmly rooted within him; now he is only interested in the fleeting, the extreme facility of everything. Children set off each day without a worry in the world.

But it is true that we would not dare venture so far. . . . Threat is piled upon threat, one yields, abandons a portion of the terrain to be conquered. This imagination which knows no bounds is henceforth allowed to be exercised only in strict accordance with the laws of an arbitrary utility; it is incapable of assuming this inferior role for very long and, in the vicinity of the twentieth year, generally prefers to abandon man to his lusterless fate.

Though he may later try to pull himself together on occasion, having felt that he is losing by slow degrees all reason for living, incapable as he has become of being able to rise to some exceptional situation such as love, he will hardly succeed. This is because he henceforth belongs body and soul to an imperative practical necessity which demands his constant attention. None of his gestures will be expansive, none of his ideas generous or far-reaching. In his mind's eye, events real or imagined will be seen only as they relate to a welter of similar events. . . .

Beloved imagination, what I most like in you is your unsparing quality.

There remains madness. . . . The insane . . . are, to some degree, victims of their imagination, in that it induces them not to pay attention to certain rules—outside of which the species feels threatened—which we are all supposed to know and respect . . . . They derive a great deal of comfort and consolation from their imagination, that they enjoy their madness sufficiently to endure the thought that its validity does not extend beyond themselves. And, indeed, hallucinations, illusions, etc., are not a source of trifling pleasure. The best controlled sensuality partakes of it . . . .

It is not the fear of madness which will oblige us to leave the flag of imagination furled.

The case against the realistic attitude demands to be examined, following the case against the materialistic attitude. . . . The realistic attitude, inspired by positivism . . . seems to me to be hostile to any intellectual or moral advancement. I loathe it, for it is made up of mediocrity, hate, and dull conceit. It is this attitude which today gives birth to these ridiculous books, these insulting plays. It constantly feeds on and derives strength from the newspapers and stultifies both science and art by assiduously flattering the lowest of tastes; clarity bordering on stupidity, a dog's life. The activity of the best minds feels the effects of it; the law of the lowest common denominator finally prevails upon them . . . .

We are still living under the reign of logic: this, of course, is what I have been driving at. But in this day and age logical methods are applicable only to solving problems of secondary interest. The absolute rationalism that is still in vogue allows us to consider only facts relating directly to our experience. . . . Under the pretense of civilization and progress, we have managed to banish from the mind everything that may rightly or wrongly be termed superstition, or fancy; forbidden is any kind of search for truth which is not in conformance with accepted practices. It was, apparently, by pure chance that a part of our mental world which we pretended not to be concerned with any longer—and, in my opinion by far the most important part—has been brought back to light. For this we must give thanks to the discoveries of Sigmund Freud . . . as he will henceforth be not to confine himself solely to the most summary realities. The imagination is perhaps on the point of reasserting itself, of reclaiming its rights. If the depths of our mind contain within it strange forces capable of augmenting those on the surface, or of waging a victorious battle against them, there is every reason to seize them—first to seize them, then, if need be, to submit them to the control of our reason.

Freud very rightly brought his critical faculties to bear upon the dream . . . this considerable portion of psychic activity . . . has still today been so grossly neglected. I have always been amazed at the way an ordinary observer lends so much more credence and attaches so much more importance to waking events than to those occurring in dreams. It is because man, when he ceases to sleep, is above all the plaything of his memory, and in its normal state memory takes pleasure in weakly retracing for him the circumstances of the dream, in stripping it of any real importance . . . . Thus the dream finds itself reduced to a mere parenthesis, as is the night. And, like the night, dreams generally contribute little to furthering our understanding. This curious state of affairs seems to me to call for certain reflections:

> . . . Dreams give every evidence of being continuous and show signs of organization. Memory alone arrogates to itself the right to excerpt from dreams . . . (Account must be taken of the *depth* of the dream. For the most part I retain only what I can glean from its most superficial layers. What I most enjoy contemplating about a dream is everything that sinks back below the surface in a waking state, everything I have forgotten about my activities in the course of the preceding day, dark foliage, stupid branches. . . . I would like to sleep, in order to surrender myself to the dreamers . . . why should I not grant to dreams . . . this value of certainty in itself . . . Why should I not expect from the sign of the dream more than I expect from a degree of consciousness which is daily more acute? Can't the dream also be used in solving the fundamental questions of life?
>
> . . . The mind of the man who dreams is fully satisfied by what happens to him. The agonizing question of possibility is no longer pertinent. Kill, fly faster, love to your heart's content. And if you should die, are you not certain of reawaking among the dead? Let yourself be carried along, events will not tolerate your interference. You are nameless. The ease of everything is priceless.
>
> . . . When, by means yet to be determined, we succeed in recording the contents of dreams in their entirety (and that presupposes a discipline of memory spanning generations . . . we may hope that the mysteries which really are not will give way to the great Mystery. I believe in the future resolution of these two states, dream and reality, which are seemingly so contradictory, into a kind of absolute reality, a *surreality*, if one may so speak. It is in quest of this surreality that I am going, certain not to find it but too unmindful of my death not to calculate to some slight degree the joys of its possession.
>
> . . . At this juncture, my intention was merely . . . noting the *hate of the marvelous* which rages in certain men, this absurdity beneath which they try to bury it. Let us not mince words: the marvelous is always beautiful, anything marvelous is beautiful, in fact only the marvelous is beautiful.

. . . At an early age children are weaned on the marvelous, and later on they fail to retain a sufficient virginity of mind to thoroughly enjoy fairy tales. No matter how charming they may be, a grown man would think he were reverting to childhood by nourishing himself on fairy tales, and I am the first to admit that all such tales are not suitable for him. The fabric of adorable improbabilities must be made a trifle more subtle the older we grow, and we are still at the age of waiting for this kind of spider. . . . But the faculties do not change radically.

Fear, the attraction of the unusual, chance, the taste for things extravagant are all devices which we can always call upon without fear of deception. There are fairy tales to be written for adults, fairy tales still almost blue.

The marvelous is not the same in every period of history: it partakes in some obscure way of a sort of general revelation only the fragments of which come down to us: they are the romantic *ruins,* the modern *mannequin,* or any other symbol capable of affecting the human sensibility for a period of time. In these areas which make us smile, there is still portrayed the incurable human restlessness. . .

We really live by our fantasies when we *give free reign to them.*

. . . It was a question of going back to the sources of poetic imagination and, what is more, of remaining there. Not that I pretend to have done so. It requires a great deal of fortitude to try to set up one's abode in these distant regions where everything seems at first to be so awkward and difficult, all the more so if one wants to try to take someone there. Besides, one is never sure of really being there. If one is going to all that trouble, one might as well stop off somewhere else. Be that as it may, the fact is that the way to these regions is clearly marked, and that to attain the true goal is now merely a matter of the travelers' ability to endure.

. . . In those [Dada] days, a man at least as boring as I, Pierre Reverdy, was writing [in *Nord-Sud*, March 1918], "The image is a pure *creation* of the mind. It cannot be born from a comparison but from a juxtaposition of two more or less distant realities. The more the relationship between the two juxtaposed realities is distant and true, the stronger the image will be—the greater its emotional power and poetic reality."

. . . One evening, therefore, before I fell asleep, I perceived, so clearly articulated that it was impossible to change a word, but nonetheless removed from the sound of any voice, a rather strange phrase which came to me without any apparent relationship to the events in which, my consciousness agrees, I was then involved, a phrase which seemed to me insistent, a phrase, if I may be so bold, *which was knocking at the window.* I took cursory note of it and prepared to move on when its organic character caught my attention. . . . Since that day, I have had occasion to concentrate my attention voluntarily on similar apparitions, and I know they are fully as clear as auditory phenomena. With a pencil and white sheet of paper to hand, I could easily trace their outlines. Here again it is not a matter of drawing, but *simply of tracing.* I could thus depict a tree, a wave, a musical instrument, all manner of things of which I am presently incapable of providing even the roughest sketch. I would plunge into it, convinced that I would find my way again, in a maze of lines which at first glance would seem to be going nowhere. And, upon opening my eyes, I would get the very strong impression of something "never seen."

. . . Completely occupied as I still was with Freud at that time, and familiar as I was with his methods of examination which I had some slight occasion to use on some patients during the war, I resolved to obtain from myself what we were trying to obtain from them, namely, a monologue spoken as rapidly as possible without any intervention on the part of the critical faculties, a monologue consequently unencumbered by the slightest inhibition.

. . . In homage to Guillaume Apollinaire . . . I baptized the new mode of pure expression which we had at our disposal and which we wished to pass on to our friends, by the name of SURREALISM.

. . . I am defining it once and for all:

SURREALISM, *n.* Psychic automatism in its pure state, by which one proposes to express—verbally, by means of the written word, or in any other manner—the actual functioning of thought. Dictated by the thought, in the absence of any control exercised by reason, exempt from any aesthetic or moral concern.

ENCYCLOPEDIA. *Philosophy.* Surrealism is based on the belief in the superior reality of certain forms of previously neglected associations, in the omnipotence of dream, in the disinterested play of thought. . . .

André Breton, "Manifesto of Surrealism" (Paris, 1924), in Breton, *Manifestoes of Surrealism*, trans. Richard Seaver and Helen R. Lane (Ann Arbor: University of Michigan Press, 1969), 1–47.

LES MOTS ET LES IMAGES

Un objet ne tient pas tellement à son nom qu'on ne puisse lui en trouver un autre qui lui convienne mieux :

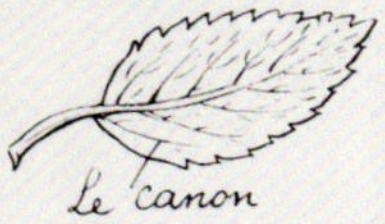

Il y a des objets qui se passent de nom :

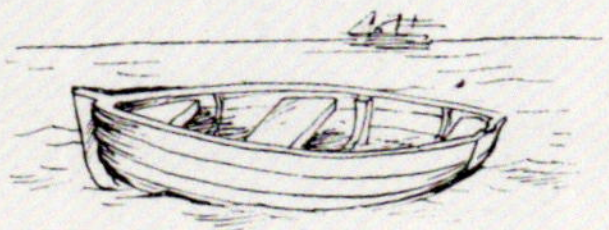

Un mot ne sert parfois qu'à se désigner soi-même :

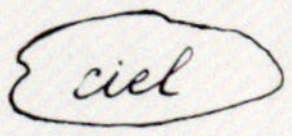

Un objet rencontre son image, un objet rencontre son nom. Il arrive que l'image et le nom de cet objet se rencontrent :

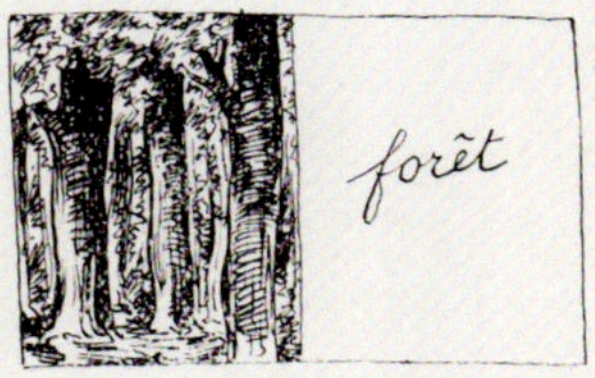

Parfois le nom d'un objet tient lieu d'une image :

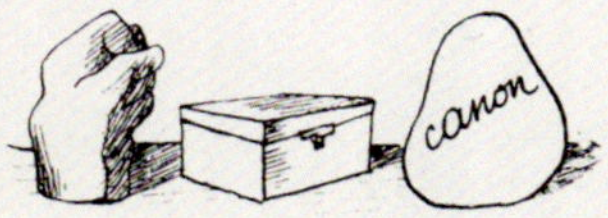

Un mot peut prendre la place d'un objet dans la réalité :

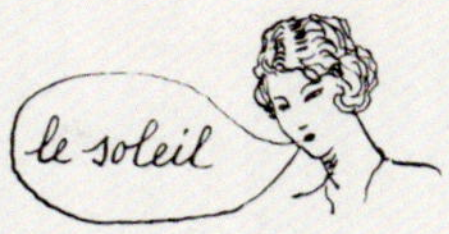

Une image peut prendre la place d'un mot dans une proposition :

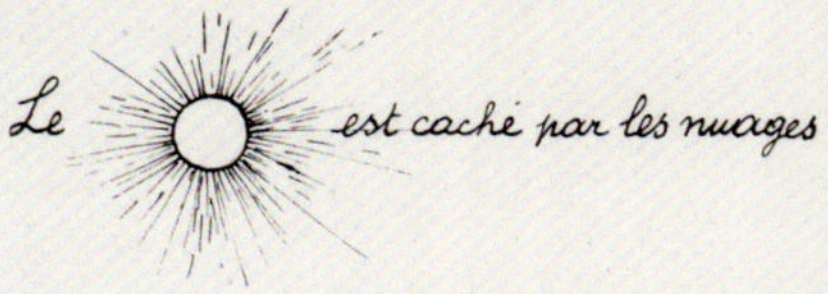

Un objet fait supposer qu'il y en a d'autres derrière lui :

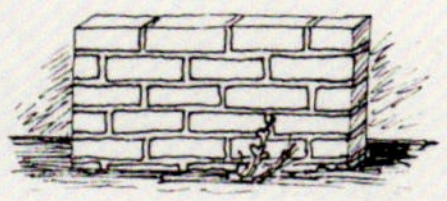

Tout tend à faire penser qu'il y a peu de relation entre un objet et ce qui le représente :

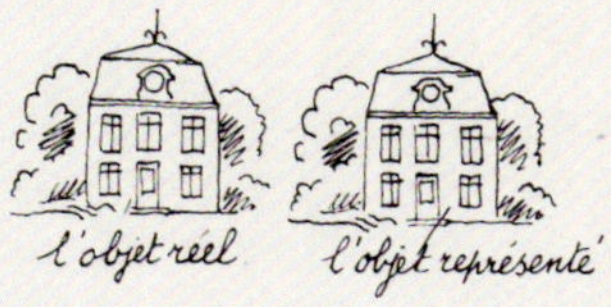

Les mots qui servent à désigner deux objets différents ne montrent pas ce qui peut séparer ces objets l'un de l'autre :

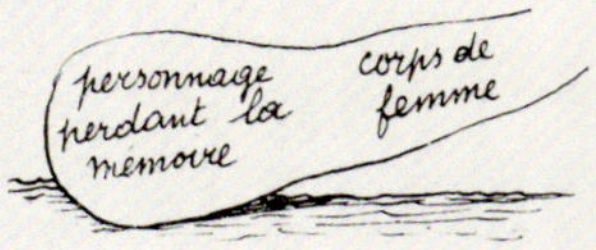

Dans un tableau, les mots sont de la même substance que les images :

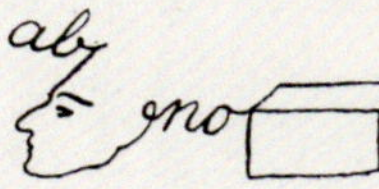

On voit autrement les images et les mots dans un tableau :

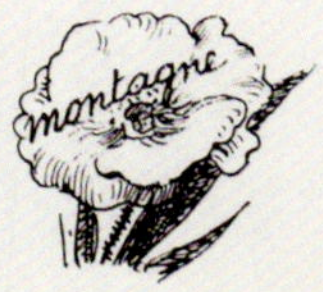

RENÉ MAGRITTE

Une forme quelconque peut remplacer l'image d'un objet :

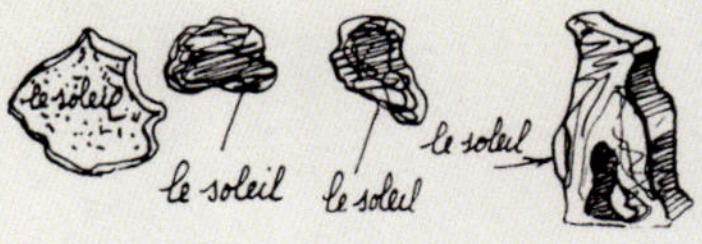

Un objet ne fait jamais le même office que son nom ou que son image :

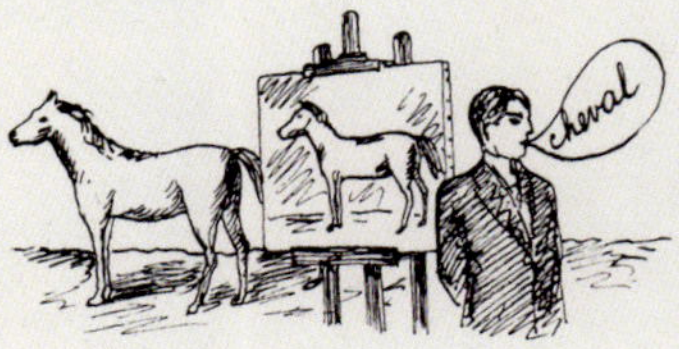

Or, les contours visibles des objets, dans la réalité, se touchent comme s'ils formaient une mosaïque :

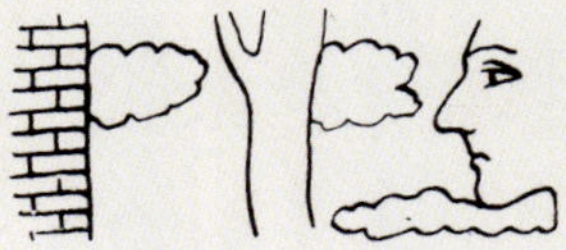

Les figures vagues ont une signification aussi nécessaire aussi parfaite que les précises :

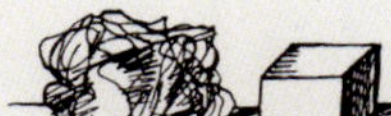

Parfois, les noms écrits dans un tableau désignent des choses précises, et les images des choses vagues :

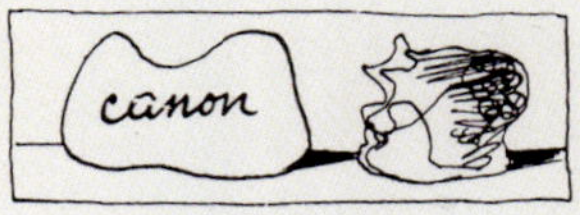

Ou bien le contraire :

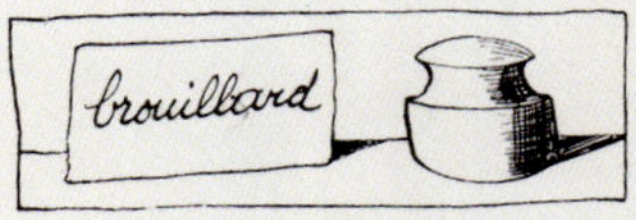

René MAGRITTE.

MONDE, SAMEDI 23 NOVEMBRE.

« Vous me demandez de participer à votre enquête sur le socialisme. Est-ce à dire que malgré tout ce qui peut nous séparer, vous me considérez comme un socialiste et non comme un social-patriote, voire comme un social-traître ? ...Marx était, malgré son génie, un homme comme un autre... Dans la Russie Soviétique, dont les conditions sociales présentent ou présenteraient des analogies saisissantes avec celles de l'Europe Occidentale de 1848... les bolcheviks ont pu emprunter à Marx, le Marx du manifeste, les formules et les mots d'ordre de leur Révolution... En attendant on voudrait croire que ce n'est pas trop demander à tous que d'essayer de se comprendre, de comprendre qu'à des milieux différents doivent correspondre fatalement des tactiques différentes et que... les travailleurs ont mieux à faire, etc. ». Qui parle? Vandervelde. Et qui lui a ouvert une tribune pour baver, faire sa propre apologie, dénigrer Marx, ignorer Lénine, et passer sous silence le roi Albert, son maître, qui tient en prison De Rosa? Barbusse, le Barbusse de *Je sais tout*, qui dirige ici le magazine *Monde*, une ordure confusionnelle, qui associe à une propagande prosoviétique dosée tout un peuple de chiens, de traîtres et de littérateurs, dont on veut nous faire croire qu'ils ont le droit d'apprécier l'œuvre de la Révolution mondiale, dont ils sont les pires ennemis.

Monde commente : *Vandervelde, auteur de plusieurs ouvrages remarquables sur le socialisme.* Remarquables? Oui, par la saloperie. Comme tout le numéro d'où ces lignes sont extraites, et où on lit encore : *« Un vol d'argenterie suivi d'une escapade à Paris, un poème philosophique qui ne vaut rien : voilà ce que la jeunesse de Saint-Just nous donne de remarquable ».* Remarquable encore cette belle petite enquête qui semble avoir été inventée pour faire aboutir Zola à l'école populiste, baptisée par le Thérive du *Temps*, jadis de *l'Action Française*. Zola dont M. Barbusse se croit propriétaire, sans doute pour ce qu'il y a de parfaitement contre-révolutionnaire chez l'auteur de *Paris*. ennemi de la violence, comme le pacifiste Barbusse, et ses collaborateurs, comme ce Bernard, que j'ai déjà entendu plusieurs fois bourdonner, qui trouve tant de talent à Cendrars (le type de *J'ai tué*, avec des réserves qui sont un bonheur : *« Cette ivresse de tuer, à laquelle il fait la part si belle, n'était-elle pas largement compensée par l'horreur du sacrifice inutile, par l'instinct de conservation?... Mais ne dramatisons pas trop ce côté de Cendrars ; il y a en lui de riches réserves humaines dont nous sommes loin encore d'avoir touché le fond ».* Cette petite annonce termine le brillant numéro que nous venons de parcourir :

Georges Danou, ami de Monde, *ingénieur-constructeur, réalise lui-même et pour vous, à des conditions tout à fait amicales, le Bien-Etre par l'Électricité, appareils médicaux, domestiques, lustrerie moderne inédite sur maquettes. Lui écrire pour rendez-vous, 11, rue Robert-Planquette, Paris* (18e).

Que voulez-vous, avec de tels *amis*, *Monde* a certainement le ton qu'il faut pour parler à un public qui cherche le Bien-Etre par l'Électricité et avec l'aide de Georges Danou et de E. Vandervelde, *Monde* collabore, c'est sûr, à l'édification du socialisme dans plusieurs pays.

ARAGON.

3

René Magritte, "Les Mots et les images" (Words and Images), *La Révolution surréaliste*, no. 12 (December 1929): 2–3.

THE OBJECT AS REVEALED IN SURREALIST EXPERIMENT

(excerpts)

The years have modified the surrealist concept of the object most instructively, showing as it were in image how the surrealist view of the possibilities of action on the external world have been and may still be subject to change. In the early experiments with poetic solicitation, automatic writing and accounts of dreams, real or imaginary articles appeared to be endowed with a real life of their own. Every object was regarded as a disturbing and arbitrary "being," and was credited with having an existence entirely independent of the experimenters' activity. . . .

The early surrealist experimenters found themselves plunged into the subterranean passages of "Revolution by Night," the passages where *The Mysteries of New York* must have just been enacted; in fact, dream passages still identifiable to-day.

[In *Wandering Footsteps* Breton recounts] *"I have in mind the occasion when Marcel Duchamp got hold of some friends to show them a cage which seemed to have no birds in it, but to be half-full of lumps of sugar. He asked them to lift the cage and they were surprised at its heaviness. What they had taken for lumps of sugar were really small lumps of marble which at great expense Duchamp had had sawn up specially for the purpose. The trick in my opinion is no worse than any other, and I would even say that it is worth nearly all the tricks of art put together."*

SALVADOR DALÍ

The semi-darkness of the first phase of surrealist experiment would disclose some headless dummies and a shape wrapped up and tied with string, the latter, being unidentifiable, having seemed very disturbing in one of Man Ray's photographs (already then this suggested other wrapped-up objects which one wanted to identify by touch but finally found could not be identified; their invention, however, came later). But how can one give the feel of the darkness which for us shrouded the whole business? Only by mentioning the way the surrealists were strongly attracted by articles shining with their own light—in short, phosphorescent articles, in the proper or improper meaning of that word. These were a paper-cutter decorated with ears of wheat, casts of naked woman hung on the walls, and T-squares and biscuits forming a Chirico 'metaphysical interior.' It is of no importance that some of these things had been covered with the luminous paint used on watch faces to make the hands and figures shine in the dark. What matters is the way in which the experiments revealed the *desire for the object,* the tangible object. This desire was to get the object at all costs out of the dark and into the light, to bear it all winking and flickering into the full daylight. That is how the *dream objects* Breton called for in his *Introduction to a Speech on the Poverty of Reality* were first met with. . . .

In the second phase of surrealist experiment, the experimenters displayed a desire to interfere. This intentional element tended more and more to tangible verification and emphasized the possibilities of a growing relation to everydayness. . . .

The awareness I was given in *The Visible Woman* that certain fulfillments were imminent led me to write, quite individually and personally, however: "I think the time is rapidly coming when it will be possible (simultaneously with automatism and other passive states) to systematize confusion thanks to a paranoiac and active process of thought, and so assist in discrediting completely the world of reality." This has led me in the course of things to manufacture quite recently some articles still undefined which, in the realm of action, provide the same conflicting opportunities as the most remote mediumistic messages provide in the realm of receptivity. . . .

Thanks to simulation in particular and images in general, we have been enabled, not only to establish communication between automatism and the road to the object, but also to regulate the system of interferences between them, automatism being thereby far from diminished but, as it were, liberated. . . .

Thereupon, however, we are seized with a new fear. Deprived of the company of our former habitual phantoms, which only too well ensured our peace of mind, we are led to regard the world of objects, the objective world, as the true and manifested content of a new dream. . . .

I have recently invited the surrealists to consider an experimental scheme of which the definite development would have to be undertaken collectively. As it is still individual, unsystematized, and merely suggestive, it is only put forward at present as a starting point.

1. *The Transcription of Reveries.*

2. *Experiment Regarding the Irrational Acquaintance of Things:* Intuitive and very quick answers have to be given to a single and very complex series of questions about known and unknown articles such as a rocking-chair, a piece of soap, &c. One must say concerning one of these articles whether it is:

Of day or night,
Paternal or maternal,
Incestuous or not incestuous,
Favorable to love,
Subject to transformation,
Where it lies when we shut our eyes (in front or behind us, or on our left or our right, far off or near, &c.),
What happens to it if it is put in urine, vinegar, &c., &c.

3. *Experiment Concerning Objective Perception:* Each of the experimenters is given an alarm-watch which will go off at a time he must not know. Having this watch in his pocket, he carries on as usual and at the very instant the alarm goes off he must note where he is and what most strikingly impinges on his senses (of sight, hearing, smell and touch). From an analysis of the various notes so made, it can be seen to what extent objective perception depends upon imaginative representation (the casual factor, astrological influence, frequency, the element of coincidence, the possibility of the result's symbolical interpretation in the light of dreams, &c.). One might find, for instance, that at five o'clock elongated shapes and perfumes were frequent, at eight o'clock hard shapes and purely phototypical images.

4. *Collective Study of Phenomenology* in subjects seeming at all times to have the utmost surrealist opportuneness. The method which can be most generally and simply employed is modelled on the method of analysis in Aurel Kolnai's phenomenology of repugnance. By means of this analysis one may discover the objective laws applicable scientifically in fields hitherto regarded as vague, fluctuating and capricious. It would in my opinion be of special interest to surrealism for such a study to bear on *fancies* and on *caprice.* They could be carried out almost entirely as polemical inquiries, needing merely to be completed by analysis and co-ordination.

5. *Automatic Sculpture:* At every meeting for polemics or experiment let every person be supplied with a fixed quantity of malleable material to be dealt with automatically. The shapes thus made, together with each maker's notes (of the time and conditions of production), are later collected and analyzed. The series of questions regarding the irrational acquaintance of things (cf. Proposal 2 above) might be used.

6. *Oral Description of Articles* perceived only by touch. The subject is blindfolded and describes by touching it some ordinary or specially manufactured article, and the record of each description is compared with the photograph of the article in question.

8. [sic] *Making of Articles* on the strength of descriptions obtained according to the preceding Proposal. Let the articles be photographed and compared with the original articles described.

9. *Examination of Certain Actions* liable owing to their irrationality to produce deep currents of demoralization and cause serious conflicts in interpretation and practice, e.g.:

a. Causing in some way any little old woman to come along and then pulling out one of her teeth,

b. Having a colossal loaf (fifteen yards long) baked and left early one morning in a public square, the public's reaction and everything of the kind until the exhaustion of the conflict to be noted.

10. *Inscription of Words on Articles,* the exact words to be decided upon. . . . I am proposing that the writing should be made to take the shape of articles and that one should write directly on the articles. There is not the slightest doubt that specific novelties would arise through the *direct* contact with the object, from this so very material and novel unifying of thought with the object—the novel and continuous flowering of fetishist "desire to verify" and the novel and constant sense of responsibility. Surely the poetry written on fans, tombs, monuments, &c., has a very particular, a very clearly distinct, style? . . . Of course I am not thinking of occasional poems, but, on the contrary, of writings devoid of any obvious or intentional relation to the object on which they are read. Thus writing would exceed the limits of "inscription" and entirely cover over *the complex,* tangible and concrete shapes of things.

Such writing could be on an egg or on a roughly cut slice of bread. I dream of a mysterious manuscript written in white ink and completely covering the strange, firm surfaces of a brand-new Rolls Royce. Let the privilege of the prophets of old be conferred on every one: let everyone be able to read from things.

In my opinion this writing on things, this material devouring of things by writing, is enough in itself to show how far we have travelled since Cubism. . . .

Nevertheless one must insist that although this attitude is a relative step forward towards the concrete, it is still on the contemplative and theoretical plane. The object's action is allowed to influence, but there is no attempt at acting on the object. On the other hand, this principle of action and of practical and concrete taking part is what presides unceasingly over the surrealist experiments and it is our submission to this principle which leads us to bring into being "objects that operate symbolically," objects which fulfill the necessity of being open to action by our own hands and moved about by our own wishes.

But our need of taking an active part in the existence of these things and our yearning to form *a whole* with them are shown to be emphatically material through our sudden consciousness of a *new hunger* we are suffering from. As we think it over, we find suddenly that it does not seem enough to devour things with our eyes and our anxiety to join actively and effectively in their existence brings us to want to *eat them*.

But the predominance of eatables or things that can be ingested is disclosed to analysis in almost all the present surrealist articles (sugared almonds, tobacco, coarse salt in Breton's; medical tablets in Gala's; milk, bread, chocolate, excrement and fried eggs in mind; sausage in Man Ray's; light lager in Crevel's). . . .

In the same way also, the edible meaning of one of Man Ray's recent articles would be revealed—an article in the middle of which a candle only has to be lit for it to set fire to several elements (a horse's tale [sic], strings, a hoop) and cause the collapse of the whole. If one takes into account that the perception of a smell is equivalent in the phenomenology of repugnance to the perception of the taste, the thing which smells may have, so that the intentional element, which is the burning of the article, may be interpreted as a roundabout desire to eat it (and so obtain its smell and even its ingestible smoke), one sees that burning a thing is equivalent, *inter alia*, to making it edible.

To sum up, the surrealist object has underdone four phases so far:

1. The object exists outside us, without our taking part in it (anthropomorphic articles); 2. The object assumes the immovable shape of desire and acts upon our contemplation (dream-state articles); 3. The object is movable and such that it can be acted upon (articles operating symbolically); 4. The object tends to bring about our fusion with it and makes us pursue the formation of a unity with it (hunger for an article and edible articles).

Salavador Dalí, "The Object as Revealed in Surrealist Experiment," *This Quarter* 5, no. 1 (1932): 197–207.

CADAVRE — « Le cadavre bat des mains comme un caillou dans une vitre » (*B. P.*)

CADAVRE EXQUIS — Jeu de papier plié qui consiste à faire composer une phrase ou un dessin par plusieurs personnes, sans qu'aucune d'elles puisse tenir compte de la collaboration ou des collaborations précédentes. L'exemple, devenu classique, qui a donné son nom au jeu tient dans la première phrase obtenue de cette manière : *Le cadavre — exquis — boira — le vin— nouveau.*

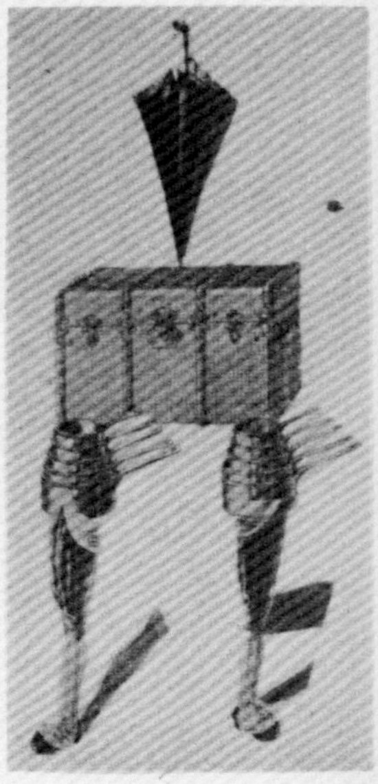

Le Cadavre exquis

CANARD — « Le canard du doute, aux lèvres de vermouth » (*Lautréamont*)

CAP — « Si le cap Horn figurait un sein, les Patagons caresseraient tous les soirs les astéries de charbon qui pullulent sur leur ventre, mais hélas ! ce cap ressemble depuis toujours à un artichaut. » (*B. P.*)

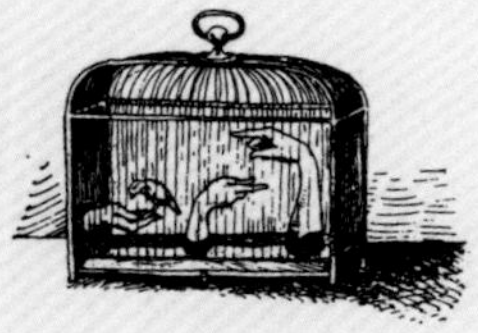

Seligmann

CAPILLAIRE — « En examinant de près le contenu de l'activité la plus irréfléchie de l'esprit, il est possible de mettre à jour un *tissu capillaire* dans l'ignorance duquel on s'ingénierait en vain à vouloir se figurer la circulation mentale. Le rôle de ce tissu est d'assurer l'échange constant qui doit se produire dans la pensée entre le monde extérieur et le monde intérieur, échange qui nécessite l'interpénétration continue de l'activité de veille et de l'activité de sommeil. » (*A. B.*)

CARACO — « Caraco est une belle garce : paresseuse comme un loir et gantée de verre pour ne rien faire, elle enfile des perles avec les dindons de la farce. » (*Cad. ex.*)

CARESSE — « D'une seule caresse — je te fais briller de tout ton éclat. » (*P.E.*)

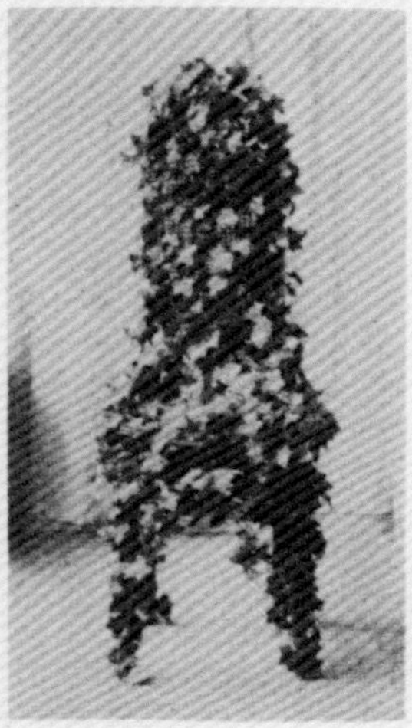

W.P.

CARROLL (Lewis), 1832-1898 — « A une époque où, dans le Royaume définitivement Uni, toute pensée était considérée comme si choquante qu'elle eût hésité à se former... qu'était devenue la liberté humaine? Elle résidait toute entière dans les frêles mains d'Alice... » (*L. A.*)

CAUSALITÉ — « Les notions de cause et d'effet se concentrent et s'entrelacent dans celle de l'interdépendance universelle au sein de laquelle la cause et l'effet ne cessent de changer de place. » (*Engels*)

CENDRE — « maladie du cigare » (*B. P.*)

CERISIER — « La branche de cerisier, haute, sans le bouton la surmontant, de 0 m. 35, est fixée par quatre vis sur le tronc d'arbre, en bois également, du modèle connu. » (*A. B. et P. E.*)

CHAISE — « les chaises dressées les pieds en haut comme les squelettes dans les fouilles archéologiques » (*V. N.*)

CHAPLIN (Charlie), né en 1888 — « Merci à celui qui sur l'immense écran oc-

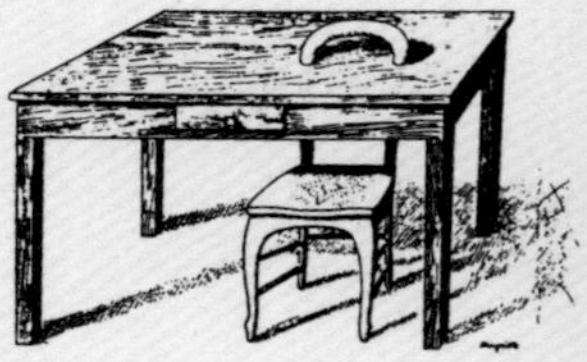

Magritte

THE ABRIDGED DICTIONARY OF SURREALISM

JAUNE — « Dans *Salammbô* j'ai voulu donner l'impression de la couleur jaune. Dans *Madame Bovary* j'ai voulu faire quelque chose qui fût de la couleur de ces moisissures des coins où il y a des cloportes. Quant au reste, le plan, les personnages, cela m'est bien égal. » (*Flaubert*)

JE — « *Je* est *un autre*. Si le cuivre s'éveille clairon, il n'y a rien de sa faute. » (*Rimbaud*).

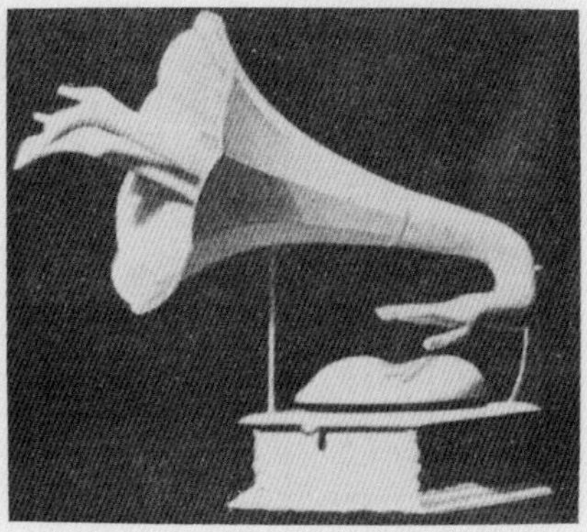

Dominguez : Jamais

KANGUROO — « Qu'il soit maudit, par ses enfants et par ma main décharnée, celui qui persiste à ne pas comprendre les kanguroos implacables du rire et les poux audacieux de la caricature ! » (*Lautréamont*)

KAOLIN — « le kaolin fourmille dans sa boîte crânienne » (*T. T.*)

LANGAGE — « Tout peut se décrire, — *verbis*. — Toutes les activités sont ou peuvent être accompagnées de mots, comme toutes les représentations peuvent être accompagnées du *moi*. » (*Novalis*). « O bouches l'homme est à la recherche d'un nouveau langage — auquel le grammairien d'aucune langue n'aura rien à dire » (*Apollinaire*). « Il nous faut peu de mots pour exprimer l'essentiel, il nous faut tous les mots pour le rendre réel... Les mots gagnent. » (*P. E.*)

LAUTRÉAMONT (Isidore Ducasse, *dit* comte de) 1846-1870. « Ce n'est pas à moi, ni à personne (Entendez-vous, messieurs? qui veut mes témoins?) de juger M. le Comte. On ne juge pas M. de Lautréamont. On le reconnaît au passage et on salue jusqu'à terre. » (*P. S.*) « J'estime que le plus beau titre de gloire du groupe surréaliste est d'avoir reconnu et proclamé l'importance ultra-littéraire de l'admirable Lautréamont. » (*André Gide*)

LÉGENDE — « Une légende disiez-vous? Non — plutôt un objet trouvé dont le géranium est le bouclier et le domino la bouche. » (*G. H.*)

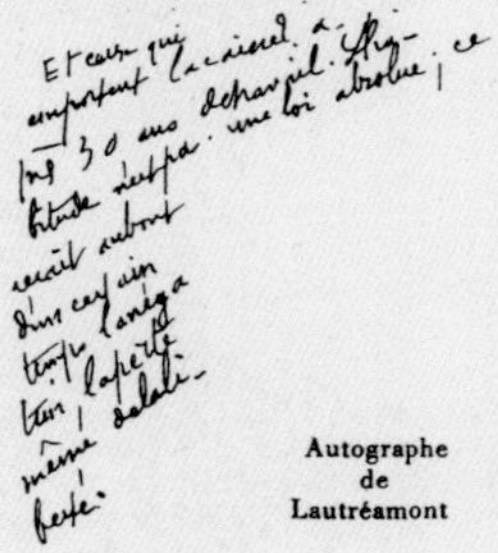

Autographe de Lautréamont

LEIRIS (Michel) — Écrivain et poète surréaliste de 1924 à 1929. (*Le Point cardinal, Glossaire*)

LÉLY (Gilbert) — « La lampe scabreuse ». Poète surréaliste (*Arden* (1933), *Je ne veux pas qu'on tue cette femme*).

LÉNINE, 1870-1924 — « De grands poètes viendront plus tard qui reliront le petit livre des enfants, qui y réfléchiront profon-

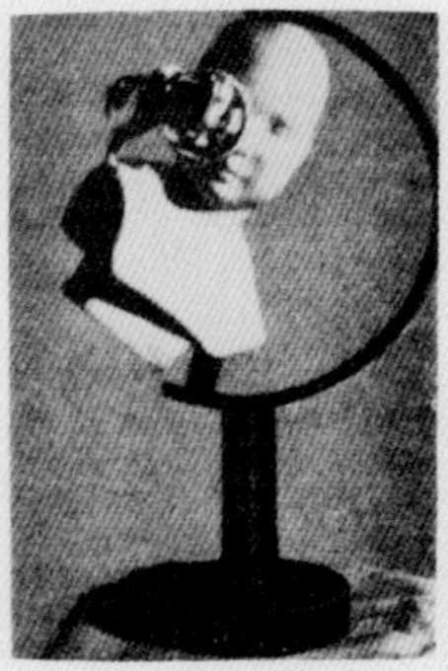

Dominguez : Larme

POUCE — « Le pouce est ce gras cabaretier flamand, d'humeur goguenarde et grivoise, qui fume sur sa porte, à l'enseigne de la double bière de mars. » (*Aloysius Bertrand*). « Dans le pouce était aménagé un théâtre d'ombres pour que les mains pussent devenir des biches, des oiseaux, des paysages. (*G. H.*). « *P'ai où ce, poue-ce, pousse.* Le sexe est le premier pouce, l'époux le poussa. Le pouce arriva à sa perfection en même temps que le sexe. Le pouce servit à prendre les poux et les puces. On vit le pouce pousser, et il servait aussi à prendre les jeunes pousses des plantes. » (*J. P. Brisset*)

POULPE — « Poulpe au regard de soie » (*Lautréamont*).

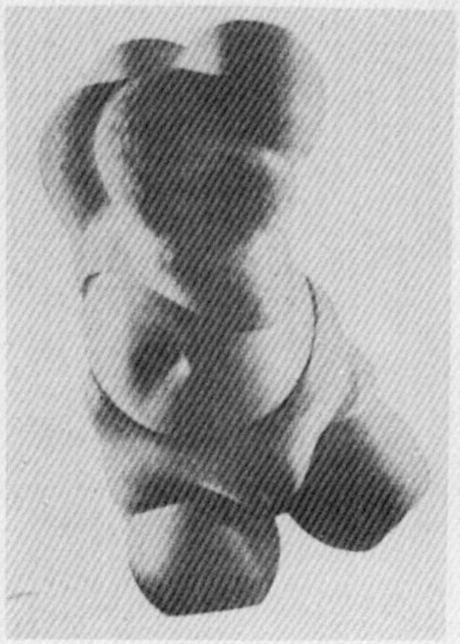

H. B.

POUPÉE — « Ne serait-ce pas dans la poupée qui, malgré sa docilité accommodante et sans borne, s'entourait d'une réserve désespérante, ne serait-ce pas dans la réalité même de la poupée que l'imagination trouverait ce qu'elle cherchait de joie, d'exaltation et de peur? Ne serait-ce pas dans le triomphe définitif sur les adolescentes aux grands yeux qui se détournent, si, sous le regard conscient pillant leurs charmes, les doigts agressifs assaillaient la forme plastique et construisaient lentement, membre à membre, ce que les sens et le cerveau s'étaient approprié. » (*H. B.*)

POUSSIÈRE — Elevage de poussière. (*M. D.*)

PRASSINOS (Gisèle), née en 1920 — « Alice II ». Poète surréaliste. (*La Sauterelle arthritique* (1934), *Quand le bruit travaille*, etc.)

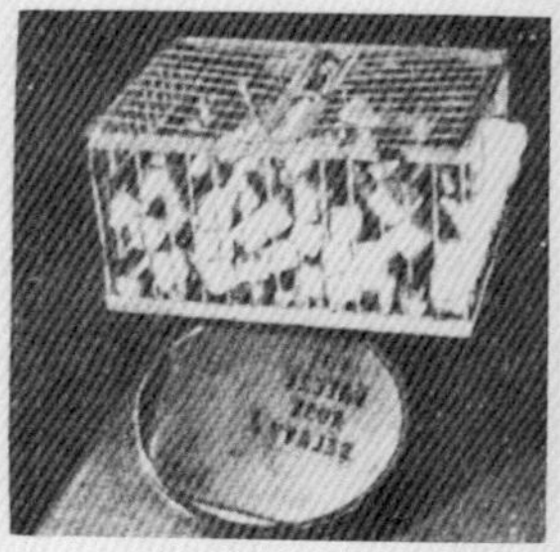

M. D. : Pourquoi ne pas éternuer ?

PRÉCIEUX — Un bonze demanda un jour au bonze Sozan Daishi : — Qu'est-ce qui est le plus précieux au monde? — N'importe quoi, une charogne, la tête d'un chat mort, répondit Sozan Daishi — Pourquoi? — Parce qu'on ne peut l'évaluer.

PRÉVERT (Jacques). — « Celui qui rouge de cœur ». Poète. Activité surréaliste proprement dite de 1926 à 1929. A pris part, depuis lors, à la réalisation de films comiques à tendances subversives. Poèmes : *Introduction à un dîner de têtes, La Crosse en l'air, Drôle d'immeuble.*

PRISME — « Plutôt la vie que ces prismes sans épaisseur même si les couleurs sont plus pures » (*A. B.*). « Les premières chaleurs florales — alliées à la fraîcheur du sang — le prisme respire avec nous — aube abondante » (*P. E.*)

PROFIL — « Gagner au jeu du profil — qu'un oiseau reste dans ses ailes. » (*P.E.*)

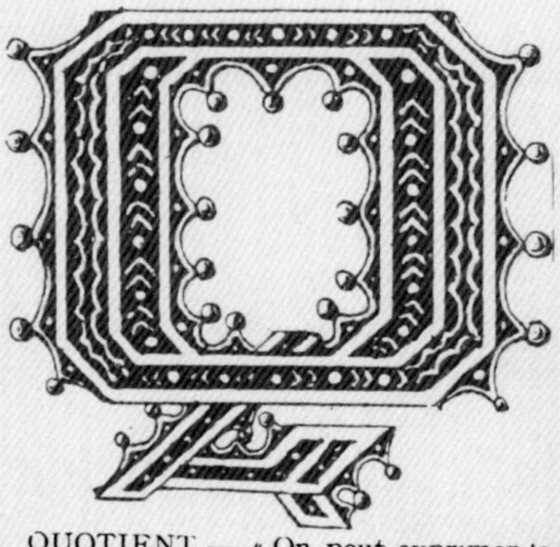

QUOTIENT — « On peut exprimer la démarche essentielle du surréalisme en disant qu'il s'agit pour lui de calculer le quotient de l'inconscient par le conscient». (*P. Na.*)

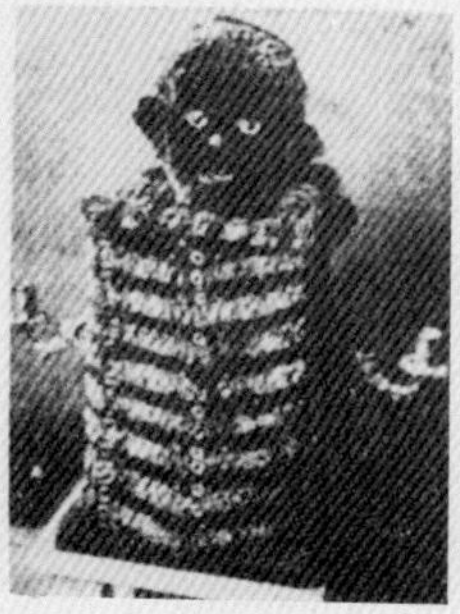

Quintessence — Objet trouvé : tabernacle en fourrure boutonné d'yeux de verre (messes noires).

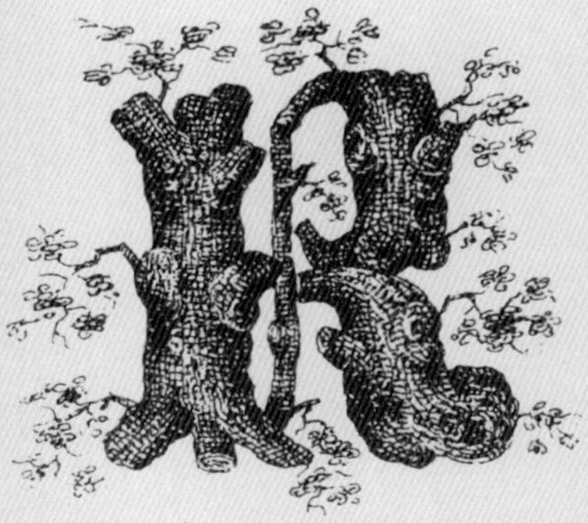

RADCLIFFE (Ann) 1764-1823 — « Le Spectre-toqué. » (*Lautréamont*)

RAISON — Nuage mangé par la lune.

RAYOGRAMME — « Photographie obtenue par simple interposition de l'objet entre le papier sensible et la source lumineuse. — Saisies aux moments d'un détachement visuel, pendant des périodes de contact émotionnel, ces images sont les oxydations de résidus, fixés par la lumière et la chimie, des organismes vivants. » (*M. R.*)

READ (Herbert), né en 1893 — Ecrivain et poète surréaliste, promoteur de ce Mouvement en Angleterre. (*Poems* (1914-1937), *Reason and Romanticism, Surrealism*, etc.)

READY MADE — Objet usuel promu à la dignité d'objet d'art par le simple choix de l'artiste. « Ready made réciproque : se servir d'un Rembrandt comme planche à repasser » (M. D.)

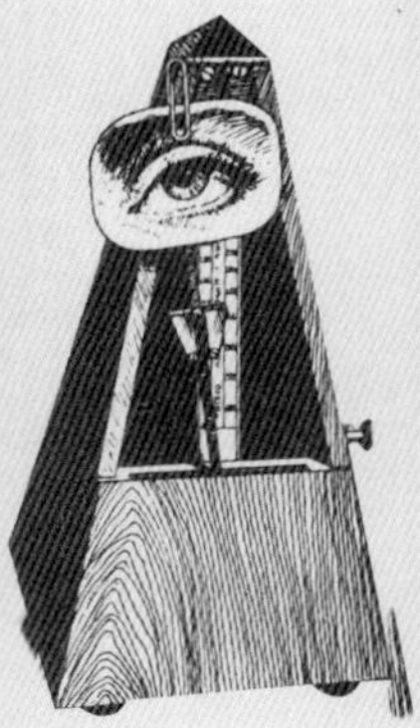

M. R.

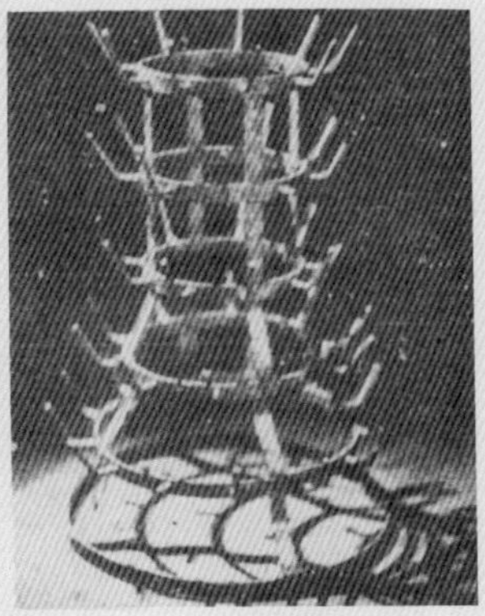

M. D. : **Ready made**

RÉALITÉ — « La *réalité* est aux doigts de cette femme qui souffle à la première page des dictionnaires. » (*A. B.*). « La Réalité devient le paravent derrière quoi se cacher et mépriser, ignorer, nier la mouvante épaisseur des réalités, leurs projections sur tous les plans — intellectuel, moral, scientifique, poétique, philosophique, etc. — eux-mêmes tour à tour émetteurs et réflecteurs, en feu d'astre à surprise ou en terre de planète habituelle » (*R. C.*)

REPOPULATION — « Reste donc celui qui spécule sur la vanité des morts, le fantôme de la repopulation. » (*M. E.*)

REPRÉSENTATION — « Les représentations conventionnelles des sources géométriques de la nature ne sont séduisantes qu'en fonction de leur puissance d'obscurcissement. »(*A. B. et P. E.*)

RETARD — « Employer « retard » au lieu de tableau ou peinture... Un retard en verre comme on dirait un poème en prose ou un crachoir en argent (*M. D.*)

RÊVE — « Le rêve n'est rien autre que poésie involontaire » (*L. H. v. Jakob*). « Des signes assez nombreux nous avertissent que la psyché du sommeil reparaît par intermittences dans la veille, et qu'inversement la psyché diurne participe à la vie endormie. » (*J. V. Troxler*). « En vérité, il y a plus d'une tête qui nous instruirait davantage avec ses rêves réels qu'avec ceux de sa fantaisie. » (*Jean-Paul*). « Le Rêve est une seconde vie. Je n'ai pu percer sans frémir ces portes d'ivoire ou de corne qui nous séparent de la mort » (*Nerval*). « Rien ne vous appartient plus en propre que vos rêves. Sujet, forme, durée, acteur, spectateur — dans ces comédies, vous êtes tout vous-même ! » (*Nietzche*) « Que le poète ne s'est-il prononcé plus nettement encore en faveur de la nature, pleine de sens, des rêves ! » (*Freud*). « ... faire valoir ce qui peut exister de commun entre les représentations de la veille et celles du sommeil. C'est seulement, en effet, lorsque la notion de leur identité sera parfaitement acquise que l'on parviendra à tirer clairement parti de leur différence, de manière à renforcer de leur *unité* la conception matérialiste du monde réel. » (*A. B.*). « Il n'y a plus de semblables dans cette solitude... je suis cette vie infinie : un être dont les origines remontent au delà de tout ce que je puis connaître, dont le sort dépasse les horizons où atteint mon regard... La solitude de la poésie et du rêve nous enlève à notre désolante solitude. » (*A. Béguin*).

REVOLVER — « L'œil du revolver regarde aux rideaux l'invisible bruit de papier gris froissé. » (*Jarry*). « Un coup de revolver serait une si douce mélodie » (*P. S.*)

REVUES SURRÉALISTES — La revue *Littérature* (33 numéros : 1919-1924) peut être considérée comme la première en date des revues surréalistes. Elle publie en effet, dès ses

23

André Breton and Paul Eluard, eds., *Le Dictionnaire abrégé du surréalisme* (The Abridged Dictionary of Surrealism), (Paris: Galerie des Beaux-Arts, 1938), 6; 15; 22–23.

DAVID SMITH

THE LANDSCAPE

I have never looked at a landscape without seeing
other landscapes

I have never seen a landscape without visions
of things I desire and despise

lower landscapes have crusts of heat—raw epidermis
and the choke of vines

the separate lines of salt errors—monadnocks
of fungus

the balance of stone—with gestures to grow

the lost posts of manmaid boundaries—in molten shade

a landscape is a still life of Chaldean history

it has faces I do not know

its mountains are always sobbing females

it is bags of melons and prickle pears

its woods are sawed to boards

its black hills bristle with maiden fern

its stones are Assyrian fragments

it flows the bogside beauty of the river Liffey

it is colored by Indiana gas green

it is steeped in veritable indian yellow

it is the place I've traveled to and never found

it is somehow veiled to vision by pious bastards
and the lord of Varu the nobleman from Gascogne

in the distance it seems threatened by the destruction
of gold

SPECTRES ARE

The race for survival—the capital dog

Banners of Royalty with Caesarian cannon

Race of stegosaurs with Queen Anne collars

The chain leg of events—a thecodonts pongee heart

Saving select bound peanut bodies for the capital
conception of natural selection

Feed by gruel spoon to stainless held chompers

Rolling bobbins trailing rotten yarns

The mothers love—the asses jaw

Rattling swords—judas pens

Fascist mothers with voluminous vitelline vesicles

Dead birds—limp curls—racist mudball lungfish

The burning bush and the chicken dinner

1914 Jean (Hans) Arp and Max Ernst meet in Cologne and start a lifelong friendship.

World War I begins (July 28).

1915–17 Arp settles in Zürich, where he co-founds the Dada group with poet Tristan Tzara, writes nonsensical poems, and makes small reliefs by superimposing shaped pieces of wood and painting the surfaces, as in the ***Earthly Forms*** series **(figs. 10–11)**.

Ernst is conscripted into the German army and serves on both the Eastern and Western fronts during World War I. Arp's letters keep him informed about Dada.

Marcel Duchamp leaves France for New York, where he coins the term "Readymade" for ***Bottle Rack*** **(fig. 2)**, assembles the Assisted Readymade ***With Hidden Noise*** **(fig. 4)**, and starts ***The Bride Stripped Bare by Her Bachelors, Even (The Large Glass)*** **(fig. 5)**.

Henry Moore serves in the British army.

André Breton serves in the French army's medical corps and sees soldiers suffering from traumatic shock.

French poet Guillaume Apollinaire coins the word "surréalisme."

1918 Twenty months after the United States enters the war, hostilities cease (November).

Apollinaire dies (November), and Breton adopts his motto "*j'émerveille*" (I marvel).

1919 Ernst co-founds the Cologne Dada group, studies Sigmund Freud's writings, and composes collages from images of objects cut from mail-order catalogues and books.

Duchamp returns briefly to Paris (July).

1920 Arp lives temporarily with Ernst in Cologne where he publishes poetry and develops his new biomorphic vocabulary more fully in wood reliefs **(fig. 12)**.

Joan Miró leaves Barcelona for Paris; thereafter, when possible, he makes annual visits to Spain.

Man Ray makes *Obstruction*, an installation of linked clothes hangers suspended from a ceiling, and *The Enigma of Isidore Ducasse* (a blanket-wrapped, twine-tied bundle, later identified as a sewing machine). He begins his career as a professional photographer.

Duchamp makes ***Fresh Widow*** **(fig. 7)** (fall).

1921 Moore studies sculpture at the Royal College of Art in London, where he learns to carve wood and stone and also studies non-Western art at the British Museum for the next three years.

Ernst's Dada exhibition in Cologne displays his collages alongside umbrellas, flower pots, and other found items. The collages are subsequently shown in Paris at the Galerie au sans Pareil (May–June).

Duchamp makes ***Why Not Sneeze, Rose Sélavy?*** **(fig. 6)** before going to Paris (June), where he meets Breton.

Ray arrives in Paris (July 22), where Duchamp introduces him to Breton. Ray makes his first photograms by exposing objects on light-sensitive paper. His exhibition of thirty-five works at Galerie Six (December 3–31) includes ***Gift*** **(fig. 8)**.

1922 Duchamp returns to New York (January).

Alberto Giacometti arrives in Paris (January) to study sculpture; he lives part-time in Switzerland until 1925.

Breton's essay "After Dada" is published in *Comedia* (March), and his essay about Duchamp is featured in *Littérature* (October).

Ernst relocates to Paris, where he joins the Dada group (August).

1923 Duchamp stops working on ***The Large Glass*** in New York and goes to Paris, where he shifts his attention to playing chess.

1924 Moore teaches at the Royal Academy's sculpture school and begins regular visits to Paris, continuing through at least 1936, sometimes with fellow sculptor Barbara Hepworth.

Ernst makes *Two Children Are Threatened by a Nightingale* (spring or summer), which incorporates small objects. He adopts a bird image as a symbol of himself and his creativity.

Breton suggests making "dream objects" in his essay "Introduction to the Discourse on the Paucity of Reality" (September).

Breton publishes the *Manifesto of Surrealism* (October).

The Bureau for Surrealist Research opens as the group's headquarters in Paris (October); among its accoutrements is a statue of a headless boar and a cast of a female nude.

Surrealists launch the journal *La Révolution surréaliste* (December 1); the first page of the inaugural issue reproduces Ray's photograph of *The Enigma of Isidore Ducasse*.

1925 Arp moves to Paris (February–March), where he lives for a while with Ernst; he meets Miró and other Surrealists who admire his whimsical biomorphic aesthetics **(fig. 14)**.

Ernst experiments with both biomorphic forms and found objects, notably in the reliefs ***Cages Are Always Imaginary*** and ***Human Figure with Two Birds*** **(figs. 16–17)**. He plans a larger multi-component *Monument to the Birds*.

Exhibition of Surrealist Painting, the movement's first group show, at Galerie Pierre (November), consists mostly of two-dimensional works but also reliefs by Arp.

1926 *Cahiers d'art* begins publication (January); the first issue illustrates a relief by Arp.

Ernst's exhibition at the Galerie Van Leer (March) presents thirty paintings and several sculptures called *Fragments of a Monument to the Birds*, 1925.

Galerie Surréaliste opens in Paris (March).

Salvador Dalí meets Breton and visits Pablo Picasso's studio during his first trip to Paris (April).

La Révolution surréaliste, no. 7 (June 15), illustrates two works by Arp and Ray's photograph of a small-jointed mannequin posed like a reclining person.

La Révolution surréaliste, no. 8 (December 1), announces an exhibition of objects, but it is not realized.

Alexander Calder lives in Paris (July 1926–autumn 1927), ostensibly to study academic sculpture, and begins fabricating *Circus*, a miniature performance piece.

David Smith starts to study painting and drawing at the Art Students League in New York (fall).

Isamu Noguchi is inspired by the *Constantin Brancusi* exhibition at the Brummer Gallery in New York (November 17–December 15), where he meets Duchamp, the curator of the exhibition.

The Société Anonyme's *International Exhibition of Modern Art* at the Brooklyn Museum (November 19, 1926–January 10, 1927) includes two reliefs by Arp (including *Bird-Man*, c. 1920) and Duchamp's ***Large Glass***.

1927 Joseph Cornell continues working for a textile company in New York and starts educating himself about modern art from publications and gallery exhibitions.

Living in New York, Smith educates himself about vanguard European art by studying illustrations in journals, including *Cahiers d'art*.

Duchamp returns to Paris (February).

Noguchi goes to Paris (March) to work as Brancusi's studio assistant for several months and participates in the international community of artists. He begins friendships with Calder and Ray before returning to New York in late 1928.

Giacometti exhibits ***Spoon Woman*** **(fig. 25)** at the Salon des Tuileries (April).

Arp's biomorphism intrigues Surrealist painters and becomes apparent in their works, notably in Miró's and Picasso's paintings. Yves Tanguy adapts biomorphic forms to a new illusionistic style, revealed in his exhibition at the Galerie Surréaliste (May 27–June 15).

René Magritte, co-founder of the Belgian Surrealist group, makes paintings and drawings of objects with unrelated or irrational words. *The Key to Dreams* presents a correctly identified image of a sponge and three misidentified images (pocket-knife as bird, satchel as sky, leaf as table). He moves to Paris (September), where he meets Arp, Ernst, Miró, and Breton.

Dalí meets Miró in Spain (September).

Arp's first solo exhibition at the Galerie Surréaliste (November 21–December 9) displays forty-six works, mostly cardboard and wood reliefs from the early and mid-1920s, including *Bottle-Navel*, *Bust-Lips-Breasts-Navel*, ***Clock*** **(fig. 15)**, *Endless Mustache*, *Nose-Appetizer*, and *Head-Landscape*. Breton writes laudatory catalogue text and acquires several reliefs, notably *Period and Comma* and ***Woman*** **(fig. 19)**. Income from sales enables Arp to make larger reliefs, such as *Dancer* and ***Three Walking Sticks*** **(fig. 21)**.

A. E. Gallatin opens the Gallery of Living Art in New York (December), where biomorphic reliefs and sculptures by Arp would be shown, including ***Shirt Front and Fork*** **(fig. 13)**, ***Torso-Navel***, and ***Head with Annoying Objects*** **(fig. 45)**, as well as Picasso's *Bather* and *Seated Bather* paintings from 1927–30.

1928 Giacometti starts a series of flat standing sculptures identified only by gender, such as ***Man*** **(fig. 26)** and *Woman*.

Breton publishes "Surrealism and Painting" as a booklet (February), adding illustrations of four reliefs by Arp, including ***The Forest*** **(fig. 10)**, *Eggboard*, and *Mountain, Table, Anchor, Navel*.

Miró makes collage "anti-paintings," including *Spanish Dancer*, using rough materials and found items (February–June).

Dalí addresses the works of Arp and Tanguy in his essay "The New Limits of Painting," *L'Amic de les arts* (February, April, and May).

Calder returns to Paris (November) and makes contour portraits and caricatures from metal wire. He and Miró meet (after December 10) and start a lifelong friendship; Calder sees at least one of Miró's anti-paintings.

Arp's exhibition at Galerie L'Époque in Brussels (November 4–17) shows eighteen reliefs, including *Flower-Head* and ***Objects Placed on Three Planes Like Writing*** **(fig. 22)**. Hubert Croxley's review in *Cahiers d'art* 3, nos. 5–6, illustrates nine reliefs and mentions Arp's influence on other artists.

Max Ernst: His Birds, His New Flowers, His Flying Forests, His Maledictions, His Santanas exhibition at the Galerie Georges Bernheim (December) presents paintings and *frottages* on motifs from nature, as well as two versions of *Monument to the Birds*, 1927.

1929 Moore, in England, learns about Surrealism from art journals. He moves to Hampstead, where he, Hepworth, Herbert Read, and Roland Penrose constitute an informal artists' colony.

Smith constructs metal sculptures inspired by recent works of Picasso and Julio González in *Cahiers d'art*.

Noguchi returns to New York (early spring) and supports himself making portrait sculptures.

Dalí spends two months in Paris (April–May) with Luis Buñuel making the film *Un Chien Andalou*. Miró introduces him to artists and galleries, where he sees works by Arp, Ernst, and Picasso. Dalí joins the Surrealist movement (October). His first exhibition of paintings at the Galerie Goemans (November 20–December 5) reveals his obsession with erotic desire, sometimes portrayed through depictions of things, as in *Accommodations of Desire* and *Illumined Pleasures*, which Breton buys.

Giacometti exhibits two flat plasters at Galerie Jeanne Bucher (May–June), where André Masson sees them and introduces him to Arp, Ernst, Miró, and the writers Georges Bataille and Michel Leiris.

Variétés magazine publishes a special issue, *Le Surréalisme en 1929* (June), with illustrations of a freestanding plaster head by Arp, Miró's collages *Portrait of a Dancer* and *Spanish Dancer*, and a primitivist assemblage figure by Tanguy.

Calder gives performances of *Circus* before going to New York (June), where he makes his first mechanical wire sculptures, including *Aquarium (Goldfish Bowl).*

"Alberto Giacometti" by Leiris in the journal *Documents*, no. 4 (September), includes photographs of his new semi-abstract sculptures with sexual subtexts, including ***Man, Man and Woman*** **(fig. 28)**, ***Reclining Woman Who Dreams*** **(fig. 27)**, and *Three Figures Outdoors.*

Arp's work is featured in *Abstract and Surrealist Painting and Sculpture* at Kunsthaus Zürich (October 6–November 3).

Arp's solo exhibition at Galerie Goemans in Paris (November) consists of eighteen works, including *Neckties and Head* and ***Objects Placed on Three Planes Like Writing.*** Leiris' review of the exhibition in *Documents*, no. 6 (November), illustrates *Head. Cahiers d'art* 5, no. 2, illustrates eight of Arp's works, including *Head-Mustaches. Das Kunstblatt* 14 (December) publishes an article about Arp by Carola Giedion-Welcker. Arp starts modeling freestanding, multi-component plasters.

La Révolution surréaliste, no. 12 (December 15), the last issue, publishes Breton's "Second Manifesto of Surrealism" and Magritte's "Words and Images."

1930 Smith learns more about developments in Paris through John Graham, meets Arshile Gorky, and begins to paint in a biomorphic style.

Exhibition of Collages: Challenge to Painting is presented at the Galerie Goemans (March). In the catalogue, Louis Aragon advocates adding manufactured objects to paintings, praises Arp for having his reliefs made by a carpenter, observes that objects can represent themselves or something completely different, and ends the essay with an exhortation to create "the marvelous."

Calder, living in Paris (March–December), visits Piet Mondrian's studio (October) and decides to develop pure geometric abstraction in his sculptures.

Miró–Arp–Giacometti exhibition at Galerie Pierre Loeb (April) brings together two biomorphic painters with the iconoclastic sculptor.

Le Surréalisme au service de la révolution, a new periodical, publishes its first issue (July) and five more through May 1933.

1931 Dalí and Giacometti play dominant roles in the group for the next three years.

Cornell makes his first collages in the manner of Ernst, including ***Untitled (Schooner).***

Ray is commissioned by a Paris electric company to make a limited-edition portfolio of ten photograms of objects **(figs. 37–40).**

Calder lives in Paris all year; in the fall Duchamp christens Calder's motorized and hand-cranked sculptures "mobiles."

Smith constructs small sculptures that incorporate wood and coral found during a trip to the Virgin Islands; he brings other materials back to his studio in Bolton Landing, New York.

Cahiers d'art 6, nos. 9–10, illustrates the first version of Ernst's ***Loplop Introduces a Young Girl*** **(fig. 18)** and four of Arp's recent works, including *Bell and Navels, Necktie and Navel,* and *Personages.*

Pierre Matisse opens his gallery in New York (October); starting in 1932 the gallery presents annual exhibitions of Miró's works.

Julien Levy opens his gallery in New York (November) and begins to promote Surrealist art.

The Newer Super-Realism at the Wadsworth Atheneum in Hartford (November 15–December 5) is the movement's first group exhibition in the United States. It showcases two-dimensional works by European painters, particularly Dalí, Miró, and Ernst.

Le Surréalisme au service de la révolution, no. 3 (December), proclaims "the object" as the new frontier of Surrealist discovery:
• Dalí's essay "Surrealist Objects" identifies six categories, primarily "symbolically functioning objects." The text illustrates four such works by Breton, Valentine Hugo, Gala Eluard, and himself. The other five categories are "transubstantiated objects," "objects for throwing," "wrapped objects," "machine objects," and "molded objects."
• Giacometti's **"Moving and Mute Objects"** text **(figs. 35)** illustrates drawings of seven sculptures, including ***The Cage, Suspended Ball, Disagreeable Object*** **(figs. 29–31)**, *Disagreeable Object to Throw Away,* and *Model for a City Square (Plaza).*
• Breton's "The Phantom Object" (an excerpt from his forthcoming book *Communicating Vessels*, 1932) describes a lost assemblage of an envelope and eyelashes by Giacometti.
• Tanguy's **"Weights and Colors"** text **(fig. 60)** is illustrated with biomorphic drawings of abstract entities intended to be fabricated as objects in pink velour, soft wax, plaster, blue chalk, and other media.
• Other illustrations include Miró's ***Personage with Umbrella*** captioned as *"Sculpture"* **(fig. 32).**

Miró: Sculptures-Objects exhibition at the Galerie Pierre (December 18, 1931–January 8, 1932) introduces his recent assemblages of found objects with painted biomorphic forms; two are illustrated and described in *Cahiers d'art* 6, nos. 9–10.

1932 Moore experiments with metamorphoses of items from nature, such as pebbles and bones, in his *Transformation* drawings.

Ray marks the end of a three-year affair with photographer Lee Miller by assembling ***Object to Be Destroyed*** **(fig. 43),** later retitled *Object of Destruction* and *Indestructible Object.*

Surréalisme at the Levy Gallery (January 9–29) is the movement's first group exhibition in New York. In addition to paintings and drawings from the Wadsworth Atheneum exhibition, Levy shows photographs of store-window props by Eugène Atget and Umbo, collages by Cornell, and several assemblages, notably Duchamp's ***Why Not Sneeze?,*** Ray's *Snow Globe,* and Cornell's ***Untitled (Glass Bell)*** **(fig. 116).** A review in *Art Digest* (January 15) is titled "Freudian Psychology Appears in the First American Surrealist Show."

Calder's motorized and hand-cranked mobiles are exhibited at Galerie Vignon (February), where Arp names the stationary constructions *stabiles.* They are subsequently shown in *Calder: Mobiles / Abstract Sculptures* at the Levy Gallery (May 12–June 11), where a review compares his style to that of Miró and other Surrealist abstractionists.

Claude Cahun meets Breton (April).

Giacometti's first solo exhibition in Paris at the Galerie Pierre Colle (May 4–17) introduces new subjects and unprecedented formats. Some allude to game-playing; others represent violent or morbid themes, as in *Caught Hand, Point to the Eye,* and ***Flower in Danger*** **(fig. 34)**. Christian Zervos's review in *Cahiers d'art* 7, nos. 8–10, illustrates eight works, including the plaster original of ***The Palace at 4 a.m.*** **(fig. 33)**, ***No More Play*** **(fig. 44)**, ***Woman with Her Throat Cut*** **(fig. 80)**, *Project for a City Plaza* and *Despite the Hands* (later retitled *Caress*).

Arp begins a series of freestanding biomorphic plasters (summer).

This Quarter 5, no. 1 (September), publishes an issue on Surrealism in English, notably the "Second Manifesto of Surrealism" and Dalí's essay "The Object as Revealed in Surrealist Experiment," which advocates practices to generate a new awareness of things and mentions recent object assemblages, such as "a paper-cutter decorated with ears of wheat, casts of naked women . . . covered with the luminous paint used on watch faces."

Objects by Joseph Cornell: Minutiae, Glass Bells, Shadow Boxes, Coups d'oeil, Jouets Surréalistes at the Levy Gallery (November–December) presents several slightly altered mechanical toys **(figs. 116–17)**, small cardboard boxes containing trivial miscellanea, and two assemblages in glass domes (one features a metronome, another a doll's hand holding a rose).

1933 Moore's and Hepworth's sculptures become fully biomorphic, as in her ***Reclining Figure*** **(fig. 61)** and his ***Reclining Figure*** **(fig. 64)**.

Cornell starts using wood boxes as containers for found objects; he lines the interiors of some of them with pages from French books.

Arp's exhibition in Paris reveals his new sculptures. Two views of ***Head Covered with Three Disagreeable Objects: A Fly, a Mandolin, and a Pair of Mustaches,*** now known as ***Head with Annoying Objects***, are published with no title in *Cahiers d'art* 8, nos. 5–6, where the caption describes it as a "poem sculpture."

Calder has an exhibition of recent works at Galerie Pierre Colle (May) before leaving for the United States (June), where he buys a farmhouse in Roxbury, Connecticut.

Le Surréalisme au service de la révolution, no. 6 (May 15), the last issue, features essays on "the object":
• Dalí's "Psycho-Atmospheric-Anamorphic Objects" recommends making erotic and edible objects.
• Giacometti's "Yesterday, Quicksand" highlights reminiscences of childhood fantasies.
• Illustrations include Ernst's *Surrealist Object* (a box containing found items from nature), Giacometti's *Hour of Footprints* construction, and Tanguy's *Life of the Object* drawing of a three-dimensional biomorphic landscape.

Minotaure, a new magazine, puts Surrealism in the broader context of vanguard art in Europe. The first issue (June) reproduces Picasso's ***Anatomy*** drawings **(fig. 58)**, photographs of his biomorphic plasters, and two metal figures, including *Woman in a Garden*.

Surrealist Exhibition: Sculptures, Objects, Paintings, Drawings at Galerie Pierre Colle (June 7–18) presents more than seventy works. Biomorphic sculptures are outnumbered by object assemblages, notably Dalí's *Retrospective Bust of a Woman* and Hugo's ***Object*** **(fig. 105)**. Miró's four ***Objects*** **(see fig. 41)** combine biomorphic shapes with found objects. Giacometti exhibits six works, including plasters *Table* and *Mannequin*, delicate constructions *The Hour of Footprints* and ***The Palace at 4 a.m.***, and *Objects* (probably *Disagreeable Object*). Ray exhibits two radically different sculptures: a kinetic object and a realistic model of his own head.
A review by Raymond Cogniat, "The Surrealists Exhibit," *Beaux Arts* (June 16), acknowledges the group's intention to be detached from reality through the systematic violence of removing utility from objects. He praises Hugo's small relief of two gloved mannequin hands.

Dalí's exhibition at the Galerie Pierre Colle (June 19–29) includes two objects.

Smith starts making welded-metal sculptures (autumn), including a *Reclining Figure,* which combine small organic elements with open structures. He incorporates industrial found objects into three constructions of heads **(figs. 156–57)**; two are exhibited in January 1934.

Duchamp meets Cornell for the first time at the *Brancusi* exhibition at the Brummer Gallery, New York (November 17, 1933–January 13, 1934).

Minotaure 1, nos. 3–4 (December), illustrates Giacometti's *Three Figures in a Field*, ***The Palace at 4 a.m.***, ***Flower in Danger***, and the original plaster of ***Woman with Her Throat Cut*** on the floor in his studio. Giacometti's short text describes ***The Palace at 4 a.m.*** as an image of the place where he lives with a lover in his dreams

1934 Moore carves *Reclining Figure* and *Figure (Torso)* with sexualized anatomies; the female torso has overly large breasts pointed upward and a hole where the face should be. He carves *Composition*, ***Bird and Egg*** and ***Two Forms*** **(figs. 63 and 65)**, and *Four-Piece Reclining Figure,* multi-component abstractions with bony and boulder-like shapes.

Duchamp and Cornell meet again at the Levy Gallery and become friends.

Ruth Bernhard makes her first photographs of female nudes and objects.

Smith sees original iron sculptures by González and Pablo Gargallo, which encourage him to explore metal constructions.

Calder refers to the works in his *Mobiles* exhibition at the Matisse Gallery (April 6–28) as "Objets Caldériens."

Minotaure 2, no. 5 (May), illustrates Giacometti's *Nocturnal Pavilion* plaster (later retitled *Cube,* although it is polygonal).

Ernst collects river stones during his vacation with Giacometti in Maloja, Switzerland (summer), paints biomorphic patterns on many, and learns to use carving tools and plaster. After returning to Paris, he starts modeling fantastic creatures, including *Lunar Frame (Woman-Bird)*, *Habakuk*, and *Oedipus*.

Dalí's exhibition at the Galerie Bonjean in Paris (June 20–July 13) includes four *Objects*.

Duchamp assembles images pertaining to ***The Large Glass*** in his *Green Box*, which is published in Paris (September).

Dalí arrives in New York (November), his first visit to the US.

Abstract Sculpture by Alberto Giacometti at the Levy Gallery (December 1, 1934–January

1, 1935) presents twelve sculptures from 1927–34, including ***No More Play***, *Disagreeable Object* (titled *Object Without a Base*), a marble *Object*, the recently completed *Head* (now known as *Head/Skull)*, and possibly ***The Invisible Object*** (as *Female Figure, plaster;* **fig. 47**). No works are sold, so Levy keeps ***No More Play*** to offset his expenses.

Hans Bellmer's photographs are published as a double-page spread in *Minotaure* 2, no. 6 (winter), entitled "The Doll—Variations on the Assemblage of an Articulated Minor."

Noguchi experiments with organic forms and metamorphosis in his plaster proposal for the ***United Hosiery Workers' Memorial***; it is illustrated in *Parnassus* 7, no. 2 (February 1935).

1935 Georges Hugnet's essay "The Useful Object: About Oscar Dominguez" in *Cahiers d'art* 10, nos. 5–6, illustrates four assemblages by Dominguez, including ***The Wanderings of Georges Hugnet*** and ***Thorn Puller*** (**figs. 46** and **55**).

Wolfgang Paalen, who knows Arp through the Abstraction-Création group, meets Breton and joins the movement.

Moore signs the British "Manifesto of Surrealism," published in *Cahiers d'Art* 10, nos. 5–6, and starts a series of large colored drawings of imagined biomorphic sculptures in landscapes and architectural settings.

Noguchi works in Mexico City on a monumental biomorphic relief *History of Mexico*; after its completion in mid-1936, he returns to New York.

Giacometti returns to making representational art based on visible reality and is consequently expelled from the group; his sculptures continue to appear in the group's exhibitions during the late 1930s and thereafter.

International Art from Cubism to Surrealism (January 15–28) in Denmark shows only a few minor sculptures.

Miró's *Rope and Personages* is included in his exhibition at the Matisse Gallery (January–February).

Breton delivers a lecture on "The Surrealist Situation of the Object" in Prague (March 29).

Matisse invites Calder (April) to exhibit at his gallery, provided that "there won't be any wall cracking or floor nailing or ceiling bursting, and . . . my carpet [must] not be eaten up by your wild menagerie," but it is postponed to early 1936.

International Surrealism, a group exhibition in the Canary Islands (May), features works by artists from eight countries, including Arp, Bellmer, Dalí, Dominguez, Duchamp, Ernst, Giacometti, Maurice Henry, Hugo, Marcel Jean, Dora Maar, Oppenheim, Ray, and Jindrich Styrsky.

Dalí's book *Conquest of the Irrational*, published by Levy in New York (July), includes photographs of his *Object Functioning Symbolically* and *Retrospective Bust of a Woman*.

Smith develops the fusion of organic forms and welded metal in *Suspended Woman*. He departs for Europe (October); in Paris he meets many artists, including Picasso and Jacques Lipchitz (who had been sculpting in a biomorphic style since 1929–30). In Greece he becomes interested in mythology. His travels end in London, and he returns to the United States in July 1936.

Lipchitz's emotive biomorphic sculptures are exhibited at the Brummer Gallery (December 2, 1935–January 31, 1936).

1936 Read's *Surrealism* book is published in London; illustrations of sculptures include a plaster *Double Head (Oedipus)* by Ernst, a *Reclining Figure* by Moore, and Penrose's ***Last Voyage of Captain Cook*** (**fig. 56**).

Levy publishes his *Surrealism* book in New York. Illustrations include sculptures by Arp, Dalí (***Aphrodisiac Jacket***, **fig. 49**), Duchamp (***Why Not Sneeze?***), Giacometti (***No More Play***, ***The Palace at 4 a.m.***, *Three Mobile Figures*), Oppenheim (***Object***, **fig. 106**), and Cornell (*Soap Bubble Set*). The book also illustrates photographs by Atget (*Shop Window*), Umbo (mannequin's legs), and Bellmer (*The Doll*).

Cahun starts taking photographs of arranged objects, including several of a small wood mannequin in a glass dome (**fig. 110**) and a number for the illustrations of Lise Deharme's children's book *Le Coeur de Pic* (*The Woodpecker's Heart*; published early 1937).

Mobiles and Objects by Alexander Calder at the Matisse Gallery (February 10–29) includes motorized and interactive constructions. Jerome Klein's review in the *New York Post* (February 15) advised visitors to "step up and whack the thing as smartly as you dare, and then be prepared to duck, for it is apt to fly at you in some unpredictable fashion."

Calder directs his energy to constructing Surrealist sculptures using organic forms; many allude to animals and insects, such as *Mantis*. He expands his repertoire to include landscapes, such as ***Gibraltar*** (**fig. 145**), and whimsically odd combinations of things, such as *Cello on a Spindle*.

Cubism and Abstract Art at the Museum of Modern Art (March 2–April 19) features an "abstract surrealism" section that includes works by Arp, Ernst, and Miró.

Surrealist Exhibition of Objects at Galerie Charles Ratton (May 22–31) is organized in categories (**fig. 50**).
• "Readymades" includes only Duchamp's ***Bottle Rack*** and ***Why Not Sneeze?***
• "Incorporated Objects" features Ernst's sculpture of a standing bird (later titled *The Beautiful German Girl*).
• "Found Objects" includes works by Ernst, Henry, Jean, Maar, Ray, Tanguy, and others.
• "Interpreted Found Objects" includes Ray's ***Varlop***.
• "Surrealist Objects" presents both organic abstractions and found-object assemblages: Biormorphic: Arp's ***Head with Annoying Objects***, Ernst's *Double Head*, and Tanguy's stuffed-fabric relief *The Other Side of the Bridge*.
Assemblages: Bellmer's ***Center of the Doll*** (**fig. 86**), Dalí's ***Aphrodisiac Jacket***, Cahun's bridal bed, Ernst's *Moving Object*, Henry's ***Homage to Paganini*** (**fig. 54**), Hugnet's ***Book-Objects***, Jean's *The Gardenia's Ghost*, Magritte's *This Is a Piece of Cheese*, Miró's ***Object*** with stuffed parrot (**fig. 48**), Oppenheim's ***Object***, Paalen's *The Exact Time* (a standing clock with mustaches as hands), Ray's ***What We All Lack*** (**fig. 53**), and five sculptures by Dominguez, including ***Thorn Puller***, ***The Wanderings of Georges Hugnet***, *The Typist* (two back-scratchers standing over broken glass), and *Exact Sensibility* (a white sphere from which a hand emerges grasping a syringe, which is plunged into the sphere).

• The show includes two geometric abstractions: Calder's minimalist *Mobile* and Ray's

Orator relief with its small distortional mirror.

Cahiers d'art 11, nos. 1–2, a special issue on *The Object*, illustrates many works from the Galerie Ratton exhibition and publishes related essays: Breton's "Crisis of the Object," Cahun's "Beware of Domestic Objects," Dalí's "Analysis of the *Aphrodisiac Jacket*," and Dalí's "Honor to the Object," which includes an illustration of Magritte's *This Is a Piece of Cheese*. Other illustrations in this issue include Ernst's *Objects Incorporated* (now called *The Beautiful German Girl*) and *Mobile Object Recommended for Families* in motion.

Minotaure 3, no. 8 (June 15), illustrates Giacometti's ***Cage*** (as *Sculpture*), where it is seen by Moore, Smith, and other international artists. The issue also features a sculpture by Moore.

International Exhibition of Surrealism at the New Burlington Galleries in London (June 11 – July 4) shows 390 works by sixty-eight artists from fourteen countries. The show—subtitled *Dreamland*—receives more than thirty thousand visitors. Works brought from the Galerie Ratton exhibition include Ernst's plaster ***Lunar Asparagus*** **(fig. 57)**, Giacometti's plaster ***Spoon Woman***, a wood assemblage by Calder, Dalí's ***Aphrodisiac Jacket***, several mannequins, Oppenheim's ***Object*** (as *Furry Cup, Saucer, and Spoon*), Ray's *Orator*, and a dozen photograms and photographs of objects, including photographs by Bellmer and Cahun. Arp shows seven works, and Penrose exhibits ***The Last Voyage of Captain Cook***. Around this time Arp visits Moore in his Hampstead studio.

Moore contributes to the *International Surrealist Bulletin* (September), which illustrates his erotic *Torso/Figure*.

Fantastic Art, Dada, Surrealism exhibition—originally called *Art of the Marvelous and Anti-Rational*—at the Museum of Modern Art (December 7, 1936–January 17, 1937) presents a historic overview of seven hundred works from medieval times to the present. After New York, the exhibition tours around the country. Surrealist sculptures include:

- Arp: Fifteen works from 1916 to 1935, including reliefs (*Mountain Table Anchor Navel*; *Shirt and Tie*; *Head*; *Woman and Mustache*) and freestanding sculptures (*Birds in an Aquarium*; *Leaves and Navels*; *Human Concretion*).

- Calder: *Mantis* and ***Gibraltar***.

- Cornell: *Natural History*, 1934 (a dozen vials are shown outside the box so their labeled contents can be seen) and *Soap Bubble Set: Composition of Objects*, 1936, also ten small glass domes, each containing a found object.

- Dominguez: ***The Wanderings of Georges Hugnet***.

- Duchamp: ***Cemetery of Uniforms and Liveries, No. 2 (The Bachelors and Nine Malic Molds)*** **(fig. 3)** and ***Why Not Sneeze?***

- Ernst: Fourteen works, including *Two Children Are Threatened by a Nightingale*, ***Loplop Introduces a Young Girl***, and the plaster ***Lunar Asparagus***.

- Giacometti: *Disagreeable Object*, ***No More Play***, *Head-Landscape*, and ***The Palace at 4 a.m.***

- Jean: ***The Gardenia's Ghost***.

- Miró: *Relief Construction* (with white biomorphic form), *Rope and Personages*, and ***Object*** (with stuffed parrot).

- Moore: ***Reclining Figure*** **(fig. 64)**.

- Oppenheim: ***Object (Breakfast in Fur)*** is the most popular work.

- Ray: *Orator* and a drawing of ***Object of Destruction***.

Dalí comes to New York for his exhibition at the Levy Gallery (December 10, 1936–January 1937). In December he designs a window display for Bonwit Teller called ***She Was a Surrealist Woman, She Was Like a Figure in a Dream*** **(fig. 51)** and sends a harp entwined with barbed wire to Harpo Marx in Los Angeles.

1937 *Max Ernst: Works from 1919 to 1936*, a special issue of *Cahiers d'art*, features Ernst's essay "Beyond Painting" and illustrates *Two Children Are Threatened by a Nightingale*, ***Loplop Introduces a Young Girl***, *Oedipus Rex*, ***Lunar Asparagus*** on a grassy lawn, *Found Objects*, three views of *Round Head* (now called *The Beautiful German Girl*), and *Mobile Object Recommended for Families*.

Breton's *L'Amour fou* cites Giacometti's discovery of a metal mask at a flea-market and its impact on the face of ***The Invisible Object*** as an example of the power of "objective chance."

Smith pushes his biomorphic style to greater abstraction and three-dimensional sophistication, notably in ***Swung Forms*** **(fig. 159)**.

Alexander Calder: Stabiles and Mobiles at the Matisse Gallery (February 23–March 13) features *Cello on a Spindle*, ***Devil Fish*** **(fig. 149)**, and ***Big Bird*** **(fig. 148)**. The latter, on much longer legs, dominates one gallery; under it are six tiny maquettes positioned like baby "chicks." Reviewer Malcolm Vaughan in *New York American* (March 6) writes: "It is not quite understandable why [these] strange contraptions . . . should be reckoned an exhibition of art objects."

Breton opens the Gradiva bookshop (May), where he exhibits Surrealist art.

Surrealism exhibition in Tokyo (June 9–14) includes at least one sculpture by Giacometti.

Minotaure 3, no. 10 (winter), illustrates Surrealist sculptures, including Cornell's ***Untitled (Glass Bell)***, Moore's sexualized *Torso/Figure*, and a satin-lined wheelbarrow by Dominguez.

The *Surrealist Objects and Poems* exhibition at the London Gallery (November 1937) shows 138 works, 88 of them by British artists. Moore's biomorphic figures are outnumbered by found-object assemblages, such as Eileen Agar's *Angel of Anarchy*.

Calder lives in London from October 1937 to February 1938. His exhibition at the Mayor Gallery (December 1–24) displays *Tightrope* and ***Devil Fish***.

1938 Roberto Matta joins the movement in Paris after several years of making automatist drawings and paintings in a biomorphic mode.

Smith's solo show at the East River Gallery in New York (January) includes seventeen welded sculptures.

International Exhibition of Surrealism at the Galerie des Beaux-Arts in Paris (January 17–February 24) presents over two hundred works by seventy artists from fourteen countries, but the show is dominated by Paris-based artists. The first gallery presents sixteen mannequins in perplexing costumes, collectively titled ***The Surrealist Street* (figs. 94–100)**, and the main gallery features Duchamp's false ceiling *1,200 Coal Sacks* (only about one-fifth of that number were actually used) illuminated by a brazier below, with leaves scattered on the floor and a small pond with reeds. Surrealist furniture—a key component of the exhibition—includes Breton's cabinet on mannequin legs, Paalen's *Ivy-Covered Chair*, Kurt Seligmann's *Ultra Furniture* hassock on four female legs, and Dominguez's female phonograph called *Never*.

• Foreign artists are limited to two works each, except for Moore, who shows several drawings and three sculptures (including *Reclining Figure*, 1934–35). Americans include Calder and Cornell.

• *The Abridged Dictionary of Surrealism*, edited by Breton and Paul Eluard, is published in lieu of a catalogue.

Bellmer moves to Paris (March) and continues making photographs of his ***Doll* (fig. 91)**.

International Exhibition of Surrealism at Galerie Robert in Amsterdam (June 3–August 1) and The Hague (September 10–30) presents a smaller version of the Paris show.

Louise Bourgeois moves from Paris to New York (October), where she studies painting at the Art Students League.

1939 Smith is intrigued by Read's *Surrealism* book, writing in his *Notebook* a quote by Hugnet: "automatism . . . aims at exteriorizing all man's desires, his obsessions, and his despairs. It gives him the means to free himself, to venture forth. What is dream, what is reality? At what point do images begin?"

Moore produces large, finely finished drawings of biomorphic Surrealist sculptures in architectural and landscape settings **(figs. 67, 69, 72–73)**, and continues until the start of World War II.

Moore's exhibition at the Mayor Gallery (February) features his drawings.

Dalí travels to New York (February) for his exhibition of paintings and objects at the Levy Gallery (March 21–April 17). He designs another window display with a fur-lined bathtub for Bonwit Teller and is involved in a fracas for which he is arrested (May 16). He designs the *Dream of Venus* pavilion (April) for the World's Fair in New York but leaves before it opens (June 6). The largest room comprises a huge aquarium with a piano and fireplace; at scheduled times young women dive into the aquarium and entertain. Other rooms include objects, such as an umbrella ceiling, intended to suggest a dream experience.

Germany invades Czechoslovakia (March); World War II begins (September).

Calder Mobiles–Stabiles at the Matisse Gallery (May 9–27) includes ***Hollow Egg* (fig. 144)**. MoMA commissions Calder to create the large mobile *Lobster Trap and Fish Tail* which will hang over the museum's main staircase for decades.

Noguchi submits three proposals for the World's Fair; only *Chassis Fountain* is completed on a monumental scale for the Ford Motor Company pavilion (May–October 1939).

Britain and France respond to Germany's aggression by declaring war (September 3). Tanguy emigrates to the United States (November) and three years later moves to Connecticut, near Calder.

The subjects of Cornell's boxes range from ballet and movies to birds and sand. A review in the *New York Times* (December 10) mentions a "whirling eyeball under a bell jar and a book which is a box in which things slide and kaleidoscope." A review in *Artnews* (December 23) describes the artist-designed environment in the *Exhibition of Objects by Joseph Cornell* at the Levy Gallery (December).

1940 *International Exhibition of Surrealism* at the Gallery of Mexican Art in Mexico City (January 17–February) includes only a few sculptures because of transportation difficulties: Arp's *Period and Comma*, Ray's photograph of Duchamp's *50 cc of Paris Air*, Oppenheim's ***My Governess* (fig. 107)**, Tanguy's biomorphic *Merchant of Sand* relief, and photographs by Denise Bellon and Raoul Ubac of the 1938 Paris exhibition.

Germany invades the Netherlands, Belgium, Denmark, and Norway (March–June), then occupies Paris (June 14). Bellmer and Ernst are interned as enemy aliens in France; Ernst is later released and goes to New York. Miró settles in Spain; Giacometti and Arp go to Switzerland. Other artists flee to Marseille to find transport to the United States. Dalí and Ray arrive in New York (August); both subsequently move to California.

Smith has a solo show at Neumann-Willard Gallery in New York (March 25–April 15) and begins living full-time in Bolton Landing in upstate New York.

Matta's exhibition at the Levy Gallery (April) presents his turbulent paintings of emotionally conceived fantastic landscapes.

Calder's exhibition at the Matisse Gallery (May 14–June 1) features *Black Beast*.

Surrealism Today exhibition at the Zwemmer Gallery in London (June) consists mostly of paintings and drawings; it marks the movement's demise in Britain. As a reviewer remarked in *Poetry and the People*, no. 20 (June 1940), "If this is all the Surrealists have to say after nine months of war, they would be better advised to remain silent." William Plomber, in *New Statesman and Nation*, June 29, 1940, noted that Surrealist imagery anticipated the reality of totalitarianism and war: "The high explosives which are going off everywhere were first detonated in the unconscious. . . . In total war the incongruous has already become the commonplace. . . . Dalí's melting watches, flesh beset by ants, disintegrating tripes . . . chests of drawers embedded in torsos, are now features of many a landscape."

London Bulletin, nos. 18–20 (June), publishes Gordon Onslow-Ford's article on Moore's large ***Reclining Figure* (fig. 68)**. Conroy Maddox's essay "The Object in Surrealism" provides detailed descriptions of certain assemblages from the previous decade and illustrates recent examples (no longer extant) by Agar and Ray.

Joseph Cornell: Exhibition of Objects (subtitled *Daguerreotypes, Miniature Glass Bells, Soap Bubble Sets, Shadow Boxes, Homage to the Romantic Ballet*) is presented at the Levy Gallery (December 10–26). Around this time Cornell decides to leave his job at the textile company and devote himself full-time to art.

1941 Levy Gallery presents *Salvador Dalí: Paintings, Drawings, and Jewels* (April 22–May 20). The artist spends the summer in Pebble

Beach, California, where he designs a décor called *A Surrealistic Night in an Enchanted Forest* for a fundraising gala for European refugees (September 2).

Calder produces Surrealist stabiles, such as *Giraffe* and *The Great Yucca*; some are exhibited in *Alexander Calder: Recent Works* at the Matisse Gallery (May 17–June 14).

Duchamp takes his *Box in a Valise* to New York (June), where Cornell helps make more. Breton arrives in New York (June). Ernst arrives (July) and is a key figure among the exiled Surrealists before moving to Sedona, Arizona.

Noguchi leaves New York for San Francisco (September) and remains in California through the end of the year.

Levy organizes the *Surrealist Paintings, Documents, Objects* exhibition in Hollywood (November 25–December 7).

The United States enters World War II after the Japanese attack Pearl Harbor (December 7).

1942 Smith works as a welder in a locomotive factory for two years, leaving him little time for art.

Cornell works increasingly in thematic series, particularly the horizontal ***Museum*** boxes neatly filled with found objects and small glass vials containing diverse items **(figs. 122 and 124)**, the vertical *Pharmacy* boxes with glass doors (Duchamp and Peggy Guggenheim each acquire one), and the *Aviary* boxes featuring images of birds.

Artists in Exile exhibition at the Matisse Gallery (March) includes biomorphic works by Ernst, Masson, Matta, and Tanguy.

Noguchi voluntarily enters a Japanese-American internment camp in Poston, Arizona (May), hoping to design improvements. After seven months he returns to New York, where he rediscovers Surrealist biomorphism.

View, a new art magazine, focuses on Surrealism. Issue no. 2 (May) prioritizes Tanguy's exhibition of recent paintings at the Matisse Gallery (April 21–May 9); its cover features an illusionistically sculptural biomorphic composition.

VVV, a new magazine conceived by Breton, Ernst, and Duchamp, with David Hare as editor, publishes the first of four issues (June). One (October) is devoted to Surrealism; another (November) features Cornell and illustrates a *Medici Slot Machine* (see fig. 128).

Guggenheim's Art of This Century gallery opens (October) with *Objects, Drawings, Photographs, Paintings, Sculpture, Collages 1910–1942*. Most works are Surrealist; Frederick Kiesler designs biomorphic furniture and pedestals.

Duchamp creates the *Miles of String* environment for the *First Papers of Surrealism* exhibition (October 14–November 7), which obscures the open space with crisscrossed twine. Calder's ***Spider*** **(fig. 153)**, is the largest work in the show.

Objects by Joseph Cornell / Marcel Duchamp: Box-Valise / Laurence Vail: Bottles is presented at Art of This Century gallery (December); most works are owned by Guggenheim, including Cornell's *Setting for a Fairy Tale*.

1943 Noguchi starts making biomorphic sculptures—some incorporating found elements—that express his dark state of mind during World War II, notably ***Untitled***, ***Monument to Heroes***, and ***This Tortured Earth*** **(figs. 134–135 and 137)**. Using a new heat-resistant cement, he molds biomorphic ***Lunars*** **(figs. 136 and 139)** and illuminates them from within. He designs abstract interlocking stage sets for dancer Martha Graham's *Herodiade*.

Calder's series of wood and wire constructions are christened *Constellations* by Duchamp and curator James Johnson Sweeney (January–February) for their exhibition at the Matisse Gallery, which also includes seven paintings by Tanguy (May–June).

Smith's exhibition at the Willard Gallery (April 6–May 1) presents eighteen sculptures and five biomorphic drawings from 1939–43, including *Widow's Lament, Atrocity, Objects Left at the Terminal Iron Works, Sewing Machine*, and *Reclining Figure*.

Moore has his first solo exhibition in New York at the Buchholz Gallery (May 11–29).

Alexander Calder: Sculptures and Constructions, the first retrospective of a living sculptor at MoMA (September 29, 1943–January 16, 1944), is hugely popular and goes on a national tour to regional art museums.

Through the Big End of the Opera Glass: Joseph Cornell, Marcel Duchamp, Yves Tanguy takes place at the Levy Gallery (December 7–28).

Natural, Insane, Surrealist Art exhibition at Art of This Century (December) juxtaposes objects from nature (skeletons, driftwood, tree roots) and Surrealist sculptures, including objects by Calder and Cornell.

1944 *Henry Moore*, a monograph by Geoffrey Grigson, is published in London.

Ernst spends the summer on Long Island, where he models biomorphic sculptures in plaster, notably *An Anxious Friend*, *The Table Is Set*, and ***Moonmad*** **(fig. 78)**.

Arp exhibition at Art of This Century gallery (February) consists of twenty-seven works from 1915–40, all from American collections.

David Hare: Sculptures at Art of This Century gallery (November) consists of twenty-six works in plaster and wire, including *Lady of Waiting* and *The Frog is a Heart*. Some works have kinetic features, using springs, suspension, and weights.

1945 After metal rationing ends, Calder makes *Man-Eater with Pennants* for MoMA's sculpture garden and creates several black-painted stabiles with war-related titles, such as ***Bayonets Menacing a Flower*** **(fig. 152)** and *The General Sherman*.

Smith has his most productive year ever, creating thirty-four sculptures that summarize themes developed during the war years. Many are biomorphic in style and depict surprising subjects, such as *Ring-Toothed Woman, Woman in the Subway, Big Rooster,* ***Ancient Household*** **(fig. 161)** and the first of the *Spectre* series of fantastic birds in flight, notably *Jurassic Bird* and *Pillar of Sunday*.

Noguchi makes interlocking sculptures, which he models in black paper. He executes *Remembrance* and *Man* in wood, ***Strange Bird (To the Sunflower)***, ***Trinity***, and *Humpty-Dumpty* in stone **(figs. 142–43)**.

Alberto Giacometti at Art of This Century gallery (February 10–March 10) presents nine of his Surrealist sculptures from American collections, including ***Disagreeable Object***, *Model for a City Plaza*, ***No More Play***, ***The Palace at 4 a.m.***, ***Walking Woman***, and ***Woman with Her Throat Cut*** (illustrated on the invitation).

Man Ray: Objects of My Affection at the Levy Gallery (April) includes a recreated *Lampshade* and ***Object to Be Destroyed***, along with recent works *Mr. Knife and Miss Fork* and *Life Saver*. The show travels to the Circle Gallery in Los Angeles (September).

Sculptures and Paintings by Max Ernst at the Levy Gallery (May 1–31) includes his new plaster hybrid figures.

World War II ends in Europe (June) and then in the Pacific (August).

Surrealism: Pictures, Objects, Photographs at La Boétie gallery in Brussels (December 1945–January 1946) is the first postwar group exhibition of Surrealist art.

1946 Arp leaves Switzerland for Paris, bringing the plasters he made during the war, notably ***Alu with Claws***.

In Spain, Miró completes small models of ***Lunar Bird* (fig. 79)**, *Solar Bird*, and *Woman*, which he will enlarge later.

Smith exhibits fifty-four sculptures from 1936–45, most from 1944–45, jointly at the Willard and Buchholz galleries in New York (January).

Sculpture by David Hare at Art of This Century (January–February) consists of twenty-three sculptures in plaster and cement, notably *The Magician's Game* and *Trap for a Gorilla*.

Breton returns to Paris (spring) and attempts to resuscitate the movement. He publishes revised editions of the two *Manifestoes of Surrealism*. He starts organizing a group exhibition, helped by Duchamp who arrives in the fall.

Dalí designs the sets for the dream portion of Alfred Hitchcock's film *Spellbound* (September).

Fourteen Americans exhibition at MoMA (September 11–December 8) includes twelve of Noguchi's biomorphic and interlocking sculptures, notably *Metamorphosis*, *Kouros*, ***Monument to Heroes***, and ***Gregory (Effigy)* (figs. 135 and 140).** Thomas Hess publishes "Contemporary Contour: Isamu Noguchi" in *Artnews* (September).

Duchamp goes to New York (December), where he collaborates with Enrico Donati on designing the catalogue for the upcoming Surrealist exhibition in Paris; the cover consists of a foam-rubber "falsie" breast titled *Please Touch*.

1947 Smith shows new sculptures on landscape themes at the Willard Gallery, along with examples from the ongoing *Spectre* series. He writes three poems in an autobiographical Surrealist mode for the catalogue.

Noguchi models ***Avatar* (fig. 141)** and carves *Night Land* in black marble, then *Cronos* in pale balsa wood.

Surrealism in 1947 at the Galerie Maeght in Paris (July–August) presents works by eighty-seven artists, mostly paintings and drawings. In addition to biomorphic sculptures by Arp, Hare, and Noguchi, a younger generation of artists emerges.

1948 *International Exhibitions of Surrealism* take place in in Santiago, Chile, and in Prague, where the movement continues with a darker mood under the Soviet regime.

Giacometti's exhibition at the Matisse Gallery (January 19–February 14) reveals his mature style of extremely thin figures, notably *Walking Man*, *Tall Figure*, and *The Nose*.

Dalí leaves the United States for Spain (July).

Objects by Joseph Cornell (September) at Copley Galleries in Los Angeles presents a survey of forty-two works from the 1930s onward (fig. 121)

1949 Ernst returns to Paris.

Les Jeux de la poupée (The Doll's Games), Bellmer's book of photographs and prose poems by Eluard, begun in 1938–39, is published in Paris (**see fig. 89**).

Noguchi's exhibition of his war-time sculptures at the Charles Egan Gallery (March) is a critical and commercial success, but the artist abandons Surrealism and the United States to travel and study globally for several years.

David Hare, Sculpture at the Levy Gallery (March–April) is the last exhibition before the gallery closes.

Cornell's exhibition *Aviary by Joseph Cornell* at the Egan Gallery (December) intrigues Robert Rauschenberg, who advises his parents-in-law to buy several boxes.

1950–52 Duchamp writes a short essay about Arp for the exhibition catalogue of *Collection of the Société Anonyme* at the Yale University Art Gallery (spring 1950).

Cornell: Night Songs and Other New Work at the Egan Gallery (December 1950) includes boxes in the *Aviary* and *Observatory* series.

Cyril Connolly's essay on Surrealism in *Artnews Annual* 21 (November 1951) considers the movement as a prewar historical phenomenon rather than an ongoing one.

EXHIBITION CHECKLIST

JEAN (HANS) ARP
(French, b. Germany, 1886–1966; also active in Switzerland)

The Forest (Earthly Forms), 1916–17
Wood and paint
12⅞ × 7¾ × 3 in. (32.7 × 19.7 × 7.6 cm)
National Gallery of Art, Washington, DC; Andrew W. Mellon Fund (1977.20.1)
fig. 10

Enak's Tears (Earthly Forms), 1917
Wood and paint
34 × 23⅛ × 2⅜ in. (86.2 × 58.5 × 6 cm)
The Museum of Modern Art, New York; Benjamin Scharps and David Scharps Fund and purchase (1197.1979)
fig. 11

Torso-Navel, 1921
Wood and oil paint
31½ × 20½ × 2½ in. (80.1 × 52.2 × 6.5 cm)
Yale University Art Gallery, New Haven; gift of Katherine S. Dreier to the Collection Société Anonyme (1950.47)
fig. 12

Shirt Front and Fork, 1922
Wood and paint
23 × 27½ × 2⅜ in. (58.4 × 70 × 6.1 cm)
National Gallery of Art, Washington, DC; Ailsa Mellon Bruce Fund (1983.3.1)
fig. 13

Man-Mustaches, 1925
Oil paint on paperboard
26⅛ × 24 in. (66.4 × 61 cm)
Private collection, courtesy Acquavella Galleries, New York
fig. 14

Objects Placed on Three Planes Like Writing, 1928
Wood and oil paint
31¾ × 39¼ in. (80.6 × 99.7 cm)
Wadsworth Atheneum Museum of Art, Hartford; purchased through the gift of James Junius Goodwin (1937.91)
fig. 22

Head with Annoying Objects (Mustache, Mandolin, and Fly), 1930
Bronze
14 × 10¼ × 7½ in. (35.6 × 26 × 19.1 cm)
Private collection
fig. 45

Torso, Navel, Mustache-Flower, 1930
Wood and oil paint
31½ × 39⅜ × 1½ in. (80 × 100 × 3.8 cm)
The Metropolitan Museum of Art, New York; the Muriel Kallis Steinberg Newman Collection, gift of Muriel Kallis Newman, 2006 (2006.32.1)
fig. 59

Configuration with Two Dangerous Points, c. 1930
Wood and oil paint
27½ × 33½ in. (69.8 × 85.1 cm)
Philadelphia Museum of Art; A. E. Gallatin Collection, 1947 (1947-88-3)
fig. 23

Alu with Claws, 1942
Bronze
22¼ × 14½ × 12⅛ in. (56.4 × 36.6 × 30.8 cm)
Hirshhorn Museum and Sculpture Garden, Washington, DC; gift of Joseph H. Hirshhorn, 1966 (66.104)
*not illustrated

HANS BELLMER
(German, 1902–1975; also active in France)

The Doll, 1933–34
Gelatin silver print
4⅝ × 3⅛ in. (11.7 × 7.8 cm)
The Metropolitan Museum of Art, New York; Ford Motor Company Collection, gift of Ford Motor Company Collection and John C. Waddell, 1987 (1987.1100.332)
fig. 82

The Doll, 1934
Gelatin silver print
2¼ × 3½ in. (5.9 × 8.9 cm)
Ubu Gallery, New York & Galerie Berinson, Berlin
fig. 87

Untitled (Reclining Doll), 1934
Graphite on paper
7⅜ × 5⅛ in. (18.7 × 13 cm)
Pace Gallery, New York
fig. 81

The Doll, c. 1934
Gelatin silver print
10 × 12⅞ in. (25.3 × 32.7 cm)
The Metropolitan Museum of Art, New York; Ford Motor Company Collection, gift of Ford Motor Company Collection and John C. Waddell, 1987 (1987.1100.261)
fig. 84

The Doll, 1934–35
Gelatin silver print
11⅝ × 7⅝ in. (29.5 × 19.4 cm)
The Metropolitan Museum of Art, New York; Ford Motor Company Collection, gift of Ford Motor Company Collection and John C. Waddell, 1987 (1987.1100.15)
fig. 85

The Doll: Ball-Joint, 1934–36
Plastic and lace on fabric on wood
20½ × 17⅞ × 2¾ in. (52 × 45.5 × 7 cm)
Herbert Lust / Greenwich Fine Arts
fig. 83

The Doll, 1935, printed 1949 or earlier
Gelatin silver print with watercolor
5⅜ × 5¼ in. (13.9 × 13.5 cm)
Ubu Gallery, New York & Galerie Berinson, Berlin
fig. 89

The Doll, 1935
Gelatin silver print
6⅝ × 6⅞ in. (16.8 × 17.5 cm)
Ubu Gallery, New York & Galerie Berinson, Berlin
fig. 92

The Doll on the Staircase, 1935
Gelatin silver print
9 × 6⅝ in. (22.9 × 16.8 cm)
Ubu Gallery, New York & Galerie Berinson, Berlin
fig. 88

The Doll, 1936, printed 1949 or earlier
Gelatin silver print with watercolor
5⅝ × 5⅝ in. (14.3 × 14.3 cm)
Ubu Gallery, New York & Galerie Berinson, Berlin
fig. 90

The Center of the Doll, c. 1936
Gelatin silver print with watercolor
3½ × 2⅝ in. (9 × 6.6 cm)
The Metropolitan Museum of Art, New York; Ford Motor Company Collection, gift of Ford Motor Company Collection and John C. Waddell, 1987 (1987.1100.333)
fig. 86

The Doll, 1938
Gelatin silver print with watercolor
7 × 7⅛ in. (17.8 × 18 cm)
The Metropolitan Museum of Art, New York; Gilman Collection, purchase, Warner Communications Inc. Purchase Fund, by exchange (2005.100.643)
fig. 91

RUTH BERNHARD
(American, b. Germany, 1905–2006)

Creation, 1936
Gelatin silver print
15⅞ × 19⅞ in. (40.3 × 50.4 cm)
Princeton University Art Museum; bequest of Ruth Bernhard (2008-424)
fig. 112

Broken Doll, 1938
Gelatin silver print
7½ × 9 in. (19 × 23 cm)
Princeton University Art Museum; bequest of Ruth Bernhard (2008-439)
fig. 111

Puppet Hand and Foot, 1938
Gelatin silver print
6¼ × 9½ in. (16 × 24 cm)
Princeton University Art Museum; bequest of Ruth Bernhard (2008-463)
fig. 114

Quicksand, 1938
Gelatin silver print
9⅜ × 7 in. (24 × 18 cm)
Princeton University Art Museum; bequest of Ruth Bernhard (2008-464)
fig. 113

CLAUDE CAHUN
(French, 1894–1954; also active in Britain)

The Hour of Flowers, 1936
Gelatin silver print with watercolor and graphite
4⅝ × 5½ in. (11.7 × 14 cm)
Ubu Gallery, New York & Galerie Berinson, Berlin
fig. 108

Untitled, 1936
Gelatin silver print
7 × 5 in. (17.8 × 12.8 cm)
Tate Gallery, London; museum purchase, 2007 (P79320)
fig. 109

Untitled, 1936
Gelatin silver print
9⅜ × 7 in. (23.7 × 17.8 cm)
Tate Gallery, London; museum purchase, 2007 (P79318)
fig. 110

ALEXANDER CALDER
(American, 1898–1976; also active in France)

Big Bird, 1937
Sheet metal, bolts, and paint
88 × 50 × 59 in. (223.5 × 127 × 149.9 cm)
Calder Foundation, New York
fig. 148

Devil Fish, 1937
Sheet metal, bolts, and paint
68 × 64 × 47 in. (172.7 × 162.6 × 119.4 cm)
Calder Foundation, New York
fig. 149

Apple Monster, 1938
Wood, wire, and paint
66 × 55½ × 32½ in. (167.6 × 141 × 82.6 cm)
Calder Foundation, New York
fig. 147

Untitled, 1938
Wood, bone, rod, wire, and paint
70¼ × 37 × 23½ in. (178.4 × 94 × 59.7 cm)
Calder Foundation, New York; gift of Holton Rower, 2014
fig. 146

The Spider, 1940
Steel and paint
95 × 99 × 73 in. (241.3 × 251.5 × 185.4 cm)
Raymond and Patsy Nasher Collection, Nasher Sculpture Center, Dallas (NC.1984.A.43)
fig. 153

Untitled (Mobile), 1942
Metal wire, paint, wood, and string
17⅜ × 21⅛ × 5½ in. (40.2 × 54 × 14.1 cm)
Hirshhorn Museum and Sculpture Garden, Washington, DC; the Joseph H. Hirshhorn Bequest, 1981 (86.744)
*not illustrated

Vertical Constellation with Yellow Bone, 1943
Wood, paint, and metal wire
22⅝ × 28⅝ × 25⅝ in. (57.4 × 72.5 × 65 cm)
Hirshhorn Museum and Sculpture Garden, Washington, DC; gift of Joseph H. Hirshhorn, 1972 (72.55)
*not illustrated

Fish, 1944
Metal, paint, plastic, wood, glass, and ceramic
16¼ × 48⅛ × 4½ in. (41.3 × 122.2 × 11.4 cm)
Hirshhorn Museum and Sculpture Garden, Washington, DC; gift of Joseph H. Hirshhorn, 1966 (66.785)
fig. 154

Scarlet Digitals, 1945
Sheet metal, wire, and paint
85 × 95 × 41 in. (215.9 × 241.3 × 104.1 cm)
Calder Foundation, New York
fig. 155

JOSEPH CORNELL
(American, 1903–1972)

Untitled (Schooner), 1931
Printed paper
4¼ × 5⅞ in. (10.8 × 14.7 cm)
Hirshhorn Museum and Sculpture Garden, Washington, DC; Joseph H. Hirshhorn Bequest Fund and partial gift from the daughter of June W. Schuster in honor of her Mother, 2003 (01.17)
*not illustrated

Jouet Surréaliste (Surrealist Toy), c. 1932
Metal toy, printed paper, paint, and ink
7/8 × 4⅛ × 3⅞ in. (2.3 × 10.6 × 9.9 cm)
Smithsonian American Art Museum, Washington, DC; gift of Mr. and Mrs. John A. Benton (1978.95.1)
fig. 117

Untitled (Harlequin Jumping Jack), c. 1935–38
Printed paper, cardboard, and string in wood box
13⅞ × 12⅛ × 2½ in. (35.2 × 30.8 × 6.4 cm)
The Fralin Museum of Art at the University of Virginia, Charlottesville; gift of the Joseph and Robert Cornell Memorial Foundation, 2002 (2002.15.1)
fig. 118

Untitled, not dated
Printed paper and string in cardboard box
1¾ × 4 × 4 in. (4.4 × 10.2 × 10.2 cm)
Joseph Cornell Study Center, Smithsonian American Art Museum, Washington, DC (JC-76)
fig. 119

Bel Echo Gruyère, c. 1939
Paper, aluminum foil, cord, and toy in painted wood box
3⅝ × 7¾ × 7¾ in. (9.2 × 19.7 × 19.7 cm)
Smithsonian American Art Museum, Washington, DC; gift of the Joseph and Robert Cornell Memorial Foundation (1985.64.42a-b)
fig. 120

Untitled (Red Sand Box), c. 1940
Driftwood, sand, shells, and glass marbles in glass-fronted wood box
4½ × 10¾ × 2⅞ in. (11.4 × 27.3 × 7.3 cm)
Collection of Robert Lehrman, courtesy of Aimee and Robert Lehrman, Washington, DC
fig. 123

Untitled, 1940s
Glass vials with cork stoppers, printed paper, paint, beads, and other media in wood box
2⅝ × 10⅞ × 7½ in. (6.7 × 27.7 × 19.1 cm)
Smithsonian American Art Museum, Washington, DC; gift of the Joseph and Robert Cornell Memorial Foundation (1985.64.56)
fig. 124

Untitled (Pink Palace), 1946
Printed paper, mirror, twigs, and glitter in glass-fronted wood box
10 × 14 × 4 in. (25.4 × 35.6 × 10.2 cm)
Smithsonian American Art Museum, Washington, DC; gift of Donald Windham (2001.39)
fig. 127

Untitled (Paul and Virginia), c. 1946–48
Printed paper, straw, bird's eggs, glass, and other media in wood box
12½ × 9⅞ × 4⅜ in. (31.8 × 25.2 × 11.1 cm)
The Robert Lehrman Art Trust, courtesy of Aimee and Robert Lehrman, Washington, DC
fig. 121

Untitled (Aviary with Yellow Birds), c. 1948
Wood, paint, and cork in glass-fronted wood box
21⅛ × 15 × 6⅜ in. (53.7 × 38.1 × 16.2 cm)
Hirshhorn Museum and Sculpture Garden, Washington, DC; gift in honor of James T. Demetrion, Director, HMSG (1984–2001), by Robert and Aimee Lehrman, 2013 (13.7)
*not illustrated

Medici Princess, c. 1948–52
Printed paper and other media in glass-fronted wood box
17⅝ × 12¼ × 4¾ in. (44.5 × 31.1 × 12.1 cm)
Hirshhorn Museum and Sculpture Garden, Washington, DC; museum purchase, 1979 (79.275)
fig. 129

Soap Bubble Set, 1949–50
Glasses, pipes, printed paper, and other media in glass-fronted wood box
14¾ × 18¾ × 4¼ in. (37.5 × 47.6 × 10.7 cm)
Smithsonian American Art Museum, Washington, DC; museum purchase made possible by the American Art Forum (1999.91)
fig. 126

Caravaggio Prince (Medici Slot Machine Variant), c. 1950
Printed paper and objects in glass-fronted wood box
15½ × 9⅝ × 4⅝ in. (39.4 × 24.4 × 11.7 cm)
National Gallery of Art, Washington, DC; Corcoran Collection, gift of the Friends of the Corcoran Gallery of Art (CGA.1978.10)
fig. 128

The Seaside, 1952–54
Printed paper, colored sand, driftwood, starfish, and other media in glass-fronted wood box
12 × 9⅛ × 3¼ in. (30.5 × 23 × 8.2 cm)
Hirshhorn Museum and Sculpture Garden, Washington, DC; the Joseph H. Hirshhorn Bequest, 1981 (86.929)
fig. 130

Suite de la Longitude, 1955–57
Glasses, marbles, printed paper, cork, and metal in glass-fronted wood box
13¼ × 19¾ × 4⅜ in. (33.8 × 50.2 × 11.2 cm)
Hirshhorn Museum and Sculpture Garden, Washington, DC; gift of Joseph H. Hirshhorn, 1966 (66.979)
*not illustrated

Sand Fountain, c. 1955–57
Sand, mirror, glass, gesso, and printed paper in glass-fronted wood box
10⅞ × 8 × 3½ in. (27.6 × 20.3 × 8.9 cm)
Hirshhorn Museum and Sculpture Garden, Washington, DC; gift of Joseph H. Hirshhorn, 1966 (66.978)
fig. 131

SALVADOR DALÍ
(Spanish, 1904–1989; also active in France)

Aphrodisiac Jacket, 1936, exhibition copy 1970s
Wool jacket, cotton shirt, brassiere, cummerbund, tie, collar, and shot glasses containing acrylic inserts and fake flies, on wood and metal hanger
34¾ × 31 × 3 in. (88.3 × 78.7 × 7.6 cm)
Collection of the Salvador Dalí Museum, Inc., St. Petersburg, Florida
fig. 49

Venus de Milo with Drawers, 1936, edition 1964
Bronze, paint, and fur
39½ × 11⅞ × 11 in. (100 × 30 × 28 cm)
Mugrabi Collection
fig. 52

Lobster Telephone, 1938
Plastic, paint, plaster, and other media
7 × 13 × 7 in. (17.8 × 33 × 17.8 cm)
Edward James Foundation, West Dean, England
fig. 103 (Alternate version illustrated)

MARCEL DUCHAMP
(American, b. France, 1887–1968)

Bottle Rack, 1914, 1960 version
Galvanized iron
23¼ × 14½ × 14½ in. (59.1 × 36.8 × 36.8 cm)
Robert Rauschenberg Foundation, New York
fig. 2

Cemetery of Uniforms and Liveries, No. 2 (The Bachelors and Nine Malic Molds), 1914
Watercolor and graphite on paper
26 × 39⅜ in. (66 × 99.8 cm)
Yale University Art Gallery, New Haven; gift of Katherine S. Dreier to the Collection Société Anonyme, 1948 (1948.311)
fig. 3

With Hidden Noise, 1916, edition 1964
Metal, twine, and unknown object
5 × 6 × 5⅞ in. (12.7 × 15.2 × 15 cm)
Collection Timothy Baum, New York
fig. 4

Fresh Widow, 1920, edition 1964
Wood, paint, glass, leather, paper, and tape
30¼ × 20⅞ × 4 in. (76.6 × 53 × 10.2 cm)
National Gallery of Art, Washington, DC; gift of Deborah and Ed Shein (2008.33.1)
fig. 7

Why Not Sneeze, Rose Sélavy?, 1921, edition 1964
Metal cage, paint, marble, thermometer, and cuttlebone
4½ × 8¾ × 6¼ in. (11.5 × 22.2 × 16 cm)
Collection of Aaron and Barbara Levine, Washington, DC
fig. 6 (Original version illustrated)

MAX ERNST
(French, b. Germany, 1891–1976; also active in the United States)

Moonmad, 1944, cast 1956
Bronze
36¾ × 13 × 12⅜ in. (93.3 × 33 × 31.4 cm)
Hirshhorn Museum and Sculpture Garden, Washington, DC; gift of Joseph H. Hirshhorn, 1966 (66.1802)
fig. 78

The Table Is Set, 1944, cast 1954
Bronze
12⅛ × 22⅛ × 23¾ in. (30.8 × 56.2 × 60.3 cm)
Hirshhorn Museum and Sculpture Garden, Washington, DC; gift of Joseph H. Hirshhorn, 1966 (66.1808)
*not illustrated

ALBERTO GIACOMETTI
(Swiss, 1901–1966; also active in France)

Spoon Woman, 1926, cast 1954
Bronze
57½ × 20¼ × 10 in. (146 × 51.5 × 25.4 cm)
Raymond and Patsy Nasher Collection, Nasher Sculpture Center, Dallas (NC.1984.A.37)
fig. 25

Woman, 1928, cast 1929
Bronze
16⅛ × 14⅞ × 3½ in. (40.9 × 37.8 × 8.7 cm)
Hirshhorn Museum and Sculpture Garden, Washington, DC; gift of Joseph H. Hirshhorn Foundation, 1972 (72.131)
*not illustrated

Man, 1929, cast c. 1950
Bronze
15½ × 12½ × 3⅝ in. (39.4 × 31.7 × 9.3 cm)
Hirshhorn Museum and Sculpture Garden, Washington, DC; gift of Joseph H. Hirshhorn, 1966 (66.2033)
*not illustrated

Reclining Woman Who Dreams, 1929
Bronze and paint
9¼ × 16⅞ × 5¾ in. (23.5 × 42.6 × 14.5 cm)
Hirshhorn Museum and Sculpture Garden, Washington, DC; gift of Joseph H. Hirshhorn, 1966 (66.2041)
fig. 27

Man, 1929–30
Plaster and paint
26¾ × 19½ × 7¾ in. (68 × 49.4 × 19.7 cm)
Hirshhorn Museum and Sculpture Garden, Washington, DC; gift of Joseph H. Hirshhorn, 1966 (66.2043)
fig. 26

No More Play, 1931–32
Marble, wood, and bronze
1⅝ × 22⅞ × 17¾ in. (4.1 × 58 × 45.2 cm)
National Gallery of Art, Washington, DC; gift of the Patsy R. and Raymond D. Nasher Collection, Dallas, in honor of the 50th Anniversary of the National Gallery of Art (1991.40.1)
fig. 44

"Objets mobiles et muets" (Moving and Mute Objects)
Le Surréalisme au service de la révolution, no. 3, (December 1931)
fig. 35

Woman with Her Throat Cut, 1932, cast 1949
Bronze
8 × 34½ × 25 in. (20.3 × 87.6 × 63.5 cm)
The Museum of Modern Art, New York; purchase, 1949 (696.1949)
fig. 80

The Invisible Object (Hands Holding the Void), 1934
Bronze
60¼ × 12¾ × 11¾ in. (153 × 32.6 × 29.8 cm)
National Gallery of Art, Washington, DC; Ailsa Mellon Bruce Fund (1973.27.1)
fig. 47

MAURICE HENRY
(French, 1907–1984)

Homage to Paganini, 1936, edition 1968
Violin, gauze, and artificial grass in glass-fronted wood box
9⅝ × 20½ × 3 in. (24.5 × 52 × 10 cm)
Private collection, Ubu Gallery, New York
fig. 54

BARBARA HEPWORTH
(British, 1903–1975)

Reclining Figure, 1933
Stone (alabaster)
7 × 12⅛ × 6⅜ in. (17.7 × 30.7 × 16.2 cm)
Hirshhorn Museum and Sculpture Garden, Washington, DC; gift of Joseph H. Hirshhorn, 1966 (66.2442)
fig. 61

GEORGES HUGNET
(French, 1906–1974)

Hans Bellmer, The Doll, second series 1934–36, 1938
Book (photographs on paper) with binding of leather, imitation hair, and lace
5⅛ × 3⅞ in. (13 × 10 cm)
Collection Timothy Baum, New York
*not illustrated

RENÉ MAGRITTE
(Belgian, 1898–1967; also active in France)

"Les Mots et les images" (Words and Images). *La Révolution surrealiste*, no. 12 (December 1929)
(see pp. 162–63)

Delusions of Grandeur II, 1948
Oil paint on canvas
39⅛ × 32⅛ in. (99.2 × 81.5 cm)
Hirshhorn Museum and Sculpture Garden, Washington, DC; gift of Joseph H. Hirshhorn, 1966 (66.3199)
*not illustrated

ANDRÉ MASSON
(French, 1896–1987)

Caryatid, 1939
Colored sand, seashells, and seaweed on wood
13⅞ × 7¼ in. (35.2 × 18.3 cm)
Hirshhorn Museum and Sculpture Garden, Washington, DC; gift of the Joseph H. Hirshhorn Foundation, 1979 (79.199)
*not illustrated

JOAN MIRÓ
(Spanish, 1893–1983; also active in France)

Painting (Circus Horse), 1927
Oil paint and graphite on burlap
76¾ × 110⅜ in. (195 × 280.2 cm)
Hirshhorn Museum and Sculpture Garden, Washington, DC; gift of the Joseph H. Hirshhorn Foundation, 1972 (72.202)
fig. 20

Object, 1932
Stone, paint, wood, shell, mirror, and sequins
5½ × 22 × 9¾ in. (14 × 55.9 × 24.8 cm)
Philadelphia Museum of Art; A. E. Gallatin Collection, 1952 (1952-61-84a-g)
fig. 41

Lunar Bird, 1945, enlarged and cast 1966–67
Bronze
89⅜ × 88½ × 58¼ in. (207 × 204.9 × 147.8 cm)
Hirshhorn Museum and Sculpture Garden, Washington, DC; gift of Joseph H. Hirshhorn, 1972 (72.204)
fig. 79

HENRY MOORE
(British, 1898–1986)

Bird and Egg, 1934
Stone (Cumberland alabaster)
8⅛ × 22 × 9¼ in. (20.6 × 55.9 × 23.5 cm)
Yale Center for British Art, New Haven; Paul Mellon Collection (B1984.6.3)
fig. 63

Composition, 1934, cast 1961
Bronze
7¾ × 17 × 8 in. (19.6 × 43 × 20.3 cm)
Hirshhorn Museum and Sculpture Garden, Washington, DC; gift of Joseph H. Hirshhorn, 1966 (66.3652)
*not illustrated

Two Forms, 1934
Wood (Pynkado)
11 × 21½ × 12⅛ in. (27.9 × 54.6 × 30.8 cm)
The Museum of Modern Art, New York; Sir Michael Sadler Fund, 1937 (207.1937)
fig. 65

Figure, 1935
Stone (Cumberland alabaster)
11½ × 11⅝ × 6¾ in. (29.2 × 29.5 × 17.1 cm)
Hirshhorn Museum and Sculpture Garden, Washington, DC; gift of Joseph H. Hirshhorn, 1966 (66.3606)
fig. 62

Untitled (Carving), 1935
Wood
10⅜ × 15⅞ × 9⅜ in. (26.2 × 40.2 × 23.6 cm)
Hirshhorn Museum and Sculpture Garden, Washington, DC; gift of Joseph H. Hirshhorn, 1966 (66.3642)
*not illustrated

Stringed Figure No. 1, 1937
Wood (cherry and oak) and string
22⅜ × 5⅜ × 6⅝ in. (56.6 × 13.5 × 16.8 cm)
Hirshhorn Museum and Sculpture Garden, Washington, DC; Joseph H. Hirshhorn Purchase Fund, 1989 (89.28)
fig. 70

Reclining Figure, 1939
Chalk, graphite, ink, and wax crayon on paper
15 × 22 in. (38.1 × 55.9 cm)
Yale Center for British Art, New Haven; gift of Jeffrey H. Loria, Yale B.A. 1962, in memory of Harriet Loria Popowitz (B2005.14.1)
fig. 67

Ideas for Sculpture, 1940
Watercolor, gouache, ink, and wax crayon on paper
16⅞ × 10 in. (42.8 × 25.4 cm)
Harvard Art Museums / Fogg Museum, Cambridge, Massachusetts; gift of Lois Orswell (1993.232)
fig. 66

Three Standing Figures, 1948
Graphite, wax crayon, ink, and gouache on paper
11½ × 9½ in. (29 × 24 cm)
Harvard Art Museums / Fogg Museum, Cambridge, Massachusetts; bequest of Meta and Paul J. Sachs, 1965 (1965.187)
fig. 73

Sculptural Objects, 1949
Lithographic ink on paper
19½ × 30 in. (49.5 × 76.2 cm)
Museum of Fine Arts, Boston; gift of Edna and Matthew Brown in honor of the 100th anniversary of the Print Department, 1987 (1987.513)
fig. 74

Reclining Figure: Internal and External Forms, 1951, cast 1952–53
Bronze
13½ × 21⅛ × 7⅝ in. (34.2 × 53.5 × 19.3 cm)
Hirshhorn Museum and Sculpture Garden, Washington, DC; gift of Joseph H. Hirshhorn, 1966 (66.3609)
fig. 76

Leaf Figure No. 4, 1953
Bronze
18⅞ × 5¼ × 4¼ in. (47.8 × 13.2 × 19.6 cm)
Hirshhorn Museum and Sculpture Garden, Washington, DC; gift of Joseph H. Hirshhorn, 1966 (66.3608)
*not illustrated

LOUISE NEVELSON
(American, b. Ukraine, 1899–1988)

Mountain Woman, 1947
Terra-cotta and paint
11 × 19½ × 9⅛ in. (28 × 49.4 × 23.2 cm)
Hirshhorn Museum and Sculpture Garden, Washington, DC; gift of Joseph H. Hirshhorn, 1966 (66.3822)
fig. 77

ISAMU NOGUCHI
(American, 1904–1988; also active in France, and Japan)

Monument to Heroes, 1943
Cardboard, paint, bones, wood, and string
28¼ × 13⅝ × 9¾ in. (71.8 × 34.6 × 24.8 cm)
Noguchi Museum, New York (190A)
fig. 135

This Tortured Earth, 1943, cast later
Bronze
29 × 28⅛ × 3 in. (73.7 × 71.4 × 7.6 cm)
Noguchi Museum, New York (195B-2/6)
fig. 137

Untitled, 1943 (on later base)
Plastic
19⅜ × 15⅝ × 11¾ in. (49.2 × 39.7 × 29.8 cm)
Noguchi Museum, New York (197)
fig. 134

Lunar Landscape, 1943–44
Magnesite cement, electric lights, plastic, cork, and string
34½ × 24¾ × 7⅞ in. (87.5 × 62.8 × 20 cm)
Hirshhorn Museum and Sculpture Garden, Washington, DC; gift of Joseph H. Hirshhorn, 1966 (66.3867)
fig. 136

Red Lunar Fist, 1943–44
Magnesite cement, plastic, resin, and electric light
7⅛ × 8⅜ × 8¾ in. (18.1 × 21.3 × 22.2 cm)
Noguchi Museum, New York (208)
fig. 139

Lunar Infant, 1944
Magnesite, wood, and electric light
22 × 16 × 16 in. (55.9 × 40.6 × 40.6 cm)
Noguchi Museum, New York (205)
fig. 138

Strange Bird (To the Sunflower), 1945
Stone (green slate)
56⅝ × 21⅞ × 20 in. (143.8 × 55.6 × 50.8 cm)
Noguchi Museum, New York (232A)
fig. 142

Trinity, 1945
Stone (slate)
55⅞ × 22 × 20 in. (141.9 × 55.9 × 50.8 cm)
Noguchi Museum, New York (234A)
fig. 143

Gregory (Effigy), 1946
Stone (slate)
69⅝ × 14⅛ × 16½ in. (176.8 × 35.9 × 41.9 cm)
Noguchi Museum, New York (242A)
fig. 140

Avatar, 1947, cast later
Bronze
78½ × 33 × 24 in. (199.4 × 83.8 × 60.9 cm)
Private collection, courtesy Pace Gallery, New York
fig. 141

PABLO PICASSO
(Spanish, 1881–1973; also active in France)

Anatomy, 1933
Ink on paper
Approx. 7⅞ × 10⅝ in. (20 × 27 cm), each
Reproduced in *Minotaure* 1, no. 1 (1933)
fig. 58

MAN RAY
(American, 1890–1976; also active in France)

Seguidilla, 1919
Gouache, ink, graphite, and colored pencil on paperboard
22 × 27⅞ in. (55.8 × 70.6 cm)
Hirshhorn Museum and Sculpture Garden, Washington, DC; Joseph H. Hirshhorn Purchase Fund and Museum Purchase, 1987 (87.15)
*not illustrated

Gift, (series II) 1921, edition 1970
Flatiron and nails
6⅛ × 3⅜ × 4¾ in. (15.4 × 8.7 × 12.2 cm)
Smithsonian American Art Museum, Washington, DC; gift of Juliet Man Ray (1983.105.3)
fig. 8

Untitled, 1921, printed 1980
Gelatin silver print
11⅝ × 8⅞ in. (29.5 × 22.6 cm)
Smithsonian American Art Museum, Washington, DC; gift of Juliet Man Ray (1983.105.14)
fig. 9

Electricity: Breeze, 1931
Photogravure on paper
10¼ × 8 in. (26 × 20.3 cm)
Smithsonian American Art Museum, Washington, DC; museum purchase (1976.84.10)
fig. 37

Electricity: Dining Room, 1931
Photogravure on paper
10¼ × 8 in. (26 × 20.3 cm)
Smithsonian American Art Museum, Washington, DC; museum purchase (1976.84.3)
fig. 38

Electricity: House, 1931
Photogravure on paper
10¼ × 8⅛ in. (26 × 20.5 cm)
Smithsonian American Art Museum, Washington, DC; museum purchase (1976.84.7)
fig. 39

Electricity: Lingerie, 1931
Photogravure on paper
10¼ × 8 in. (26 × 20.3 cm)
Smithsonian American Art Museum, Washington, DC; museum purchase (1976.84.6)
fig. 40

Object to Be Destroyed (Indestructible Object), 1932, edition 1965
Metronome and photograph
8½ × 4½ × 4½ in. (21.6 × 11.5 × 11.5 cm)
Smithsonian American Art Museum, Washington, DC; gift of Samuel M. Greenbaum and Helen Mark families in memory of Helen Mark Greenbaum (1993.43)
fig. 43

Self-Portrait, 1933
Bronze, eyeglasses, and paper in wood box
14 × 8¼ × 5⅜ in. (35.6 × 21.1 × 13.7 cm)
Smithsonian American Art Museum, Washington, DC; gift of Juliet Man Ray (1983.105.2)
fig. 42

Surrealist Exhibition at the Galerie Pierre Colle, Paris, Showing objects by André Breton, Salvador Dalí, Marcel Duchamp, Max Ernst, and Man Ray, 1933
Gelatin silver print
7⅞ × 10⅞ in. (20 × 27.7 cm)
Philadelphia Museum of Art; 125th anniversary acquisition, the Lynne and Harold Honickman Gift of the Julien Levy Collection, 2001 (2001-62-797)
fig. 36

Varlop, 1935, edition later
Carpenter's plane
23¼ × 7⅞ × 9½ in. (59 × 20 × 24.2 cm)
Hirshhorn Museum and Sculpture Garden, Washington, DC; the Joseph H. Hirshhorn Bequest, 1981 (86.3140)
*not illustrated

Nut Girls (Les Filles des Noix), 1941
Photograph, printed papers, and walnut
10½ × 8½ in. (26.7 × 21.6 cm)
Hirshhorn Museum and Sculpture Garden, Washington, DC; gift of Joseph H. Hirshhorn, 1966 (66.3236)
*not illustrated

DAVID SMITH
(American, 1906–1965)

Chain Head, 1933
Steel and paint
19 × 10 × 7 in. (48.3 × 25.4 × 17.8 cm)
The Estate of David Smith, New York
fig. 157

Saw Head, 1933
Iron and bronze objects with paint
18½ × 12 × 8¼ in. (47 × 30.5 × 21 cm)
The Estate of David Smith, New York
fig. 156

Swung Forms, 1937
Steel
23 × 11 × 23 in. (58.4 × 27.9 × 58.4 cm)
The Estate of David Smith, New York
fig. 159

Ancient Household, 1945
Iron on artist's wood base
24¾ × 17⅝ × 15⅞ in. (62.9 × 44.8 × 40.3 cm)
Hirshhorn Museum and Sculpture Garden, Washington, DC; gift of the Joseph H. Hirshhorn Foundation and Lily Harmon, 1979–80 (80.148)
fig. 161

Big Rooster, 1945
Steel
16½ × 21¼ × 15⅝ in. (41.7 × 54 × 39.6 cm)
Hirshhorn Museum and Sculpture Garden, Washington, DC; gift of Joseph H. Hirshhorn, 1966 (66.4629)
*not illustrated

Study for "Question and Answer," 1951
Gouache on paper
17 × 22⅛ in. (43.2 × 56.1 cm)
Hirshhorn Museum and Sculpture Garden, Washington, DC; gift of Joseph H. Hirshhorn, 1966 (66.4620)
*not illustrated

Agricola I, 1951–52
Steel and paint
73½ × 55¼ × 24⅝ in. (186.5 × 140.3 × 62.5 cm)
Hirshhorn Museum and Sculpture Garden, Washington, DC; gift of Joseph H. Hirshhorn, 1966 (66.4638)
fig. 162

Spectre Riding a Headless Horse, 1951–52
Steel and bronze
25⅜ × 24⅛ × 11¼ in. (64.4 × 61.3 × 28.5 cm)
Hirshhorn Museum and Sculpture Garden, Washington, DC; gift of Joseph H. Hirshhorn, 1966 (66.4624)
fig. 160

YVES TANGUY
(American, b. France, 1900–1955)

"Poids et couleurs" (Weights and Colors)
Le Surréalisme au service de la révolution, no. 3 (December 1931)
fig. 60

Naked Water, 1942
Oil paint on canvas
35⅞ × 28 in. (91.1 × 71 cm)
Hirshhorn Museum and Sculpture Garden, Washington, DC; gift of Joseph H. Hirshhorn, 1972 (72.286)
fig. 133

RAOUL UBAC
(Belgian, 1910–1985; also active in France)

Dalí's "Rainy Taxi" at the International Exhibition of Surrealism, Paris, 1938 (detail)
Gelatin silver print
6¾ × 8⅝ in. (17 × 22 cm)
Collection Timothy Baum, New York
fig. 93

Dalí's "Aphrodisiac Table" in the International Exhibition of Surrealism, Paris, 1938
Gelatin silver print
9 × 6¾ in. (23 × 17.2 cm)
Collection Timothy Baum, New York
fig. 102

Ernst's and Miró's Mannequins in the International Exhibition of Surrealism, Paris, 1938
Gelatin silver print
9½ × 6⅞ in. (23.4 × 17.3 cm)
Collection Timothy Baum, New York
fig. 94

Dominguez's Mannequin in the International Exhibition of Surrealism, Paris, 1938
Gelatin silver print
9½ × 6⅞ in. (23.4 × 17.3 cm)
Collection Timothy Baum, New York
fig. 97

OTHER ILLUSTRATED WORKS

JEAN (HANS) ARP
(French, b. Germany, 1887–1966; also active in Switzerland)

Clock, 1924
Wood and oil paint
20⅞ × 21 × 2⅜ in. (53 × 53.5 × 6 cm)
Kunstmuseum Basel; gift of Marguerite Arp-Hagenbach (1968.31)
fig. 15

Three Walking Sticks, 1927
Wood relief and oil paint
44½ × 57⅛ × 1½ in. (113 × 145 × 3.8 cm)
Kunstsammlung Nordrhein-Westfalen, Düsseldorf
fig. 21

Woman, 1927
Wood and oil paint
53½ × 39⅜ × 1½ in. (136 × 100 × 3.8 cm)
Musée national d'art moderne, Centre Georges Pompidou, Paris (AM2003-580)
fig. 19

LOUISE BOURGEOIS
(American, b. France, 1911–2010)

Cell (Choisy), 1990–93
Marble, metal, and glass
120½ × 67 × 94⅞ in. (306 × 170.2 × 241 cm)
Courtesy the Easton Foundation, New York
fig. 165

JOSEF BREITENBACH
(American, b. Germany, 1896–1984; also active in France)

"The Surrealist Street" installation in the International Exhibition of Surrealism, Paris, 1938
Gelatin silver print
7 × 9½ in. (17.8 × 24.1 cm)
The Getty Research Institute, Los Angeles (94.R.26)
fig. 96

Duchamp's 1,200 Coal Sacks installation in the International Exhibition of Surrealism, Paris, 1938
Gelatin silver print
9⅜ × 11½ in. (24 × 29.2 cm)
The Getty Research Institute, Los Angeles (94.R.26)
fig. 101

ALEXANDER CALDER
(American, 1898–1976; also active in France)

Gibraltar, 1936
Wood (lignum vitae and walnut), steel rods, and paint
51⅞ × 24¼ × 11⅜ in. (131.7 × 61.3 × 28.7 cm)
The Museum of Modern Art, New York; gift of the artist (847.1966.a-b)
fig. 150

La Demoiselle (Young Lady), 1939
Metal, wire, and paint
58½ × 21 × 29½ in. (148.6 × 53.3 × 74.9 cm)
Glenstone
fig. 150

Hollow Egg, 1939
Metal wire and paint
54 × 39½ × 38⅛ in. (137.2 × 100.3 × 96.8 cm)
The Phillips Collection, Washington, DC; partial and promised gift in memory of Betty Milton, a close friend of Louisa Calder, 2001 (2001.012.001)
fig. 144

Bayonets Menacing a Flower, 1945
Metal, paint, and wire
45 × 51 × 18½ in. (114.3 × 129.5 × 47 cm)
Mildred Lane Kemper Art Museum, Washington University in St. Louis; University purchase, McMillan Fund, 1946 (WU 3770)
fig. 152

Stegosaurus, 1973
Steel and paint
60 × 171 × 96 in. (406.4 × 434.3 × 243.8 cm)
Ella Burr McManus Trust, Hartford
fig. 151

JOSEPH CORNELL
(American, 1903–1972)

Untitled (Glass Bell), 1932
Wood, paint, printed paper, plaster, and metal in glass dome
15¾ × 8⅝ × 8⅝ in. (40 × 21.9 × 21.9 cm)
Private collection
fig. 116

Untitled (Museum Box), early 1940s
Wood, found objects, and shot glasses
5¾ × 16 × 9¼ in. (14.6 × 40.6 × 23.5 cm), closed
Wadsworth Atheneum Museum of Art, Hartford; gift of the Joseph and Robert Cornell Memorial Foundation (2002.35.4)
fig. 122

A Pantry Ballet (for Jacques Offenbach), 1942
Wood, plastic, paper, metal, and thread
10½ × 18⅛ × 6 in. (26.7 × 46.1 × 15.2 cm)
The Nelson-Atkins Museum of Art, Kansas City; gift of the Friends of Art (F77-34)
fig. 125

SALVADOR DALÍ
(Spanish, 1904–1989; also active in France)

She Was a Surrealist Woman, She Was Like a Figure in a Dream, 1936
Gelatin silver print
Dimensions unrecorded
Museum of the City of New York (37.67.8)
fig. 51

OSCAR DOMINGUEZ
(French, b. Spain, 1906–1957)

Thorn Puller, 1934
Plaster, paint, wood, and metal
18⅞ × 8¼ × 12⅜ in. (48 × 21 × 31.5 cm)
Museo Nacional Centro de Arte Reina Sofía, Madrid
fig. 55

The Wanderings of Georges Hugnet, 1935
Wood, metal, and oil paint
18⅞ × 16⅜ × 4¾ in. (48 × 41.5 × 12 cm)
Museo Nacional Centro de Arte Reina Sofía, Madrid
fig. 46

MARCEL DUCHAMP
(American, b. France, 1887–1968)

The Bride Stripped Bare by Her Bachelors, Even (The Large Glass), 1915–23
Oil paint, varnish, lead foil, lead wire, and dust on two glass panels
109¼ × 69¼ in. (277.5 × 175.9 cm)
Philadelphia Museum of Art; bequest of Katherine S. Dreier, 1952 (1952-98-1)
fig. 5

MAX ERNST
(French, b. Germany, 1891–1976; also active in the United States)

Cages Are Always Imaginary, 1925
Plaster, metal, wood, and paint
17¾ × 10⅜ × 2 in. (45 × 26.5 × 5 cm)
Kunsthaus Zürich
fig. 16

Human Figure with Two Birds, 1925/1929
Wood, paint, and sandpaper
45⅞ × 15½ in. (116.4 × 39.4 cm)
The Art Institute of Chicago; through prior gift of the Albert Kunstadter Family Foundation (1989.386)
fig. 17

Loplop Introduces a Young Girl, 1930/1936
Oil paint on wood, with plaster and found objects
76⅝ × 35 × 4 in. (194.5 × 89 × 10 cm)
Musée national d'art moderne, Centre Georges Pompidou, Paris (AM1982-187)
fig. 18

Lunar Asparagus, 1935, cast 1972
Plaster
65¼ × 15¾ × 9⅛ in. (165.7 × 39.9 × 23.4 cm)
The Museum of Modern Art, New York; purchase (273.1937)
fig. 57

LEONOR FINI
(Argentine, 1907–1996; active in France)

Corset Chair, 1939
Wood, iron, and mother-of-pearl
38½ × 18 × 19 in. (97.8 × 45.7 × 48.3 cm)
Bauer Collection
fig. 115

ALBERTO GIACOMETTI
(Swiss, 1901–1966; also active in France)

Man and Woman, 1929
Bronze
15¾ × 15¾ × 6½ in. (40 × 40 × 16.5 cm)
Musée national d'art moderne, Centre Georges Pompidou, Paris (AM1984-355)
fig. 28

The Cage, 1930–31
Wood
19⅝ × 10⅝ × 10⅝ in. (49.8 × 27 × 27 cm)
Moderna Museet, Stockholm; purchase, 1964 (NMSK 1843)
fig. 29

Suspended Ball, 1930–31
Wood, iron, and cord
23¾ × 14⅜ × 13⅜ in. (60.4 × 36.5 × 34 cm)
Musée national d'art moderne, Centre Georges Pompidou, Paris (AM1996-205)
fig. 30

The Palace at 4 a.m., 1932
Wood, glass, wire, and string
25 × 28¼ × 15¾ in. (63.5 × 71.8 × 40 cm)
The Museum of Modern Art, New York; purchase (90.1936)
fig. 33

Flower in Danger, 1932–33
Wood, metal, plaster, and string
22 × 30¾ × 7 in. (55.9 × 78.1 × 17.8 cm)
Kunsthaus Zürich
fig. 34

BARBARA HEPWORTH
(British, 1903–1975)

Pendour, 1947–48
Wood and paint
12⅛ × 29⅜ × 9⅜ in. (30.6 × 74.5 × 23.8 cm)
Hirshhorn Museum and Sculpture Garden, Washington, DC; gift of Joseph H. Hirshhorn (66.2444)
fig. 75

VALENTINE HUGO
(French, 1887–1968)

Object, 1931
Wood hands and leather gloves on fabric with dice
12¾ × 9 × 3¾ in. (32.5 × 23 × 9.5 cm)
Musée national d'art moderne, Centre Georges Pompidou, Paris (AM2003-3)
fig. 105

SEYMOUR LIPTON
(American, 1903–1986)

Imprisoned Figure, 1948
Wood and lead
84¾ × 30⅞ × 23⅝ in. (215.2 × 78.3 × 59.9 cm)
The Museum of Modern Art, New York; gift of the artist (507.1969)
fig. 163

DORA MAAR
(French, 1907–1997)

Untitled (Hand-Shell), 1934
Gelatin silver print
15¾ × 11⅜ in. (40 × 29 cm)
Musée national d'art moderne, Centre Georges Pompidou, Paris (AM1991-34)
fig. 104

RENÉ MAGRITTE
(Belgian, 1898–1967; also active in France)

The Treachery of Images (This Is Not a Pipe), 1929
Oil paint on canvas
23¾ × 32 in. (60.3 × 81.1 × 2.5 cm)
Los Angeles County Museum of Art; purchased with funds provided by the Mr. and Mrs. William Preston Harrison Collection (78.7)
fig. 24

The Future of Statues, 1937
Plaster and oil paint
13 × 6½ × 8 in. (33 × 16.5 × 20.3 cm)
Tate Gallery, London (T03258)
fig. 1

JOAN MIRÓ
(Spanish, 1893–1983; also active in France)

Personage with Umbrella, 1931
Wood furniture frames, dowel, umbrella and artificial flowers
H: 70⅞ in. (180 cm)
Reproduced in *Le Surréalisme au service de la révolution,* no. 3 (December 1931)
fig. 32

Object, 1936
Wood, parrot, silk stocking with velvet garter and doll's paper shoe and hat, cork ball, celluloid fish, and engraved map
31⅞ × 11⅞ × 10¼ in. (81 × 30.1 × 26 cm)
The Museum of Modern Art, New York; gift of Mr. and Mrs. Pierre Matisse (940.1965.a-c)
fig. 48

HENRY MOORE
(British, 1898–1986)

Reclining Figure, 1931, cast 1963
Bronze on marble base
9⅞ × 21 in. (25.3 × 53.3 cm)
The Henry Moore Foundation, Much Hadham, England; gift of the artist
fig. 64

Five Figures in a Setting, 1937
Charcoal, pastel, and wax crayon on paper
15 × 21⅞ (38 × 55.5 cm)
Private collection, London
fig. 71

Reclining Figure, 1939
Wood
37 × 79 × 30 in. (94 × 200.7 × 76.2 cm)
Detroit Institute of Arts; Founders Society Purchase
fig. 68

Sculptural Object in a Landscape, 1939
Ink and watercolor on paper
15 × 21¾ in. (38 × 55.3 cm)
Sainsbury Centre for Visual Arts, University of East Anglia, Norwich, England
fig. 72

Two Heads (Drawing for Metal Sculpture), 1939
Ink and charcoal on paper
11 × 15 in. (27.7 × 38.1 cm)
The Henry Moore Foundation, Much Hadham, England
fig. 69

ISAMU NOGUCHI
(American, 1904–1988; also active in France and Japan)

United Hosiery Workers' Memorial, 1933–34
Plaster
Dimensions unrecorded
Courtesy the Noguchi Museum, New York
fig. 132

CLAES OLDENBURG
(American, b. Sweden, 1929)

Proposal for a Cathedral in the Form of a Colossal Faucet, 1972
Lithographic ink on paper
32⅜ × 24⅝ in. (82.2 × 62.4 cm)
Hirshhorn Museum and Sculpture Garden, Washington, DC; the Joseph H. Hirshhorn Bequest (86.3489)
fig. 164

MERET OPPENHEIM
(Swiss, b. Germany, 1913–1985; also active in France)

My Governess, 1936
Leather shoes and paper on metal tray
5½ × 13 × 8¼ in. (14 × 33 × 21 cm)
Moderna Museet, Stockholm (NMSK 1972)
fig. 107

Object, 1936
Fur-covered cup, saucer, and spoon
Cup 4⅜ in. (10.9 cm) in diameter; saucer 9⅜ in. (23.7 cm) in diameter; spoon 8 in. (20.2 cm) long, overall height 2⅞ in. (7.3 cm)
The Museum of Modern Art, New York; purchase (130.1946.a-c)
fig. 106

ROLAND PENROSE
(British, 1900–1984; also active in France)

The Last Voyage of Captain Cook, 1936, 1967 version
Plaster and steel on wooden base
27¼ × 26 × 32½ in. (69.2 × 66 × 82.5 cm)
Tate Gallery, London; presented by Mrs. Gabrielle Keiller through the Friends of the Tate Gallery, 1982 (T03377)
fig. 56

Photograph of *The Dew Machine,* 1937
Gelatin silver print
15 × 10 in. (38 × 25.4 cm)
Scottish National Gallery of Modern Art Archive, Edinburgh
p. 191

MAN RAY
(American, 1890–1976; also active in France)

Woman Holding Giacometti's Disagreeable Object, 1931
Photograph
4¾ × 3½ in. (12 × 9 cm)
Musée national d'art moderne, Centre Georges Pompidou, Paris (AM 1994-393 [6768])
fig. 31

What We All Lack, 1935
Clay pipe with glass ball
14¾ × 8 × 3½ in. (37.5 × 20.3 × 8.9 cm)
The Art Institute of Chicago; gift of Mary P. Hines in memory of her mother, Frances W. Pick (1995.238)
fig. 53

Surrealist Exhibition of Objects, Galerie Ratton, Paris, 1936
Gelatin silver print
Birger Raben-Skov Collection, Copenhagen
fig. 50

Dalí's Mannequin in the International Exhibition of Surrealism, Paris, 1938
Gelatin silver print
7⅜ × 5½ in. (18.8 × 14 cm)
The J. Paul Getty Museum, Los Angeles (84.XO.1194.6)
fig. 95

Masson's Mannequin in the International Exhibition of Surrealism, Paris, 1938
Gelatin silver print
7¼ × 5½ in. (18.3 × 13.8 cm)
The J. Paul Getty Museum, Los Angeles (84.XO.1194.10)
fig. 98

Paalen's Mannequin in the International Exhibition of Surrealism, Paris, 1938
Gelatin silver print
7⅛ × 5¼ in. (18.2 × 13.5 cm)
The J. Paul Getty Museum, Los Angeles (84.XO.1194.8)
fig. 100

Seligmann's Mannequin in the International Exhibition of Surrealism, Paris, 1938
Gelatin silver print
7½ × 6 in. (18.9 × 14.4 cm)
The J. Paul Getty Museum, Los Angeles (84.XO.1194.3)
fig. 99

DAVID SMITH
(American, 1906–1965)

Reclining Construction, 1936
Iron and paint
14 × 27 × 6⅛ in. (35.6 × 68.6 × 15.6 cm)
Yale University Art Gallery, New Haven; gift of Caral and M. J. Lebworth, B.A. 1948 (2009.28.1)
fig. 158

Credits

We would like to thank all those who gave their kind permission to reproduce material. Individual works of art appearing herein may be protected by copyright in the United States of America or elsewhere, and may not be reproduced in any form without the permission of the rights holders. In reproducing the images contained in this publication, the Museum obtained the permission of the rights holders whenever possible. In those instances where the Museum could not locate the rights holders, notwithstanding good-faith efforts, it requests that any contact information concerning such rights holders be forwarded so that they may be contacted for future editions.

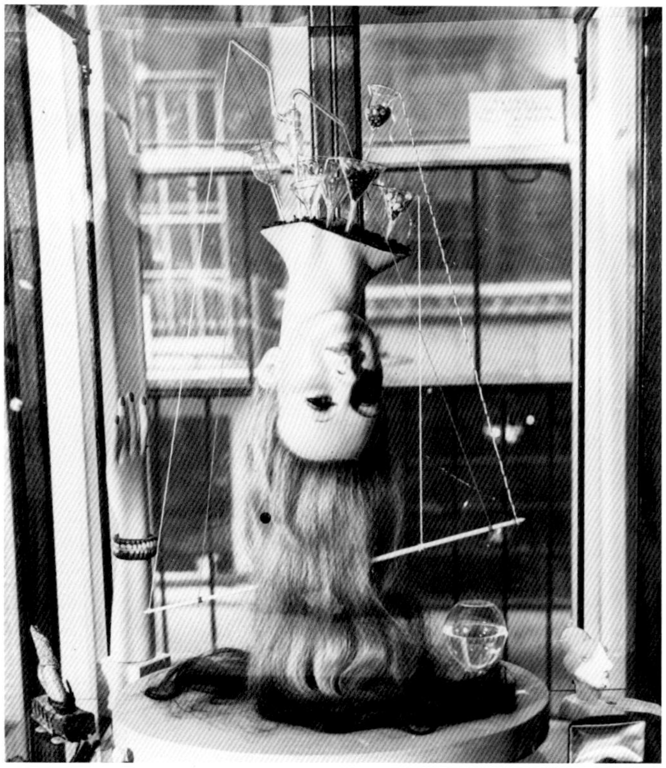

Artists' Copyrights

All works by Jean (Hans) Arp: © 2015 Artists Rights Society (ARS), New York / VG Bild-Kunst, Bonn. All works by Hans Bellmer: © 2015 Artists Rights Society (ARS), New York / ADAGP, Paris. All works by Ruth Bernhard: © Ruth Bernhard Archive, Princeton University Art Museum. © Trustees of Princeton University. All works by Louise Bourgeois: © The Easton Foundation / Licensed by VAGA, New York, NY. All works by Josef Breitenbach: © The Josef and Yaye Breitenbach Charitable Foundation. All works by Claude Cahun: © Estate of Claude Cahun. All works by Alexander Calder: © 2015 Calder Foundation, New York / Artists Rights Society (ARS), New York. All works by Joseph Cornell: © The Joseph and Robert Cornell Memorial Foundation / Licensed by VAGA, New York, NY. All works by Salvador Dalí: © Salvador Dalí, Fundació Gala-Salvador Dalí, Artists Rights Society (ARS), New York 2015. All works by Oscar Dominguez: © 2015 Artists Rights Society (ARS), New York / ADAGP, Paris. All works by Marcel Duchamp: © Succession Marcel Duchamp / ADAGP, Paris / Artists Rights Society (ARS), New York 2015. All works by Leonor Fini: © 2015 Artists Rights Society (ARS), New York / ADAGP, Paris. All works by Max Ernst: © 2015 Artists Rights Society (ARS), New York / ADAGP, Paris. All works by Alberto Giacometti: © 2015 Alberto Giacometti Estate / Licensed by VAGA and ARS, New York, NY. All works by Maurice Henry: © 2015 Artists Rights Society (ARS), New York / ADAGP, Paris. All works by Barbara Hepworth: © Bowness. All works by Valentine Hugo: © 2015 Artists Rights Society (ARS), New York / ADAGP, Paris. All works by Seymour Lipton: © The Estate of Seymour Lipton; Courtesy of Michael Rosenfeld Gallery LLC, New York, NY. All works by Dora Maar: © 2015 Artists Rights Society (ARS), New York / ADAGP, Paris. All works by René Magritte: © 2015 C. Herscovici / Artists Rights Society (ARS), New York. All works by André Masson: © 2015 Artists Rights Society (ARS), New York / ADAGP, Paris. All works by Joan Miró: © Successió Miró / Artists Rights Society (ARS), New York / ADAGP, Paris 2015. All works by Henry Moore: Reproduced by the permission of The Henry Moore Foundation. All works by Louise Nevelson: © 2015 Estate of Louise Nevelson / Artists Rights Society (ARS), New York. All works by Isamu Noguchi: © 2015 The Isamu Noguchi Foundation and Garden Museum, New York / Artists Rights Society (ARS), New York. All works by Claes Oldenburg: © 2015 Claes Oldenburg. All works by Meret Oppenheim: © 2015 Artists Rights Society (ARS), New York / ProLitteris, Zurich. All works by Wolfgang Paalen: © Succession Wolfgang Paalen und Eva Sulzer. All works by Roland Penrose: © Roland Penrose Estate, England 2015. All works by Pablo Picasso: © 2015 Estate of Pablo Picasso / Artists Rights Society (ARS), New York. All works by Man Ray: © Man Ray Trust / Artists Rights Society (ARS), NY / ADAGP, Paris 2015. All works by Kurt Seligmann: © 2015 Orange County Citizens Foundation / Artists Rights Society (ARS), New York. All works by David Smith: © The Estate of David Smith, Licensed by VAGA, New York, NY. All works by Yves Tanguy: © 2015 Estate of Yves Tanguy / Artists Rights Society (ARS), New York. All works by Raoul Ubac: © 2015 Artists Rights Society (ARS), New York / ADAGP, Paris.

Photographic Credits

Courtesy Acquavella Galleries, New York: fig. 14. © The Art Institute of Chicago: figs. 17, 53. Courtesy Timothy Baum and Di Donna Galleries: figs. 4, 93–94, 97, 102. Ruth Bernhard Archive, Princeton University Art Museum. © Trustees of Princeton University: figs. 111–14. Birger Raben-Skov Collection, Copenhagen; courtesy Galerie 1900–2000, Paris: fig. 50. Calder Foundation, New York / Art Resource, NY: figs. 146–49, 151; Photo by Jimi Billingsley: fig. 155. © 2014 Christie's Images Limited: fig. 116. © CNAC/MNAM/ Dist. RMN-Grand Palais / Art Resource, NY: figs. 28, 31; Photo by Jacques Faujour: fig. 104; Photo by Georges Meguerditchian: fig. 30; Photo by Philippe Migeat: figs. 18–19, 105. Salvador Dalí Museum, Inc., St. Petersburg, Florida: fig. 49. Courtesy the Easton Foundation, New York: fig. 165. Courtesy the Fralin Musuem of Art at the University of Virginia: fig. 118. The J. Paul Getty Museum, Los Angeles: figs. 95, 98–100. The Getty Research Institute, Los Angeles: figs. 96, 101. Courtesy Glenstone; Photo by Tim Nighswander / Imaging4Art.com: fig. 150. Mark Gulezian, Quicksilver Photography: figs. 121, 123. Harvard Art Museums/ Fogg Museum, Imaging Department © President and Fellows of Harvard College: figs. 66, 73. Hirshhorn Museum and Sculpture Garden: Photo by Cathy Carver: p. 12; figs. 20, 26–27, 61, 70, 75–78, 129–31, 136, 162, 164; Photo by Mysti Scott: figs. 32, 35, 58, 60; Photo by Lee Stalsworth: figs. 62, 79, 133, 154, 160–61. Kunsthaus Zürich: figs. 16, 34. Kunstmuseum Basel; Photo by Martin P. Bühler: fig. 15. Kunstsammlung Nordrhein-Westfalen, Düsseldorf; Photo by Walter Klein, Düsseldorf: fig. 21. Mildred Lane Kemper Museum, Washington University in St. Louis: fig. 152. Courtesy Herbert Lust / Greenwich Fine Arts: fig. 83. © The Metropolitan Museum of Art / Art Resource, NY: figs. 59, 82, 84–86, 91. Moderna Museet, Stockholm / De Agostini Picture Library / Bridgeman Images: figs. 29, 107. The Henry Moore Foundation: figs. 64, 68–69, 71–72. Courtesy Mugrabi Collection: fig. 52. Photographic Archives Museo Nacional Centro de Arte Reina Sofia, Madrid: figs. 46, 55. Museum of the City of New York: fig. 51. © 2015 Museum of Fine Arts, Boston: fig. 74. © The Museum of Modern Art / Licensed by SCALA / Art Resource, NY: pp. 4–5; figs. 11, 33, 48, 57, 65, 80, 106, 145, 163. © 2015 Museum Associates / LACMA. Licensed by Art Resource, NY: fig. 24. Raymond and Patsy Nasher Collection, Nasher Sculpture Center, Dallas; Photo by David Heald: figs. 25, 153. National Gallery of Art, Washington, DC: figs. 7, 10, 13; 44, 47, 128. Nelson-Atkins Museum of Art, Kansas City; Photo by Melville McLean: fig. 125. © Isamu Noguchi Foundation and Garden Museum, New York: figs. 132, 134–35, 137–40, 142–43. Courtesy Pace Gallery, New York: fig. 141; Photo by Kerry Ryan McFate: fig. 81. The Phillips Collection, Washington, DC: fig. 144. Philadelphia Museum of Art: pp. 2–3; figs. 23, 36, 41, 43. Philadelphia Museum of Art / Art Resource, NY: figs. 5, 6. Courtesy private collection: fig. 45. Robert Rauschenberg Foundation, New York: fig. 2. Scottish National Gallery of Art Modern Archive, Edinburgh: p. 191. The Estate of David Smith, New York: fig. 156; Photo by Ellen Page Wilson: fig. 157; Photo courtesy Pace Gallery, New York: fig. 159. Smithsonian American Art Museum, Washington, DC: figs. 8–9, 37–40, 42–43, 117, 119–20, 124, 126–27. © Tate, London 2015: figs. 109–10. Tate, London / Art Resource, NY: figs. 1, 56, 103. Courtesy Ubu Gallery, New York: fig. 54. Courtesy Ubu Gallery, New York & Galerie Berinson, Berlin; Photo by Joelle Jensen: figs. 87–90, 92, 108. Wadsworth Atheneum Museum of Art, Hartford: figs. 22, 122. Courtesy Weinstein Gallery, San Francisco; Photo by Nicholas Pishvanov: fig. 115. Yale Center for British Art, New Haven: figs. 63, 67. Yale University Art Gallery, New Haven: figs. 3, 12, 158.

This catalogue is published in conjunction with the exhibition *Marvelous Objects: Surrealist Sculpture from Paris to New York*, organized by the Hirshhorn Museum and Sculpture Garden, Smithsonian Institution, Washington, DC, October 29, 2015–February 15, 2016.

Leading support for *Marvelous Objects: Surrealist Sculpture from Paris to New York* has been provided by the Jerome L. Greene Foundation, with major funding from the Terra Foundation for American Art, and lead corporate sponsor Altria Group. Additional support has been provided by the Swiss Arts Council Pro Helvetia, the Hirshhorn International Council, and the Smithsonian Institution's Scholarly Studies Program, and from Barbara and Aaron Levine and Robert Mnuchin.

ISBN: 978-3-7913-5465-1

LIBRARY OF CONGRESS CONTROL NUMBER: 2015944274

EDITED BY RHYS CONLON AND AMY PASTAN

DESIGNED BY EILEEN BOXER

PRODUCTION COORDINATION BY LUKE CHASE, DELMONICO • PRESTEL

PUBLISHED BY
HIRSHHORN MUSEUM AND SCULPTURE GARDEN

AND

DELMONICO BOOKS, AN IMPRINT OF PRESTEL,
A MEMBER OF VERLAGSGRUPPE RANDOM HOUSE GMBH

PRESTEL VERLAG
Neumarkter Strasse 28
81673 Munich
Tel. +49 89 4136 0
Fax +49 89 4136 2335

PRESTEL PUBLISHING LTD.
14-17 Wells Street
London W1T 3PD
Tel. +44 20 7323 5004
Fax +44 20 7323 0271

PRESTEL PUBLISHING
900 Broadway, Suite 603
New York, NY 10003
Tel. +1 212 995 2720
Fax +1 212 995 2733
sales@prestel-usa.com

WWW.PRESTEL.COM

Smithsonian
Hirshhorn Museum and Sculpture Garden

Cover: Salvador Dalí, *Venus de Milo with Drawers*, 1936 (detail). Mugrabi Collection.

Back Cover: Alexander Calder, *The Spider*, 1940. Raymond and Patsy Nasher Collection, Nasher Sculpture Center, Dallas.

Endpapers: Pablo Picasso, *Anatomy*, 1933. Reproduced in *Minotaure* 1, no. 1 (1933).

Pages 2–3: Jean (Hans) Arp, *Configuration with Two Dangerous Points*, c. 1930 (detail). Philadelphia Museum of Art; A. E. Gallatin Collection.

Pages 4–5: Alberto Giacometti, *Woman with Her Throat Cut*, 1932; The Museum of Modern Art, New York; purchase.

Page 12: Isamu Noguchi, *Lunar Landscape*, 1943–44 (detail); Hirshhorn Museum and Sculpture Garden, Washington, DC; gift of Joseph H. Hirshhorn.

Page 191: Photograph of *The Dew Machine* by Roland Penrose, 1937. Scottish National Gallery of Modern Art Archive, Edinburgh.

PRINTED AND BOUND IN CHINA

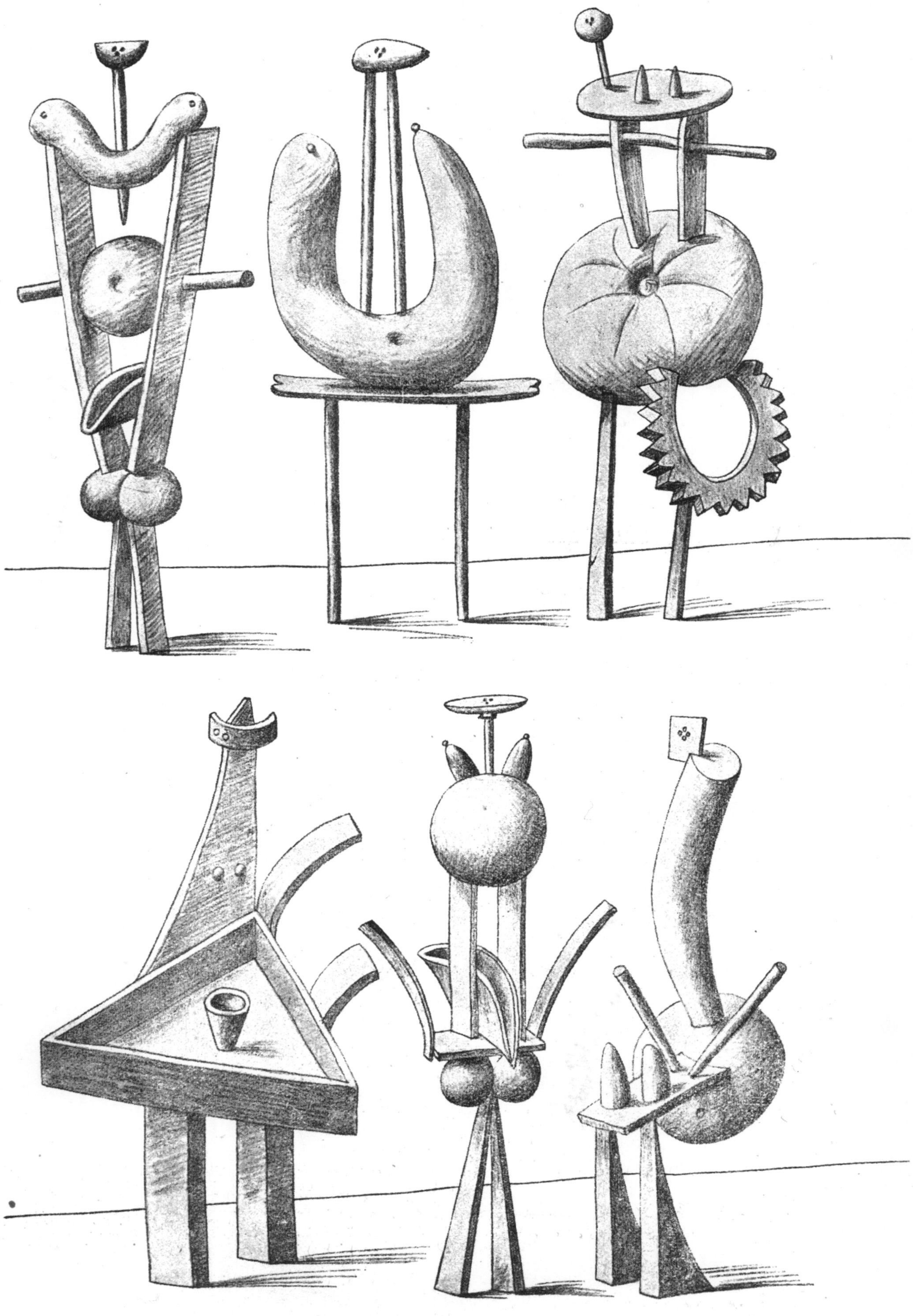